Quests & Quandaries

A Human Development Workbook

Second Edition

Written and compiled by Carol W. Hotchkiss

Illustrations by Whitney Abbott

Avocus Publishing, Inc.
4 White Brook Road
Gilsum, NH 03448

(800) 345-6665
FAX: (603) 357-2073
www.avocus.com
Info@avocus.com

Disclaimer: This book has no definitive answers. It provides a framework wherein the reader is invited to participate in expanding and defining her/his horizons. The response will be different for each reader and should be approached with an open mind. Any other interpretation of our printing is erroneous and therefore misunderstood.

The following portions of *Quests & Quandaries* have been reprinted with permission:

"Body Maintenance Check-up" was excerpted from *The Wellness Encyclopedia* from the editors of the "University of California at Berkeley Wellness Letter" copyright 1991, Health Letter Associates, 632 Broadway, New York, NY 10012.

"Looking at Myself" with permission of Community Intervention, 529 South 7th Street, Suite 570, Minneapolis, MN 55415.

"Breaking an Addiction" with permission of the American Lung Association, 1740 Broadway, New York, NY 10019.

"Alcoholism and the Family" with permission of Al-Anon Family Group Headquarters, Inc., P.O. Box 862, Midtown Station, New York, NY 10018.

"The Invisible Knapsack" with permission of Peggy McIntosh, Wellesley College Center for Research on Women, Wellesley, MA 02181.

ISBN 1-890765-08-2. $29.95 Softcover

Acknowledgments

One of the real pleasures of working in schools and attempting to address the difficult issues of human development is that there is an incredibly talented, generous, and committed group of colleagues who have identified that same need. There are wonderful programs and classes addressing these issues in public and private schools all over the United States. As pioneers of a relatively new curriculum, we have relished the opportunity to share our ideas, our successes, our failures, and our determination. Everything in this book is a combination of the many discussions, risks, and accomplishments that we have individually and collectively undertaken. Many exercises and approaches in this book are "tools of the trade" that we have evolved from this rich and interdependent network.

I would like to acknowledge all of the educators whose shared ideas and genuine commitment to students have added to this book. I hope that in turn, this resource will make their jobs easier and more fun. I would like to especially thank my human development teaching partners at Cate School, Sandy Ellis, David Mochel, Janey Cohen, Nori Burk, Floyd Grant, and Jose Munoz. Their suggestions, criticism, encouragement, and wisdom permeate every page.

Equally important has been the honesty, direction, and feedback of the students who have shaped our course in human development. They have always let us know when we were addressing their needs and questions and when we had strayed into less relevant adult speculation. Special thanks must go to the seniors who have worked and taught with us as teaching assistants. They have provided the perspective and power that has educated both their peers and their teachers.

I would like to thank Cate School for providing the basis for the human development courses that shaped and developed this curriculum. Special thanks to Headmaster Scott McLeod for believing in the importance of this project right from the start. My deep respect and appreciation goes to Ellie Griffin and all the participants over the years at the Human Development Institute for our yearly dialogue and transfusion as we attempt to address these difficult and important topics with our students. Steve Ruzicka, Ed Kowalchick, and Liz Fleming Powell at TABS have provided unending support and encouragement for me both personally and professionally. Watching them work with both teachers and students continues to instruct and inspire as they dedicate themselves to building healthy educational communities.

Craig Thorn at Avocus Publishing has been a wonderful editor and colleague in the development of this second edition. Craig's many excellent suggestions and the dogged pestering of Ernest Peter, president of Avocus, made this edition come together. Thanks to them both for their patience and perseverance. Thanks also to Theo Coonrod for reading my endless copy with her finely honed English teacher's pen.

Finally, I would like to thank my youngest son, Sam, for living many of these quests and quandaries with me over the past seven years. His wisdom, confidence, resilience, and love have helped me understand and articulate many of the questions that young people today are asking of themselves and of their teachers. If all young people could be so wise and so unwavering, we will be in fine shape.

Dedication

Since the first edition of Quests & Quandaries, *two of my then teenage children have grown, married, and developed five beautiful new humans.*

**This second edition is dedicated to my grandchildren
—Alicia, Zoe, Silas, Noah, and Maddy—
and to their generation.**

*May the teaching and learning that we do today
create a safer, less troubling world for them
when they begin their quests.*

Continuing thanks to all the teachers and students who have used Quests & Quandaries *and shared their questions, comments, and suggestions. Much of that feedback helped to create this second edition.*

Thanks to Dr. Ed Koffenberger and his AP Psychology students for helping to evaluate the Web sites listed after each chapter.

Special thanks to Avocus Press for giving me the time and space to complete this work.

Contents

Quandaries

How to Use This Book . . .

This book has been designed to be used as a part of courses on human development. Each class can pick specific exercises and areas of focus. It can also be used independently by those who would like to explore their own developmental issues. *Even if you are using this book as part of a course, you are encouraged to tailor the material to meet your specific needs and interests.* While we share many common human experiences, you have your own important questions, challenges, and special needs to address. Part of the change that takes place during adolescence is a growing ability to separate yourself from others—to distinguish how you are like others and how you are different. By necessity, education often focuses on how we are alike by using the common themes we share. Human development courses are no exception, but this focus often filters out the rich, personal differences that distinguish your life. I have tried to include a broad range of topics and experiences that reflect both human similarities and differences. It will be up to you, however, to find and define yourself within this context. Some issues will be immediately relevant and helpful. Some, you may tuck away for future reference or "planning ahead." Others may give you some insight into a friend or into an experience that you have never encountered. Those that appear to have no relevance to you at all may either be studied on a purely intellectual level or skipped altogether. In the end, your experience with this workbook should be completely different from anyone else's. It will address *your human development* to the extent that you can actually explore and use it.

Process: a series of actions, choices, and changes leading to an end result.

> *Men and nations behave wisely once they have exhausted all the other alternatives.*
>
> —*Abba Eban*

This book is primarily about *process*, not facts or results. You will find some basic information and some interesting theories. The focus, however, will be on how to gather, question, and use the information that is available to you from many sources. The final answers or ideas are up to you. Most unplanned teenage pregnancies, for instance, are not the result of ignorance or stupidity. Teenagers today are intelligent, informed, and relatively sophisticated about sex and birth control. Yet only 25 percent who are sexually active use birth control on a regular basis. The problem lies in the *process*—putting what you know into the context of your life in a realistic and self-caring way. As teenagers and adults, we often act in spite of what we know, not because of it.

Sometimes, we just don't take the time to think things through. Rational thought and planning can appear to be the antithesis of fun, romance, and adventure. Students often moan when I suggest that one should carefully plan and decide when, how, and if they are going to have sexual intercourse. How unromantic! What about passion and spontaneity? Spontaneity is a precious, joyous part of life and risk-taking is an important element in both growth and learning. By definition, however, a risk is "exposure to the chance of injury or loss; a hazard or dangerous chance."[1] Individual maturation is the gradual process of learning to think about the risks involved and make quick, conscious decisions whether or not it is worth the risk. Risking a picnic on a cloudy day may involve a wet lunch and a laughing scramble for the car. The consequences of unprotected sex (which can be much more tempting than a picnic) can be much more life altering, and today, even life threatening.

> *A life without adventure is likely to be unsatisfying, but a life in which adventure is allowed to take whatever form it will is sure to be short.*
>
> —*Bertrand Russell*

One of the biggest obstacles to rational evaluation and planning is an apparently limitless human capacity to convince ourselves that IT WILL NEVER HAPPEN TO ME. Often enough, it doesn't. Russian roulette can be fatal, but five out of six people get a lucky break. Every close call feeds our sense of invulnerability rather than makes us more cautious in the future. Each time we survive a ride with an intoxicated driver, have unprotected sex without getting pregnant, or take a drug without any clear negative effects, we feel a little bolder. We become more convinced that the odds don't really apply to us. Your brain may tell you that you were lucky and not to risk it again, but the spunky, playful kid in you becomes convinced that you have a special set of powers and luck. "I'm different—too lucky, too smart, too quick, too unique; I can handle it." Often, a tragic or near tragic occurrence is the only way to shake this form of denial. One-third of all girls requesting birth control do so because they are afraid that they might already be pregnant. Students Against Drunk Drivers groups are always most active in schools where a drunk driver has killed one or more of the students' friends. People are more likely to wear seat belts *after* an accident. Accepting your own vulnerability and mortality is a difficult and evolving part of taking responsibility for yourself.

Another processing roadblock to taking good care of ourselves is the discomfort and frustration of learning something new. Nobody likes to feel or look like an idiot. When you are learning or trying something for the first time, you fail, you make mistakes, you don't know what you are doing, you ask dumb questions, you are awkward and it is hard to feel confident, talented, and nonchalant. Luckily, kids learn how to ride a bike before they start worrying about looking cool or none of us would know how. We wobbled; we fell; we looked scared and screamed for our parent not to let go; we probably got mad, cried, and certainly skinned various parts of our bodies. And, gradually, we learned how to ride a bike. Learning a new skill implies that you initially lack this ability. This takes time, practice, thought, and experience. By about the age of ten, most of us would rather skip the awkward, embarrassing part of learning and become instantly skilled, confident, and wise. For most adult development, this means we either have to avoid the situation completely or fake it. Avoiding it means we never do learn, and faking it usually leads to a lot of dumb mistakes. We have all laughed at jokes we didn't understand and gotten ourselves into situations we were not really prepared for. It takes a lot of self-confidence to say "I don't know" and confidence is usually one of the things we have least of in a new situation. It is always true masters of a skill or situation who are most comfortable admitting what they don't know. Teenagers are learning so many new skills at once, it is easy to feel inept, frustrated, and impatient. Hiding these feelings and trying to appear more savvy and competent than you are can create an uncomfortable difference between the image you project to others and your true self. Building the inner confidence that allows you to grow, ask questions, and learn from your mistakes is a critical step in mastering the skills you need to manage your own life.

Another related problem is learned social embarrassment. Many of the topics and issues that are important to our personal and social well-being are difficult to talk about in this culture. We learn early in our childhood that certain topics make the grown-ups around us uncomfortable. Most families don't talk openly about sexuality, fears or inadequacies, death, drug use, or family problems. Even close friends may avoid talking honestly about some of these subjects. Most students agree that it is much less embarrassing to *have* sexual intercourse than to *talk* about it. Most couples finally discuss birth control *after* they have had intercourse. Communicating honestly and comfortably about the issues which affect you is important to healthy development and well-being.

The last and most important processing hurdle is the critical step of taking charge and really being responsible for yourself. Human beings are pretty helpless when they are born. Compared to any other animal, even bugs, we are weak and dependent on people around us for our survival. When you were born, your internal systems were working moderately well and you could blink, but you couldn't walk, talk, feed yourself, protect yourself, or even roll over if you wanted a different view. Most of your basic survival needs were met by your parents.

Life is like playing a violin solo in public and learning the instrument as one goes on.
—Edward Bulwer-Lytton

Experience teaches you to recognize a mistake once you've made it again.
—Unknown

Parents can only give good advice or put them on the right paths, but the final forming of a person's character lies in their own hands.

—Anne Frank

Luckily, most parents do that sort of thing and you probably have come to expect them to meet your basic needs, protect you from danger, comfort you when you are hurt, and to think you are pretty wonderful. It is not a bad deal actually, but they get tired of dirty diapers and you get tired of being told what to do. So the inevitable trek toward autonomy begins.

Adolescence is the period when this transfer of responsibility is most obvious and dramatic. While most teenagers are ready and excited to gain more control over their lives, the full implications of these new responsibilities can be both subtle and scary. When my son first got his driver's permit, he took his younger brother and me for a drive. He admitted that he was a little nervous. I replied, "As well you should be; you have your life and your brother's and mother's lives in your hands." While this did not appear to comfort him much, it was the simple truth. Independence takes away the safety nets. It puts you in charge of your own needs, safety, comfort, and self-worth—and, at times, those of others. These are important responsibilities that will require thought, planning, effort, practice, and an ever-increasing amount of wisdom. When you are new at this, tired, confused, or just in a particularly tough situation, it is tempting to forget who is in charge. This is dangerous thinking and will keep you from growing up.

Security is mostly a superstition. It does not exist in nature nor do the children of men as a whole experience it. Life is either a daring adventure or nothing.

—Helen Keller

Luckily the transition into adulthood in our society is gradual with some room for mistakes and regression. This workbook will assume each of you is at a different point in the process of taking responsibility for your life, but the journey has begun.

OBJECTIVES AND VALUES

To address the *process* of human development, this book will use a different format and set of objectives than many texts. It is quite literally, a *work book*. (You may have already noticed there are a lot of blank spaces and places for you to complete.) You will find a lot more questions than answers. You will be expected to search actively for the information and insights that you need. Some of these questions only you will be able to answer for yourself. Some information you will learn from your friends and families. Some you will find in this book, reference books, or by consulting with professionals or other sources. Some of the questions will only raise deeper questions and may take most of your life to answer. *The objective is to know which questions to ask and to know how to get accurate, realistic answers that will enrich your personal, social, and ethical development.* **This is the Quest.**

Exploring, clarifying, and questioning your own values will be an important part of this work. You will not be told what is right or wrong, but there are some values that are implicit in the ideas and assumptions presented in this book. No education or theory is valueless—especially where it involves human behavior. This book is based on four basic value assumptions:

1. **All ideas and human behaviors exist within an ethical framework.** A sense of personal integrity and honor is basic to higher levels of human development. Individually, we must explore, articulate, and act upon our values.

2. **Each individual has the responsibility and right to respect, maintain, nurture, and protect her or his self.** Irresponsibility or self-destructive behaviors undermine a person's self-worth and potential. It is each person's challenge to stretch and meet the possibilities, obstacles, and quandaries that life presents to him or to her.

It's not what we don't know that hurts, it's what we know that ain't so.
—Will Rogers

3. **Equally important, each person has the responsibility to respect the safety, integrity, and value of others.** Empathy and awareness of differing personalities, experiences, and values enrich our understanding of ourselves and human development on a larger scale. Our personal decisions, attitudes, and values should embody this respect both for ourselves and for others.

4. **Relationships, self-awareness, and personal growth are best accomplished through honesty and communication.** Becoming comfortable with the full range of our thoughts, feelings, experiences, hopes, and questions is the foundation of self-esteem and self-actualization. Listening to another person without judgment or advice, and honestly sharing our own life experiences and issues is the basis of healthy, enriching relationships.

These values are implicit in everything you will read or do in this workbook. You may want to question or at least be aware of some of their implications. This workbook will not sanction any behavior that *only* hurts yourself. Your own well-being is your most basic responsibility. The writing and exercises will assume that good decisions consider the needs, safety, and dignity of others as well as your own. Discussions will assume that every situation has an ethical dimension that is as important, if not more important, than expediency, self-interests, or even short-term well-being. This book will address many sensitive subjects in a direct, nonjudgmental way. This is based on the assumption that it is better to talk honestly about these issues than to avoid, deny, or misunderstand them. This will not always be comfortable and may occasionally raise conflicts or questions within your own belief systems. Use those conflicts to help define what is right and true for you. Talk to a friend, teacher, religious adviser, or family member about your questions. Ask for whatever guidance and support you need to deal with these complex and sometimes confusing issues.

CHAPTER FORMAT

This workbook provides a variety of information, ideas, and exercises for you to use as you study human development issues. If you are in a class, your teacher and class will select the areas that you will cover as a group. Don't let that stop you from exploring sections of the rest of the book on your own.

The following descriptions should give you an idea of the different sections that are included in each chapter.

➡ *GENERAL TEXT:*   This is the basic background information that will introduce the chapter topics. This text comes in two types—the regular, old-fashioned text that you read and try to remember, and a more do-it-yourself, fill-in variety. The fill-in text sections outline the main ideas of a topic and leave spaces for you to fill in the information yourself. This information will usually be provided through a class lecture or research assignment. Filling in the subheadings yourself will help you remember and articulate the information.

➡ *EXERCISES AND QUESTIONNAIRES:*   Each chapter will have several exercises you can do by yourself, for yourself. Most of these activities do not have a set of right or wrong answers. They are an opportunity for you to explore your own ideas, opinions, and experiences. These sections are for your own use and should remain confidential. It is always tempting to give the obvious and noble response when we fill out questionnaires. That will not prove to be very useful or enlightening. Take the opportunity to be honest with yourself.

➡ *QUANDARY MASTER:*   This section is a series of letters that describe problems or questions that individuals have encountered related to the chapter topic. The letters are fictitious, but based on real situations. Use this exercise as an opportunity to apply what you have learned to the complex situations that can arise. Write your responses to each letter in a way that considers both the facts and the human realities of each situation.

> ➡ ***Boxes***
>
> *Scattered throughout each chapter will be boxes of incidental or related information—quotes, studies, biographies, statistics, or resources. These boxes will add to the basic text and suggest related issues that you may want to explore further.*

> ➡ **Quandaries**
>
> Each chapter will contain some Quandaries boxes that present a practical or ethical question related to the topic at hand. A Quandaries box may present a dilemma or it may outline various positions on a question. These issues are not supposed to be easy and there are no answers at the back of the book. If you think the answer is simple or obvious, you probably need to read it again. The aim of these boxes is to help you begin to identify important issues and formulate your own opinions and values.

> • **A Note on Gender Language:** She and he are used interchangeably throughout this workbook. Whenever you see one or the other, assume that it means either or both unless it is an obviously gender specific situation (her menstrual cycle or his vas deferens). Occasionally, I have purposefully violated gender stereotypes to raise your awareness of some of the unconscious assumptions that we make. See Chapter 4 on Relationships for information and discussion of gender and language.

---

[1]Websters College Dictionary. New York: Random House, 1991.

Chapter 1

Questing: Coming of Age

Quest: the act of seeking or looking for something, a search; an adventure or expedition, as in medieval romance.[1]

Quandary: a state of hesitation or perplexity, a predicament or dilemma.[2]

> It is good to have an end to journey towards; but it is the journey that matters, in the end.
> —Ursula K. LeGuin

In days of old, young people often set off on a quest as a rite of passage into adulthood. Adolescent boys were sent off into the woods to capture a lion. Indian braves went off alone to fast and experience a spiritual awakening. Knights rode off to slay dragons. Poor boys ran off to sea to seek their fortunes. While young girls were usually not permitted such adventurous questing, they were carefully taught the skills and wisdom of mending and maintaining the fabric of home, family, and society. Both faced new responsibilities and the questions and challenges that accompany them. Mistakes were inevitable and sometimes costly. Through this questing, young people gained the skills, character, and humility needed to take their places as competent, responsible, and ethical adults.

Modern youth do not usually have such exciting or tangible opportunities to grow into their man or womanhood. With the coming of the industrial revolution, adult skills and responsibilities became more complex, involving more sophisticated training and education. Physical maturity was no longer enough. Young people are actually physically mature at an earlier age, but need more years of education and experience in order to successfully function in modern adult society. In earlier times, fifteen-year-olds were often married and supporting their own household. Today a person may not finish her education and be on her own until she is in her mid to late twenties or even her thirties.

While adult status has been delayed, the philosophical and personal quests of adolescence remain. The traditional search for separation, identity, character, and independence still begins at the end of childhood. Increasingly complex and abstract situations must be faced and mastered as modern-day dragons. Taking responsibility for your own life and well-being no longer requires hunting, weaving, or surviving in the wilderness for most teenagers, but it demands no less courage, skill, or risk-taking. We carry the dragons within ourselves: challenges of individuality, relationships, personal decisions, our responsibility to others and the survival of our planet. Our quests have become symbolic, exploring the nature of life itself and our own unique challenges within it.

- *What kind of person do I want to be?*
- *What skills and knowledge do I need to take care of myself?*
- *Who am I as a sexual person?*
- *How do I deal with failure, disappointment, and loss?*
- *How do I come to know and respect what is special about me?*
- *What are the hurdles inside and outside of me that I must face?*
- *What is my obligation to others and the world at large?*
- *What makes me happy?*
- *What is the meaning of my life?*
- *What do I believe in?*

The first real jolt of adulthood occurs when you realize that the answers to these questions are indeed a *quandary*. The answers contain ambiguities and contradictions. The deeper you look, the more complex and confusing the questions become. Your parents will share their ideas, hopes, and expectations, but even if they try, they cannot answer the questions for you. Religions, philosophy, and politics offer answers to consider. Within a chosen faith or political affiliation, each must still question and strive to understand on a personal level. Many wise and respected people have come up with very different answers.

Life is like a ten-speed bike. Most of us have gears we never use.
—Charles M. Schultz

Life offers a series of experiences, mistakes, accomplishments, challenges, relationships, and losses that help each of us explore these questions. This exploration will require information, reflection, and a certain amount of resiliency. The next series of exercises explores what you bring along as you begin this quest.

Quandary: The Age of Innocence or Loss of Innocence?

In trying to understand the universal qualities of human development, some researchers look at the impact of a given time in history. The following two writers have taken different points of view about adolescence in the United States during the 1980s and 1990s. How do you see your generation? Have you been pushed to deal with adult problems at too early an age or have you been pampered and overprotected from adult responsibilities?

Children Without Childhood[3] In her book, Marie Winn states, "We are at the beginning of a new era. Once parents struggled to preserve children's innocence, to keep childhood a carefree golden age. The new era operates on the belief that children must be exposed early to adult experience in order to survive. The Age of Protection has ended. An Age of Preparation has set in."[4] Changes in the basic family structure, the media, and new adult attitudes about child rearing have exposed children to adult problems, information, frailties, and freedoms for which they are not emotionally or intellectually ready. The result has been a loss of childhood innocence and play, a loss of respect for adult authority, early sexual experimentation and drug use, and a youthful cynicism and indifference.

The Postponed Generation[5] Susan Littwin writes that adolescents today are actually much less adult and independent than previous generations. Raised in a time of unprecedented prosperity and consumption, they were protected from scarcity and struggle. They grew up believing that whatever they wanted or needed would come easily and quickly. This sense of entitlement did not prepare them to cope with the economic, personal, and professional realities of the '80s and '90s—a lowered standard of living, steep competition for college and jobs, changing roles and relationships. The result is a generation that is anxious, dependent, apolitical, and disillusioned. "It is hard enough to establish an adult identity, even in the best of times. But to do it with such a jarring conflict between expectation and reality is a stunning task."[6]

My Opinion:

Questing Shield Exercise Instructions:

On each section of this shield, you will draw symbols to represent the qualities and ideals that you are carrying with you on your personal quest. Read each section carefully before deciding what you most need and value. Write your item on the lines below and then decide what symbol or design you would like to put on your shield. You may decorate it anyway you would like.

1. Pick one animal whose character and strengths you admire and would like to emulate in yourself. Example: the power of a lion, the determination of a beaver, the beauty of a butterfly, the playfulness of a dolphin, etc. _____

2. Pick one person whose love, wisdom, and support you will use to strengthen and guide you. Example: someone that you respect and admire; a friend or family member; a personal hero or heroine of yours; a historical, religious, or fictional character that you admire.

3. Pick one activity or skill that gives you pleasure and makes you feel good about yourself. Example: playing an instrument, making something, surfing, camping, community service, hang gliding, etc. _____

4. Pick one personal strength that will help you through good and bad times. Example: your sense of humor, intelligence, perseverance, friendliness, self-confidence, helpfulness, sensitivity, dependability, etc. _____

5. Pick one personal weakness you must work on to accomplish successfully your goals. Example: lack of confidence, stubbornness, laziness, fear, jealousy, shyness, prejudices, disorganization, etc. _____

6. Pick one important issue or principle you would like to address or change in your life. Example: an environmental issue, prejudice, disarmament, individual freedom, poverty, the homeless, AIDS, drunk driving, etc. _____

7. Pick a life goal or quality for which you would most like to attain or to be known. Example: a particular talent, wealth, friendship, courage, humor, helping others, honesty, adventure, spirituality, an accomplishment, etc. _____

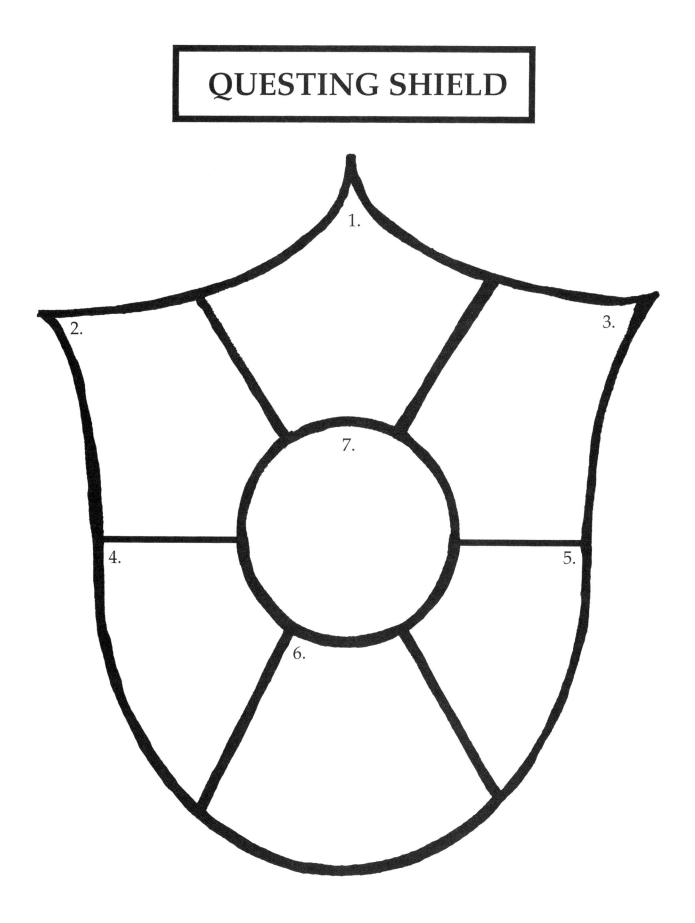

WHO AM I NOW?

Fill in the following twenty blanks with nouns, adjectives, or phrases that describe how you see yourself at this point in your life. You can use anything that you think describes who you are—put down whatever comes to your mind. *Examples: A man, friendly, a stamp collector, an excellent chess player, a student, afraid of snakes, one of six children, Samantha's boyfriend, etc.*

I AM:

1. _____

2. _____

3. _____

4. _____

5. _____

6. _____

7. _____

8. _____

9. _____

10. _____

11. _____

12. _____

13. _____

14. _____

15. _____

16. _____

17. _____

18. _____

19. _____

20. _____

The Story of My Life

Robert Coles, a well-known psychiatrist, writer, and teacher, has said that true understanding and development lies in the literary understanding of the stories of our lives. After listening to thousands of children and adults, he believes that our moral understanding arises not so much from psychiatric theories as from literature, religion, and learning by example.[7] It is in the stories of our lives that we gain meaning and understanding.

Make a list of five or six turning points in your life so far. These can be grand events where your life took an important change, or simple moments when something changed inside of you. They can be wonderful, exciting times or sad, painful times. Try to come up with the events or forces which have really made you who you are.

Using these turning points as a guide, write an autobiography of your life so far. Write about your life as a novelist might. Examine your surroundings and the impact they have had on you. Describe yourself and your list of supporting characters. What are the themes and lessons that you have learned? What would you entitle your autobiography? Take some time with this exercise to explore your life and your stories. Come back to it at various times during the course to check your perceptions and self-understanding. Reading autobiographies of other people may give you a richer understanding of yourself and others.

My Turning Points

1. Age _____   What happened _____

   How I changed   _____

2. Age _____   What happened _____

   How I changed   _____

3. Age _____   What happened _____

   How I changed   _____

4. Age _____   What happened _____

   How I changed   _____

5. Age _____   What happened _____

   How I changed   _____

6. Age _____   What happened _____

   How I changed   _____

MENTORS: PERSONAL GUIDES AND HEROES

A *mentor* is a person in your life who has been a trusted counselor or guide. This could be a friend or family member who has supported you throughout the years. It might be a coach or teacher or even a stranger who helped you through a difficult situation and taught you something that developed new strength or understanding. Through actions, writings, or philosophy, a famous or literary personality may have become a mentor for you. Most mentors teach by example. They are someone you respect and would like to emulate. Part of the person you will become is shaped by the personal mentors that you choose.

Complete the information listed below on four people in your life who have influenced you in important, lasting ways. Try to include people you have known personally and people you have read or studied whose ideas or actions have influenced you. This might be a literary character, a performer, writer, politician, scientist, activist, or historical or religious figure.

> *Each of us is the pupil of whichever of us could best teach what each of us needed to learn. When the pupil is ready, the teacher appears.*
> —*Maria Barreno*

Mentor #1 _____   Relationship _____

Why do I respect this person?

What have I learned from this person?

What qualities of this person would I like to develop in myself?

Mentor #2 _____   Relationship _____

Why do I respect this person?

What have I learned from this person?

What qualities of this person would I like to develop in myself?

Mentor #3 _____   Relationship _____

Why do I respect this person?

What have I learned from this person?

What qualities of this person would I like to develop in myself?

Mentor #4 _____   Relationship _____

Why do I respect this person?

What have I learned from this person?

What qualities of this person would I like to develop in myself?

ADOLESCENCE

> (Teenagers) today are tyrants. They contradict their parents, gobble their food, and tyrannize their teachers.
> —Socrates (470–399 B.C.)

"It was the best of times and it was the worst of times" (Dickens, *Tale of Two Cities*). Some people believe that adolescence inevitably includes problems, rebellious behavior, and trouble. Others think back romantically to the freedom and excitement of adolescence. In truth, the experience of adolescence varies from person to person and from day to day. Some people confront many difficult and painful obstacles to growing up. Many individuals never experience the alienation and confusion so often portrayed in books and movies about teenagers. Most teenagers have their good days and their bad days, experience both insecurity and exhilaration, make mistakes, learn important new skills and, day by day, become more comfortable and confident in their new adulthood.

Technically, adolescence is the period of physical, psychological, and social change from childhood to adulthood. As your body goes through puberty, your mind, relationships, status in the world, and sense of who you are stretches and matures. During this transitional period, a young person gains the skills, values, self-concept, and social competence to function as an adult member of society.

Adolescence is:

- *a time of rapid physical growth and sexual maturation.*

- *a time of intellectual growth from the concrete, cognitive logic of a child to the adult ability to think abstractly.*

- *a time of values clarification and development of moral autonomy.*

- *a time to achieve a coherent and unique sense of personal identity.*

- *a time to make a shift in identification and emotional attachment from parents to peers and members of the opposite sex.*

Physical Growth and Sexual Maturation:

At some time between the ages of nine and fifteen, every child begins what is known as the *adolescent growth spurt.*

➡ The hypothalamus energizes the pituitary gland which is located at the base of the brain.

➡ The pituitary gland then activates the ovaries, testes, and adrenal glands which secrete estrogen and androgens into the bloodstream.

Then the fireworks begin! The development of the head and brain is mostly completed during infancy, but general body growth and the development of the lymphoid system take a second spurt during adolescence. Skeletal and muscular changes affect the feet and hands first. The legs then grow before the upper body, often making the growing adolescent feel out of balance and awkward. Changes in blood pressure, heart rate, red blood cells, respiratory rate, and metabolic rate also occur. Hormones stimulate the development of new sexual interests and appearances. The average peak growth age is 12 for girls and 14 for boys. During this time, both sexes are likely to be growing faster than any other time in their lives since early childhood. Most adults forget what it is like to wake up with a slightly different, somewhat unpredictable body every morning.

The rate and onset of growth varies greatly between individuals and also between cultures. The average age of menarche (the first menstrual period) in young women is 12.5 to 13.2 years of age in most western societies, but the median age varies from 13 to 16 years worldwide. In the isolated highlands of New Guinea, girls do not begin to menstruate until around 18 years of age. The age of menarche has also declined at least two years since the late 1800s—the average age of menarche in 1880 was 16. Nutrition, sleep, and exercise habits can significantly affect adolescent growth. Both the timing and shape of your physical development will usually follow your parents' pattern of maturation.

There is not enough research to support the suggestion that that age is declining even more rapidly in the twenty-first century, but early physical maturation and breast development has raised questions about this trend and the possible influence of hormone additives in our food. Estrogen and other growth hormones are often used to increase production and weight in cows, pigs, and chickens. Most studies have indicated that the milk and meat from these supplemented animals are safe, but objectors question the credibility of these studies and believe that the long-term and subtle effects are not yet known.

Changes Boys Experience

♂ You may grow from three to twelve inches in a single year, reaching close to your full height (usually by around age seventeen).

♂ Your voice changes, lowering and usually going through a period of unpredictable variation.

♂ Your skin becomes oilier, often causing pimples on your face, neck, and upper body.

♂ Your body hair gets thicker and facial hair begins to develop.

♂ Your sweat glands begin working, causing more sweat and stronger odor.

♂ Your muscles and strength develop.

♂ Your penis and testicles get bigger. Pubic hair begins to grow around your anus, testicles, and penis.

♂ Sperm and semen begin to be produced in your testicles. You will probably have "wet dreams," nocturnal emissions of semen ejaculated during your sleep.

♂ Sexual feelings and urges begin to intensify.

Before adolescence, boys and girls are generally similar in strength and physical ability. After puberty, boys' muscles tend to be both bigger and stronger than girls'. Boys also develop larger hearts and lungs and a lower heart rate. Adult males have a lower proportion of fat to muscle than adult females. On the average, adult male voices will be about an octave lower than a female's, but both male and female individuals vary.

Many boys experience some growth of the breast tissues during puberty. This is called *gynecomostia* and it is normal and temporary. It will disappear within six months to a year and has nothing to do with your sexual orientation or prowess.

Several studies have examined the effects of early and late development on personality variables. Early maturing boys are more often accepted as adults and given more recognition, responsibility, and popularity by both adults and their peers. By age thirty, they were more confident, responsible, and self-controlled. Late maturing boys often appeared more childish, restless, and rebellious during adolescence. As adults, they were still more dependent, impulsive, and self-indulgent, but "coping with being small and weak (even temporarily) in a world that values size and strength seemed to have given the late maturers some insights and flexibility that the early maturers lacked."[8]

Changes Girls Experience

♀ You may grow from three to twelve inches in a single year, reaching close to your full height (usually by around age sixteen).

♀ Your skin becomes oilier, often causing pimples on your face, neck, and upper body.

♀ Hair will begin to grow under your arms and your leg hairs will become thicker and maybe darker.

♀ Your sweat glands begin working, causing more sweat and stronger odor.

♀ Your muscle tone will become more flexible and better suited for endurance than strength.

♀ Your breasts will grow and your hips will widen.

♀ Pubic hair will grow around your genital area (*vulva*).

♀ Your uterus and vagina will grow. The eggs in your ovaries have been there since birth, but now they will begin to mature.

♀ Menarche, the beginning of your menstrual cycle, usually comes at the end of this growth spurt and will probably be irregular for the first year.

♀ Sexual feelings and urges begin to intensify.

Girls' early start on puberty brings about those awkward eighth-grade dances, where your dance partners come up to your chin. Or the boys may have been wrestling around in the parking lot while you and your girlfriends were thinking a bit more romantically. These differences even out within a year or two.

While adult males are stronger, adult females show greater endurance for long-term stress. Their bodies tend to use energy more efficiently. The first woman to swim the English Channel, Gertrude Ederle, beat all previous times. As adults, women tend to be healthier, have greater resistance to diseases and, for a variety of physical and social reasons, live six to eight years longer.

Studies have not shown any significant long-term personality patterns for early or late development in girls. Since girls develop about two years earlier than boys, late maturers may not appear as young in a group of their peers. Early maturers, however, often gain temporary status and sexual attention. This can have both advantages and disadvantages. Early sexual pressures from older boys may be difficult to handle emotionally. Girls who are accustomed to socializing with older students may be isolated by their peers and feel socially frustrated within their age group. These differences will even out by the end of high school, but some early maturing girls find it difficult to reestablish ties with their classmates.

Intellectual and Moral Development:

At the same time your body is changing and developing, your ability to think, reason, and make judgments changes as well. This is called *cognitive development.* You don't just get smarter, you begin to think about things in substantially different ways. Research has suggested there are two periods of rapid change in cognitive processes. One is between ten and twelve years of age and the second is between fourteen and sixteen years. These times appear to coincide with the physical growth spurts of the brain.[9]

Jean Piaget, a Swiss psychologist, studied children's thought processes. He noted, as a child grows, significant changes occur in the way human beings think about their world. As a child, one can only think logically about concrete, real objects. During adolescence, one begins to develop a sophisticated ability to reason and make judgments based on hypothetical logic. Piaget called this *formal operations.* Adolescents can think about what is possible as well as about what is concrete and actual. They can identify common themes and contradictions in ideas, people, and within themselves. They can examine abstract ideas such as love, justice, art, truth, and integrity. They begin to measure themselves and their world against these ideals. They can consider ideas, decisions, relationships, and their lives both logically and abstractly.

Along with the development of cognitive reasoning, *ethical reasoning* also undergoes some significant changes during adolescence. As an individual becomes able to think abstractly and consider different perspectives, ethical considerations shift from purely conventional measures of right and wrong to more independent judgments based on ethical principles.

Lawrence Kohlberg and his associates at Harvard University have outlined six stages of moral development which they have observed in their research. In early adolescence, most individuals base their ethical decisions on the approval and consideration of others or on the letter of the law and a sense of duty to the status quo. *Good* behavior pleases others and conforms to general rules, expectations, or the majority opinion.

During adolescence, most individuals begin to shift to a more *autonomous* (*independent; self-governing*) or principled level of thinking. Individuals make a clear effort to define general ethical principles for themselves. This may or may not conflict with prevailing opinions, rules, or authority. When adolescents question authority, they are beginning to contrast the values of the adults around them to a new personal system of ethical principles.

A growing awareness of cultural and personal relativism leads many young adults to abandon any moral judgment of differing viewpoints at all—*"different strokes for different folks."* Others adopt a philosophy of individual existentialism—*"whatever gets you through the night is all right."* Some teenagers form a strong set of personal beliefs without judging different points of view. Others decide if ethics are just a matter of personal

I do not think that I will ever reach a stage when I will say "This is what I believe. Finished." What I believe is alive . . . and open to growth. . . .
            —*Madeleine L'Engle*

opinion or social control, why bother? Personal advantage, whim, or convenience may temporarily replace ethical considerations. Eventually, both of these positions tend to raise some logical and ethical dilemmas which lead to the development of a more universal-ethical-principle orientation.

Dr. Carol Gilligan was one of Dr. Kohlberg's research assistants. She noticed that the large majority of subjects used to formulate Kohlberg's stages of ethical development were men. She also noted that even thoughtful adult women tended to score lower on this scale than their male counterparts. Dr. Gilligan speculated that perhaps there was a gender difference in the way individuals viewed ethical questions, and that Kohlberg's stages were, more accurately, the stages of *male* ethical development. Gilligan theorized that not only may females answer ethical dilemmas differently; they may view the dilemmas and base their answers on a different set of criteria. In her book, *In a Different Voice*,[10] Dr. Gilligan presents the theory that girls and women are more likely to define an ethical dilemma in terms of connections or relationships, and boys and men tend to view these dilemmas in terms of the stated rules or principles. Both adult males and females understood the ethical dynamics involved, but framed both the question and answer differently. If a problem arose during an elementary school game, the boys would look to the rules and stated procedures to resolve it. Girls tended to define the problem in terms of the people and relationships involved, and might even end the game rather than damage these connections. Where Kohlberg's theory might have concluded that the girls' responses were not as developed, Gilligan made a strong case that the female ethical voice was simply based on different criteria and should not be judged by the male model. If the original subjects had been mostly female, the theory that emerged would have been quite different.

Many interesting studies and books have been based on Gilligan's ideas. Her pioneering work made people aware of two fundamental considerations. *First, we must pay careful attention to the population on which we base our ideas and assumptions.* The researchers did not account for gender when they interpreted their data. They assumed that their subjects, mostly college-age, white males in Cambridge, Massachusetts, were representative of everyone. In effect, this established a white, male, affluent, east coast American standard by which everyone would be judged. This bias was not set up intentionally or carelessly. We all assume on some level that our perceptions and realities are universal—that other people think and feel the same way we do. In some cases, we are correct. In other matters, gender, ethnicity, culture, socioeconomic background, and even geography can make a significant difference. On the first intelligence tests, the testers did not account for language and, not surprisingly, found that people who did not speak or read English (the language in which the test was written) did not score as highly. In order to assert that a theory or characteristic is universal, one must carefully consider, balance, and account for all of these factors.

Second, and perhaps more important, Gilligan's work questions the assumption that different approaches to ethical questions must be ranked or devalued. The ethic of caring evident in the girls' responses was not superior or inferior. It was based on a different set of assumptions and objectives. In the

Quandary: *What Is the Ethical Dilemma?*

In their research, Kohlberg and his associates posed ethical dilemmas and studied the responses and reasoning they heard at different ages. These dilemmas involve a conflict that can be viewed on different levels. Here are two examples of problems that were used.

- *Henri's Dilemma—Henri's wife is critically ill and will die if she does not get a special medication. The druggist is selling the drug for ten times what it costs to make it. Henri cannot raise the money and the druggist refuses to lower the price or wait for payment. What should Henri do?*

- *Helga's Dilemma—Helga is asked by a Jewish good friend, Rachel, to hide her from the Nazi Gestapo. If they are discovered, Rachel, Helga, and Helga's whole family will be killed. If Helga does not hide her, Rachel will probably be deported to a concentration camp. What should Helga do?*

What do you think? What guidelines or principles do you consider to arrive at your judgment—laws, public opinion, religious principles, fairness, personal advantage, possible punishment, strategic considerations, relationships, social justice? How difficult is it to put yourself in Henri or Helga's place? What considerations affect your answer?

Present these dilemmas to six people of different ages—*(6–12 years old, 13–18 years old, 19–24 years old, 25–35 years old, 36–50 years old, over 50)*. Be careful not to influence the answers by the way you present the question or react to the answer. *Do you see any ethical differences in the way each age group goes about resolving the dilemmas?*

OR, you may choose to interview three boys and three girls of the same age range to test Dr. Gilligan's argument. *Do you see any differences between the way boys and girls approach these problems? Was there any gender difference between the two questions?*

Researchers have to question a large number of subjects in order to account for the individual differences at each age. With just six subjects, you may not have noticed any consistent differences. Trends and stages are generalizations that the majority of people in any given group tend to favor.

example of the interrupted game, the desired outcome for the girls was not winning or losing; it was to keep everyone cared for and connected. This orientation might not work well for a World Series, but may be exactly what we need to resolve some of the important political and ecological conflicts throughout the world today. When we learn to value different voices, strengths, and perspectives, we have a stronger repertoire of talents and insights with which to address the problems we face.

A Coherent and Unique Sense of Personal Identity:

Perhaps the most universally discussed characteristic of adolescence is the development of a sense of individual identity. Who am I? How am I different from others? How am I the same? How do I change in different situations and what characteristics are consistently *ME?* What do *I* think? What do *I* feel? What do *I* believe? A person begins to identify his own personal qualities, his own preferences and goals, and begins to take control of his own life. Instead of being defined and identified by others, she begins to recognize her own talents, skills, relationships, impulses, needs, defenses, and aspirations.

Erik H. Erikson, a well-known psychoanalyst, researcher, and professor of human development, was the first to write extensively about this important part of human development that begins during adolescence. Erikson theorized that children (and adults) go through a predictable series of *life crises*—specific changes or important junctures in their development. The resolution of each crisis sets up the groundwork for later development. During adolescence, the important task or life crisis is the formation of an independent ego identity. This identity includes a sexual identity, a work identity, and an ethical identity. Confusion about these roles creates feelings of isolation, indecision, and anxiety. Discovering who you are and would like to become is the foundation of all self-esteem, development, and healthy relationships.

> *Trouble is only opportunity in work clothes.*
> —Henry Kaiser

> *We are the hero of our own story.*
> —Mary McCarthy

Creating an Identity

One of the wonders of great literature is that it captures the essence of a character's personal, yet universal, identity. We identify with some qualities and contrast ourselves with others. Each memorable character encompasses a unique but recognizable segment of the human experi-

---

Writing in the third person, see yourself as objectively as possible and write a brief character description of yourself under the following circumstances:

1. Think back to early elementary school and describe yourself in the classroom or playground. What did you look like? How did you relate to others? What did you do well and what did you have difficulty with? How did your feelings differ from the way you acted? Identify the qualities that were a part of you then that are still central to who you are today.

2. Next, picture yourself today at a party or informal gathering of some of your peers. Try to describe objectively your character in this group. What do you look like? How are you different and the same as the other people at the party? What would you be doing? How would others respond to you? How would you be feeling on the inside that may contrast with the ways you look and act?

3. Now, using some artistic license, describe your ideal self. Go back to the same party and describe yourself as you would like to appear and feel. What type of person would you like to be? How would your appearance, feelings, relationships, and role in this group be different?

4. Then jump ahead and create the adult that you would like to become. What personal qualities and talents have you developed? What kinds of relationships are you involved in? What do other people see and respect in you? What kinds of work and play have you included in your life? What is important in your life?

5. Finally, imagine that your life is nearing its end. What will you want to have accomplished and become? What regrets would you want to have avoided? What will give you pride and comfort in your old age? How do you want to be remembered by others? What will be important to you as you face your own death?

ence, just as your life does. Now step back and try to look at yourself as the hero or heroine in your life novel. What qualities are central to your unique identity?

A Self Profile

In this list of personality characteristics, circle any of the words which you believe describe you. Don't worry about contradictions—we are all full of them!

Absentminded	Demanding	Imaginative	Nonconformist	Satisfied
Active	Dependable	Impulsive	Observant	Self-assured
Adventurous	Determined	Inconsiderate	Old-fashioned	Selfish
Aggressive	Different	Independent	Open-minded	Sensible
Ambitious	Diplomatic	Insecure	Optimistic	Sensitive
Angry	Disorganized	Insensitive	Organized	Serious
Anxious	Easygoing	Insightful	Outgoing	Shy
Apathetic	Efficient	Intelligent	Outspoken	Silly
Artistic	Emotional	Intimidating	Passive	Skeptical
Assertive	Energetic	Introverted	Patient	Sociable
Athletic	Even tempered	Irresponsible	Peacemaker	Spontaneous
Bitter	Fearful	Kind	Pessimistic	Strong
Blunt	Feisty	Lazy	Playful	Tactful
Bossy	Forceful	Lively	Pleasant	Tender
Calm	Friendly	Logical	Powerful	Tolerant
Candid	Funny	Lonely	Prejudiced	Tough
Careless	Generous	Loner	Proud	Traditional
Cautious	Gentle	Loving	Questioning	Trusting
Cheerful	Gifted	Macho	Quiet	Understanding
Clever	Happy	Miserly	Realistic	Unpredictable
Competent	Helpful	Modest	Rebellious	Well-liked
Composed	Honest	Moody	Relaxed	Wise
Confident	Hot tempered	Musical	Religious	Withdrawn
Courageous	Humble	Nervous	Responsible	Witty
Creative	Hyperactive	Noisy	Risk-taker	Worried

1. Pick the five words from the list that you believe *best* describe you. List them in order of their importance to you.

2. What qualities have you circled that you would rather you did not have? Why? Are they changeable or are you stuck with them?

3. What qualities that you have circled do you feel best about? Why? How do you use and develop these qualities?

Adoption and Identity

Being adopted may create some unique questions in your efforts to establish your own identity during adolescence. A big piece of the puzzle, your genetic makeup, is often missing. Your adoptive family has provided your environment and the love and care you have needed growing up. Your life in this family is a large, important part of who you are, but it doesn't explain your red hair, some physical characteristics, and even some genetically determined elements of your temperament. It may be important for you to know that there is a long line of heart disease or alcoholism or arthritis in your genetic background so that you can make good decisions about your health to avoid these problems.

Some adopted teenagers have little or no interest in knowing more about their birthparents. Others are mildly curious and some become determined to find out the circumstances of their adoption. Some adopted children have emotional, eating, or drug-related problems during adolescence that might be avoided by recognizing these normal questions of identity and history. It is not always obvious that adoption is an issue, but if you are adopted and run into problems during this time of your life, you should think about how your adoption may play into your sense of yourself at this time.

Birth information is not always an easy or simple topic for families to talk about. Your adoptive parents may be quite helpful to you when they understand your need to have all the pieces of your identity puzzle. They may already have access to information about your birthparents or genetic background. Some states seal adoption records, but there is a lot of nonidentifying information about your adoption that is available to you. Many states are beginning to recognize the rights of adopted individuals to access this information about themselves. At twenty-one, you may have more legal rights in this quest.

It is quite normal to speculate about what your birthparents look like, what kind of people they are and why you were put up for adoption. You may wonder if you have brothers or sisters or if your birthmother ever thinks about you. Giving a child up for adoption is a very difficult and caring decision, usually made to provide you with opportunities and security that your birthmother could not offer at that time in her life. It is safe to assume that she thinks about you often and hopes you are having a good life. Some birthparents welcome contact or information about a child they have put up for adoption; others may have blocked out what was a painful and buried decision and may not want to deal with it. If you decide to search for your birthparents, you will need support from your family and enough personal confidence to understand what you discover. The way your birthparents have handled your adoption is all about them—it tells you nothing about your character or worth. It is wonderful if your birthparent becomes an added support person in your life, but if she or he cannot handle a relationship with you, that is because of her or his own problems and fears. There can be some very powerful feelings around these issues, so be sure that you have an objective adult to talk to.

The increase in international adoptions may add another dimension to individual identity questions. You may have no memory of your birthplace or culture, but physical or racial differences can make your adoption a visible part of your everyday life. You have been raised as an American child in an American environment, quite different from your birth parents' culture. The influence of heredity and environment is very real for you. If you are genetically Korean, but raised by American parents in the United States, what part of you is Korean and what part American? Strangers may expect you to be more like their stereotype of your national heritage when, in fact, it may be very foreign to you. Korean nationals may be offended by your lack of cultural identity or awareness. You are, first and foremost, a unique and distinct individual. Your bicultural makeup may give you a valuable insight into our international commonality and the limitations of judging people by appearance or nationality. Celebrate all of the interrelated parts of your identity and don't let others define you by their assumptions. Some international adopted children may feel "less than" either their adopted identity or their birth identity, but, in reality, they are "more than" either part. This awareness can significantly enrich your understanding of yourself and our world.

Circles of Identity

We all have different levels of identity and group memberships that help define who we are at any given moment. Each level adds a different piece to the overall puzzle and affects each other part of who we are.

- To begin to fill in your circles, start with the five adjectives that you selected as best describing you from the adjectives list in the exercise on page 24. Write them in the center section that is labeled **SELF**.

- In the **PHYSICAL** circle, list any words that describe your physical appearance. *For example: male, tall, skinny, strong, etc.*

- In the **FAMILY** circle, write in any words that describe your role or position in your family. *For example: oldest, the black sheep, only boy, the smart one, the baby, etc.*

- In the **CLOSE FRIENDS** circle, write any words that describe your role with that group and qualities that they would ascribe to you. You may want to ask them for words they would use to describe you and write them in. *For example: leader, funny, helpful, good listener, crazy, bossy, dependable, etc.*

- In the **PEER GROUP** circle, we begin to deal more with generalizations and stereotypes. Identify the group of people your own age that you are most closely associated with—it may be a social group or a team, a school, neighborhood, or special interest group. *For example: jocks, Deadheads, eggheads, preppies, theater group, etc.* Fill in the circle with adjectives that describe qualities that group tends to have in common. Include both qualities that you have noticed to be true and qualities that people from the outside believe to be true.

- Do the same thing for the remaining parts of the circle.

    ETHNIC (racial and cultural background)

    SOCIOECONOMIC (income and social class)

    RELIGIOUS (if you ascribe to no particular religion, use agnostic or atheist)

    GEOGRAPHIC (state or section of the country)

    NATIONAL (the country you identify with—if you identify with both your current location and your country of origin, divide this part of the circle in half and include both)

Be sure to include both qualities that you have observed and the more general stereotypes of that group.

As you move farther from the center of this circle, the characteristics may describe you personally less and less even though you are a member of these larger groups. Our personal identity, however, is shaped by all the groups we belong to. This may also influence the expectations and assumptions of people who do not know you well. When you travel abroad, people may make certain judgments about you because you are from the United States. Strangers may expect you to behave in a certain way because of your physical build, racial background, or socioeconomic group.

In the outer circles, underline or highlight any characteristics that you believe do accurately describe a part of your personality. Consider how the others may affect the way you think about yourself and the way others react to you. For example, if you are a jock and also a serious, intelligent student, how has the stereotype of the "dumb jock" affected who you are? Is it annoying, but easily dispelled? Do you ever find yourself underplaying one part of your personality when you are with a particular group? Have you rebelled against the stereotype and made a point to prove that jocks are not dumb? Have you ever used one stereotype as an excuse not to develop another part of your personality? (I don't need to study because nobody really expects me to do that well anyway.)

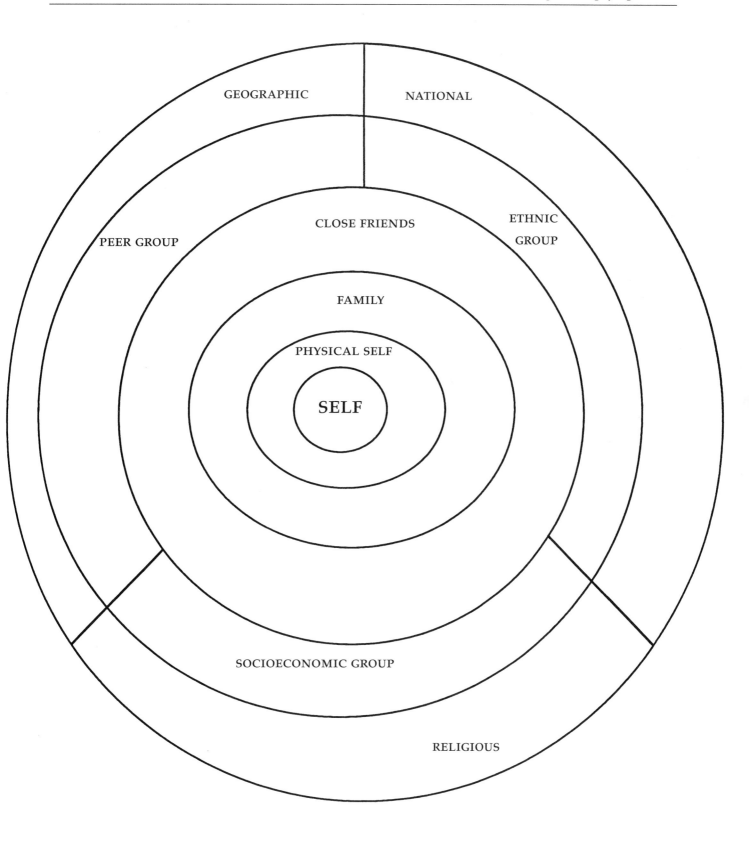

CIRCLES OF IDENTITY

Quandary: *Nature versus Nurture*

How much of your appearance, physical and psychological makeup, intelligence, behavior, and gender characteristics are determined by your genetic makeup (NATURE)? How much is influenced or determined by the physical and social factors in your environment (NURTURE)? Are you physically healthy because you inherited a strong physique or because you have a healthy diet and sanitary living conditions? Did you inherit your sunny disposition from your easygoing father or are you easygoing because you have been raised and nurtured by his example? Are boys more aggressive than girls because of some hormonal difference or because they have been given aggressive toys and encouraged to be strong and competitive? Do children inherit a vulnerability to mental illness, criminal behavior, or alcoholism or do they learn these behaviors growing up in disruptive home environments?

It is very difficult to separate the influences of nature and nurture and most scientists agree that every individual is the product of both. The research that has been done raises some interesting questions. Studies of twins are often used to look at this distinction. Remember, identical (monozygotic) twins come from the same egg and sperm which has split. Therefore they have the exact same genetic makeup. Fraternal twins (dizygotic) are born at the same time, but from separate egg and sperm. They are genetically like brother and sister.

Consider the following research carefully and begin to formulate your own opinions.

- In an adoptive study, Rosenthal looked at four groups.

    1. Children of mentally ill parents who were raised by those parents.
    2. Children of mentally ill parents who were adopted by normal parents.
    3. Children of normal parents who were adopted by mentally ill parents.
    4. Children of normal parents who were adopted by normal parents.

    Groups 1 and 2 *both* had a high percentage of mental illness as adults, demonstrating the strong influence of heredity. Group 3 had a somewhat higher rate of problems than Group 4, but this was strongly influenced by the *quality* of the relationship they had with their parent, whether that parent was mentally ill or not.

- Children with one alcoholic parent have a 26 percent chance of becoming an alcoholic; with two alcoholic parents, the risk goes up to 60 percent. Children of alcoholics adopted at an early age into a nonalcoholic family still had an alcoholism rate of 18 percent. This is significantly higher than the average 5 percent rate for children without an alcoholic parent.

- A study at Washington University looked at the children of mentally ill parents who were raised in severely disruptive home situations. Sixteen percent became severely mentally ill; 31 percent became withdrawn, odd, and reclusive; 32 percent were mildly maladjusted; and 12 percent became average, functioning adults. A surprising 9 percent, however, developed into exceptional, creative people, apparently strengthened rather than destroyed by both nature and nurture.

- Environment begins to have an impact long before a child can be separated from her biological parent—in the uterus. A mother's nutrition, use of drugs, state of mind, and general environment have been shown to influence the development, health, size, intelligence, and potential problems of the growing fetus.

MULTICULTURALISM IN THE UNITED STATES

The United States has always been a diverse combination of many cultures, races, languages, religions, and backgrounds. When Europeans first landed on this continent, there were over 500 distinct nations of people that the colonists decided to call "Indians." These tribal nations had a rich diversity of language, lifestyle, customs, and spiritual tradition. Immigrants from around the world streamed onto the continent, introducing the languages, foods, customs, music, architecture, religion, art, holidays, clothing, and stories of their homelands. Some settlers came in search of adventure, land, or wealth. Some came looking for religious freedom or escape from political prosecution. Others were brought forcibly as slaves or indentured servants. Some founding fathers and mothers were exported convicts or castoffs from other nations. As the new nation spread and became established, new immigrants from Asia and other countries came looking for work or gold. Some "immigrants" didn't even migrate. Mexicans, living in north Mexico, became Mexican-Americans in what was annexed to be California, New Mexico, Arizona, or Texas. By the late 1800s, the country had been wrestled from the American Indian Nations to accommodate people from over fifty countries representing almost every race, religion, language, and ethnic background on the planet. The United States was the new "melting pot" of immigrants, the first grand experiment of global diversity.

As the ignoble treatment of the American Indian tribes attested, this experiment was not based on cultural sensitivity or a celebration of differences. The "melting pot" was about *assimilation*. *Assimilation* is the process by which one group or individual takes on the characteristics of, or becomes like, the dominant group or culture. We were all to become a new culture of *Americans,* united in one government, language, and tradition. Irishmen dropped their accents. Teenagers abandoned the "old-fashioned" traditional dress of their homelands. Banjoes and bluegrass replaced European music. Bold, new writers heralded a new "American" voice in literature; and second-generation children exchanged their parents' language and traditions for the new American ways. This was not done quickly or easily. Each new immigrant group suffered economic and social hardships as they "melted." And it didn't take too long to figure out that some people or groups did not "melt" very well. Racial differences made it especially hard for some groups to blend in. Some individuals, particularly the older, first-generation folks, wanted a new home, not a new culture; and they clung stubbornly to the clothing, traditions, food, and language of their homeland. Economic differences continued to separate people as they always had in human society. Some individuals rejected the whole idea of any cultural identity in favor of the American promise of gallant individualism.

As we begin the twenty-first century, many of our original cultures have blended. Most Caucasian Americans no longer think of themselves by their ethnic origin. The groups who have not assimilated, either by choice or by exclusion, have challenged the melting pot analogy, and asserted that the United States should be more like a great tossed salad bowl—rich and wonderful because of its distinct, diverse, and delicious parts. African-Americans, Mexican-Americans, Asian-Americans, American Indians, and other groups attempt to celebrate BOTH their connection to their racial or cultural origin AND their American identity.

At the same time, the ethnic makeup of the United States has been steadily shifting away from any ethnic majority in the United States at all. In the 2000 Census, 48 percent of the Americans in California are white, 28 percent are Hispanic, 10 percent Asian-American, 7 percent African-American, and 1 percent American Indian. By 2025, it is projected that 44 percent of those living in California will be Hispanic, 34 percent white, 17 percent Asian-American, and 5 percent African-American—the first statewide Caucasian minority.[11] Texas, Hawaii, New Mexico, and the District of Columbia are projected to be at least 50 percent citizens of color by 2025, and Caucasians are projected to make up less than half of the entire population of the United States by 2050. With this shift comes a diversity of foods, languages, religions, music, and fashion. In our schools, in the media, on the Internet, in our cities, and on the main streets of our smallest towns, cultures already mix and share and overlap.

Some people think that this is a wonderful turn of events. They love Thai food, listen to African music, make Russian friends on the Internet, wear Guatemalan pants, learn Tai-Chi, watch Italian movies, celebrate Kwanza, practice their Spanish over a burrito at the Tex-Mex restaurant, study Buddhist meditation, and attend the Greek Dance Festival right in their own city square. The Red Cross and Doctors Without Borders join humanitarian workers from many countries to help victims of natural catastrophes. High school and college exchange students from all over the world join families in distant countries to learn a foreign language, broaden their horizons, and discover what we all have in common.

Some people are not as comfortable with diversity, and prefer things to be a little more predictable and customary. When they want a multicultural experience, they travel—but are happy to get back to their own hometown neighborhood, food, and language. They are content to "live and let live," but when people in their own town or country dress differently or speak another language or demand cultural respect for differences that are hard to understand, these people may feel uncomfortable or invaded. This is a personal inclination, and there are members of every culture, dominant or minority, who feel this way. They prefer to live as homogeneously as possible, with people more like themselves. This may work smoothly, and is very common in the United States, but these segregated lives can also become a source of misunderstanding or discrimination. It may be helpful to remember the initial tendencies that established the segregation in the first place, and find ways to increase multicultural understanding that recognize this underlying comfort level.

A small number of people seem to strongly dislike, fear, or devalue people who are culturally or racially different from them. History has witnessed terrible atrocities that have attempted to wipe out or disparage diversity. Wars and hate crimes continue to plague us as we learn how to live together. Supremacist groups around the world believe strongly that conflicting cultures or beliefs should be segregated or destroyed. Differences are viewed as a threat to the values or purity of the group, not an enhancement. Intolerance, of one sort or another, played into several of the violent school shootings in the late 1990s. There are hate group sites on the Internet, and violent crimes against minorities, gays, and women highlight the news on a regular basis.

Schools are laboratories for diversity issues and tensions. Students from many backgrounds and racial or ethnic groups learn together, play on teams together, forming friendships or rivalries. This mix can be rewarding and it can be difficult, but the understanding that can develop is critical to our evolving ability to live together on this increasingly diverse and interdependent planet. Young people bring the flexibility and idealism that we will need to resolve these complicated matters. We have *all* been raised with prejudices and assumptions about the world, and about people who are different from ourselves. Some prejudices are obvious, and some are illusive and subtle. Your assumptions about our own culture, as well as your beliefs about other cultures, become a part of your personal identity. In your personal quest, you will learn how you have assimilated your own culture, and what preferences and dislikes are cultural in nature. Ultimately, we must all discover what we have in common, and how we can benefit from our multicultural differences.

Quandary: What Is Your Cultural Identity?

Many of the cultural beliefs and attitudes that you have been taught are very subtle—in fact, most of us assume they are just facts or reality. When we are with our own cultural group, no one questions these assumptions and we don't have to explain or defend them. When another culture has different assumptions about these same things, we may be shocked and genuinely believe our way is the best or proper belief. We tend to put value judgments on these differences and on the people who behave differently. Identify your culture's value of each of the following by completing each sentence with a judgment (*i.e., Burping is . . . rude and disgusting*).

- *Eating insects is . . .*

- *Swearing is . . .*

- *Piercing parts of your body is . . .*

- *Talking back to your parents is . . .*

- *Fist fighting is . . .*

- *Fat women are . . .*

- *People who do well in school are . . .*

- *Standing close to someone when you talk is . . .*

- *Leaving your house during menstruation is . . .*

- *Long hair on men means . . .*

- *Women who fight are . . .*

- *Raising your voice during a discussion is . . .*

- *Going to college is . . .*

- *Killing a person is . . .*

- *Eating an animal is . . .*

- *Living with your parents when you are an adult is . . .*

- *Shaving your armpits is . . .*

- *Boys who like ballet are . . .*

- *Sarcasm is . . .*

- *Being on time is . . .*

- *Eating human flesh is . . .*

All of these things, to one degree or another, are culturally determined. Insects are a delicacy and important source of protein in many parts of the world. You would probably swear, or not swear, very differently if you had been raised in a different culture or family. Some cultures accept talking back to parents, while other cultures judge it unthinkable. Time may be based on the clock in one culture and on a natural cycle or the completion of tasks in another. Culture dictates how close or far you should stand when talking to someone and whether you should look at that person directly or cast your eyes to the side. Weight, grooming, and clothing all carry cultural values and meaning. Long hair in men may indicate a loose lifestyle in one culture, and strength and purity in another. It may be OK in one culture to eat a cow, and in another to eat a cat. Murder is outlawed in some cultures and required in others. Even cannibalism has been regarded differently by different groups throughout history.

There are often good reasons for cultural judgments, and some cultures do not prosper because of one or more of their cultural values. Many of your values are based on the wisdom and experience of your culture. When different cultures interact, however, these ingrained assumptions may cause us to make cultural judgments out of context. Burping may be rude in Philadelphia, but it is a compliment to the cook in Saudi Arabia.

Separation and Independence

Ever since your journey through the birth canal and your first breath of air on your own, you have been gradually separating from the mother and father who have given you life and nurturance. In the beginning, of course, you were physically part of the same body as your mother, created from the sperm and egg of your mother and father. For nine months, everything that you felt, ate, or experienced was through your mother's physical and emotional system. Your cells divided and specialized according to the combined genetic codes of your father's and mother's chromosomes. Seeds of independence stirred as your heart started to beat on its own. By five months, you began to kick and move about on your own within your mother's uterus.

At birth, your physical system was separated from your mother's. The umbilical cord which supplied you with food, oxygen, and circulation was cut and you began to breathe, feed, and heat yourself. During your first year of independence, most of your efforts went into physical development. Your internal systems matured, stabilizing your digestion, circulation, nervous system, vision, and muscular coordination. You learned to turn over, hold your head up, sit up, control your hand to reach for what you want, to grasp it and let it go, crawl, stand and take your first steps. No wonder the two-year-old is so cocky and proud of himself.

In more subtle ways, you were also beginning to become psychologically independent. By about six months of age, you had the skills, charm, determination, and wit to initiate and control the activities and people around you. You could clap your hands to start a game of patty-cake, hold up your arms so that your father would lift you up, bang on toys to make wonderful, loud noises, throw food off your tray to watch Mom pick it up, or smile sweetly to calm your exasperated parents.

At the same time that you discovered your own powers, you began to realize that you are indeed separate from these much loved, much needed grown-ups. Independence and separation come hand in hand. At eighteen months of age, you decided that this was not such a good thing. This is the age when you cried whenever Mom or Dad left the room, and shied away from strangers. You spent the next six months trying to resolve this conflict. You learned many tricks and social behaviors to get your parents to stay close by and respond to your needs and wishes. Once you reestablished this sense of safety and control, you felt safer to assert yourself as an individual. By age two, you had an independent self-concept and a mind of your own. You rejected suggestions and help from your parents and wanted to do things for yourself. Thus, the *terrible twos* gave a loud and determined send-off to your personal quest for independence.

Early friendships with other children . . . taking the school bus by yourself . . . tying your own shoes . . . choosing your own clothes . . . riding a two-wheeler . . . reading your first book by yourself . . . resolving difficulties with other children without the help of adults . . . secret thoughts, feelings, and experiences. All of these experiences made up the gradual separation that prepared each of us to become unique and independent adults.

The hardest years in life are those between ten and seventy.
—Helen Hayes at age 83

To have a sacred place . . . is an absolute necessity for anybody today. You must have a room, or a certain hour or so a day, where . . . you can simply experience and bring forth what you are and what you might be. This is a place of creative incubation. At first you may find that nothing happens there. But if you have a sacred place and use it, eventually something will happen.

—Joseph Campbell,
The Power of Myth

Taking Charge: Who's responsible for what?

As you separate from your parents, you take on more and more responsibility for yourself. Check who in your life is in charge of the areas listed below. If something is still completely your parents' responsibility, check **5**. If it is completely your responsibility, check **1**. If you share this responsibility, place a check somewhere along the line that shows how much of each of you is responsible.

Your Physical Well-Being	YOU				YOUR PARENTS
What you eat	1	2	3	4	5
How/when you exercise	1	2	3	4	5
Bathing/hair care	1	2	3	4	5
Tooth and braces care	1	2	3	4	5
Taking medication	1	2	3	4	5
Doctors appointments	1	2	3	4	5
Treating injuries/illnesses	1	2	3	4	5
Dental appointments	1	2	3	4	5
Visual needs (glasses, checkups)	1	2	3	4	5

Your Physical Appearance					
What clothes you wear	1	2	3	4	5
How you wear your hair	1	2	3	4	5
Makeup, tattoos, jewelry	1	2	3	4	5
Hair color	1	2	3	4	5
Your weight	1	2	3	4	5
Skin problems	1	2	3	4	5
Repair/replacement of clothing	1	2	3	4	5
Washing/ironing of clothing	1	2	3	4	5

Finances—Who pays for . . .					
Medical appointments	1	2	3	4	5
Hygiene (soap, toothpaste, etc.)	1	2	3	4	5
Medications	1	2	3	4	5
Braces/retainers	1	2	3	4	5
Glasses/contacts	1	2	3	4	5
Food	1	2	3	4	5
Clothing	1	2	3	4	5
Shoes	1	2	3	4	5

Sports equipment	1	2	3	4	5
Cosmetics	1	2	3	4	5
Housing expenses	1	2	3	4	5
Education expenses	1	2	3	4	5
Transportation	1	2	3	4	5
Stereo/ tapes/ music	1	2	3	4	5
Entertainment	1	2	3	4	5

Relationships

Time spent with family	1	2	3	4	5
How you interact with parents	1	2	3	4	5
Contact with grandparents	1	2	3	4	5
Contact with siblings	1	2	3	4	5
Who you spent time with as friends	1	2	3	4	5
Who you have over to your home	1	2	3	4	5
Selection of romantic boy/girlfriend	1	2	3	4	5
Decisions about sexual activity	1	2	3	4	5
Procuring birth control	1	2	3	4	5
Paying for birth control	1	2	3	4	5
Unplanned pregnancy	1	2	3	4	5
Resolving school problems	1	2	3	4	5
Resolving conflict with peers	1	2	3	4	5
Resolving legal problems	1	2	3	4	5

Activities

Where/if you go to school	1	2	3	4	5
Sports you play	1	2	3	4	5
Extracurricular activities	1	2	3	4	5
Lessons or special interests	1	2	3	4	5
School performance/grades	1	2	3	4	5
Parties you attend	1	2	3	4	5
Time you must be home	1	2	3	4	5
Concerts you attend	1	2	3	4	5
Where you go when not home	1	2	3	4	5
With whom you may ride in a car	1	2	3	4	5

Smoking	1	2	3	4	5
Use of alcohol	1	2	3	4	5
Use of drugs	1	2	3	4	5
Use of your free time	1	2	3	4	5
Bedtime	1	2	3	4	5
Getting up in the morning	1	2	3	4	5
Chores around the house	1	2	3	4	5
Cleaning your room					

Values and Future

Your religious affiliation	1	2	3	4	5
Church attendance	1	2	3	4	5
Political views/activities	1	2	3	4	5
Colleges you apply to	1	2	3	4	5
Whether or not to go to college	1	2	3	4	5
Possible career choices	1	2	3	4	5

Many of these responsibilities you have probably taken over completely and others your parents still take care of for you. Which areas do you see changing over the next five years?

Can't/Won't: Taking Charge of the Possibilities

Most of us are actually more in charge of our lives than we realize. Our language can affect the way we view the power and choices that are available to us.

Before reading any further, write ten things on the lines below that you cannot do.

1. I cannot _____

2. I cannot _____

3. I cannot _____

4. I cannot _____

5. I cannot _____

6. I cannot _____

Deadly Persuasion

Notes from Jean Kilbourne[12] on advertising.

- *If you are like most people, you think that advertising has no influence on you. This is what advertisers want you to believe. But if that were true, why would companies spend over $200 billion a year on advertising?*
- *The average American is exposed to at least 3000 ads every day and will spend three years of her life watching television commercials. Advertising makes up about 70 percent of our newspapers and 40 percent of our mail.*
- *Advertising often sells a great deal more than products. It sells values, images, and concepts of love and sexuality, romance, success, and perhaps most important, normalcy. To a great extent, it tells us who we are and who we should be.*
- *A study of seven- to ten-year-old children done by researchers at Columbia University in 1975 found that heavy viewing of advertising led to cynicism, not only about advertising, but about life in general.*
- *The story that advertising tells is that the way to be happy, to find satisfaction, is through consumption of material objects.*

7. I cannot _____

8. I cannot _____

9. I cannot _____

10. I cannot _____

How did you feel as you listed all of these limitations? For most people, this is a pretty discouraging and frustrating list. It may include personal weaknesses (*I cannot do physics*) or frustrations (*I can't get organized*). It may include things that other people won't let you do (*I can't stay out past 11:00 PM* or *I can't skip my classes and go to the beach*).

But how many of the things that you listed are *really* impossible? Did you include things like *I cannot walk through walls* or *I can't live without oxygen?* Most of us list things that we actually have chosen not to do. I *could* do physics, but I choose not to spend the time and effort that it would require for me to learn it. I *could* get organized, but it's such a hassle and I muddle by. I *could* stay out after 11:00 PM, but my parents would be angry and worried and probably ground me. I choose to come in by 11:00 to avoid the consequences of violating their curfew. I *could* skip my classes, but I might miss information that would be needed later and I choose not to risk the consequences of the school rule against skipping class.

Most of our limits are choices that we have made because we either don't like the consequences or value something else more. Saying "I can't" implies a power outside of yourself that is controlling your behavior. By changing *can't* to *won't*, you can clarify the personal decision you are making. This brings the power to change or control the situation back to yourself.

Consider the difference between these two statements.

I can't quite smoking.

I won't quit smoking.

The first sentence is not true, of course. You *can* quit smoking at any moment. When you change the sentence to "I won't," the focus shifts to the personal decision that you have made to continue smoking. You can then explore the reasons why you *won't* quit.

Go back over the list you made and substitute "won't" for "can't." By realizing that you are actually making choices, you begin to understand and use the power in your life. You can evaluate whether or not your reasons are really important and take action.

Assertiveness

You have the right to . . .

➡ judge your own behavior, thoughts, and feelings

➡ not defend or excuse your decisions

➡ change your mind

➡ make mistakes—and be responsible for them

➡ be illogical

➡ say "I don't know"

➡ say "I don't understand"

➡ decide if you are responsible for solving someone else's problem

➡ refuse help from others

An important part of being independent is being able to think for yourself and follow through on your convictions. Assertive behavior enables you to:

- *act in your own best interests*
- *stand up for yourself without undue anxiety*
- *express honest feelings comfortably*
- *exercise your personal rights without denying the rights of others.*

Assertiveness requires confidence, honesty, and clear thinking. Faced with a possible conflict, many of us choose to act less directly. Let's suppose that a friend has borrowed a favorite CD and returned it with a big scratch through it.

A *PASSIVE* response would be to quietly buy a new CD and never mention it to your friend. This sends a clear message to your friend that he doesn't need to respect your property or rights. You may be left feeling frustrated and misused, particularly when it happens again—because if you are *really* passive, you won't be able to say no when he asks to borrow something else.

An *AGGRESSIVE* response would be to attack your friend and tell him how irresponsible and inconsiderate his is. Your friend's immediate reaction may be to feel hurt or humiliated, but most of us respond to an attack by defending ourselves. In the argument or fight that ensues, you may lose both your CD and a friendship.

You could also respond in an indirect or *PASSIVE AGGRESSIVE* way. Don't mention anything to your friend, but complain to all your other friends about what a jerk he is. Guilt trips and manipulation are passive aggressive ways of getting what you want without having to ask for it. Passive aggressive behavior is hard work and makes others feel confused and resentful.

To be *ASSERTIVE,* you must respect your own rights and feelings. You must also respect the rights and feelings of others. Without attacking or letting others walk all over you, you need to identify your own needs and wishes and state them clearly. "George, there is a big scratch on the CD I lent you. I would like you to replace it." George can now apologize and replace the disk. Or he can deny it or become aggressive or try to make you feel guilty for holding him accountable for his actions. Those are George's problems. You may or may not get your disk replaced, but, more important, you have respected yourself and insisted that other people respect you.

How do you tend to respond to the following situations? Use these letters to indicate what your most typical response would be:

P = *Passive*   **AG** = *Aggressive*   **PA** = *Passive Aggressive*   **and**   **A** = *Assertive*

_____ Speaking up when you disagree with something in class or a meeting

_____ Offering an idea or suggestion to a group

_____ Joining a group at a party that you don't know very well

_____ Responding to someone who interrupts you

_____ Requesting an expected service that you didn't receive

_____ Requesting the return of a borrowed item that is overdue

_____ Reacting to personal criticism

_____ Responding to an unfair grade

_____ Responding to a friend's behavior that is bothering you

_____ Discussing your curfew with your parents

_____ Saying no to a request that you don't want to do

_____ Expressing anger

_____ Covering for a friend that gets you into trouble

_____ Being unfairly blamed for something

_____ Disagreeing with your friends on a matter of principle

_____ Expressing your choice when a group is trying to decide what to do

_____ Being asked to do something you believe is wrong

_____ Standing up for someone you think is being unfairly judged or picked on

The Effective "I" Statement

One way to stay assertive under pressure is to use an "I" statement. This is a little formula for expressing yourself without becoming passive or aggressive. When a person feels threatened, angry, scared, or hurt, it is an instinctive reaction to fight or to run and hide. In order to stand your ground, it is nice to have a simple tool to help you stay centered and assertive.

I feel/think _____ *when* _____.

I would like _____.

- Always start the sentence with the word "I." "YOU" invariably turns into an attack. "I" takes responsibility for the ideas and feelings you are about to express.

- Next comes "feel" or "think" followed by what you are honestly feeling or thinking. *I feel <u>uncomfortable</u> when <u>you make racial jokes</u>.*

- Be careful not to slip "YOU" in at this point. There is not much difference between *I think you are a jerk* and *You are a jerk*.

- Avoid using "that" after *I feel*. What follows is usually a thought, not a feeling—*I feel that you should be more considerate*. You may think that, but it is not a feeling. A true feeling can follow directly from *I feel*. *I feel hurt when you don't keep your word*.

- Next, describe the specific situation that you are reacting to. *I think that you are not really listening to me when you interrupt before I have finished*. Try not to make judgments (*You are rude*) or overgeneralize (*You never listen to anyone*).

- Finally, if it's appropriate, ask for what you want. Again, start with "I" and make your request clearly. *I want you to let me finish before you start talking, please*.

Go back to your checklist and see if you can come up with strong "I" statements in the situations that you had trouble with.

VIOLENCE IN SCHOOLS AND AMERICAN CULTURE

The late 1990s saw a dramatic rise in random violence and shootings in schools across the country.

- Feb. 2, 1996, *Moses Lake, Washington*—14-year-old opened fire in his classroom, killing the teacher and two students.

- Feb. 19, *Bethel, Alaska*—16-year-old shot and killed the principal and another student.

- Oct. 1, 1997, *Pearl, Mississippi*—16-year-old kills mother then opens fire at school, wounding nine, and killing two.

- Dec. 1, 1997, *West Paducah, Kentucky*—14-year-old kills three and wounds five during prayer meeting in school hallway.

- Mar. 24, 1998, *Jonesboro, Arkansas*—Two boys, ages 11 and 13, open fire on classmates during false fire alarm, killing four students and a teacher, and wounding ten others.

- Apr. 24, 1998, *Edinboro, Pennsylvania*—14-year-old shoots and kills 48-year-old science teacher who was chaperoning a graduation dance.

- Apr. 28, 1998, *Pomona, California*—14-year-old shoots and kills two boys, and wounds a third, during an after-school basketball game at the elementary school.

- May 19, 1998, *Fayetteville, Tennessee*—In the school parking lot, three days before graduation, 18-year-old honor student kills classmate who was dating his ex-girlfriend.

- May 21, 1998, *Springfield, Oregon*—15-year-old student kills parents, then opens fires in the school cafeteria, killing two.

Can you judge a book by its cover?

If you look around your school, you will probably notice that there is an unspoken dress code among students. Certain brand names, colors, and styles are "in" while others are considered pathetically out of style. There are probably days when you want to blend in and other days when you feel more like dressing to fit your own mood and comfort. Some students love standing out from the crowd in the way they dress, and different groups may have a different dress code within the same school.

We all tend to make assumptions about a person by the way they dress—everything from their personal sense of style to their economic background, the kind of music they probably like, how smart or nice they are, if they do drugs, if they are a virgin, and if we would want them as a friend. Like any other stereotype, sometimes we are right and sometimes we are very wrong. Groups or cliques tend to gravitate together because they have things in common, but the individual differences are likely to be just as pronounced. Football players all may like to play football, but that tells you nothing about the rest of their lives or personalities. Even when you know *a lot* of football players who love to ski and hate sushi, that doesn't guarantee anything about the next football player you meet.

Dress and hair are two easy ways to play around with your identity and try out different styles. You will find that some people will react more to the way you look than to who you really are as a person. Don't make that same mistake with others. The way a person looks or dresses may give you some good information about who she is—or it may be just a cover.

- June 15, 1998, *Richmond, Virginia*—Student shoots teacher and guidance counselor in the school hallway.

- Apr. 20, 1999, *Littleton, Colorado*—Two students open fire in suburban high school, killing thirteen students before shooting themselves.

- Nov. 19, 1999, *Deming, New Mexico*—12-year-old shoots and kills a classmate during lunch hour.

- Dec. 6, 1999, *Gibson, Oklahoma*—13-year-old opens fire with his father's 9mm semiautomatic handgun, injuring five of his classmates.

In addition to these more notable events, in 1999 the teenage homicide rate was up 300 percent, firearm deaths were up 43 percent, and the suicide rate for 15- to 19-year-olds had tripled since 1970. Eighty percent of all teenage deaths in 1999 resulted from homicide, suicide, or violent accidents. An estimated 100,000 students carried a gun to school on a regular basis. Parents had become increasingly concerned about their child's safety at school—55 percent said that they feared every day for their child's safety at school.

Why is this happening?   Fighting is not new in high schools, but the use of guns, and of random mass shootings, is. In a Gallup Poll conducted in 1999,[13] students believed that peer issues and personal problems were behind most of the violent behavior in schools. Parents were more likely to blame the availability of guns, poor parental supervision, and the amount of violence portrayed in the mass media. Educators agreed that parents appeared to be less available, and less involved in their child's education. Some parents sided with their child against the school on even minor disciplinary questions, undermining the school's authority and respect for school personnel and policies. "Strict" teachers, who enforced high standards for behavior and academic performance, were at the highest risk of being attacked or shot. This threat lowered educational standards and expectations, and drove off good teachers.

Researchers point to a combination of factors contributing to the rise of violence. Today's students, in general, seem to have a lower tolerance for frustration, are less able to control impulses, or manage their anger. The availability of guns, and the prevalence of violence on television, in computer games, and in popular music have created a channel for this frustration. Shooters often feel isolated, or maligned by their peers. Therapists have identified a deep-seated rage in many of the young people who have brought this kind of violence to the schools. Most lack empathy for others, feel very sensitive to criticism, and are likely to feel depressed and isolated. The Columbine (Littleton, Colorado) shootings also suggested the role of personal and racial intolerance as a factor. The shooters had been regularly harassed by some of the popular athletes in the school, and, in turn, specifically targeted some of the school's minority students. More and more students report feeling disconnected or alienated from their families, their schools, and their peers. An increasingly diverse student body may challenge a sense of connection and community, and provide disenfranchised scapegoats for this sense of rage and loneliness as well.

What can be done?   Many schools across the country have initiated programs aimed at developing student skills for handling conflict and anger. Mediation teams and teen courts are attempting to provide peaceful avenues for resolving disagreements. Many student groups and support organizations are looking at ways to improve tolerance, and establish a common ground of inclusion for all students. Some students, parents, and political representatives have mounted campaigns for stricter gun control laws. A government commission has been established to investigate the impact of violence in the mass media, and explore ways this can be addressed. Educators and therapists are attempting to improve their ability to identify warning signs, and intervene with children who may fall into this pattern of violence. Some schools have increased the security and surveillance in their buildings. Parents are examining their own role in providing supervision, social skills, emotional connections, and ethical standards for their children.

These incidents make everyone feel a bit helpless and confused. Even students or teachers who cannot imagine this kind of thing ever happening at their school, stop to wonder. Why are young teens so angry and desperate? What about the young lives and families that have been so randomly destroyed? How would I feel if it happened to me or to my friends? What can anyone do? *It is important to continue to be shocked and saddened by these tragedies.* If we start to accept this kind of violence as normal or tolerable, we lose perspective and reasonable expectations of safety and community. History has shown us that we tend to get what we expect, so it will be important to set our sights higher and work to reclaim both potential victims and potential perpetrators.

Quandary: Living with Violence

With the spread of violence to rural and suburban schools across the country, teachers, parents, and students are less confident that this sort of thing could never happen in their school. Nine percent of all public school students and 7 percent of all private school students report being the victim of a violent or property crime at school.

Which of the following factors do you think are responsible for the increase in violence in our schools?

Alcohol or drug use

Availability of guns

Boredom

Computers/Internet

Decline in religion

Depression

Emotionalism—valuing feelings above reason

Exposure to adult pressures without adult coping skills

Feeling out of control

Hazing in schools

Inadequate supervision or security in schools

Increased diversity in schools

Intolerance or racism

Jealousy

Lack of parental supervision

Lack of values

Loneliness

Low tolerance for frustration

Personal insecurity

Personal problems

Rage

School pressures

Sense of entitlement

Social peer pressures

Stress

Violence on TV & in movies

Violent computer games

Violent role models

Warning signs ignored

Weak coping skills

OTHER:_____

Which of the following solutions do you think will most effectively help us to address these problems?

Anger management training

Better discipline in schools

Better identification and intervention

Better teachers

Conflict resolution training

Control of hazing and harassment in schools

Counseling/therapy

Dress code or uniforms

Guards in schools

Gun control laws

Improve parent/child relationships

Increased respect for teachers/schools

Increased security

Isolate or expel troublemakers

Less media violence

Less stress in schools

Metal detectors in schools

More homogeneous schools

More interesting classes

More parental involvement in schools

More parental supervision

Peer mediation

Positive nonviolent role models

Regulate Internet

Religious training

Stronger laws and punishment

Tolerance training

OTHER: _____

Locus of Control

For each of the following statements, mark whether you strongly agree **(SA)**, agree **(A)**, disagree **(D)**, or strongly disagree **(SD).**

_____   In the long run, people get the respect and good outcomes they deserve.

_____   Becoming a success is a matter of hard work; luck has little or nothing to do with it.

_____   Trusting to fate has never turned out as well for me as making a decision to take a definite course of action.

_____   Capable people who fail to become leaders have not taken advantage of their opportunities.

_____   There is a direct connection between how hard I work and the rewards that I get.

_____   The average citizen can have an influence in government decisions.

_____   People do not realize how much they personally determine their own outcomes.[14]

> *Whether you think you can do something or you think you can't, either way, you are right*
> *—Henry Ford*

All of these statements are an expression of personal control. Do you see yourself as able to exert control over your environment or as a passive victim of fate? Do you make things happen or watch things happen to you? Psychologists have called this difference in perspective your *locus of control.* If you believe that events are generally a consequence of your own actions and thereby under your control, you have an **internal** locus of control. *If I study, I will do well on the test. If I am friendly and reach out to people, I will have friends.* If you believe that events are generally unrelated to your own behavior and most often beyond your control, you have an **external** locus of control. *People either like me or they don't; there's not much I can do about it. It doesn't matter how long or hard I study history— I always get a C.*

While each of us may take a different approach in different situations, our general outlook has a strong effect on our performance and self-esteem. Research has shown that an internal locus of control is closely related to academic and professional achievement. It is a better predictor of success than intelligence, socioeconomic background, family characteristics, and education. **PEOPLE WHO BELIEVE THAT THEY MAKE A DIFFERENCE, DO.**

COMPUTERS AND THE INTERNET[15]

Computers are an important and fascinating part of the twenty-first century and teenagers are especially adept at exploring this brave new world. You probably know more about the Internet than your parents and most of your teachers. In fact, they may come to you for advice and information. Efforts to put up firewalls or restrict student use of the Internet are often seen as an entertaining challenge to particularly adept computer hackers. In many ways, cyberspace is more your world than that of the adults who are trying to keep up with you. This fact can be quite amusing, but it also leaves a lot of responsibility in your hands to control and protect yourself.

The Internet provides both advantages and disadvantages for you as you work to establish yourself as an independent, competent adult. The time spent on the computer and surfing the Net has probably given you some very useful skills. Hours of practice at anything produce competence, and many teens spend enough time exploring the Internet to have

---

The Multitasking Generation

Multitasking got its name from the computer's ability to run several programs at once, and teens who have grown up with computers are experts at doing several things at once. Seated at a computer, many teens can work on homework, check their e-mail, keep up with ten different instant messenger conversations, talk on the phone, burn a CD, play an ongoing computer game, and listen to their favorite CD—all pretty much at the same time.

The research is not in yet, but some experts worry about the effect of multitasking on the developing brain and personality. Dr. Jane M. Healy believes that young people are not learning to focus and persevere with one thing (*Failure to Connect: How Computers Affect Our Children's Minds;* Simon & Schuster, 1999). David Shenk worries that we are raising a generation of kids who will be addicted to the thrill of multitasking and fail to develop patience, sacrificing quality and tranquillity in the process (*Datasmog: Surviving the Information Glut;* Harper, 1998). Dr. Todd E. Feinberg points out that the brain cannot actually focus on more than one task at a time—multitasking is actually the rapid shift from one focus to the next (*Altered Egos: How the Brain Creates the Self;* Oxford, 2001). Dr. Alvin Rosenfeld worries that multitasking skills are being refined at the expense of an ability to reflect and know who you are (*The Overscheduled Child;* Griffin, 2001).

When asked about their elders' concerns, most teens respond: *Get over it.*

Multitasking is a way of life for many busy, technically sophisticated teens. Some say that it is actually relaxing. Others say it is the only way they can keep up with their busy lives. Even critics admit that the ability to multitask will probably be an important skill in the future work force. The influx of information and stimulation in the world puts heavy demands on the human brain. Teens today are a living experiment on how the brain adapts and is affected by these demands.

Adapted from the New York Times, Technology, April 12, 2001.

a master's degree. Without ever taking a course, most teens can find information quickly and ingeniously, create a PowerPoint presentation, join a chat room anywhere around the world, develop a Web site, scan pictures, wander through virtual art museums, learn new software, and resolve any hardware or software problem as it arises. These skills will be very valuable in your adult career in almost any field. Many a fourteen-year-old techie can carry on a sophisticated, complex conversation with a professional adult computer analyst.

In the process, you have probably increased your writing skills (certainly your typing speed!). While Internet grammar and shorthand may horrify your English teacher, many teens are expressing themselves in writing more than ever before. Finding information and resolving problems on the Internet involve high-level thinking skills—identifying key words and concepts, trial and error problem solving, memory, and transferring concepts from one situation to another. Designing a Web site requires technical know-how, but also requires skill in graphics, page layout, and writing.

Cyberspace is a virtual mega-library of information. Right from your computer, you can probably answer any question that pops into your mind or up on your homework. You can access original documents from the Library of Congress, read the transcript of a court case, find out what teens in Palestine think about the war, or get the latest information and music from your favorite rock band. In this maze of helpful and not so helpful information, you have to become a savvy consumer of information. Anyone can declare anything on the Internet and make it look like a fact. You must learn to separate fact from fiction, judge the source of information, and do some good comparison shopping. Teenagers are well aware of some of the junk that is on the Internet, but a slick Web site and showy graphics can sometimes obscure weak research or hidden messages.

The anonymity and vastness of the Internet has created an ethical quandary for high school and college students as well. A quick cut and paste from the Internet can make short work of a homework assignment or paper. Indeed, some Web sites offer completed papers already done for you. Even properly identifying your sources from Internet sites has sent the plagiarism police scrambling for new guidelines and procedures. *Plagiarism,* using the words or ideas of others without proper acknowledgment, is serious academic dishonesty that could cost you more than the grade on the paper. Information from the Internet seems so free floating that it may be hard to keep it straight and give proper credit. Check with your school or teachers to find out how you should footnote your Internet research. There is much to learn from the Internet; but if you just cut and paste, you will rob yourself of the skills that you need to develop your own ideas.

One of the most exciting opportunities of the Internet is that you can meet and talk to people from all around the world. Cross-cultural discussions and newsgroups abound on the Internet. You can learn about world events or natural disasters directly from people who are right there as it is unfolding. The pen pals and personal relationships that can develop out of chat rooms or forums may help you relate to people in very different cultures or circumstances. This kind of international connection and understanding can help your generation resolve some of the conflict that is inevitable in an increasingly multicultural and interconnected world. Take advantage of this amazing opportunity—practice your French with someone in France, participate in newsgroups or forums about world issues with people from all over the world, find out what music teens in Japan or South Africa are listening to. Enter with an open mind and heart—the world is a fascinating place.

Some of the more popular uses of the Internet are the chat rooms and quick e-mail exchanges. E-mail or instant messenger services can be a high-tech form of note passing that keeps you in touch with friends and family who live at a distance. Or, they can be one more weapon in your procrastination arsenal. Time can evaporate when you are online and, before you know it, it is bedtime and your homework is still sitting there. Taking a minute to check your e-mail can mushroom into an hour of online chatting or interesting diversions with very little effort on your part. Set your timer; do your work first; program your computer to shut down if you get carried away. Some people do get "addicted" to cyberspace. Especially if "offline" is getting a bit overwhelming, the Internet can provide escape and a sense of control, providing online friends and a place to vent. You might want to talk to someone about how to get a grip if you find yourself (or a friend):

- *Denying how much time you are online*

- *Lying about what you are doing online*

- *Excessively tired because of online hours*

- *Slipping in your grades*

- *Spending less time with your offline friends and activities*

Most people who get hooked on the Internet are experiencing problems in their real lives. The Internet may provide some comfort and escape, but it won't necessarily help you cope with the real dilemmas.

Chat rooms are like the "Cheers" or Disneyland of relationships. You can make friends and establish an identity in a place where you feel like you belong. If you are having a major problem with acne or a gangly growth spurt, your appearance doesn't matter. If you are having trouble fitting in at school, you can get a fresh start and practice your social skills online. The anonymity of the Internet allows a lot of people to be more honest and talk about things they don't yet have the confidence to talk about in person. One very poised and popular eleventh-grade student said that the Internet had saved his life during eighth grade. He had been very lonely and unable to fit in with any of the groups at school. His parents were going through a divorce and nothing seemed to be going right. His online friends had given him advice and confidence during this rough time. It is sort of like having "invisible friends" who actually talk back. Being invisible can help you take the risk of being who you really are, and that can be the basis for establishing your true identity. Invisible friends, however, have a way of disappearing and they should only be a warm-up for establishing strong attachments with the people in your real life.

On the other hand, some people use the anonymity of the Internet to make up an identity and act out different characters or fantasies. This can be creative and interesting, but it can also get a little strange. Hiding behind a fake identity or even just not really knowing or seeing their target, some people give themselves license to throw out profanities, inappropriate sexual remarks, or abusive comments. Easy access to the "send" button can make impulsive e-mails hard to reconsider. If you make up an identity and create your own fantasy world, it may be hard to remember that the others you are interacting with are real people (maybe . . .). Your charade may take advantage of their honesty and make it impossible to have a genuine relationship with them even if you come to like them a lot. They don't really know you for yourself and probably wouldn't like the idea that you have been lying to them. If you have a good imagination, your fake identity can also leave you feeling that your real identity is pretty lame by comparison.

Just as in the real world, there are some pretty raunchy, untrustworthy people on line. It may be harder to pick them out because you can't see them or know much about them except what they tell you. A flirtatious 16-year-old girl could be a 45-year-old man. A sympathetic adult confidante could take advantage of the information shared online. You need to be cautious.

- *Don't divulge personal information to strangers. Never give out your phone number or address, and be careful about other identifying information such as your school, neighborhood, or daily schedule.*

- *Log off if someone makes you uncomfortable or asks you to do something that is wrong. Write down the username of that person, tell your parents, and contact the chat room.*

- *Never accept gifts from strangers online or call strangers you have met online even if they invite you to call collect.*

- *Never meet anyone offline without adult supervision and knowledge.*

The Internet is a powerful tool that will continue to shape our lives and relationships until the next technological shift comes along. It will help you in your quests and provide its share of quandaries as well. The Web site listings at the end of each chapter are meant to provide answers, information, and resources for you in this journey. There are many, many more out there, some of them very good and others laughable. Explore critically and enjoy the process.

Dear Quandary Master . . .

Here are some letters asking for advice and information about some difficulties encountered growing up. Make your answers as realistic and helpful as possible. Be sure to include any relevant information or resources that might be helpful.

#1.

Dear Quandary Master,

I am fifteen years old, but I still look about ten. Everyone in the world has had that famous "growth spurt" except me. Don't laugh because this is definitely not funny. The girls all treat me like their kid brother. I'm not a bad athlete, but I can't make any team because I'm too small. My friends have all filled out, gotten lower voices, and one of them is even shaving. My parents and teachers still treat me like a kid—nobody takes me seriously. When I try to strike a macho pose even I know I look ridiculous. My dad says not to worry—he didn't grow until his senior year and now he's 6'2". Great. What do I do in the meantime?

Signed, Delayed Darrell

#2.

Dear Quandary Master,

I had the luck of being the first in my group of friends to get my driver's license. It was great at first, but lately I am feeling like everyone's unpaid chauffeur. My friends call me whenever they want to go anywhere. They act like they want my company, but they really just want a ride—shopping, errands, cruising by their boyfriend's house, or just driving around to kill time. If they run into a guy they like who offers them a ride, they make all these gushy apologies, but in the end, they take off with him leaving me alone in a place I didn't want to be in the first place. I like my friends, but I am feeling used and I don't know how to say no. My parents are threatening to charge me gas money because I have put so many miles on the car. I like to drive, but this is ridiculous.

Signed, Chauffeur Charlotte

#3.

Dear Quandary Master,

I think I must be a little wacko. This is supposed to be the best time of my life and all I ever do is worry. I worry about whether or not people like me or if I will ever have a serious boyfriend. Then if a guy does show an interest in me, I worry about sex and don't know when or if I want him to touch me. My parents are usually pretty terrific, but even they get on my nerves. They always want to "understand" or help me out. Most of the time, I just want them to leave me alone—then I feel guilty because I know they love me a lot. I worry about my weight and what to wear, what to say, what to do. I worry about the environment and all of the dumb wars and just the way people treat other people in this world. I know this all sounds pathetic, but I just don't seem to know what I want or what I feel anymore. Why can't I just relax and be me*—whoever that is?!*

Signed, Who Knows?????

#4.

Dear Quandary Master,

I used to go to a pretty crummy school in the city where I lived, but I got a scholarship from <u>A Better Chance</u> to go to a good boarding school about 500 miles from home. This is my third year.

It has hard adjusting at first—everybody talked different, dressed different, acted different . . . they were just different. I had a lot of catching up to do in my studies too. But people were pretty nice and I have made some good friends, both black and white. I have done pretty well and it looks like I will get into one of the top colleges.

There are two things that still bother me. One is that no matter how hard I work or how successful I am, there are people, students and some teachers, who think I got some kind of break because I'm black, that I didn't really earn the grade or the college accept or even to be in this school. There is no way for me to prove myself to them; they just think what they think.

The other thing that worries me is how much I have changed since I came to this school. Hey, I am three years older and I have learned a lot, but I worry that I may have lost <u>me</u>. My family is very proud, but sometimes I don't feel like they really understand me anymore—there are so many things in my life I just can't explain to them. I don't hang out much with my friends at home anymore either—they're cool, but our schedules don't match and it seems like I spend more and more time at school or with school friends. Last time I was home, my old best buddy told me he didn't even know me any more—I had changed, sold out, thought I was too good for the neighborhood.

I know it's more complicated than that, but he made me feel real bad. Now I am looking at an Ivy League college even farther from home and the people I grew up with. I'm not the "black freeloader" my schoolmates see or the "preppie sell-out" my old friends imagine. Or am I?

Signed, Just Me

Do-It-Yourself Quandary

Identify an important dilemma related to adolescence and coming of age in our culture today that was not discussed in this chapter.

- *What factors make this issue particularly complicated or difficult to resolve?*

- *What values or ethical considerations are involved?*

- *What solutions or choices are available?*

WEB SITES

Adolescence
www.advocatesforyouth.org
www.teenwire.com
www.youthresource.org
www.teenadviceonline.org
http://education.indiana.edu/cas/adol/adol.html
http://aspe.os.dhhs.gov/hsp/adolescent99
www.goaskalice.columbia.edu
www.healthcentral.com/Centers/OneCenter.cfm?Center=TeenHealth

Adoption
www.calib.com/naic/index.htm
www.almanet.com
www.adoptioncrossroads.org
www.ncfa-usa.org
www.birthquest.org
www.bastards.org
www.adoption-research.org
(international adoptions)

Computers and the Internet
www.rider.edu/users/suler/psycyber/cybaddict.html
www.concentric.net/~Astorm
www.hno.harvard.edu/gazette/1999/01.21/computer.html
www.cgrg.ohio-state.edu/Astrolabe
http://members.aol.com/internetethics
www.itvs.org/digitaldivide

Culture and Environment
www.worldwatch.org
www.geocities.com/~acunu
www.un.org/esa/earthsummit
www.oneworldmagazine.org
www.wsu.edu:8001/vcwsu/commons/topics/culture/culture-index.html
www.peopleandplanet.net
www.oceanintl.org

Ethics
www.ethics.ubc.ca/resources
www.publicintegrity.org
www.secure.law.cornell.edu/ethics/index.html
www.globalethics.org
www.josephsoninstitute.org
www.giraffe.org
www.gratzclusterydslc.org
www.fiu.edu/~time4chg/Library/ideas.html
www.sgr.org.uk/index.html
www.ethics.acusd.edu/resources.html

Media and Advertising

http://www.mediawatch.com

http://www.about-face.org

http://www.adbusters.org

http://www.med.sc.edu:81/medialit/

Violence

www.ncsu.edu/cpsv/

www.keepschoolssafe.org

www.jointogether.org

http://eric-web.tc.columbia.edu/monographs/uds107/preventing contents.html

www.josephsoninstitute.org/Survey2001/violence2000-pressrelease.htm

www.pta.org/events/violprev

---

[1] *Random House Webster's College Dictionary.* New York: Random House, 1991.

[2] Ibid.

[3] Winn, Marie. *Children Without Childhood.* New York: Pantheon Books, 1983.

[4] Ibid.

[5] Littwin, Susan. *The Postponed Generation.* New York: William Morrow and Company, 1986.

[6] Ibid.

[7] Coles, Robert. *The Call of Stories: Teaching and the Moral Imagination.* Boston: Houghton Mifflin Company, 1989.

[8] Fischer and Lazerson. *Human Development.* New York: W. H. Freeman and Company, 1984.

[9] Epstein, H. T. EEG developmental stages. *Development Psychobiology,* 1980, 13:629-621.

[10] Gilligan, Carol. *In a Different Voice.*

[11] http://www.ppic.org/publications/CalCounts2.

[12] Kilbourne, Jean. *Deadly Persuasion: Why Women and Girls Must Fight the Addictive Power of Advertising.* Simon and Schuster, 1999.

[13] www.time.com/time/magazine.

[14] Adapted from Rotter, J. B. Generalized expectancies for internal versus external control of reinforcement. *Psychological monographs,* 1966, 80 (1 Whole no. 609).

[15] Special thanks to John Suler at Rider University for his wisdom and guidance in this area. Much of the ideas in this section were taken from his article, Adolescents in cyberspace: The good, the bad, and the ugly. *Psychology of Home,* June, 1998.

Chapter 2

Wellness and Your Body

One of your primary responsibilities as an independent adult is to take care of your body. As a child, your parents managed your health, hygiene, diet, and safety by providing you with a balanced diet, nagging you to brush your teeth, caring for you when you were sick, and setting limits to protect you from danger. Even as a teen, responsibility for many of these things has shifted to you. Your parents may still cook your meals, but you have much more freedom about when and what you eat. You have probably taken over almost complete responsibility for your personal hygiene. You are able to work with your doctor and dentist as an adult, capable of understanding and questioning their treatment. You can read and learn about your body and health and make intelligent decisions about how to care for yourself.

It is very easy when we are young to take good health for granted. Most bodies are strong and resilient. They take years of abuse and neglect without showing the negative effects. When you are sixteen, it is hard to imagine having heart problems at age forty or having false teeth at age fifty or being an invalid at age seventy. Indeed, it is hard even to imagine *being* forty or seventy, much less figuring out how it might feel. Nevertheless, the choices and care that you take now will determine the quality of life that you will have then.

Take a minute to try to imagine your life at age seventy. Think of the different older people that you know. Some are good-natured and active,

Living to 100[1]

In his interviews with centenarians (people who are 100 or older), Dr. Thomas Perls, at Harvard University, discovered the following traits that appear to play a part in healthy aging.

- Flexible
- Assertive
- Independent
- Handle emotional stress well
- Don't dwell on problems
- Meaningful relationships with family and friends
- Rich spiritual or religious life
- Mentally and physically active
- Good sense of humor
- Positive attitude

At 101, Abraham Goldstein attributed his life and health to "being persistent—I just keep breathing."

traveling and enjoying their retirement. They are in good health, good spirits, and fun to be around. Many are still involved in sports, gardening, hiking, swimming, and are intellectually alert and interesting. They have a good sex life, a good sense of humor, and enjoy their children, grandchildren, and spouses. Others are plagued with physical problems and limitations. They seem unhappy and cranky, difficult to be around. They may seem dull and forgetful, struggling with poor hearing, memory loss, and depression. They aren't able to get around on their own or enjoy the last part of their lives.

While life is never totally predictable, many of the decisions and habits that you choose today will determine what kind of person you will be when you are seventy. With the current life expectancy in the U.S. being 72 for men and 78.8 for women, you need to plan on making your body last at least 80 years! Imagine trying to keep a car running for that amount of time. Your body will go through many changes during those years, but there are many things that you can do to keep it running and comfortable so that you can enjoy *all* of your life.

The human body is a complex, intricate organism. Each day your mind and body must coordinate the work of 206 bones, over 600 muscles, 45 organs and glands, 23 hormones, and trillions of nerve cells. Ninety-six percent of your body is made up of oxygen, carbon, hydrogen, and nitrogen. The other 4 percent contains calcium, phosphorus, potassium, sulfur, sodium, chlorine, and magnesium. There are also traces of iron, iodine, copper, zinc, manganese, cobalt, chromium, selenium, molybdenum, fluorine, tin, silicon, and vanadium. (You are beginning to sound more like a car all the time.) Each of these elements and minerals, even the smallest trace elements, must be maintained and replaced if your body is to function smoothly.

Body Maintenance Checkup

Many factors are involved in maintaining your body. Like a car, it needs careful use, a good grade of fuel, regular tune-ups, and careful attention to any funny knocks or noises. In addition to these mechanical checks, you must also be aware of how your mind and lifestyle are affecting your body and wellness. Rate yourself on each of the questions below to get an idea of how well you are taking care of yourself. *Each of these questions has been shown to be closely related to general health and longevity.*

*Give yourself: 5 points for **always**, 3 points for **usually**, and 0 points for **not really**.*

*1. Do you exercise or play a sport at least four times a week? _____

2. Does your weight fall into the appropriate weight for your height? _____

*3. Does your diet include vegetables, fruit, dairy, and protein? _____

4. Do you eat fish and poultry more than red meats? _____

5. Do you include high-fiber foods in your diet several times a day? _____

*6. Do you drink 6–8 glasses of water each day? _____

7. Do you avoid fad diets or binge eating? _____

8. Do you limit your intake of sugar, fats, and cholesterol? _____

*9. Do you smoke cigarettes? (5 = never, 3 = sometimes, 0 = yes) _____

10. Do you brush and floss your teeth daily? (3 points if you don't floss) _____

11. Do you know what to do in case of injury or illness? _____

*12. Do you get 8–9 hours of sleep each day? _____

13. Do you use sunscreen and avoid getting sunburned? _____

14. Girls: Do you examine your breasts for unusual changes or lumps once a month?
     Boys: Do you examine your testicles for unusual changes or lumps every 3 months? _____

*15. Do you ever drive after drinking or using other drugs or ride with drivers who have been drinking or using other drugs? (5 = never, 3 = sometimes, 0 = yes) _____

16. Do you feel like you have a reasonable amount of control in your life? _____

17. Do you include relaxation and play as a regular part of your day? _____

*18. Do you have a good amount of laughter in your life? _____

*19. Do you hold in your angry feelings? (5 = never, 3 = sometimes, 0 = yes) _____

20. Do you worry a lot? (5 = never, 3 = sometimes, 0 = yes) _____

21. Do you do some type of meditation or relaxation on a regular basis? _____

22. Do you have a hobby or pastime that gives you particular pleasure? _____

23. Is there at least one person you can turn to for support and comfort? _____

*24. Are your decisions and behavior consistent with your personal values? _____

25. Do you feel respected and cared for in your family? _____

26. Do you live in an environment that has a high level of air or noise pollution? _____

27. Are you able to make decisions without excess stress or worry? _____

28. Do you have one skill or talent of which you are especially proud? _____

29. Do you have a spiritual or religious base in your life? _____

*30. Do you feel connected and obligated to a family or community of people? _____

Total raw score _____

Total your scores for #1, 3, 6, 9, 12, 15, 18, 19, 24, and 30 _____

Add these two scores together to make up your composite score _____

If you scored between 175 and 200   *You are taking good care of yourself, and should have a long, healthy life.*
If you scored between 150 and 175   *Not bad, but you have some important areas to work on.*
If you scored between 100 and 150   *Identify your problem areas, and make some serious changes.*
If you scored under 100   *You need to sit yourself down, and come up with a new, healthier lifestyle!*

In the human being, the mind and body are very closely interconnected. Thoughts and feelings can create strong physical responses. Imagine that while you are quietly sitting here reading this chapter, a crazed grizzly bear suddenly breaks through your door and starts toward you. Very likely, you will experience some immediate physical changes. Your heart starts beating quickly, raising your blood pressure and rushing blood to your brain and major muscles. Your breathing becomes rapid and shallow. Adrenaline and other hormones are released into your blood causing you to be faster and stronger than you were a minute ago. Your liver releases sugar to heighten your energy level. Your pupils dilate and your senses are heightened. Your thighs, hips, shoulders, jaws, and face muscles all become tense and ready for action. Blood flow is constricted to your stomach and extremities. Your body may begin to perspire.

The need is now for a gentler, a more tolerant people than those who won for us against the ice, the tiger and the bear.
—*Loren Eisley*

All of these physical changes are in response to your mental perception of danger and prepare you to fight or run for your life. You will have many of the same responses when the danger is psychological—approaching an important examination or stepping up to bat at the bottom of the ninth with bases loaded. You will also have the same response when you perceive a danger that is not real—riding on a safe, but scary roller coaster, standing up before a large audience to give a speech, or not recognizing your friend dressed up as a grizzly bear. **Your response is a reaction to your state of mind, not an actual danger.**

As much as 90 percent of all illnesses can be directly or indirectly related to mental stress. Ulcers, allergies, asthma, high blood pressure, insomnia, headaches, muscle tension, stomach pain, and digestive disorders are all directly related to mental disturbances. Chronic stress creates high levels of adrenaline and cortizone. These hormones reduce your immune functioning, increasing your vulnerability to colds, infections, viruses, even cancer. Grieving adults have a much higher risk of cancer during the first eighteen months after the death of a spouse.

On a more positive note, mental relaxation and visualization can also be used to successfully fight cancer. Biofeedback is a relaxation technique that teaches individuals how to lower their blood pressure, reduce pain, lower body temperature, or relax muscles by using their mind. The subject is hooked up to a machine that measures systolic blood pressure or whatever function he is trying to control. The measurements are displayed on a screen or in the form of a sound pitch—this is the feedback. The subject is then instructed to concentrate on relaxing and lowering the wave or pitch. He is not instructed how to do this, just to use whatever sensations or thoughts that work for him. Amazingly, most people are able to learn to do this within a short period of time. After the individual technique is thoroughly learned, the subject is able to repeat this control without the visual or auditory feedback from the machine. Meditation, hypnosis, and guided imagery can have similar results.

Being loved and productive also has a strong impact on your physical health. Happily married people live longer than unmarried people. Older people with a loving pet live longer than those who are alone. Babies thrive physically and mentally when they are held and talked to.

Without this loving interaction, they are slow to develop. They are often sickly and many die. In 1915, a study of infants raised in foundling homes with very little individual attention reported death rates ranging from 32 percent to 75 percent before the age of two. This effect is called *failure to thrive.* Harry Harlow did a study of monkeys deprived of early attachment and contact with an affectionate adult. These unmothered infants were frail and depressed, and became neurotic and aggressive adults. Studies of institutionalized or abandoned children throughout the world show similar results.

While the mind can have a positive or negative impact on the body, the reverse is also true. Mental tension can be released and eased by physical activity. Aerobic exercise such as running, swimming, biking, skiing, or any exercise that speeds up your system, actually manipulates your brain chemistry by inducing the brain to release an excess of brain opiads called **endorphins,** our brain's natural painkillers. This accounts for what is known as a "runner's high." During childbirth, our body releases ten times the normal level of endorphins, creating increased energy and a sense of joy. Conversely, the flooding of hormones after childbirth and during certain periods of the menstrual cycle can create depression and irritability known as postpartum depression and PMS.

Schizophrenia and manic-depression have been shown to have a physical basis and can be successfully treated by adding chemicals which block the transmission of a neurotransmitter called **dopamine.** Anxiety, hyperactivity, memory, depression, and mental alertness can all be dramatically affected by diet and exercise. The brain, which is a physical part of your body, controls both your health and your mental perceptions. It can be affected both mentally and physically to create a healthier body and outlook.

WELLNESS

Wellness is not just the absence of disease. It is a way of life and state of awareness that allows you to function at your physical and mental best. It involves knowing your body and what it needs. It also involves knowing when something is wrong and what to do. Taking responsibility for your well-being means making daily choices that support and enhance your life. This involves both information and active caring for yourself.

In order to take care of yourself you need to:

- *Know what your body needs to run efficiently.* In addition to diet and exercise, examine your life for psychological and environmental stresses that wear down your health. Learn how your body works and what factors are of particular importance to you.

- *Be an informed medical consumer.* Know how to actively use the medical information and professional help available to you. Read labels, ask questions, and be an active partner in your medical treatment. Any good doctor will welcome your questions and encourage your willingness to take responsibility for your health.

What's Normal?

"Normal" may vary some from person to person, so it is good to know what is normal for you in a healthy state.

Temperature ⇨ 98.6° taken orally (rectal temperatures register about 1 degree higher). Individual normal temperatures may vary between 97.6 and 99.6

Pulse ⇨ 60 to 100 beats per minute while resting.

Respiration ⇨ 10 to 20 breaths per minute while resting.

Blood Pressure ⇨ Varies considerably but should be under 140/90. The first number is your *systolic pressure* which is the pressure when the heart contracts and pumps blood through your body. The second number is your *diastolic pressure* or the pressure between pumps when your heart is resting.

- *Respond to warning signs and symptoms that indicate that something is not functioning properly.* Male life expectancy is seven years shorter than females. One of the important factors in this difference is that, in our culture, men are taught to ignore warning signs from their bodies and are less likely than women to see a doctor or respond to physical discomfort. Illness and pain are indicators that something needs attention. Don't ignore them any more than you would ignore a strange knock in your car engine.

- *Know how to respond to medical problems and emergencies.* Learn how to take care of yourself instead of expecting parents or doctors to take responsibility for your well-being. Read, ask questions, and know when to get help when you need it. Parents spent a lot of time when you were young protecting you from illness and danger. Now you are in many situations where you must think and respond for yourself in order to be safe and healthy.

- *Make healthy choices and decisions and live by them.* Researchers at Emory University found that fourteen primary causes of illness and premature death—about two-thirds of the deaths under age sixty-five—were potentially preventable. It doesn't really matter if you know what is healthy if you don't actively incorporate this information into your life.

- *Actively care about yourself.* Some people take the attitude that "if I am only hurting myself, it is OK." Often, we take better care of our friends and family members than we do of ourselves. Many people take risks with themselves that they would never want someone whom they loved to take. You need to respect and value your own life; respect your body and its needs; protect and nurture yourself. You are unique and invaluable; no one else can know and care for you as well as you can.

Breast Self-Exam

Women should examine their breasts once a month for any lumps, thickening, or changes. A few days after your menstrual period is a good time. Do your first check in the shower or bath when your hands are wet and soapy. Using the flat surfaces of your fingers, gently move over every part of each breast, checking for unusual lumps or thickening. Squeeze each nipple gently to check for a discharge. The second check should be done on a comfortable flat surface. Lie down and place a pillow or folded towel under your left shoulder and place your left arm under your head. Use your right hand to gently move your fingers in a circular motion around the surface of your left breast. Be sure to include the nipple, breastbone, and armpit. Repeat on the other side.

Each woman's breasts are unique and may include normal lumps or shape differences. Getting to know what is normal for you will help you to notice when there is a potential problem. Breast cancer is the most common form of cancer among women and can be cured 90 percent of the time if it is caught early.

Testicular Self-Exam

A three-minute self-exam of the penis and testicles once a month can allow early treatment of penile infections, STDs, and testicular cancer. The best time is during or after a warm shower. Stand with your right leg resting on an elevated surface. Gently roll the right testicle between your thumb and forefinger, feeling for any hard lumps or nodules. Notice any enlargement or changes in the testicle or dull ache or pain in the groin or lower abdomen. Repeat, lifting the left leg and examining the left testicle. Check the foreskin and glans of the penis for any sores, warts, or discharge.

You should check with your doctor if you notice any changes or lumps. Testicular cancer spreads quickly, but can usually be controlled if discovered early. STDs are best treated at the earliest possible time, since some external symptoms disappear while the disease is still spreading within your body.

A Patient's Bill of Rights
Developed by the American Hospital Association, 1973

1. The patient has the right to considerate and respectful care.

2. The patient has the right to obtain from his physician complete current information concerning his diagnosis, treatment, and prognosis in terms that she can understand. When it is not medically advisable to give such information to the patient, the information should be made available to an appropriate person in her behalf.

3. The patient has the right to receive any information necessary to give informed consent prior to the start of any procedure and/or treatment. The patient has the right to know the risks involved, the probable duration of incapacitation, and may request information concerning medical alternatives.

4. The patient has the right to refuse treatment to the extent permitted by law and to be informed of the medical consequences of his action.

5. The patient has the right to every consideration of her privacy concerning her own medical care program. Case discussion, consultation, examination, and treatment are confidential and should be conducted discreetly. Those not directly involved in her care must have the permission of the patient to be present.

6. The patient has the right to expect that all communication and records pertaining to his care should be treated as confidential.

7. The patient has the right to expect that within its capacity a hospital must make reasonable response to the request of a patient for services.

8. The patient has the right to obtain information as to any relationship of her hospital to other health care and education institutions insofar as her care is concerned.

9. The patient has the right to be advised if the hospital proposes to engage in or perform human experimentation affecting his care or treatment. He has the right to refuse to participate in such research projects.

10. The patient has the right to expect reasonable continuity of care.

11. The patient has the right to examine and receive an explanation of her bill, regardless of the source of payment.

12. The patient has the right to know what hospital rules and regulations apply to his conduct as a patient.

Federal law requires each state to provide you with information about your health care rights. Every competent adult has the right to accept or refuse medical treatment. In some cases, an illness or injury may make it impossible for you to indicate how you would like to be treated. In most states, you can complete a "living will" or "directive to physician" to express your wishes in advance and to designate who you would like to make these decisions for you if you are unconscious or incapacitated. This document may direct your doctor or hospital to withhold or withdraw life-sustaining procedures in the event that you suffer from a terminal illness and are near death. It can be very helpful to your family and doctor to know what you would have wanted in a situation when you cannot speak for yourself. Some people rightly argue that it is impossible to really know what you would want until you are actually in a terminal situation, but a living will gives your family and medical providers some direction and guidance as they attempt to make these decisions for you.

The law varies from state to state, but most living wills require that you be eighteen years or older, of sound mind, and be witnessed by two persons who are not related or have any claim on your estate. If you list someone as a power of attorney to make health care decisions for you, that person or persons must sign an agreement. Forms for your area may be obtained at your local hospital or a stationery store that carries legal documents. The Oregon Directive to Physician shown here is an example of the kind of document that may be used.

Oregon Directive to Physician[2]

Directive made this _____ day of _____ 20 _____

I, _____ , being of sound mind, willfully and voluntarily make known my desire that my life shall not be artificially prolonged under the circumstances set forth below and do hereby declare:

1. If at any time I should have an incurable injury, disease or illness certified to be a terminal condition by two physicians, one of whom is the attending physician, and where the application of life-sustaining procedures would serve only to artificially prolong the moment of death and where my physician determines that my death is imminent whether or not life-sustaining procedures are utilized, I direct that such procedures be withheld or withdrawn, and that I be permitted to die naturally.

2. In the absence of my ability to give directions regarding the use of such life-sustaining procedures, it is my intention that this directive shall be honored by my family and physician(s) as the final expression of my legal right to refuse medical or surgical treatment and accept the consequences from such refusal.

3. I understand the full import of this directive and I am emotionally and mentally competent to make this directive.

_____   _____
Signature   City   County   State

This is a serious document that raises many important questions. *At what point do you believe that it is medically and ethically permissible to terminate your life? To what lengths do you believe that a doctor should go to keep your body alive if you are comatose and your death is imminent? At what point does your spirit or person cease to exist? Is your vital essence located in your body? In your brain? In your heart?* A body can function either mechanically or artificially long after the more sophisticated centers in your brain have stopped. *Should your body be kept alive even if your higher levels of awareness have died? How can one know for sure what is still functioning? What if a medical discovery or miracle suddenly occurred that could reverse your condition? Is it permissible* **not** *to use medical knowledge to sustain any form of life?*

As a minor, your family and physician take responsibility for these decisions, but your thoughts and wishes are clearly important. **Discuss these questions with your parents.** Find out what they believe is the best thing to do. Listen carefully and let them know what you think. You may want to write out your wishes and give the paper to them. If you are under eighteen, this will not be legally binding, but it does give your parents some indication of what you believe if they should ever have to act in your interests.

Dr. Death—Saint or Sadist?

April 13, 1999, seventy-year old Dr. Jack Kevorkian was sentenced in Michigan to ten to twenty-five years in prison for assisting in the direct injection, or voluntary euthanasia, death of Thomas Youk, a fifty-two-year-old man who was suffering from Lou Gehrig's disease. An outspoken proponent of euthanasia and doctor-assisted suicide, Dr. Kevorkian had publicly acknowledged helping at least 130 other people end their lives. He took a tape of Mr. Youk's death to the television show, *60 Minutes*, challenging prosecutors to take the case to court. On the tape, Thomas Youk clearly requested the injection and participated willingly in his own death. Kevorkian served as his own attorney and argued that his actions were a justifiable act of mercy and the law should be changed. After eight years and eleven previous court appearances, Dr. Kevorkian was convicted of second-degree murder and use of a controlled substance (lethal drug).

Dr. Kevorkian was born in May, 1928, in Pontiac, Michigan. He graduated from the University of Michigan with a specialty in pathology and actually got his nickname, Doctor Death, from his journal article on his efforts to photograph the eyes of dying patients. He was subsequently asked to leave the University of Michigan for advocating medical experimentation on consenting convicts during executions and later published an article detailing his experiments on transfusing blood from cadavers to live patients. In the 1980s be began to write about the ethics of euthanasia and death counseling. In 1989, he built a rudimentary "suicide machine" and, in 1990, first used it to assist in the death of Janet Adkins, a fifty-four-year-old sufferer of Alzheimer's disease.

Obsessed with death and odd by nature, Dr. Kevorkian is alternately seen as a pathological serial killer or a prisoner of conscience, a martyr to the cause of the right to choose to die. His patients have described him as a caring angel of mercy; his opponents see him as a dangerous and arrogant psychopath attempting to play God with other people's lives. What do you think?

Quandary: *Ethics on the Care of the Terminally Ill*

Advances in modern medicine have made it possible to sustain physical life under circumstances where a terminal patient is in a coma or in extreme pain. This has raised many controversial issues of ethical responsibility. Euthanasia, also called mercy killing, is the act of putting to death painlessly or allowing someone to die by withholding medical assistance. Some people believe that this is an easily abused form of murder. Others believe that to terminate a painful or comatose life that is being sustained by medical technology is the humane and caring response.

In June of 1990, the Supreme Court ruled that a person has the right to refuse life-sustaining medical treatment, but that family members may not make this decision for an unconscious patient. In 1991, the Council on Ethical and Judicial Affairs of the American Medical Association adopted the position that physicians must respect a patient's right to forego life-sustaining treatment (including mechanical ventilation, renal dialysis, chemotherapy, antibiotics, artificial nutrition and hydration), but must not perform euthanasia or participate in assisted suicide. If the patient is unconscious, the family may become the surrogate decision maker, basing their decision on the patient's previous values and preferences. Individuals were encouraged to complete a living will to make their wishes known in advance.

The ethical issues and dilemmas of euthanasia are quite complex. A distinction is usually made between active euthanasia (actually causing or assisting the death of a terminal patient) and passive euthanasia (withholding treatment that could save the life of a terminal patient). The issue of voluntary consent is also complex and becomes paramount when the patient is mentally or physically unable to give consent.

Consider the arguments in each of the following situations and formulate your own opinions.

1. **Passive, voluntary euthanasia:** A patient who is suffering in the advanced stages of AIDS refuses antibiotic treatment of a dangerous, but treatable infection of pneumonia.

   PRO: Every person has the right to shorten the physical and emotional pain of an incurable illness and choose when and how he will die. A physician and the law must respect this basic human freedom.

   CON: The medical community is charged with the ethical and legal responsibility to save a life whenever possible. The sanctity of life is more important than the relief of pain. Withholding available treatment has the same consequences as actively assisting a suicide. A cure may be found at any time that will make this death unnecessary.

2. **Passive, nonvoluntary euthanasia:** A family decides to remove artificial respiration and IV from an infant who is born with severe physical and mental disabilities and cannot survive without extensive medical technology.

   PRO: Without sophisticated medical intervention, this infant would have died immediately. Medical technology has already played God with this human life, sometimes only for financial or professional profit. Even if she is able to one day breathe or eat on her own, she will live in a painful, vegetative state causing great emotional pain and financial expense to her parents.

   CON: We have neither the right nor the wisdom to play God with human life. There is no such thing as a life not worthy of being lived. Miraculous improvements and accomplishments have occurred in even a short, painful lifetime. The newborn infant has had no chance to defend her own life. Once we begin to make decisions about who will live and who will die, it is a short step to the political euthanasia of socially undesirable persons such as that which occurred in Nazi Germany.

3. **Active, voluntary euthanasia:** A severely disabled person with cerebral palsy is in extreme physical and mental pain, but cannot physically end his life. He has chosen to starve to death, refusing intravenous feeding.

   PRO: No one can judge or experience the pain of another's life. The final decision to continue or discontinue that life must be up to the individual. Physically able persons easily retain this freedom and it is not fair that a severely disabled person have this power taken away because of her disability.

   CON: Voluntary consent is a difficult choice to judge. Statements made in living wills are out of context and may not really reflect a person's wishes when actually faced with a terminal illness. The wish to die may be the result of momentary desperation, temporary instability, or a clouded, pain-drugged mind. Patients may not really want to die, but may feel guilty about the financial or emotional burden they are creating for their loved ones. Life is sacred and must be protected even against a person's wishes.

4. **Active, involuntary euthanasia:** A family requests a lethal injection that will painlessly end the life of their daughter who has been pronounced "brain dead" and has been in a coma for eight years.

   PRO: Based on the previous values and preferences of their daughter, the parents are genuinely positive that she would agree with their decision and wish to have her body at peace. There is no chance of any recovery and her current vegetative state is an insult to the value and dignity of her life. Slowly allowing her to die is a painful and expensive process for everyone involved. It is more humane to actively end the suffering.

   CON: The purpose and value of each life is a matter not to be judged or determined by mere human beings. Murder cannot be condoned under any circumstances and families must not be allowed to weigh their own emotional or financial burdens against a human life. How are we to know the internal or spiritual experience of another, even if by our crude measures she is "brain dead"? Diagnosis may be wrong and there are cases of totally unexpected recoveries.

EMERGENCY FIRST-AID

> It's better to be careful a hundred times than to get killed once.
> —Mark Twain

Accidents are the leading cause of death for persons under twenty-four. When you were a child, you could usually depend on some adult to know what to do in an emergency. As you spend more time on your own or with groups of your friends, it is important that you be able to respond to first-aid situations for yourself.

Emergency first-aid training is too critical and complicated to learn primarily from a book. There are excellent courses in first-aid and cardiopulmonary resuscitation offered by the American Red Cross for a nominal fee. You can find out where a course is being offered by calling the American Red Cross listed in your phone book. This training will teach you what to do until you can get professional help and may save your own life or the life of a friend.

There are a few guidelines that every adult, young and old, should know. Your immediate response is very important. General guidelines suggested by the American Red Cross are:

Universal Precautions for HIV

- Practice abstinence or safer sex.
- Avoid IV needles and definitely don't share.
- Do not share your razor or toothbrush.
- Keep a pair of disposable gloves in your home and car first-aid kits.
- Use disposable gloves whenever possible if you are assisting someone with a bleeding injury or nosebleed.
- Clean your hands and surface area with chlorine bleach if you have handled blood or other bodily fluids.
- Allow trained coaches and health officials to handle friends or teammates who have been injured and are bleeding.
- Ask your dentist to use gloves when cleaning or working on your teeth.
- Be sure that any tattooing or body piercing is done under sterile, safe conditions.

E.G.B.O.K.

One reminder that emergency team members often use to stay calm and keep people from panicking in an emergency is the acronym E.G.B.O.K.— which stands for Everything's Going to Be O.K. By reassuring and comforting the victim and yourself, the body and mind are able to relax and focus on what needs to be done to respond to the emergency.

✚ **Do the best you can given your training and the circumstances.**

✚ **Stop the bleeding when possible.**

✚ **DO NOT MOVE the individual if there is any chance of head or neck injury.**

✚ **Be comforting and reassuring to the injured person. Keep other people at the site calm and busy helping or going for help.**

✚ **IN ALL CASES, GET EMERGENCY ASSISTANCE AS SOON AS POSSIBLE.**

Listed below are some common first-aid emergencies that you may encounter. *The descriptions and suggestions given are very general and should not replace comprehensive first-aid training.* They are provided to help you identify a medical emergency and keep things from getting worse until you can get help.

✚ **ALCOHOL POISONING** ➜ Symptoms of alcohol poisoning include nausea, vomiting, disorientation, and a weak pulse rate. Try to keep the person awake and moving. If she is unconscious, do not lie her on her back—she can choke on her vomit. Keep checking for breathing and pulse. Do not leave her unattended but get help as quickly as possible.

✚ **BLEEDING** ➜ Apply direct pressure on the wound for ten minutes without peeking or removing the pressure. Elevate that part of the body if possible. Get help.

✚ **BROKEN BONES** ➜ Keep the break and area above and below the break from moving. Be sure not to cut off circulation if you use any kind of splint or tie.

✚ **BURNS** ➜ Submerse the burn in cold water and watch for shock. **Do not** apply grease or put water on a deep open burn. Do not break blisters. For **SUNBURN,** apply a cold cloth or water and take vitamin C and aspirin. Vinegar or wet tea bags may reduce the sting.

✚ **CHOKING** ➜ If a person cannot talk, cannot breath, and begins to turn blue, she is probably choking. Stand behind her and wrap your arms around her waist with your fist against her stomach just above the navel, but below the ribcage. Keep the thumb side of the fist against the stomach and grasp the fist with the other hand. Thrust your fist upward, forcing the object out. Repeat up to ten times or until the airway is cleared.

✚ **DRUG OVERDOSE** ➜ Try to keep the person awake and moving if possible. If he is agitated, try to restrain in as comforting and reassuring a way as possible. Remove any dangerous or sharp objects from the area. Do not leave him alone and get him to a hospital or a clinic as quickly as possible. Try to determine what drugs and how much were taken. Take a sample to the hospital with you if possible so it can be analyzed.

✚ **FROSTBITE →** Warm slowly, do not rub or heat by flame or hot water.

✚ **HEAD INJURY OR INTERNAL BLEEDING →** Keep the person quiet, lying down with his head slightly elevated. Reassure him and get help quickly.

✚ **HYPERVENTILATION →** When too much oxygen is taken in and the level of carbon dioxide in the blood is lowered, a person hyperventilates. He may be breathing quickly and may feel tingling or numbness. Breathing into a paper bag which covers the nose and mouth will increase the level of carbon dioxide. Continue for 5–15 minutes.

✚ **SHOCK →** A person can go into shock whenever vital tissues do not get enough blood. This can happen with severe bleeding or less serious injuries if the body is stunned and loses control of the circulatory system. Symptoms of shock include cold, clammy skin, a fast, weak pulse, paleness, dizziness, nausea, and dilated pupils. Have the victim lie down and elevate her legs two or more inches unless there is an injury to the chest or head. Keep her warm but not hot, and give her small amounts of water unless there is an abdominal injury. Take her pulse every five minutes. Comfort and reassure her to relieve anxiety. Get help.

✚ **SPINAL INJURY →** In any injury involving the neck or back, you must be concerned about spinal injury. Other symptoms include back or neck pain which increases with movement, loss of sensation or a tingling feeling in hands, feet, arms, or legs, or numbness on one side of the body. ***Do not move him*** unless there is an immediate threat to life. If in the water, float him face up until help arrives.

SLEEP

Most human beings will spend about a third of their life sleeping. Scientists are not exactly sure what sleep is or why we need it, but many studies have shown the adverse effects of sleep deprivation. Important reaction time slows significantly in sleep-deprived individuals. Sleep deprivation also interferes with "divergent thinking"—your creativity, flexibility, and problem-solving skills. Other studies have shown that emotional stability, irritability, and cross-temporal processing are negatively affected. Cross-temporal processing allows a person to use past experience and information to make decisions about behavior. This allows a mature individual to establish long-term goals, learn from experience, and delay gratification for the sake of future rewards. Without this processing, children are more prone to emotional outbursts and have a limited ability to learn from their experience. You develop these skills as you mature, but sleep deprivation slows down this development and may contribute to the emotional roller coaster some teenagers experience.

Apparently, sleep helps rid the brain of a chemical called adenosine, but we are not sure why adenosine must be cleared out or what other chemicals may be involved. Rapid eye movement (REM) sleep, that usually accompanies dreams, is also important to your physical and psychological

Can't Sleep?

- **Avoid caffeine for six hours before bedtime.** It takes three to six hours for your body to fully eliminate the effects of caffeine. Coffee and tea are not the only sources of caffeine. Chocolate contains both caffeine and another stimulant, theobromine. Pepsi (37 milligrams), Tab (44 milligrams), Mountain Dew (52 milligrams), and even Sunkist Orange soda (42 milligrams) contain significant amounts of caffeine and other stimulants. Coca-cola originally contained both caffeine and a low dose of cocaine. In 1903, cocaine was no longer added, but a 12-ounce serving of Coke still contains about 35 milligrams of chemically pure caffeine.

- **Quit smoking.** Nicotine reaches the brain in about eight seconds and increases alertness. It also causes the release of adrenaline and noradrenaline, which increase heart rate and blood pressure. Smokers have trouble falling asleep and do not sleep as deeply. Constricted air passages and reduced oxygen intake may produce interrupted sleep patterns as the body briefly awakes to get more air.

- **Avoid sugar at bedtime.** Try eating lighter at your evening meal.

- **Exercise for ten to twenty minutes about an hour before bedtime.** This releases mental and physical stress, and allows your body to unwind from the day.

- **Try a glass of warm milk.** The tryptophan in milk helps create serotonin, the neurotransmitter that stimulates sleepiness in the brain. Vitamin B_6 helps tryptophan convert more rapidly.

- **Take two aspirin and call me in the morning.** Several studies have demonstrated that aspirin, which comes from willow bark, does help people sleep, decreasing the number of awakenings during the night. *Be sure to wash the aspirin down with a large glass of water* so that it doesn't sit in your stomach overnight, causing a stomach ulcer.

- **Try meditation, deep breathing, or gradual relaxation exercises.**

state. This phase of sleep occurs in the last hour of sleep and allows you to awake rested and refreshed. In one experiment, subjects were awakened every time they began REM sleep, thus allowing them sufficient sleeping time, but no dreaming time. Over a short period of time, these subjects became irritable and disoriented. Extended periods without dreaming caused confused thinking, depression, and some actual hallucinations. Alcoholics, whose drinking may interfere with their REM sleep, can also experience hallucinations and distorted thinking. These side effects may be caused by a chemical reaction related to alcohol, but some researchers believe that sleep or dream deprivation could be involved. For reasons that are still not clear, we need both to sleep and to dream.

How much sleep is enough?

- *Full-term newborns need about 18 hours of sleep each day.*

- *Toddlers and young children need about 12 hours of sleep, usually divided between night sleep and naps.*

- *Eight- to twelve-year-olds need 8¼ to 9¼ hours of sleep each night.*

- *Twelve- to twenty-two-year-olds also need 8 to 9 hours of sleep each night.*

- *Adults on the average need 8¼ hours of sleep each night.*

- *Older adults typically sleep less, but it is not clear if they need more sleep than they get because of an age-related decline in melatonin, a brain chemical that regulates sleep.*

Within these age groups, individual sleep needs may vary from person to person. Some people can get by on as little as 4½ hours of sleep and others really need 9 or 10 hours. Studies have also confirmed the fact that some people are indeed morning people or "larks" (about 30 percent) and others, the "owls" (about 70 percent), reach their stride later in the day and evening.

Before you decide that you are an "owl" who only needs 4½ hours of sleep, preferably in the morning, check out this list of sleep-deprivation symptoms.

- Are you hard to wake in the morning?

- Do you get cranky or irritable late in the day?

- Do you ever have brief, unpredictable micro-sleeps during a class or quiet period, particularly in the afternoon or after a meal?

- When you stay up late to study for a test, are you able to remember the material for the test, but not recall much of it the next day?

- Could you easily sleep for 12 or more hours a night on weekends or over holidays?

- When you have a big paper or test or a late social activity, do you tend to take the extra time from your sleep?

- Do you find yourself looking forward to a good night's sleep?

Recent studies have provided some interesting information about the physiological need for sleep during adolescence. Mary Carskadon, at Brown University, has discovered that adolescent biological clocks, or circadian rhythms, undergo a hormonal "phase shift" which delays the nightly release of melatonin from the preadolescent time of 9:30 P.M. to about 10:30 P.M. in older adolescents. Melatonin is released from the pineal gland in the brain, inducing sleepiness and establishing your biological clock. While teenagers are hormonally triggered to be alert until around 11:00 and often stay up much later than that, they still need 8¼ to 9¼ hours of sleep. Waking at 6:30 or 7:00 to get ready for school cuts sleeping time short, particularly the REM time in the last hour of sleep. Some schools are experimenting with later starting times and have had some intriguing results. Several school districts in Minnesota delayed their first class period one hour, beginning class at 8:30 A.M. Particularly among eleventh and twelfth graders, preliminary results seem to suggest that grades are up; disciplinary, health, and counseling problems are down; and students are no longer falling asleep in class.

Until your school is more accommodating, you may want to organize your studies and activities so that you can get to sleep by 11:00 P.M. as often as possible. Don't be fooled by the second wind of wakefulness that often comes between 8:00 and 10:00 at night. This burst of alertness may give you a false reading of your need for sleep. By 10:30 or 11:00, your body will be ready. If you don't feel tired, quiet your music and settle in to bed with a good book. You will probably fall asleep quickly and naturally. Most people can recover from a single night of insufficient sleep by catching up the next night. Two or more late nights in a row create more of a problem. One study found that students limited to 5 hours of sleep each night for one week took two full 10- to 12-hour sleep days to return to normal scores on tests of divergent thinking and mood. Imagine how brilliant and good-humored you might be if you actually got enough sleep!

NUTRITION AND EXERCISE

Acne

*Acne is caused by the increase in oil in the hair follicles below the surface of the skin as a result of normal increases of androgen during adolescence. **It is NOT caused by greasy foods, chocolate, or a frustrated sex drive.** It can be increased by greasy lotions or makeup, emotional stress, high levels of iodine, and certain drugs (birth control pills, lithium, steroids). You can minimize blemishing.*

- Wash skin several times a day with soap and water. Massage gently.
- Use a fresh washcloth each day.
- Don't squeeze, scratch, or poke at pimples.
- Use over-the-counter medication containing benzoyl peroxide.
- Wash well immediately after strenuous exercise.
- Keep hair clean and off your face.
- Avoid oil-based creams, lotions, or makeup.
- Benzoyl peroxide, azelaic acid, or specialized antibodics may help control mild acne.
- See a dermatologist if your acne has not improved within three months. A doctor may be able to prescribe retinoids, tetracycline, or isotretinoin for serious or persistent acne.

Diet

Deciding when and what you eat is one of the most important ways you can keep your body and mind running well. Since the food you eat provides all of the energy and nutrients to build and rebuild the cells of your body, in a very real sense **you are what you eat.** To stay healthy, you need to eat a diet that includes a variety of foods, at least half of which are fruits, vegetables, grains, and legumes, and not eat more than your body uses. While diet is a complex and sometimes controversial subject, the researchers at the School of Public Health at the University of California in Berkeley have suggested twelve basic guidelines for a healthy diet.[3]

1. *Keep your total fat intake at or below 30 percent of your total daily calories.* Eat lean meats, low-fat dairy products, and cut back on vegetable oils, butter, mayonnaise, and fried foods.

2. *Limit your intake of saturated fat to less than 10 percent of your fat calories.* Saturated fats from animal products and tropical vegetable oils contribute to high blood cholesterol levels.

3. *Keep your cholesterol intake at 300 milligrams per day or less.* Cholesterol is only found in animal products such as meat, poultry, dairy, and egg yolks.

4. *Eat a diet high in complex carbohydrates.* Carbohydrates should make up at least 55 percent of your intake. This means five or six servings of fruit and/or vegetable and six or more servings of whole grains or legumes.

5. *Maintain a moderate protein intake.* Low-fat sources of protein should make up about 12 percent of your total daily calories.

6. *Eat a variety of foods.* Eating a wide assortment of foods assures you of getting all the vitamins and minerals that you need—even the ones we don't know about.

7. *Avoid too much sugar.* Sugar is a source of empty calories—not much good for anything except body fat after the initial, short-lived energy boost.

Never eat more than you can lift.

—Miss Piggy

8. *Limit your sodium intake to no more than 2,400 milligrams a day.* This is about 1 teaspoon of salt a day—watch food labels and cut back on how much salt you add to your food.

9. *Maintain an adequate calcium intake.* You need calcium to keep your bones and teeth strong. If you don't drink milk, try low-fat yogurt and extra helpings of broccoli, kale, collard, and fortified tofu.

10. *Get your vitamins and minerals from foods, not from supplements.* A good diet should provide you with what you need. Especially avoid supplements that have megadoses of any one nutrient.

11. *Maintain a desired weight.* Use exercise, not restrictive dieting, to regulate your weight. Judge your body weight by a doctor's recommendation for your height and build, NOT by the media or other social pressures.

12. *If you drink alcohol, do it in moderation.* Alcohol inhibits the small intestine's ability to transport and absorb nutrients, can lead to a variety of other health problems, and adds many calories to your diet without supplying any nutrients.

There are six essential nutrients that are necessary to sustain human life.

Got Enough Sugar?

The average twelve-ounce can of cola contains 10 teaspoons of sugar (40 grams).

Protein

Proteins make up 18 to 20 percent of your body. Protein is needed to build skin, hair, nails, muscles, and bones and forms antibodies to fight infection. Proteins are made up of 22 amino acids, 14 of which can be manufactured by your body. The other eight must be supplied through your diet. Food sources that contain all eight of these amino acids, such as meat, fish, eggs, milk, soybeans, and nuts, are called *complete proteins. Incomplete proteins,* like most grains and vegetables, can be eaten in the right combinations to make complete proteins—rice with beans, cheese with whole wheat bread, or peanut butter on whole wheat bread, for instance. Combinations do not have to be eaten together, but should be eaten within three or four hours. Most Americans eat nearly twice as much protein as their bodies need.

Carbohydrates

Carbohydrates provide a quick, short-lived energy boost and are your most common source of food energy. Unrefined or complete carbohydrates such as vegetables, fruits, whole grains, and potatoes provide a wide range of vitamins, minerals, and fiber. Sugar, bleached flour, and white rice are simple carbohydrates which provide a quick pick-me-up, but little else—except calories. Beans and rice, pasta with vegetables, potatoes, bran, and whole grain breads are good sources of complex carbohydrates.

Water

Two-thirds of your body is made up of water. Your brain is 75 percent water. Water provides a valuable source of minerals, helps digest food, cools the body, transports nutrients, and carries away waste. The exact amount of water that you need will vary depending on temperature, humidity, the foods you eat, and the amount of exercise you do, but, on the average, you should drink six to eight glasses of water a day.

Fats

Fats are the slowest burning energy food source, containing twice as much energy per gram as proteins or carbohydrates—about 9 calories per gram. Fats are filling, maintain healthy skin and hair, are an efficient way to store energy, regulate levels of cholesterol in the blood, and are also an important source of vitamins A, D, K, and E. Too much fat and too little exercise creates a buildup of fatty tissue on your body and vital organs, especially your heart. No more than 30 percent of your caloric intake should come from fat.

Vitamins and Minerals

Vitamins and minerals regulate your body's metabolic processes, promote good vision, form normal blood cells, regulate the functioning of your heart and nervous system, and provide the building material for your teeth and bones. Most vitamins are fat soluble and can be stored for long periods of time, but vitamin C and the B vitamins are water soluble and must be replaced regularly. You should be able to get all of the vitamins and minerals from the foods you eat without a vitamin supplement. Steaming or stir-frying your vegetables—or better yet, eating them raw—will help to preserve as many essential vitamins as possible. There is current research that seems to suggest that beta carotene (a form of vitamin A), vitamin C, and vitamin E may have some cancer-prevention properties. Most minerals are needed in very small quantities and are plentiful in a normal diet. Calcium, iron, and zinc are the most likely to be deficient and can cause a variety of health problems. Women need more iron than men, particularly during their menstrual period.

Two other important variables in your diet are **fiber** and **cholesterol**.

Fiber is found exclusively in plant foods and is not easily digested by human digestive enzymes. It passes through your digestive system without being completely broken down. Because of this, fiber does not contribute any nutrients to your body, but it does perform other important functions. Fiber promotes efficient waste elimination, preventing constipation and intestinal disorders, and seems to lower the risk of colon cancer, the second most common form of cancer in the United States. Fiber also appears to lower blood cholesterol levels which lowers the risk of heart disease and slows down the entry of glucose into the bloodstream which is of special help to diabetics. High-fiber foods are usually low in fat which makes them helpful for individuals attempting to control their weight.

You should take in 20 to 30 grams of fiber each day. The average American only consumes about 12 grams. You can increase your intake of fiber by eating a variety of unprocessed foods. Fruits and vegetables are a valuable source of fiber, especially when eaten with their skins. Legumes are particularly high in dietary fiber. Try not to eat all your daily fiber in one sitting, and drink plenty of liquids. Otherwise fiber can slow down your digestion and be uncomfortable.

Cholesterol is a white, waxy, fat-like substance that is present in all of your body's tissues. In the right amounts, it is used in the outer membrane of cells, insulates nerve fibers, and helps to build certain hormones. All the cholesterol that you need is produced by your own body from the foods that you eat. You also can add cholesterol to your body through the cholesterol already present in the food you eat, primarily meats, eggs, and

Wash Your Hands

The increase of drug-resistant, infectious diseases has served as an important reminder to wash your hands before eating or handling food; after using the bathroom, sneezing, or coughing; or handling objects that may be carrying viral or bacterial infections left by other hands. In an outbreak of the E. coli virus in Washington State, 501 people got seriously ill—151 had to be hospitalized, and three died. Forty-eight of these patients, including two of the children who died, had not eaten the infected hamburger, but contracted the virus from someone who had—most spreading the infection through unwashed, or poorly washed, hands. The Mayo Clinic recommends using soap, and rubbing vigorously for at least 10 seconds, frequently throughout the day. Keep your hands away from your mouth, eyes, or ears until you've had a chance to wash.

Vitamins You Need

Vitamin*	Where to get it	What it does	Deficiency
A (1000) RE)	Liver, eggs, dairy Carotene (green vegetables, deep yellow fruits)	Skin; hair; vision; tooth and bones; resistance to infection	Night blindness; dry eyes; dry, rough skin; poor tooth enamel; weak bones
Thiamin B_1 (1.5 mg)	Lean meat, liver, peas, legumes, oranges, grains	Releases energy; muscle tone; appetite regulation; heart and nervous system	Fatigue; loss of appetite; moodiness; mental confusion; leg cramps; muscle weakness
Riboflavin B_2 (1.8 mg)	Dairy, chicken, lean meat, dark green vegetables, eggs, tuna, whole grains, legumes	Helps cells use oxygen; metabolism; keeps skin and membranes healthy	Skin disorders; digestive disturbances; light sensitivity
Niacin B_3 (20 mg)	Liver, fish, poultry, nuts, green vegetables, grains (milk, eggs, lean meat)	Metabolism; helps cells use oxygen; healthy skin, nerves, and digestion	Skin disorders; depression; anxiety; confusion; digestive disturbances; diarrhea
Pyridoxine B_6 (2 mg)	Lean meat, liver, fish, nuts, legumes, grains, corn, poultry, bananas	Metabolism; formation of red blood cells and antibodies	Dermatitis; anemia; dizziness; depression; irritability; convulsions; smooth tongue
Cyano- cobalamin B_{12} (6 mg)	Lean meat, egg yolks, dairy, fish, shellfish	Red blood cells; healthy nervous system; metabolism; normal development	Anemia; numbness and tingling in fingers; fatigue; poor growth; peripheral nerve endings
Folic Acid (400 mg)	Dark green leafy vegetables, lima beans, grains, legumes	Formation of hemoglobin, enzymes, and other cells	Anemia; diarrhea; smooth, swollen tongue; poor growth
Pantothenic (10 mg)	Whole grains, egg yolks, fresh vegetables, liver	Metabolism; formation of hormones and nervous system	Fatigue; abdominal cramps; nausea; sleep problems
Biotin (300 mg)	Liver, egg yolks, legumes, cauliflower, vegetables	Releases energy from protein metabolism	Deficiencies very rare
C (60 mg)	Fruit, green vegetables, cauliflower, tomatoes	Maintains cell connections; blood vessels; bones; teeth; heals wounds; absorbs iron; resists infection	Weakness; fatigue; weight or appetite loss; increased risk of infection; slow healing; bruise; nosebleed; swollen gums
D (400 IU)	Fortified milk, egg yolks, fortified breakfast cereal, sunlight	Assists absorption and metabolism of calcium; aids bone and tooth growth	Poor bone and tooth formation; bowed legs, stunted growth; muscle weakness
E (30 IU)	Plant oils, wheat germ, vegetables, grains, eggs, legumes, fruits	Protects cell membranes, fatty acids, vitamin A, and red blood cells. Oxygen use	Red blood cell breakage and muscle weakness. Deficiency very rare
K (70 mg)	Green leafy vegetables, cabbage, egg yolks, milk	Aids in blood clotting and regulation of calcium	Hemorrhaging and delayed blood clotting

Includes Recommended Dietary Allowances for 15–18 year olds by the National Academy of Sciences, 1989.
g = gram   mg = milligram   mc = microgram   IU = International Unit   RE = retinol equivalent

Minerals You Need

Mineral*	Where to get it	What it does	Deficiency
Calcium (1000 mg)	Dairy, sardines, oysters, tofu, green vegetables, fruit	Strong bones and teeth; muscle contraction; heart and nerve function	Stunted growth; weak bones; osteoporosis
Chromium	Brewer's yeast, meat, grains, cheese, nuts	Involved in breakdown of sugar to release energy	Impaired glucose metabolism
Copper (2 mg)	Liver, shellfish, grains, nuts, legumes, lean meat, fish, fruits, vegetables	Hemoglobin and red blood cells; part of enzymes, respiration, and energy	Anemia; bone defects; stunted growth; impaired metabolism
Iodine (150 mc)	Iodized salt, seafood, some dairy products	Helps regulate growth, development, and metabolism	Enlarged thyroid; sluggish; weight gain
Iron (15 mg)	Liver, red meat, fish, egg yolks, legumes, leafy green vegetables, dried fruits	Hemoglobin which carries oxygen to cells, needed for use of energy by cells	Anemia; fatigue; headaches; muscle weakness; pale skin; inability to concentrate
Magnesium (400 mg)	Whole grains, nuts, legumes, dark green vegetables, seafood, chocolate	Builds protein; relaxes muscles; resists tooth decay; nerve functioning	Confusion; nervousness; muscle weakness; disorientation; hallucinations
Phosphorus (1200 mg)	Dairy, fish, meat, poultry, egg yolks, legumes, peas, grains, soft drinks	Strong bones and teeth; activates vitamins; releases energy; nerve functioning	Muscle weakness; loss of appetite; bone pain
Potassium	Lean meat, fresh fruit and vegetables, dairy, legumes, bananas	Muscle contraction; heart action; nerve functioning; use of proteins and glycerin	Muscle weakness; irregular heartbeat; apathy; confusion; loss of appetite. (Deficiencies occur with vomiting, diarrhea, sweating, or use of diuretics)
Selenium (50 mc)	Liver, seafood, lean meats, grains, wheat germ, milk	Works with vitamin E to protect cell membranes	Heart abnormalities; anemia. Rare
Sodium	Salt, most processed foods, dairy, meats	Normal fluid balance; nerve functioning; muscles	Muscle cramps; weakness; loss of appetite; apathy
Zinc (15 mg)	Liver, egg yolks, lean meat, fish, poultry, dairy, grains, vegetables	Works with enzymes; sense of taste; reproductive hormones; healing wounds	Retarded growth and sexual development; loss of taste and appetite; slow healing

Includes Recommended Allowances for 15–18 year olds by the National Academy of Sciences, 1989.
g = gram   mg = milligram   mc = microgram   IU = International Unit   RE = retinol equivalent

Checking Up On Your Diet

Take some time to keep track of your diet. Write down everything that you eat and then check off on the nutrient list those that you have included in your diet. Check one box for each food that provides each nutrient. If you include good servings of the nutrient-rich foods, you will easily meet the recommended dietary allowance, but you can check the amounts you are getting for any vitamin or mineral that you are low in or concerned about in a book like *Let's Eat Right to Keep Fit* by Adele Davis. Make a special note of the foods you eat that may provide unwanted calories, fat, or cholesterol but do not significantly add to your nutrition. Note any strengths, weaknesses, or changes you would like to make in your diet. Try keeping track for several days in a row to see if your diet balances out.

Breakfast:

Lunch:

Dinner:

Snacks:

Nutrients

Protein	▢▢▢▢▢▢ ▢
Unrefined Carbos	▢▢▢▢▢▢ ▢
Refined Carbos	▢▢▢▢▢▢ ▢
Fat	▢▢▢▢▢▢ ▢
Fiber	▢▢▢▢▢▢ ▢
Thiamine	▢▢▢▢▢▢ ▢
Riboflavin	▢▢▢▢▢▢ ▢
Niacin	▢▢▢▢▢▢ ▢
B_6	▢▢▢▢▢▢ ▢
B_{12}	▢▢▢▢▢▢ ▢
Folic Acid	▢▢▢▢▢▢ ▢
Biotin	▢▢▢▢▢▢ ▢
Vitamin C	▢▢▢▢▢▢ ▢
Vitamin D	▢▢▢▢▢▢ ▢
Vitamin E	▢▢▢▢▢▢ ▢
Vitamin K	▢▢▢▢▢▢ ▢
Calcium	▢▢▢▢▢▢ ▢
Chromium	▢▢▢▢▢▢ ▢
Copper	▢▢▢▢▢▢ ▢
Iodine	▢▢▢▢▢▢ ▢
Iron	▢▢▢▢▢▢ ▢
Magnesium	▢▢▢▢▢▢ ▢
Phosphorus	▢▢▢▢▢▢ ▢
Potassium	▢▢▢▢▢▢ ▢
Selenium	▢▢▢▢▢▢ ▢
Sodium	▢▢▢▢▢▢ ▢
Zinc	▢▢▢▢▢▢ ▢

NOTES:

Modern Mystery Foods

Most processed foods in the markets today are required by law to list their ingredients in descending order by weight. While the print is always small and many of the ingredients sound like something from a chemistry lab, it is worth reading carefully to see what you are buying. Look carefully for fat and cholesterol—avoid saturated fats like coconut, palm, or palm kernel oils or animal fats such as butter or lard. Polyunsaturated vegetable oils (corn, safflower, sunflower, sesame, or soybean) or mono-unsaturated oils (olive, peanut, or canola) help keep your blood cholesterol levels lower. Hydrogenation makes fats more saturated. Sugar also comes in many forms (sugar, brown sugar, corn syrup, honey) and each will be listed separately. Added together, sugar may actually be the predominant ingredient.

See if you can figure out what each of these commonly known products are from their list of ingredients.[4]

1. _____ Corn meal, vegetable oil, whey, cheddar cheese, salt, sour cream, artificial flavoring, monosodium glutamate, lactic acid, artificial coloring, citric acid.

2. _____ Sugar, gelatin, adipic acid, disodium phosphate, fumeric acid, artificial flavor, artificial color.

3. _____ Corn flour, sugar, oat flour, brown sugar, cottonseed oil, salt, niacianude, reduced iron, calcium, pantothenate, yellow 5, zinc oxide, yellow 6, pyridoxine hydrocholoride, thiamin monocitrate, BHT, riboflavin, folic acid, vitamin B_{12}.

4. _____ Water, meat by-products, poultry by-products, beef, fish, heart, wheat gluten, vegetable gums, whole wheat, bone meal, whole corn, whole egg, calcium sulfate, sodium tripolysphophate, natural flavoring, hydrogenized vegetable protein, onion powder, garlic powder, tetra-potassium, calcium chloride, potassium chloride, caramel coloring, artificial coloring, zinc sulfate, vitamin A, D, and E supplements, calcium pantothenate, thiamin mononitrate.

5. _____ Sugar, fructose citric acid, magnesium oxide, natural and artificial flavoring, calcium silicate, titanium dioxide, ascorbic acid, red 40, BHA.

6. _____ Water, flour, chicken, shortening, potatoes, carrots, chicken skin, modified food starch, peas, salt, dextrose, soy protein concentrate, chicken broth replacer, flavorings, hydrolyzed plant protein, partially hydrogenated soybean oils, sugar, sodium trypolyphosphate, monosodium glutamate, cellulose gum, paprika, oleoresin tumeric, beta carotene.

7. _____ Water, corn syrup, hydrogenated coconut and palm kernel oils, sugar, sodium caseinate, polysorbate 60 and sorbitan monostearate, natural and artificial flavors, xanthan gum and guar gum, artificial color.

8. _____ Water, corn syrup, graham cracker meal, shortening, sugar, molasses, dextrose, salt, leavening, part hydrogenated soybean and cottonseed oil, sugar, milk replacer, lemon concentrate, modified food starch, gelatin, cellulose gum, nonfat dry milk, salt, polysorbate 60, sorbitan monostearate, lecithin, dry whole milk, artificial flavoring, artificial coloring.

dairy products. If your body has more cholesterol than it needs, it begins to accumulate on the arterial walls. This slows down the flow of blood, leading to arteriosclerosis, blood clotting, heart attacks, and strokes. Blood cholesterol levels are measured through a sample of blood drawn from your arm. The test results measure the number of milligrams of cholesterol per deciliter of blood, usually between 150 and 300. The average American has a cholesterol level of 210, but doctors believe that a level between 180 and 200 is better to lower the risk of heart disease and stroke.

Being overweight, eating foods which are high in saturated fats and cholesterol, and smoking all raise your cholesterol level. Eating foods high in fiber, substituting polyunsaturated and mono-unsaturated fats in your diet, and eating fatty fish all tend to lower your cholesterol level. Aerobic exercise also helps your body to process cholesterol efficiently. People over thirty are at highest risk for cholesterol problems, but younger people establish dietary habits and cholesterol levels that can lead to problems when they are older.

Vegetarian Diets

Some people today choose to eliminate most or all animal products from their diet. Total vegetarians eliminate all foods of animal origin, but some vegetarians may include dairy products, eggs, fish, or poultry. Other people just prefer a non-meat diet and eat meat only occasionally. While we are still a meat-and-potatoes society, fruits and vegetables are usually high in fiber, low in fat and cholesterol, and can provide a healthy and nutritionally adequate diet. Studies have shown that vegetarians are at less risk for heart disease, diabetes, and some cancers, and tend to have lower blood pressure and cholesterol levels.

It does take some thoughtful planning to make sure that you get all of the vitamins, minerals, and protein that your body needs. Vitamins B_{12} and D are found only in animal products and are needed for healthy blood and nerves. Dairy products and eggs are a sufficient source of these vitamins. Broccoli and almonds are also a good source of the B vitamins. If you do not eat any dairy or eggs, you will need to get your B_{12} from fortified products such as tofu or from a vitamin supplement. You can usually get enough vitamin D from exposure to the sun.

Calcium, zinc, and iron are the minerals most difficult to get if you do not eat meat products. Peas, lentils, and wheat germ are good sources of zinc. The calcium in broccoli, kale, collard, and fortified tofu is not as easily absorbed as that in milk products, so you will need to eat a lot. Iron is available in beans, potatoes, dried fruit, and fortified cereals and can be enhanced by eating these foods with others rich in vitamin C—berries, citrus fruits, tomatoes, or broccoli.

Vegetarians can get an adequate supply of protein from grains and legumes, but remember that these are incomplete protein sources and must be combined in order to form a complete set of amino acids. Legumes (peas, nuts, peanut butter, beans) and whole grain breads, rice, or cereal, for example, form a complete set. If you are considering a vegetarian diet, be sure to study your nutritional needs carefully and learn to include all the nutrients that you need.

Why Won't Grown-Ups Eat Their Veggies?

The National Cancer Institute, a government nutrition education program, estimates that approximately 35 percent of all cancer deaths in the United States may be related to diet—specifically too much fat and not enough fruits and vegetables. The Institute recommends at least five servings of fruit and vegetables each day and reports that only 9 percent of adults in the U.S. are meeting this requirement. Almost half aren't eating even one piece of fruit a day. (A serving is 1/2 cup of cooked or raw vegetables or fruit, 1 cup of leafy vegetables, 1 medium piece of fruit, or 3/4 cup of vegetable or fruit juice.)

Quandary: *Diet for a Small Planet*[5]

In 1971, Frances Moore Lappe wrote a book titled *Diet for a Small Planet* in which she questioned how we use the earth's resources to provide protein nutrients for human life. Lappe collected data showing that developed countries use practically as much grain as feed for livestock as the majority of people in the world have available as food. We use 16 pounds of edible grain and 2,464 gallons of water to produce one pound of edible beef. The "feed cost" of one eight-ounce steak could provide 45 to 50 people with a full cup of high-protein cereal grains.

Since 1971, many health and environmentally conscious groups and individuals have become concerned about our global diet. *Beyond Beef*, an international coalition of environmental groups, cites the following concerns:

1. **PERSONAL HEALTH:** The Surgeon General has reported that 70 percent of deaths in the U.S. are related to diet, mainly the overconsumption of saturated fats like those contained in meat.

2. **ANIMAL SUFFERING:** In the United States, more than 100,000 cows are slaughtered every day. Cows and other animals are branded, dehorned, and castrated and fed masses of drugs and hormones to increase their market value. Veal calves are taken from their mothers at birth, force-fed, and held in tiny wooden crates where they are allowed no exercise, sociability, or sunlight. Feedlots and cattle cars jam cattle together where they have little room to move and are often trampled and injured.

3. **RAIN FOREST DESTRUCTION:** Twenty-five percent of the Central American rain forest has been cleared to create pasture for beef cattle, mostly for the American fast-food hamburger. It has been estimated that every four-ounce hamburger made from rain forest beef destroys 55 square feet of tropical rain forest.

4. **GLOBAL WARMING:** In addition to the clearing of the rain forest trees, in their normal digestive processes cattle belch up to 60 million tons of methane gases each year—12 percent of the total methane released into our atmosphere.

5. **WATER POLLUTION AND SCARCITY:** Cattle produce nearly one billion tons of manure each year, much of which pollutes our rivers and streams. Also, nearly half the water consumed in the United States goes to grow feed to raise cattle and other livestock. It takes the equivalent of eight months of daily showers to produce one pound of beef.

6. **DESERTIFICATION:** In addition to using or polluting the earth's scarce supply of fresh water, each cow eats approximately 900 pounds of range vegetation each year. Without this water-absorbing range vegetation, the land becomes increasingly vulnerable to wind and water erosion.

7. **WORLD HUNGER:** While nearly one billion people suffer from hunger and malnutrition and over 40 million die of starvation each year, more than one-third of the world's grain harvest is used to feed livestock. In the U.S., livestock consume 70 percent of all grain produced in this country.

8. **FAMILY FARMS:** Livestock can only be raised humanely by smaller family farmers which can provide the time and space for ecologically responsible cattle raising. Corporate farming uses large factory feedlots and vast amounts of chemicals, hormones, and pesticides to increase their profits. Large corporate farming concerns have high-tech production processes, massive lobbying groups, and have forced the small farmer out of the market.

In Europe, the trend is to look not only at the nutritional content of your diet, but to consider the environmental impact of what you eat. Hardy Votgmann, director of the Division of Alternative Agriculture Methods in Germany reports, "A large proportion of consumers has become aware of the wider context of food production. To be acceptable, food must be healthy and healthfully produced, not only for oneself, but for the environment and the larger society as well."

Exercise

Diet provides you with the fuel or energy to run your body. Exercise is the way that you use that energy and tone your body. It is important to keep a balance between the calories that you take in and the energy that you burn in your daily activity. Leftover calories are stored as fat on your body and vital organs. When you do not take in enough calories to support your activity, your body begins to break down the protein in your muscles and organs. A good balance will provide you with the energy that you need without building up excess fatty tissue.

Everyday activities like walking, gardening, or household chores are all forms of exercise, but most of us do not have a vigorous enough lifestyle to match our nutrient-rich diet. Some form of physical exercise, whether it is recreational or structured, is usually necessary to keep your body fit and strong.

There are four basic elements of physical fitness: ***cardiovascular endurance, muscular strength, muscular endurance,*** and ***flexibility.*** Different forms of exercise develop different elements of fitness. Weight lifting develops muscular strength and endurance, but does little to improve your cardiovascular endurance. Running is good for cardiovascular endurance, but does little to improve your upper body strength. You should evaluate and vary your exercise program to make sure that you are developing all four elements.

Cardiovascular Endurance

Cardiovascular endurance is the ability of the heart, blood vessels, and blood to carry oxygen to the cells and the ability of the cells to process the oxygen. This ability is critical to every cell in your body. Cardiovascular endurance is most effectively developed through aerobic exercise—exercise that demands large quantities of oxygen to be delivered to the large muscle groups for a sustained period of time. Regular aerobic exercise trains your heart to be able to pump more oxygen and your muscles to use that oxygen more efficiently. This helps keep blood pressure low, reduces the risk of heart disease, helps to control weight gain, and reduces mental stress and depression.

For most aerobic exercise, you should spend five to ten minutes warming up slowly. This can be a slower or less strenuous version of whatever exercise you plan to do—fast walking before running, slow swimming before laps, etc. Then take ten to fifteen minutes to stretch and loosen up your body. The aerobic part of your exercise should last fifteen to sixty minutes. You should end with five to ten minutes of cool down, allowing your heart and body to return to its normal state.

An Exercise Plan

- Studies have shown that people who exercise in the morning are more likely to keep at it than people who exercise later in the day.
- Warm up gradually. Take 5 minutes to build up to your regular level of exertion, allowing your heart rate to speed up slightly before going full speed.
- Always take time to warm up properly **before** you stretch! Stretching cold muscles can injure them. After a gentle warm-up, take 5 to 10 minutes to stretch your arms, back, and legs. Stretch slowly and gently—don't bounce.
- "No pain, no gain" is NOT a productive approach to exercise. Push to the point of tension, but stop before you feel any pain or discomfort. Your body will gradually become stronger without stressing your system or muscles.
- Always allow 5 minutes to cool down, let your heart rate and muscle tension return to normal. Slow down your exercise rate and end with slow stretches.
- Replace the fluids that you lose through sweat and exertion. In hot weather, you can lose more than a quart of water in an hour. Drink 16 to 20 ounces a couple of hours before you exercise and, afterward, enough fluid to replace the fluid you've sweated—even if you aren't thirsty.

The American College of Sports Medicine recommends:

- FREQUENCY: 3 to 5 times a week

- DURATION: 15 to 60 minutes

- INTENSITY: raise your heart level to 60 to 80 percent of its maximum (training heart rate)

There are many enjoyable forms of aerobic exercise:

Walking: Brisk walking averages about 3.5 to 4.5 miles per hour, that is, approximately 120 to 160 2.5 foot steps per minute. It should take you about fifteen minutes to walk a mile. Wear good shoes, vary your route, and take a friend. Swing your arms or carry extra weights to increase the aerobic impact.

Hiking: Hiking can provide a good workout with the added benefit of nature and variety. Hiking along a rough but level trail requires about 50 percent more energy than walking on a paved road. Hiking at a normal pace over a varied terrain for eight hours uses up about 3,500 calories—1000 more than most runners will use during a marathon. Wear shoes that support your ankles and loose clothing. Don't forget to replace your fluids.

Running: Running for a half hour three or four days a week will lower your heart rate and blood pressure and help reduce your weight quickly. A moderate pace for thirty minutes is better than working harder for fifteen, so pace yourself and gradually work up your endurance. Don't get carried away—running more than twenty miles a week does not greatly enhance your fitness, but does increase your chance of injury.

Swimming: Swimming works out more than two-thirds of your body's total muscle mass and develops muscle strength, endurance, and flexibility. It also places very little stress on your bones and joints. Use the crawl stroke and start slowly with four 25-yard laps, resting when necessary. Eventually you will want to swim continuously for thirty to forty minutes at least three times a week.

Biking: Biking is an excellent form of exercise, giving you a good cardiovascular workout, building large leg muscles, and burning between four and seven hundred calories per hour. A good workout can be achieved in three twenty-minute rides a week depending on the terrain and traffic. Keep pedaling even when you go downhill so that the lactic acids don't build up in your muscles—that's what makes them sore.

Measuring Your Heart Rate

With the palm of your hand facing you, locate your pulse with the index and middle finger of your other hand. While looking at a clock, begin counting your pulse beginning with zero. After 10 seconds, stop and multiply that number by 6 to get the number of beats per minute. This is your **pulse rate.** To get your **training heart rate,** subtract your age from 220 then multiply by 0.6 and 0.8 to get your lower and upper training limits.
Example:
220 minus 16 years = 204
204 times 0.6 = 122
204 times 0.8 = 163
Your body is in a recommended aerobic state when your heart rate is between 122 and 163.

🦶 **Cross-Country Skiing:** If you have the snow, cross-country skiing is about the best aerobic exercise you can do. It uses the muscles in the shoulders, back, chest, abdomen, buttocks, and legs and can burn as much as 900 calories per hour. Dress in layers because you will heat up quickly, and don't forget to replace your fluids.

🦶 **Sports:** Many sports provide an excellent cardiovascular workout combined with camaraderie and high interest. Racquet sports develop agility, coordination, and concentration and if you push yourself and maintain your training heart rate for at least twenty minutes three times a week, you can get a good cardiovascular workout. Soccer, football, jumping rope, and even ultimate Frisbee can give you a good workout plus build muscular strength and endurance. Low-key, recreational sports should probably be supplemented by some additional workouts—both to prepare for the game and maintain a desired, well-rounded fitness.

🦶 **Aerobics:** Many people prefer the fun and convenience of aerobic dance or exercise. Classes or videotapes are available to take you through an aerobic routine that will give you a good workout with the fun of dancing and groaning along with a group. You will need to do a thirty to sixty minute aerobic workout three to six times a week to develop cardiovascular fitness or any significant weight loss. Build up gradually and watch your heart rate. Studies have shown that low-impact aerobics—at least one foot is almost always on the ground and your arms are used to raise your heart rate—can be just as effective and easier on your joints and muscles.

🦶 **Machines:** Rowing machines, cross-country ski machines, exercise bicycles, and stair-climbing machines provide effective ways of getting in your exercise. Most gyms will have a variety of exercise machines and may be a better investment than a single machine in your home which you may tire of.

Muscular Strength and Endurance

Well-conditioned muscles keep your body strong and flexible enough to function smoothly, maintain good posture, and prevent injury. **Muscular strength is the maximum force that you can exert in a single effort and muscular endurance is your ability to sustain and repeat that effort.** Both strength and endurance are improved through exercise that applies resistance to your effort or movement. Working out with weights is probably the best way to enhance muscular strength. Free weights or weight machines allow you to increase the resistance and quickly build muscle strength. Endurance is improved by many repetitions of an exercise. You can use weights or exercise machines, but old-fashioned calisthenics are equally effective.

The best exercise for your **abdominal muscles** is a *sit-up*. Sit-ups tone all three abdominal muscles that protect your back, tone your mid-section,

---

R.I.C.E.

If you injure a joint or muscle during sports or exercise, remember the following treatment formula to avoid further injury and speed recovery.

- **R**est the injured area for 24 to 48 hours.
- **I**ce the area for 5 to 20 minutes each hour until there is no further swelling or heat.
- **C**ompress the area by wrapping it tightly for 30 minutes, then unwrap for 15. Repeat several times.
- **E**levate the area to reduce swelling: Prop it up while you sleep if necessary.

Jock Itch

Jock itch is caused by a fungus infection that develops in exercise clothing that is stored in a dark, poorly ventilated place such as a locker or gym bag after exercise. Its symptoms are redness, itchiness, and scaliness in the groin and thigh area. It is most closely associated with male athletic supporters, but can develop in tight women's clothing as well.

To avoid and treat jock itch:

- *Don't wear tight, close fitting clothing.*
- *Change underwear frequently, especially after exercise.*
- *Wash clothes after a workout—don't store in your locker or gym bag.*
- *Shower after a workout, applying powder to the groin area afterward.*
- *Sleep in loose, airy nightclothes or in the buff.*

If you have a bad case, an antifungal cream or lotion can be bought at the pharmacy. It will take about two weeks to clear up.

and give your torso more strength and power. The safest, most effective sit-up is to lie on your back with your knees bent and your feet flat on the floor. Don't put your hands behind your head or neck—this can jerk your neck muscles and allows your arms to do a lot of the work. You can put your hands at your sides, crossed over your chest or, when your abdominal muscles become strong enough, cross them behind your head with each hand on the opposite shoulder.

Contract your abdominal muscles and press your lower back into the floor. You only need to come up to about a 45-degree angle to effectively work your abdominal muscles. Start out with three sets of five, resting between sets. Work up to three sets of 15, three times a week. You can further work your side muscles by twisting your body up and toward the opposite knee from the regular sit-up position. Hold for three seconds and return to the center. Do this twist ten times to each side, three times a week.

The best exercise for developing **upper body strength** is the old-fashioned standard *push-up*. The push-up works the muscles in the shoulders, upper arms, and chest, but also tones the abdomen, hips, and back and helps develop good posture. Place your hands slightly wider than your shoulders, feet and legs close together, knees straight, and arms perpendicular to the floor. Lower your chest to the floor and push back up. Breathe out as you go down and breathe in as you push up. Be sure to keep your body straight—don't sag. Start out with three sets of as many as you can, but don't strain and don't worry if you can't do many at first. You will be impressed by your progress. You can also start with *modified push-ups*. Keep your body straight from your head to your knees and do your push-up from there. You can also start with *let-downs*. Start in the standard push-up position and slowly lower your body inch by inch, keeping your body straight, until your chest reaches the floor. Then relax (or collapse, as the case may be) and using your knees, return to the starting point.

Most of your **lower body workout** will come from aerobic exercise such as running, biking, swimming, or cross-country skiing. You can also do isometric exercises that lift or tighten your leg muscles.

Flexibility

Stretching leads to greater agility, muscle speed, and a lower risk of injuring your muscles, tendons, and ligaments. It also relieves stiffness, prevents sore muscles, and releases mental stress. And it feels good! You should always stretch before **and** after you exercise to keep your muscles flexible and to release the lactic acids that can get stored up in your muscles when you exercise—that's what makes you sore. Don't bounce or jerk your muscles; stretch slowly and gently until you feel resistance. Hold this position for 20 to 30 seconds and then relax. Allow your body some time to incorporate the stretch before going on to the next one.

You should see a doctor if there is severe pain and swelling, numbness, discoloration, or inability to move the injured part.

Remember to warm up your muscles before you stretch—cold muscles tear more easily. Always stop **before** the pain. Pain means straining or tearing, not stretching. Isolate different muscles groups, stretching them one by one. Try to keep your other muscles relaxed while you are working on one. Stretch three to four times a week for at least ten to twenty minutes. Always stretch before exercising or playing a sport to reduce the risk of muscle strain or injury. Flexibility develops gradually, so don't get discouraged. Little by little, you will become more limber and comfortable.

Use your breath to coordinate and release your stretch. As you stretch, take a deep abdominal breath, filling your lungs and chest cavity. Then, as you release the breath, let go of the stretch and completely relax, allowing your muscles to go limp. Don't rush; follow each muscle group stretching with three or four slow, deep breaths to allow the muscles to stay stretched. Visualize your breath going into your muscles, making them more flexible and relaxed.

Your Perfect Workout Week

Exercise can make you feel terrific and it does terrific things for your body, but it can be difficult to keep at it. In spite of all the books, videos, classes, and equipment available, the only exercise program that will really work for you is one that you devise yourself—one that fits your time schedule, fitness level, interests, and facilities. In devising your own program, set realistic goals that are important to you. Look at the four elements of fitness—*cardiovascular endurance* [CE], *muscular strength* [MS], *muscular endurance* [ME], and *flexibility* [F] and make sure that you address them all. Start slowly and celebrate your improvement as you gradually increase your time and performance. Don't overexert yourself or set your immediate goals too high—strained muscles and perfectionist expectations are usually good excuses to give up. Make sure that you have found a convenient time, place, and activity for you. Make it easy to exercise. And be sure to set up a program that is fun and interesting to you. Exercise to music that you like. Be playful and find exercise that is genuinely rewarding and enjoyable to you. Do you like having a set routine that you do every day or is it more fun for you to vary your exercise from day to day? Do you like to exercise alone or does it help to have a friend to commiserate and laugh with? Experiment with different combinations, times, and activities until you find the mix that fits conveniently and enjoyably into your life.

Set up what you think might be the perfect exercise week for you. Try it out and make whatever changes you need.

Day of Week	Time	Exercise	Goal	CE	MS	ME	F
MONDAY				❏	❏	❏	❏
TUESDAY				❏	❏	❏	❏
WEDNESDAY				❏	❏	❏	❏
THURSDAY				❏	❏	❏	❏
FRIDAY				❏	❏	❏	❏
SATURDAY				❏	❏	❏	❏
SUNDAY				❏	❏	❏	❏

EATING/WEIGHT DISORDERS

Problems with eating, exercise, and weight have become increasingly prevalent among young people in the last twenty years. It is estimated that about one out of every 200 people between twelve and thirty have *anorexia nervosa*. Estimates for *bulimia* in college-age women vary from five to twenty out of every 100. While more women than men are affected by eating disorders, an increasing number of men do struggle with compulsive eating and bingeing or may attempt to control their weight and body image through compulsive exercise or steroid use. Male eating and weight disorders are less likely to be diagnosed, but experts estimate that at least several hundred thousand men are affected.

While we are not sure exactly what causes eating and weight disorders, biological, psychological, and social factors all appear to play a part. Biologically, depression, mood disorders, and alcoholism tend to run in the families of patients with weight disorders. Some bulimics have been helped by treatment with antidepressant medication.

Psychologically, weight disorders are often associated with a high need for control. Patients are often high achievers or perfectionists who are lacking in self-confidence in spite of obvious achievements. They may fear abandonment or betrayal and have difficulty establishing close relationships. They often feel out of control, anxious, and confused. Adolescents and adults with weight disorders were often "model children" who are intelligent, perfectionist, and have high personal standards and unrealistic family expectations. Current research has also traced the beginnings of some weight disorders to early sexual assault or abuse.

There are also many social or cultural pressures that influence how both girls and boys feel about their bodies. Historically, women have often been judged and valued by the shape of their body—as one nineteenth-century critic described it, "Men have a body; women are their body." In the 1800s, females were fitted into tightly-laced corsets that exerted as much as eighty pounds of pressure. Girls were fitted for hour-glass shaping corsets as young as one year of age. The effect of these body-binding devises was devastating to a woman's health and strength. Their ribs were turned inward and compressed, organs were squeezed, and backs and stomach muscles were weakened. These conditions often led to fainting spells, menstrual problems, constipation, and difficulty during childbirth. Women often cooperated with this abuse by having lower ribs surgically removed to achieve a smaller waist or eating small amounts of arsenic to whiten their complexion. More recently, males too have been encouraged to achieve an "ideal" body type instead of appreciating a wider range of normal body development. Advertising, with its anorexic models and photo touch-ups, has contributed to a general dissatisfaction with how we look.

Anorexia Nervosa

Anorexia is a life-threatening weight disorder that is marked by a consuming obsession with thinness. Anorexics develop an intense fear of gaining weight and gradually stop eating. While there is a noticeable weight loss (at least 25 percent of original body weight), most anorexics have a *distorted body image* and see themselves as much fatter than they are. Anorexia quickly results in malnutrition and can lead to permanent physiological problems and death. One anorexic in ten dies of the disease.

There are several serious medical complications that result from the starvation associated with anorexia. Malnutrition can cause muscle weakness, fatigue, hypothermia, and an impaired ability to concentrate. This weakening of the heart muscle can cause a slow or irregular heartbeat and lead to permanent heart damage. The kidneys can be damaged by a lack of potassium and anorexics often have chronic problems with digestion and elimination. The loss of nutrients and water causes a serious fluid and electrolyte imbalance which can lead to heart and kidney failure. Karen Carpenter, a popular rock singer in the seventies, actually died of heart failure after she had begun recovering from anorexia.

Treatment of anorexia usually involves both medical and psychological care. In the advanced stages of weight loss, the individual may require hospitalization with physical and nutritional intervention. Individual and group counseling work to address underlying problems and develop alternate coping skills.

Some signs of anorexia are:

- *strict dieting and excessive weight loss*
- *intense fear of weight gain and getting fat*
- *in females, loss of the menstrual period*
- *abuse of laxatives, diuretics, or diet pills*
- *obsessive interest in diet books, meal planning, etc.*
- *bizarre or ritualistic eating habits*
- *complaints of feeling cold*
- *hyperactivity—excessive exercising*
- *emaciated, skeletal appearance*
- *brittle fingernails*
- *hair pulls out easily or hair loss*
- *growth of fine, downy body hair especially on arms and legs*
- *poor concentration and disorganized thinking*
- *social withdrawal*
- *perfectionist expectations of self and others*

Like an alcoholic or drug addict, most anorexics experience a sense of **denial** about their weight loss and related problems. He tends to be comforted by the weight loss, see himself as chronically overweight, and will avoid most attempts to get him to eat or get help.

Bulimia or Binge Eating

Binge eating or **bulimia** is the rapid, uncontrolled consumption of large quantities of food during a short period of time. Foods eaten are often high in fat and sugar. Purging is the attempt to get rid of the food eaten during a binge. The most common method is by self-induced vomiting. Other methods include the use of laxatives, diuretics, vigorous exercise, severe dieting, or fasting.

Bulimia is a more chronic and inconspicuous disorder than anorexia. Bulimics may be of normal body weight and can be involved with bingeing and purging for many years without being discovered. This long-term disruption of nutrition and the digestive system can create serious physiological problems. Frequent vomiting can erode the enamel on your teeth, create irregular heart rhythms or cardiac failure, cause irritation and infection of the salivary glands, and cause bleeding or perforation of the esophagus or stomach. The reduced level of nutrients that actually reach the body creates muscle weakness, disruption of the menstrual cycle in females, and damage to the liver and kidneys.

Treatment of bulimia also usually involves both medical and psychological care. It is important to have a complete physical to determine what physical dangers have evolved. Group therapy has been most successful in helping bulimics recover from their binge/purge habits and strengthen their coping skills and self-image.

Some signs of bulimia are:

- *preoccupation with food, weight, body size, and fat*
- *secret bingeing followed by fasting, self-induced vomiting, or laxatives*
- *purging*
- *low self-esteem or self-loathing especially after eating*
- *depression or mood swings*
- *frequent visits to the bathroom immediately after meals*
- *loss of tooth enamel and increased tooth decay*
- *low frustration tolerance and poor impulse control*
- *unexplained disappearance of food*
- *swollen glands that lead to "chipmunk cheeks"*
- *excessive dieting and exercise*
- *frequent weight fluctuations*
- *frequent sore throats*
- *signs of secrecy including social withdrawal and eating alone*
- *may be accompanied by other compulsive behaviors such as substance abuse, shopping, shoplifting, or stealing*

Some bulimics cannot compensate for their compulsive overeating and do become overweight. Others, sometimes known as **bulimarexics,** swing back and forth between overeating and self-starvation. Most bulimics realize that they do have a problem with their eating, but feel too ashamed and confused to seek help.

Compulsive Exercising

Compulsive exercising has many of the same characteristics as anorexia and bulimia, but the central obsession is exercise. Exercise can provide a sense of control and, because it is generally seen as a healthy activity, may satisfy the exerciser's high perfectionist needs to be good and disciplined. Many exercisers become addicted to the natural painkilling endorphins that the brain releases during extensive aerobic exercise.

Compulsive exercisers also tend to develop compulsive interests in food and diet. They may become fanatical about health foods and restrict the range of foods that they eat. Because of their compulsive exercising, they frequently do not eat enough to maintain the energy that they are expending. At that point, their body actually begins to eat itself—to use up the protein stored in muscles and organ tissues. This can result in permanent heart damage and death. A fluid and electrolyte imbalance raises the risk of heart and kidney failure.

Compulsive exercising is often unrecognized and undiagnosed until weight loss is severe or other medical problems develop. Like the other weight disorders, treatment involves both medical and psychological intervention. Most compulsive exercisers do not see their behavior as a life-threatening problem and are resistant to concern or treatment.

Some sighs of compulsive exercising are:

- *excessive exercising, often several hours a day*
- *compulsive need to exercise every day*
- *exercise begins to take time from work, school, and relationships*
- *preoccupation with exercise, diet, food preparation, and body weight*
- *exercise is not relaxing and playful; it is approached with serious determination and discipline*
- *constantly increasing the level and length of exercise sessions*
- *never satisfied with victories or accomplishments; always setting new goals*
- *gradual but noticeable weight loss, accompanied by a tight, gaunt appearance*
- *social withdrawal and preoccupation*
- *mood swings and/or depression and paranoia*
- *poor concentration and disorganized thinking*
- *perfectionist expectations of self and others*
- *in females, loss of menstrual period*

Steroids

Growing girls aren't the only ones influenced by social and media body images. Between 7 percent and 11 percent of all high school boys have tried steroids, many just to improve their masculine appearance. Dr. Gary English, an expert on steroid use, said, "The fastest growing group of adolescents using steroids aren't competing on teams. They're just kids who want to have a Body Beautiful like the ones they're bombarded with on television."

Anabolic-androgenic steroids are a synthetic derivative form of the male hormone testosterone. They were originally developed in the 1930s in Germany to help develop normal male characteristics in young men who were not producing enough testosterone. In normal males, steroids produced larger muscle mass, more aggression, and allowed them to work harder and longer. These were valuable qualities during wartime and the German soldiers used steroids extensively during World War II.

After the war, the Germans were the first to experiment with the use of steroids to enhance athletic performance. The long-term dangers of steroids had not yet been explored. We now know that steroid use is associated with damage to the liver, cardiovascular system, and reproductive organs. Only one member of the 1964 steroid-enhanced East German women's swim team is still alive.

> *I'd compare steroid use among boys to anorexia and bulimia for girls. It's an extreme reaction to a normal adolescent concern—body image.*
>
> *—M. J. Carlson, nurse practitioner*

In spite of recent legislation to restrict the sale and use of steroids, they are not hard to get on the black market or by mail order. Many bodybuilding magazines promote the use of steroids and carry classified ads that sell them. Some parents and coaches actually encourage steroid use to increase athletic performance. With these mixed messages from adults and professional athletes, boys using steroids may disregard the long-term damage to their systems in favor of a desired body image. Like anorexics, some steroid users develop a distorted body image and increase their steroid use in an effort to keep getting bigger and stronger.

Some signs of steroid use are:

- *Rapid muscle and weight gain—a 20 to 30 percent increase over a four- to eight-week period*

- *Puffiness or bloating, especially of the upper body and face*

- *Severe acne, especially across the back*

- *Small purple or red spots on the skin*

- *Persistent bad breath*

- *Unexplained aggressiveness or mood swings*

Taken alone, many of these signs are normal during adolescence, but a combination of two or three at once does suggest steroid use.[6]

What can you do to help a friend?

Having a friend or family member with an eating or weight disorder can be very confusing and difficult. A person struggling with t his problem can seem helpless and pathetic one minute and fiercely stubborn and hostile the next. Often, she will deny that there is any problem and reject your offers of concern. You may feel powerless to help or protect her, and worried that she will seriously harm herself. Most likely, you will begin to feel angry and uncomfortable around this person. Here are some suggestions to help you deal honestly and helpfully with your friend.

1. Know the signs of eating and weight disorders. Notice what your friend does or says that concerns you.

2. You are not responsible for controlling or curing your friend's eating problems. You can express your concerns, refuse to contribute to the problem, or alert a knowledgeable adult, but don't become obsessed with his eating or exercise.

3. If you do decide to talk to your friend, pick a quiet, confidential time and place. Use "I" statements that describe specific behaviors that you have noticed and how you feel about them—*I have noticed that you just pick at your food and have lost a lot of weight lately and I am worried that you may be hurting yourself.* Speak honestly and specifically, stressing your care and concern for her. Then ask for her reaction and listen carefully. You don't have to agree, but try to understand what she is telling you.

4. Don't avoid expressing your concerns because you are afraid of hurting your friend's feelings or making him worse. Blaming and denial are the worst things you can do; what he needs is your concern, honesty, and support.

5. Don't let the disorder monopolize your relationship. Speak your mind, but develop interests, topics of conversations, and ways to let her know you care that don't involve food or exercise.

6. Avoid power struggles over eating and weight. The person with a weight disorder will always win.

7. Be a good listener. You don't have to listen to hours of brooding about food or weight, but listening to what she feels and thinks can be very helpful.

8. Don't enable your friend's disorder by allowing his eating or exercise habits to dominate your activities or schedule. Set limits of what you will put up with and don't make excuses for stolen food or abusive behavior.

9. Realize that most people with eating and weight disorders are ambivalent about getting better. Sometimes they really do want to have more normal eating habits, but at other times, they want the comfort and security that eating, not eating, or exercise gives them.

10. Realize that you are a caring friend who is sincerely trying to do what is right in an extremely difficult situation. Don't blame yourself or hold yourself responsible for your friend's problems or improvement. Talk to someone about your feelings and needs as you attempt to understand and help.

Self-Injury

A growing number of teens have engaged in behaviors defined as *moderate* or *superficial self-mutilation*. This can include cutting, burning, scratching, skin-picking, hitting, or other deliberate forms of inflicting damage on your body. These acts are usually not suicidal, but can be dangerous and may indicate a deeper level of depression or suicidal thinking in some cases. Some who injure themselves, in fact, see the cutting or injury as a release of tension or anxiety that actually protects them from being suicidal. Reasons most commonly given for self-injury are

- *Escape from emptiness, depression, and feelings of depression*

- *Stress or tension reducer*

- *Relief: when intense feelings build, self-injurers are overwhelmed and unable to cope. By causing pain, they reduce the level of emotional and physiological arousal to a more bearable level.*

- *Expression of emotional pain: many who self-injure say they do it in order to feel something, to know that they're still alive.*

- *Punishment for being "bad"*

- *Relief from anger: many self-injurers have enormous amounts of rage and are afraid to express it outwardly.*[7]

Females are more likely to engage in this behavior than males, perhaps due to the social inhibitions about anger for girls. Self-injurers often don't understand the behavior themselves and may feel ashamed or confused by it. Self-injury usually involves unacceptable anger and may be a part of other psychiatric disorders.

When a person decides to stop, she will need strong emotional support from friends and family. It is important to work with a therapist to find alternative coping skills and outlets. If you have a friend or family member that you think is self-injuring or has come to you for support, don't panic. Let her know that you care about her, and are concerned or worried about this behavior. Be prepared to listen, but set limits on what you are willing to tolerate, or keep confidential. Talk with your school counselor about the situation, both for your friend's sake and for your own. Most important, don't take it personally if your friend doesn't stop, or gets angry with you. This is one of those times when being a good friend may not always be doing what your friend wants, but what she needs.

GLOBAL NUTRITION

Nutrition is not merely a matter of personal hygiene and food choices, but of global resources and distribution. Most of us will never be truly hungry. We throw away food and each day we feed our pets enough food to meet the nutritional needs of hundreds and thousands of people. At least 10,000 people die each day of starvation. Twelve thousand children in India alone go blind each year from lack of iodine. Two-thirds of the world is undernourished.

Many people throughout the world have been left hungry as the result of political exploitation and terrorism. Natural disasters, poor land resources, and overpopulation create large-scale hunger. Bangladesh, the poorest country in the world, has one-half the population of the United States living in a country the size of Wisconsin. A number equal to the population of New York City are homeless in that country. In South America, many people live in a poverty of contaminated water and no medical supplies. Thousands are still dying of cholera and other diseases that no longer threaten more privileged countries. In the U.S., we are a country of relative privilege although we too have a rising rate of homelessness and true pockets of poverty and malnutrition.

With television coverage, modern travel, and mutual interdependence, we have become a global village. Like never before, we are aware of these differences and deficits throughout the world. It can be uncomfortable and thought-provoking to compare our lives with the less privileged and malnourished lives of the majority of people on this planet. How does it feel to be so privileged? What have we done to deserve our privilege? What, if any, responsibilities does our privilege entail?

These are difficult moral, political, and personal questions. The distribution of wealth in any society is a basic political issue which becomes even more complex when considered within the context of the whole planet. We are increasingly interdependent. Trees cut down in the South American rain forest to feed a starving people exacerbates a global warming which threatens the entire planet. First-world businesses often depend on the low paid work force of underdeveloped nations to maintain their own standard of living. Small and aggressive countries control world resources of oil, and nuclear technology creates power on a global scale.

Quandary: *Moral Positions on World Hunger*

Consider the following positions on world hunger. What do you think is the appropriate moral position? What are the political and practical realities that come into play? How do you think we should deal with both the realities and ethics of this situation? What do you think that you personally should or can do?

1. All human beings have equal rights to the necessities of life.
One-third of the world is consuming two-thirds of the world's resources at the expense of the rest of the world. Children are starving or overfed based merely on where and when they were lucky enough to be born—none of us did anything to deserve either our privilege or poverty. Those of us who were fortunate enough to be born into privilege have a moral obligation to use our advantage and resources to benefit those who are starving and suffering.

2. Helping less fortunate nations will not solve the problem and may actually endanger the human species.
While it is unfortunate that many people are starving, the truth is that there simply is not enough food to go around. Survival of the fittest is the law of nature and by rescuing nations and people who are unfit, we are weakening and potentially destroying human life on this planet. We would be exceeding the "carrying capacity" of the earth and we will all sink. We have a moral obligation to future generations, to our species, to protect our resources and our prosperity by NOT helping weaker nations.

3. No principle of morality absolves one of behaving immorally simply to save one's life or nation.
Even if the human species perishes, it is immoral for one segment of the world to live in excess while another segment starves. Food is a basic right of all people and it must be shared equitably. Every human life is of equal value and deserves an equal share no matter what the consequences. Even survival is less important than human justice and mercy.

4. If we can prevent something bad without sacrificing anything of comparable moral significance, we ought to do it.
While we are not morally obligated to help those who are less fortunate than ourselves, it is the good and noble thing to do if we can do so without endangering ourselves. As a nation, we use more than our fair share of the world's resources and much more than we need for adequate survival. We are a society of excess and waste because we think that we can afford to be. We have a moral obligation to separate our "wants" from our "needs," trim back our excessive lifestyle, and share what we can comfortably do without.

5. Life is not and never will be equitable and we have the right to the advantages that our society has earned and developed.
Our system of government, natural resources, and individual efforts have created the wealth and privileges that we enjoy. We should not be punished for hard work, success, or even good luck by being obliged to share with individuals or nations that have failed. Whether it is inherent superiority or the luck of the draw, we are entitled to the privilege and relative wealth that we have built up.

6. We are an interdependent world. The problems and needs of developing nations will destroy us all if we do not work together to create a healthy planet.
World hunger, ecological crises, and poverty create a reservoir of violence and loss that is destroying our human and natural resources. It is in our own best interests to help those less fortunate than ourselves; there is no way that our wealth can protect us indefinitely. Working together, we can resolve our common problems of limited resources, pollution, and poverty. By pretending these are foreign, unrelated problems, we are burying our head in the sand.

Dealing with Stress

Stress is and always has been a basic element of being alive. It is a physical, mental, or emotional tension that creates the energy we need to deal with problems. An interesting study done by Seymour Levine and his colleagues at the Stanford University Medical School seems to show that a certain amount of stress in our lives prepares us to deal with the inevitable stress of adulthood. They compared groups of young rats. One group was subjected to stressful handling and manipulation and the other group was kept in a placid, unstressed environment. The stressed group grew faster, gained weight more rapidly, and developed a good coat of fur sooner. As adults, they responded to an emergency and learned problem-solving behavior more quickly and lived longer. The rats in the unstressed group were timid and often paralyzed with fear. At least in rats, a degree of adversity appears to be good training for strong psychological development.

In a stressful situation, our bodies respond immediately. The pituitary gland, located at the base of the brain, releases a hormone called ACTH or *adrenocorticotropic hormone*. This hormone triggers the adrenal glands above the kidneys to release several hormones including adrenaline. This action puts our body into a **FIGHT/FLIGHT** mode. We become instantly ready to fight whatever danger we are in or get the heck out of there—fast. When faced with a physical emergency, your heart will probably start beating rapidly, your breathing will change, your muscles tense, your stomach tighten, your eyes open widely, and you may break into a sweat.

This physical reaction evolved during a time in human history when our survival, as it would with your uninvited tiger, depended on quick physical action. Adrenaline causes your heartbeat to increase quickly, pumping blood to your system. Your breathing becomes rapid and shallow to supply your body with increased oxygen. Your liver automatically releases sugar to give you much more strength and speed than usual. There are many cases of individuals in an adrenaline state picking up cars or trees that have fallen on someone. Your pupils dilate, allowing you to see any approaching danger. All of your senses are heightened, creating a protective sense of alertness. The muscles in your thighs, hips, shoulders, jaw, face, and arms tense for movement. The blood flow is increased to your brain and major muscles so that you can think and act quickly. Your stomach shuts down—it is not needed—and may feel tight and upset. Blood flow is constricted to your hands and feet so that if they are injured in battle you won't bleed to death. Your body begins to perspire to cool you down in preparation for action.

All of this is extremely important for fighting saber-toothed tigers and other physical dangers. We are all here today because our cave ancestors developed this important capacity. Psychological stress, however, causes the same physical responses without the physical release in fight or flight. When our brain perceives danger, whether it is a tiger or an SAT test, it sends our body into this automatic response. Forced to sit for

---

Productive Stress

You can control and use the stress in your life through your mental attitude.

- *View problems as opportunities to learn and grow.*

- *Evaluate criticism objectively and learn what you can from it. Never let it define who you can be.*

- *Don't try to please everyone—you can't.*

- *Don't expect yourself to be perfect—you're not and you can always learn more from your mistakes than your successes.*

- *Give yourself a break. Know when you need to ease up and take some time to relax and reflect. Einstein came up with many of his best ideas while sailing.*

- *Identify the strengths and possibilities of even the worst situation.*

- *Remember a batting average of .500 is pretty darn good.*

three hours and concentrate on multiple-choice questions, our physical condition becomes counterproductive. It is something like pushing the accelerator of a car to the floor and holding down the brake at the same time. It is at these times that we need to control and rechannel our body's response to stress.

Chronic, undischarged stress wears down your immune system. Health experts suspect that chronic stress is directly or indirectly responsible for about 90 percent of all disease. The anxiety caused by stress is not inherently in a situation, but in our response or thoughts about a situation. If you did not know there was a crazed saber-toothed tiger creeping up behind you, you might feel completely relaxed and unstressed. Conversely, we have all experienced an irrational fear that put our body through all of the stress reactions when there was actually no danger at all.

One study suggests that the amount of control that we believe we have over the stresses in our life actually reduces the negative impact. Subjects were asked to complete a complicated questionnaire in a room right next to some noisy, irritating construction work. Half of the subjects were told that if the noise became too distracting they could ring a button and be moved to a quieter room; the other half were not given that option. Although none of the subjects actually used the button, the first group all reported less stress and completed the questionnaire in less time. In the workplace, research has shown that this sense of personal control can be a critical factor to good health. People with high-stress jobs that allow them little control or decision making are two to four times more likely to develop serious illnesses. Taking control over the stress level and relaxation in your life may be a lifesaving skill.

> *I made some studies and reality is the leading cause of stress among those in touch with it. I can take it in small doses, but as a lifestyle, I found it too confining.*
>
> *—Lily Tomlin*

Personality and Stress

Different personality types seem to increase or decrease the amount of dysfunctional stress that they carry around with them. High stress, Type A personalities tend to increase their stress level and put themselves at higher risk for such physical problems as high blood pressure, heart attacks, and ulcers. Check how often you tend to experience the following feelings or situations. How can you reduce the pressure that these actions may create?

Always	Sometimes	Never	
❐	❐	❐	1. Move, walk, and eat rapidly.
❐	❐	❐	2. Get very irritated and upset when I have to wait in traffic, at a restaurant, or when performing repetitive tasks.
❐	❐	❐	3. Feel anxious when I relax and do absolutely nothing for several hours.
❐	❐	❐	4. Feel competitive with most people that I work with.
❐	❐	❐	5. Keep trying to schedule things tighter and tighter so that I can get more done.

❐	❐	❐	6. Try to do two or more things at once (read while eating, etc.).
❐	❐	❐	7. Complete others' sentences or hurry them in conversation.
❐	❐	❐	8. Believe that my success is due to my ability to get things done faster.
❐	❐	❐	9 Habitually clench my jaw or grind my teeth.
❐	❐	❐	10. Have difficulty admitting any defect or emotional difficulty.
❐	❐	❐	11. Find that my day is so tightly scheduled that by the end of the day I am always behind.
❐	❐	❐	12. Complete work being performed by others because they are not doing it fast enough.
❐	❐	❐	13. Value myself and others more by accomplishments than personal traits.

Finding Time for Your Life

Everyone is busy these days. Dads are working later and moms have a career of their own. Some elementary school children need a day planner to organize their lessons and play dates, and many high school students have four or more hours of homework every night. The number one reason high school students give for drinking or partying on weekends is to release stress and take a break.

The way that you spend your time determines the quality of your life. Everything that you do should fit into one of three categories:

1. Things I enjoy and value.

2. Things I do to *get to* the things I enjoy and value.

3. Things I do to take care of myself and the relationships I care about.

The first category is easy. We all understand the time we put into the things we love. It can be a little more complicated when the things you enjoy and the things you value are in conflict. You may not enjoy a homework assignment, but you value being a good student and doing your best on your work. You may enjoy spending hours on a computer game, but you may not value that way to spend your time.

Some of the things that you value and enjoy require planning, working, and waiting. In the second category, we *delay gratification* and use our time to do things that will eventually help us accomplish an important goal. You save your money instead of spending it as soon as you get it, because you want to buy an expensive stereo setup or you value thriftiness. You may really want to run in a marathon, so you block out some of your personal time to do a daily workout. Children don't delay gratification very well. They have a hard time waiting, and may throw a fit if they can't have what they want right away. As a young adult, you have learned to be more patient, but there are times when it isn't easy. Many of the goals you care about take weeks, or even years, of self-discipline and patience. Sometimes you may work hard, restrain yourself, and still not get what you wanted. It is easy to get discouraged, and talk yourself out of all that waiting and planning. Some people think that the future is too unpredictable; you should just grab what you can. By choosing not to delay gratification, they may have given up many of the things they enjoy and value because they require too much waiting. You will have to decide what things you value enough to work and wait for.

The third category is maintenance time. This is time that you must spend to keep your body, your mind, and your relationships in strong, healthy condition. You obviously have to eat and sleep, but you can choose to put aside time to exercise or see the dentist or call a friend or do a favor for your grandmother. You may plan time to meditate or attend a religious service; time for your girlfriend or to walk your dog or to wash your car. This time is usually not terribly exciting, but it is essential to maintaining the quality of your life, and the things you care about.

Just about everything you do should fit into one of these categories in one way or another. If you find yourself spending a lot of time doing things you don't enjoy that do not contribute to your goals, your health, or your relationships, you should probably stop and question why you

Panic Attacks

Panic is a healthy part of the body's natural alarm system. In the face of danger, adrenaline is produced, and the body goes into a *fight-flight* mode that gives us the strength and speed that may be needed to avert danger. In our increasingly complex and occasionally overwhelming world, some individuals experience what is called a ***panic attack***—a sudden, physiological panic response, without any apparent danger or trigger. A panic attack begins suddenly, as an inexplicable feeling of terror accompanied by pounding heartbeat, trembling, sweating, chest pain, nausea, dizziness, shortness of breath, and obsessive thoughts of dying or going crazy. This attack reaches a peak within five to ten minutes, and subsides within an hour. Fear of recurring panic attacks can set up a cycle of anxiety that is very debilitating.

If you think you are having a panic attack, remind yourself that, no matter how uncomfortable and overwhelming the attack feels, *it will pass.* Just ride it out, and know that you will be fine when your body has worked through the physiological cycle. Try taking slow deep breaths from the diaphragm. If you are especially worried about this experience, or have more than one in a short period of time, check with your doctor or school counselor. About 35 percent of the general population have had a single panic attack at some point in their life, and only about half of those have a second or repeated attack. Look for ways that you can reduce the overall stress in your life; practice meditation or some form of regular relaxation; and keep your body healthy with a good diet, exercise, and enough sleep.[8]

are doing what you are doing. Since time is a limited resource, you may need to be sure that you are spending enough time on the things that are most important to you. If you have a part-time job that you hate, but you are saving up for a car, that fits. If the job is taking up so much time that your grades are falling, you may need to balance your need for a car and your desire to get into a good college. If you keep the job and decide to stay up until 2:00 A.M. each night to study, your need for sleep and your health will suffer.

Good time management is knowing what you really want and value, being realistic about how much time you have, and finding a balance between the two. In spite of advertising and fantasies to the contrary, *you cannot have it all and you cannot do it all.* Establish your priorities, get organized, and set realistic goals for yourself.

1. **Know what is important and set realistic goals to accomplish the things you value.** Write an action plan that lists all the steps that will help you meet your goal. Identify obstacles and look for solutions. Put a picture on your mirror and note on your locker to remind you of the end result. Visualize the fame, glory, and satisfaction you will have when you finally reach your goal!

2. **Get organized.** Establish a daily routine that includes the things you value and need to do to take care of yourself. Organize your room and your schoolwork so you don't waste a lot of time finding things or getting started. Identify the time when you work best, and schedule your most important tasks at that time. Build in slack time and flexibility. Keep a to-do list and enjoy checking things off, one by one.

3. **Do it now.** Avoid procrastination by breaking big tasks into smaller parts. Set a timeline and deadline for each part. Be realistic; then just get down to it. The first step is usually the hardest and once you get going, you are on the way. Think of a nice reward for yourself when you finish.

4. **Don't get overwhelmed by perfectionism.** Do your best in the time available. Learn from your mistakes and don't avoid life because you are afraid you might fail. If you do fail, you will have learned a lot from the effort—probably more than you would have learned if everything went perfectly.

5. **Slow down.** The pace of life has gotten so fast that many people develop stress-related illnesses or depression. Learn how to say NO— know your limits and don't take on too much work. Set aside time for yourself and time to play. Take up a hobby, go for a walk, get a massage. Concentrate on one thing at a time and don't let your mind dart around from one worry to the next. Life is a journey, not a destination.

Learning How to Relax

There are many ways that you can train yourself to relax and ease the physical stress on your body. By relaxing your body, your state of mind also relaxes. The easiest, most effective way to relax your body is through your breathing. Under stress, we tend to hold our breathe and take short shallow breaths. By consciously slowing your breathing and taking deep calming breaths, your whole body responds by becoming calm. Followers of yoga believe that your breath is your primary life force—it controls your energy and clears your mind. It is easy to focus on your breathing any time you want to relax—during a test, before a speech or stress-producing activity, while you are walking or to help you get to sleep. You should take at least forty deep breaths every day.

A deep, *cleansing breath* slowly fills your entire lungs and is held slightly when your lungs are full and again after you have completely breathed the air out. You should breathe in slowly through your nostrils, counting to yourself as the air fills your lungs. At first you may find that you have breathed in as much as possible to the count of four, but with practice, you will be able to breathe slowly in to the count of eight or ten. Concentrate on filling your lungs from the abdomen up to the top of your lungs. When your lungs are full, hold the breath for a count about half as long as your intake count. Then breathe out slowly and completely for the same count that it took you to fill your lungs. Again hold your breath out for half of the count. For example, breathe in for a count of six, hold for a count of three, breathe out for a count of six and hold for a count of three. Gradually you will be able to increase your holding time to match your inhalation/exhalation time. Your breathing will become slow and regular and you will notice your body and mind relaxing and becoming clearer.

Another way that you can use your breathing to relax is to combine your breathe with relaxing messages or *visualizations.* After you have done four or five slow, deep breaths, allow your breathing to return to normal. It will probably be slower than before. As you continue breathing, visualize the number eight in your mind as you breathe out. Breathe in again and as you breathe out, visualize the number seven. Continue this countdown to zero, focusing on the visual number and allowing yourself to relax more deeply as you get closer and closer to zero. Let yourself become completely relaxed as you breathe out and visualize zero. This is a simple form of meditation and it works because you are shutting out all of your distracting, worrisome thoughts as you use your brain to focus on your breathing and visualizations. This can be a very effective way of relaxing and getting to sleep after a stressful day or when you have a lot on your mind. Instead of numbers, you can also repeat a word or *mantra,* a soothing sound, to yourself on each exhalation. Some people say "relax" or "release" or hum a note quietly to themselves. Experiment around for the word or sound that is most soothing for you. The vibration of different sounds and pitches can be felt in different parts of your body.

Each of us must overcome trauma to achieve adulthood. Birth is trauma. So is toilet training, learning to crawl, walk, entering school, the first date and so on. The question is whether trauma can be turned into an opportunity or whether it will remain an obstacle. It should be viewed as something to build on.

—*Dr. Rudolph Ekstein*

For centuries, people around the world have used *meditation* to focus attention and to calm both the body and mind. Regular meditation generates a neurological "relaxation response" that has been shown to lower heart rate, blood pressure, and muscular tension. Recent studies at Harvard's Mind-Body Institute also found that regular meditation impacts the brain in the areas of attention and the autonomic nervous system.[9] Other studies have demonstrated that meditation may be even better than other relaxation techniques at lowering blood pressure or reducing physical and mental stress. Meditation has been used effectively to control the pain and anxiety related to serious physical ailments. In *mindfulness meditation,* you begin your focus on a particular point, such as your breath or a candle flame. Then you allow your thoughts, emotions, or sensations to filter through your mind. Observe and identify each thought as it passes through your mind and then let it go by saying a key word (*"release"* or *"thinking"* or *"poof"*—*whatever works for you*) or image (*watching it float off like a cloud or balloon.*) The idea is to remain somewhat detached and nonjudgmental, but to quietly observe your own mind. This exercise calms your mind, and awakens self-awareness and acceptance. The technique is simple, but it is not always easy to shut out the world and turn off your own mental chatter. In this fast-paced world where we are bombarded with so much information and stimulation, this may be a practice well worth developing, for both your health and state of mind. If you can't sit still, you might try mindfulness meditation while you run, do routine tasks, or are stuck waiting somewhere.

Another way to relax your body, developed by Dr. Edmund Jacobson, is called *progressive muscle relaxation.* Lie comfortably on your back and take three or four slow, cleansing breaths, dismissing any thoughts or distractions from your mind with each breath. Then slowly focus on different muscles in your body, starting with your feet. Isolate one set of muscles, for example the muscles in your left foot, and tense them as tightly as you can. Hold the tension for about thirty seconds, then completely release all tension in those muscles as you breathe out. Feel that completely relaxed state. If there is still some tension remaining, repeat the tension/release with the same set of muscles. Continue throughout your body, giving extra attention to the areas where you tend to carry most of your tension—usually back, shoulders, neck, and face. This exercise can be especially helpful if you have or make a tape instructing you to tense and release each muscle group. After you have become good at isolating and relaxing your muscles, you can do the relaxing without tensing the muscle first. You will also learn how to scan your body to recognize any tension in your muscles and only work on relaxing the muscles that need it. Progressive muscle relaxation has been shown to lower blood pressure by 8 to 10 percent and can be effective in alleviating backaches and headaches.

Yoga is an integrated system of exercise, breathing, relaxation, diet, and meditation that began in India thousands of years ago. Many Americans and people around the world have adopted some or all of the yoga practices to reduce stress, and to tone and strengthen their bodies. Yoga

---

Tears and Laughter

Research has shown that there are two important chemicals in emotionally shed **tears**—*leucine-enkephalin and prolactin. These chemicals may be natural endorphins or pain killers released by the brain to reduce stress. Resisting tears may actually be harmful to your health.*

Laughter *promotes blood circulation, stimulates digestion, lowers blood pressure, and prompts the release of pain-reducing endorphins. Some people believe that the chemicals released during laughter are important to healing both the body and mind.*

Our breath is the bridge from our body to our mind. . . . Breath is aligned to both body and mind, and it alone is the tool which can bring them both together, illuminating both, and bringing both peace and calm.
    —*Thich Nhat Hanh,*
The Miracle of Mindfulness

Are Herbs Drugs?

Herbal medicines such as ginseng, echinacea, arnica, and St. John's wort have gained popularity as natural remedies without the side effects and by-products of conventional, synthetic drugs. Many of these remedies and alternative medicines have been used effectively for centuries and the modern medical establishment is beginning to study and teach these alternative and holistic approaches.

While herbs have fewer side effects than most over-the-counter medications, they should be used properly and are not always safe for everyone. Echinacea helps mobilize your immune system at the first signs of a cold, but can actually deplete your immune system if it is taken on a regular basis. Ginkgo increases memory only if the cause of memory loss is decreased blood flow to the brain, only one of many reasons for poor memory. St. John's wort has been shown effective in mild cases of depression, but should never be mixed with prescribed antidepressants and doesn't work to make nondepressed individuals happier.

Herbs need to be stored in a cool, dark place in order to remain potent. Most herbs work gradually, building on your body's self-healing mechanisms. It may be tempting to take too much or abandon your efforts if you don't get instant results. Some herbs can interact with other medications in a bad way. Check with a holistic doctor or naturopath to make sure that you are taking the proper dosage and that the herb will not interfere with medications you are taking or any other preexisting conditions.

---

exercises, or *asanas*, are gentle stretching poses that loosen the joints and muscles, improve circulation, release tension, and increase flexibility. Deep breathing and other breathing techniques are an essential part of yoga movement, serving to center the mind and provide oxygen to the brain and muscles. Yoga also teaches relaxation and meditation techniques. There are many videotapes and books that teach yoga, but you may want to start with a guided class in order to understand how all of these teachings work together. Yoga is a slow, gentle form of exercise that should never be forced. The *asanas* allow your body to stretch and realign without injury or strain. You will be surprised at how much of a workout you will get with very little movement.

Aerobic exercise is also an excellent way to release physical tension from your body. Running, swimming, biking, fast walking, or aerobic exercise all help your body reestablish a healthy balance. If you can exercise until you increase your heart rate and get out of breath at least twenty minutes a day, you should be able to release most of the stresses in your life. Studies have shown that students who exercise regularly are less anxious, have fewer stress-related medical problems, and have better coping skills in stress-related situations.

What you eat also affects the way your body handles stress. Certain foods and drugs—sugar, caffeine, alcohol, nicotine, stimulants, and some food additives—actually produce physical stress in many people. Any foods that you are allergic to also create stress in your body. While vitamins and minerals do not actually reduce stress, certain ones may be worn down by stress and need to be replaced when you are under more than normal stresses. The B-complex vitamins (thiamin, riboflavin, niacin, pyridoxine, pantothinic acid, biotin) are heavily taxed during physical and psychological stress and can be replenished from molasses, whole grains, wheat germ, brewer's yeast, liver, leafy greens, and beans. Vitamin C can be replenished from citrus fruits, green peppers, papaya, and cantaloupe. Calcium and magnesium are easily depleted by stress and can be replaced by milk, cheese, liver, yogurt, greens, and soybeans. Extra potassium can be gotten from bananas as well as other fruits and vegetables. Zinc can be replaced with brewer's yeast, liver, seafood, soybeans, spinach, sunflower seeds, and mushrooms. A well-balanced diet and regular exercise will go a long way to keep your body functioning in good health even during periods of high stress.

Dear Quandary Master . . .

Here are some letters asking for advice and information about some health situations. Make your answers as realistic and helpful as possible. Be sure to include any relevant information or resources that might be helpful.

#1.

Dear Quandary Master,

I have been a vegetarian for almost a year now. I have no interest in eating meat of any kind (including fish or chicken), but I do include dairy products and eggs. I am healthy, but I have lost some weight and lately, I just feel tired all the time. My skin seems pale and I tire out real quickly when I exercise. I am worried that I'm not getting some vitamin or mineral that my body needs. What might be causing the problem? Should I take a vitamin supplement?

Signed, Vegetarian Victor

#2.

Dear Quandary Master,

My boyfriend and I have been dating for quite a while now and began having sex about a month ago. We use condoms and a spermicide, but we have talked about my going on the pill in order to be really safe—neither of us wants to deal with a pregnancy. The problem is, my doctor is the same doctor that I have been seeing since I was two years old. She's a great doctor, but she still thinks of me as a little kid. She is also good friends with my parents. She would be shocked if I asked about birth control. Would she tell my parents? There are no clinics around and I don't know how to find another good doctor that I can trust. How much is all this going to cost? I want to be responsible, but when you get right down to it, it isn't that easy.

Signed, Where do I turn?

#3.

Dear Quandary Master,

My psychology teacher told us about some study in which these little kids were asked to pick out other kids they would like as friends just from their picture. There were all kinds of racial groups and handicapped kids and a fat kid—they almost always picked the fat kid last. Well, that's the story of my life. I'm a nice guy, but I am definitely overweight. It seems like people don't give me a chance, especially girls. I have tried diets and weight-reducing drinks. My parents even sent me to a fat camp one summer. Nothing has worked. I try to exercise, but it is tiring and I'm no good at sports because I'm so slow. I know I eat too much, but I can't seem to stop—besides, there's not much else to do. I'm sick of the fat jokes and feeling lonely. What can I do?

Signed, Obese Otis

#4.

Dear Quandary Master,

I can't believe I am writing to you, but there is no one I dare talk to. I am so ashamed and disgusted with myself. A couple of years ago, I went through a tough time during my parents' divorce and I started eating a lot. I mean a lot. I ate so much that sometimes I would throw up because I was so full and uncomfortable. I know this sounds weird, but that actually made me feel better. My stomach stopped hurting and I had sort of punished myself for eating all that food. And I didn't gain weight. I have pretty much gotten over my parents' divorce, but to make a long, ugly story short, I still have these binges and I almost automatically throw up whenever I eat much. It has become like a habit and I can't stop. NO ONE knows I do this; I would just die if anyone found out. I have tried to stop and I am really worried about what I am doing to myself. What can I do? Please don't say counseling—I could never talk to someone face to face about this.

Signed, Disgusting Delores

#5.

Dear Quandary Master,

I am sixteen years old and my doctor just told me I have an ulcer. This is sick. I mean, this is supposed to be the wild and carefree time of my life, and I spend most of it trying to get my work done, or worrying about what I will never get finished. I am taking three AP courses with a zillion hours of homework so I can get into that college that is supposed to make all this work worth it. I play two sports—I am pretty good at soccer, and basketball is my love, but practice and games take up a lot of time. I am president of the International Club. We have two big programs a year that are a lot of work, but worth it, though I am a nut-case while it is all going on. I volunteer once a week at a Senior Center—that takes about three hours every Tuesday evening, but I really love my time there. I don't get started on my homework until about 9:00 that night, so that is always a late night. Not that Tuesday is my only late night; I rarely get to bed before 1:30 or 2:00. Did you notice I haven't mentioned friends or free time? I haven't seen either since school started. Something has got to go. I don't know what to give up or how to manage all these things. Help.

Signed, Maalox Melanie

Do-It-Yourself Quandary

Identify an important dilemma related to health and wellness in our culture today that was not discussed in this chapter.

- *What factors make this issue particularly complicated or difficult to resolve?*

- *What values or ethical considerations are involved?*

- *What solutions or choices are available?*

WEB SITES

Diet and Nutrition
www.noah.cuny.edu/nutrition/nutrition.html
www.mayo.ivi.com/common/htm/dietpage.htm
www.wellweb.com/nutri/usdaguid/contents.htm
www.ganesa.com/food/index.html
www.thp.org
www.vegweb.com
www.dietitian.com

Eating Disorders
www.anred.com
www.edap.org
www.nedic.on.ca/guide
www.edreferral.com
www.overeatersanonymous.org

Exercise
www.msnbc.com/news/EXERCISEfront.asp
www.fitnessonline.com
www.yogasite.com
www.workout.com
www.shapeup.org
www.caloriecontrol.org/exercalc.html
www.highschoolrunner.com
http://lifematters.com/taijin.html

Holistic Health
www.altmedicine.com
www.wellweb.com/altern/index.html
www.naturalhealth1.com
www.stud.lunit.no/studorg/ikstrh/ed/ed.html
www.webideas.com/biofeedback

Stress

http://content.health.msn.com/content/article/1758.healthink-785.html

www.mentalhealth.com/mag1/p51-str.html

www.teachhealth.com

www.imt.net~randolfi/StressLinks.html

www.futurehealth.org/stresstips.htm

www.meditationcenter.com

www.zenmind.com/meditation.html

Wellness and General Health

http://lifematters.com/index.html

www.abouthealth.com/teens

www.zaphealth.com

www.redcross.org

www.wellweb.com

www.noah.cuny.edu

www.cdc.gov

www.healthfinder.gov

www.medicinet.com

www.nethealth.com/intro.html

www.cmhc.com/selfhelp.htm

www.intelihealth.com

www.adolescenthealth.org/html/alphabetical.html

www.ama-assn.org/adolhlth

www.hify.com/index.html

www.4woman.org/faq/adoles.htm
   (girls)

www.wellnessletter.com

www.bu.edu/wellness

www.healthcentral.com/peoplespharmacy/peoplespharmacy.cfm

---

[1]Perls, Thomas. *Living to 100.* Basic Books, 1999.

[2]Prepared by the Health Law Section of the Oregon State Bar, 1991.

[3]*The Wellness Encyclopedia* from the editors of the University of California, Berkeley Wellness Letter. Boston: Houghton Mifflin Company, 1991.

[4]1. Cheetos, 2. Jell-O, 3. Captain Crunch, 4. dog food, 5. KoolAid, 6. chicken pot pie, 7. CoolWhip, 8. frozen banana cream pie!

[5]Moore Lappe, Frances. *Diet for a Small Planet, Revised Edition.* New York: Ballantine Books, 1975.

[6]*The Temptations of Taking Steroids.* Beth Mullally, Ottaway News Service, 1992.

[7]"Self-Injury: You are not the only one . . ." http://www.palace.netllama/psych/intro.html.

[8]Harvard Women's Health Watch, Volume VII, Number 12, August 2000. Panic: Worry in the Extreme.

[9]Harvard Women's Health Watch, Volume VIII, Number 5, January 2001. Is Mediation Good Medicine?

Chapter 3

Chemicals and Your Mind

HOW YOUR BRAIN WORKS

The human brain is a fascinating, complex organ that operates your body, interprets your senses, processes your feelings, stores your memories, learns new information, formulates ideas, processes language, dreams, imagines, creates, and interprets both pleasure and pain. It even has a censoring system that can repress certain thoughts, memories, or feelings out of your conscious awareness. It is the one organ in your body that cannot be altered or transplanted without significantly changing who you are. Before we look at how chemicals interact with your brain, it is important to understand how the brain works and what it is capable of doing.

Your brain is about the size of a grapefruit and weights 2.5 to 3 pounds when fully mature. If you place your two fists together at the heel of your hand, they approximate both the size and structure of your brain. Each fist represents one hemisphere and the brain stem and limbic system would fit between your two fists and extend down your wrists. Add a pair of thick gloves for the cortex and you can visualize how your brain is set up.[1]

When a human baby is born, his brain is only 25 percent of its adult size—that is what makes us so helpless. When human beings first began to stand erect, the pelvic structure of the female became smaller to support this new distribution of weight. Babies needed to be delivered sooner and smaller to pass through the birth canal. By age one, a baby's head circumference has increased by four inches. By age five, the child's brain will have reached 90 percent of its adult size and most skulls are fully grown by age ten. The brain itself has a second growth spurt around ages fourteen to sixteen to reach its full cognitive functioning abilities.

As we grow, the billions of connections in our brain are actually pruned or streamlined to become more efficient. Babies lose the ability to make certain sounds which are not included in the language they are being taught. When we learn a second language, our first language may be shifted to another part of the brain or we may store the new language in the right hemisphere. We learn to discriminate between different stimuli and ignore ones that are not useful to our survival or experience. Experience and exposure to different stimuli actually exercise and enlarge the brain. Children who are raised in dull, nonstimulating environments actually stop growing and may be permanently retarded in their mental development. Roseweig and Diamond[2] did a study of rats placed in *enriched* (lots of toys and materials to explore), *standard* (normal rat stuff), or *impoverished* (nothing to do or play with) environments. The enriched environment increased the actual brain weight of the rats by 10 percent. Other studies have shown that the ions in the air on mountaintops, around waterfalls, and near the ocean create distinct changes in brain chemistry.

Studies have also shown some interesting differences between different groups of people. Left-handers may have the same brain setup as right-handers, but most have either the functions of the hemispheres reversed or *non-lateralized*. Speech, for instance, normally processed in the left hemisphere, may be processed in both hemispheres. Left-handers are more likely to have language or spatial problems, but they also tend to recover from brain injury or surgery more quickly because their brain is more flexible.

Males and females also have some distinct brain differences. On the average, the male brain is about 10 percent heavier. Girls tend to develop verbal skills more quickly than boys, and boys develop spatial acuity at a younger age. Physically, male and female brains look different. Females have a larger corpus collosum connecting the two hemispheres. This difference is observable as early as twenty-six weeks in utero. While it is difficult to know exactly what the difference in this structure means, right-handed males do tend to separate the functions of the left and right hemispheres more than females or left-handed individuals. This may make them more efficient at tasks requiring *specificity* and less efficient at tasks requiring coordination of the two hemispheres. Like lefties, females tend to recover from strokes or specific brain injuries more quickly.

Brain Chemistry

The brain is an incredibly complex and efficient organism. It contains over 100,000,000,000 neurons with at least 100,000,000,000,000 potential points of communication. The basic structure of this communication system is the neuron. Unlike other cells of the body, neurons do not reproduce after birth—we are born with all the brain cells that we will ever have. Before birth, these nerve cells reproduce at the amazing rate of 250,000 per minute.

Each neuron contains an elaborate system of *dendrites* which receive messages from other neurons in the form of a chemical *neurotransmitter.* These dendrites are small hair-like tentacles extending from the cell body that wave around looking for neural messages which apply to their particular function. Each of these minute dendrites contains a set of *receptor sites* which magnetically attract certain neurotransmitters. Each receptor site has a unique shape which will only accept certain messages—much as a keyhole will only work with specifically shaped keys.

When a chemical message fits, it is processed through the cell body. The cell body contains a *nucleus* which contains the DNA of the cell and controls the balance and reproduction of the individual neurons and *mitochondrion,* which are simple cells that metabolize glucose and other food substances into biological energy.

The message is then carried through a long fiber called the *axon.* The axon can be anywhere from a fraction of an inch to three feet in length. While neurons do not reproduce, life experience and use may increase the number and connections of axons attached to each neuron.

The entire nerve cell is covered by the *cell membrane,* a wall that is composed of fat molecules and complex protein molecules. These molecules are arranged in patterns according to the functions of each specific cell type. Chemical messages, food, and energy must pass through the cell membrane in order to keep the cell alive and functioning properly.

The end of the axon is called the *synaptic button.* This slightly enlarged portion of the axon contains more mitochondrion and *vesicles,* which are spheres that contain chemical neurotransmitters that carry the neural message across the space between neurons called the *synapse.* The neurotransmitters then attach to the matching receptor sites on the next neuron and the message continues.

Each chemical excites, relaxes, or changes the neuron as it passes through, according to the programmed function of that neuron and the specific chemical message being relayed. All this takes place in a fraction of a second until the desired muscles and parts of the brain have been notified. There are probably hundreds of different chemicals that serve as neurotransmitters.

To process these neurotransmitters and their information accurately, each neuron must perform the following functions in less than a thousandth of a second:

1. The **neurotransmitter** must find the proper fit in the **receptor site** of the dendrite.

2. The **channels** into the cell must open.

3. The **neurotransmitters** are positively charged and rush down the **axon.**

4. The **neurotransmitters** attach to the **vesicles.**

5. The **vesicles** carry the **neurotransmitters** across the **synapse** to the **dendrite** of the next **neuron.**

6. **Enzymes** on the dendrite will clear the **vesicles** and send them back to their original cell.

7. After the **neurotransmitter** is taken in and the **vesicle** sent back, the **channels** close.

8. The **neuron** must make new **neurotransmitters** to replace what has been lost in the process.

Since our brain's communication system is based on a relay of chemical information, adding foreign chemicals to our body can affect this communication. Many drugs, both legal and illegal, as well as the chemicals in the food we eat, can mimic our natural neurotransmitters and change the way our brain works. As you study the drugs in the rest of this chapter, carefully identify how each drug affects this communication system of the brain in order to produce the subjective response that we feel.

The Two Hemispheres of Your Brain

The Theory of Relativity occurred to me by intuition, and music was the driving force behind that intuition. My discovery was the result of musical perception.
—Albert Einstein

I have no special gift, I am only passionately curious," Albert Einstein (1879–1955) said.

The brain is divided into two equal hemispheres that are connected through a series of nerve fibers called the *corpus callosum.* While structurally similar, each hemisphere has a distinct function. In general, the left hemisphere controls the right side of your body and the right hemisphere controls the left side of your body. Each hemisphere also has some specific responsibilities. The left hemisphere organizes, analyzes, and rationalizes information sequentially. It controls your speech, your sense of time, and your ability to recall and use language. The left hemisphere processes information efficiently in a linear, logical way. The right hemisphere, on the other hand, is very spatial and holistic. It processes whole images and allows us to conceptualize the big picture. The right hemisphere is very visual, responding to pictures, colors, and shapes. It also processes emotions, music, touch, and imagination. The right hemisphere reasons more by intuition than logic. Dreams are usually created by our more intuitive right hemisphere; therefore, it is sometimes difficult to describe them in words or follow their sequential logic. Some mind-altering drugs depress the left hemisphere and stimulate the right hemisphere, lifting our holistic thinking out of its logical context. This hemispheric switch produces the hallucinations, flashes of nonverbal insight, and disconnected spatial images.

Albert Einstein's brain wasn't any bigger than yours, but a study at McMaster University in Canada in 1999 found that there were two significant differences. The inferior parietal lobe, located in the center of the brain, was found to be 15 percent wider than normal. This part of the brain has been linked with higher-level thinking including mathematics, music, and processing visual images. There is some debate about whether Einstein's parietal lobe was always larger or if it had become larger through extensive use. The second difference, however, appears to have always been part of Einstein's brain structure. The sylvan groove that normally separates the lobe into two sections did not extend all the way to the back in Einstein's case. Dr. Sandra Witelson, the McMaster neuroscientist who led the study, hypothesized that this partially missing groove may have allowed more connections to be established in this part of the brain, allowing Einstein to think in such complex and innovative ways.[3]

In summary, the right hemisphere sees the forest and the left hemisphere sees the trees. The right hemisphere processes the color, shading, and beauty of the image, while the left hemisphere describes the image and creates a more scientific assessment. Speech is learned and stored in the left hemisphere; the right hemisphere can then put those words to music and allow us to sing. Your left hemisphere can write and spell a word, but your right hemisphere may notice that it doesn't "look right." Conceptual mathematics is developed in the right hemisphere and translated into numbers and theorems by the left hemisphere. "Aha" moments occur when your left hemisphere is finally able to articulate or organize a concept from your right hemisphere. The corpus callosum coordinates these two hemispheres and allows them to work together. A writer can use his left hemisphere to describe and articulate the images, feelings, and intuitions of his right hemisphere. An engineer can use her right hemisphere to conceptualize the size and shape of a structure to be analyzed and designed by her left hemisphere.

The brain is a muscle, however, and with exercise, one side of the brain usually becomes larger or dominant. A talent, interest, or activity in one area can lead us to specialize and develop that part of the brain. Reading is processed through the left hemisphere and, in literary cultures, tends to build up the left hemisphere and make it dominant. Artists and musicians draw on the right hemisphere more regularly and may develop their holistic skills. You can probably think of individuals whom you would describe as very left brained or very right brained. When one hemisphere markedly dominates the other, this dominance is called *hemisphericity.* Research suggests that if your brain gets too far out of balance, you are not able to think as productively, and the imbalance can actually lead to physical problems, such as headaches, fatigue, and insomnia. If you are working your left hemisphere a great deal in school all day, take some time for physical activity, music, or a hobby that re-

Are Females More Intuitive?

Female intuition has long been viewed with both skepticism and awe. Women are more likely to act on a hunch or "just have a feeling" about a person or event (right hemisphere thinking). Men are more likely to require proof and apply logic to a solution (left hemisphere thinking). On the other hand, boys tend to be better at visuospatial tasks (right hemisphere) while girls tend to be better at verbal and associative tasks (left hemisphere). Evolution, expectations, and experience clearly shape many of these differences.

The most significant biological difference between the male and female brain appears to be the thickness of the corpus callosum. The female corpus callosum is thicker, allowing more neural connections between the right and left hemispheres. These neural connections may allow females to be better at integrating the two hemispheres and may make it more difficult to isolate one from the other. With fewer neural connections between the hemispheres, males may filter out cross-hemispheric distractions and focus more exclusively on either spatial or linear thought. Intuition is not usually logical. Males may overrule their intuition in the mental shift from the right hemisphere to the more logical left hemisphere. By integrating the left and right hemisphere, females may be more likely to let their incongruent logic and intuition coexist.

Building a Brain

As a group, you are to create a large-scale model of how information is communicated within the brain using members of your group as different parts of the brain and communication system. You should include *neurotransmitters, dendrites, cell body, a nucleus, mitochondrians, axon, synapse button, vesicles, synapse* and *receptor sites*. Your model should demonstrate how the system is set up and how chemical messages are relayed. Be creative. Remember to work together as a group and listen to everyone's ideas before proceeding. Everyone and everything must be labeled and a part of the finished model. You have the following materials and thirty minutes to complete your model. (Use only whatever materials you need.)

Materials:
string/yarn	scissors	marking pens
name tags	paper cups	food coloring
colored paper	Hula Hoops	marshmallows
(other odds and ends as available)		

Demonstrate how a specific message would pass through your model.

As you learn about how different drugs work within your brain, go back to your model and demonstrate what happens at the various sites. For example, you might assign someone to be cocaine and have her travel through the brain telling each site or chemical how she affects them. Or you might just want to send her through and have each site demonstrate what would happen to him when he meets cocaine.

quires your hands or mind in a more right-brained way. Look up from your work on the computer to focus your eyes on something in the distance. Brush your teeth or tie your shoes with your nondominant hand. This change will wake up your right hemisphere and create new connections between the hemispheres. Get out of your thinking head when you take a walk or drive the car, and let your right hemisphere take in the scenery. Cook, knit, dance, paint, or go to a movie. If you find your right hemisphere taking over with daydreams, panicky feelings, or problems paying attention, do a crossword puzzle, play chess, or organize your closet to refocus your left hemisphere. Reading a book, cleaning your room, or writing in a journal will give your left hemisphere a workout, and put your brain in better balance.

Memory and Learning

Memory is a complicated brain process that involves both storage and retrieval. First, you must collect and store the information to be remembered and second, your brain must be able to find and retrieve that information. Individual brains may have different strengths and weaknesses in this area.

Some people record information better if it is seen and have difficulty processing things they have only heard (*visual learners*). This can be a problem taking notes in lectures without any written or visual component. Foreign languages may be particularly difficult. Others may be able to process things they have heard very well, yet have difficulty with visual or spatial memory (*auditory learners*). Spelling, geometry, or reading may pose problems for these people. Other people have problems with focus or attention—in order for your brain to process information, you must first focus on the material and have it register in your brain. You may have noticed if you are tired or distracted, you can read a whole page of an assignment and have no idea what you have just read. Individuals with attention deficit disorder often have a difficult time focusing on the information to be remembered and filtering out distractions.

Once the brain focuses and stores information, it must also be able to find that information when it is needed. Some people seem to have a very efficient retrieval system while others know that the information or word is in their brain somewhere, but have difficulty finding it. An example of this annoying phenomenon occurs when a word or name is on the "tip of your tongue," but you can't remember it.

Stress or anxiety can also exacerbate memory problems. Taking a test or giving a speech may raise your anxiety level to the point that you cannot remember what you knew perfectly well both before and after. Test anxiety can make it very difficult for a student to demonstrate what he or she knows and understands. When you freeze during a test or performance, your stress level rises, making it even more difficult to remember anything.

Here are some tools that may improve your memory.

- **Make friends with your brain.** Figure out how you learn and remember things best, and be sure to use your strengths in the classroom and when you study. If you are a visual learner, write things down; use colored pens and highlighters to make them stand out in your mind. Ask your teacher to provide visual notes or models to help you learn the material. If you are an auditory learner, read aloud to yourself when you study and ask your teacher to explain assignments and information verbally. Books-on-Tape may help you process your reading assignments.

- **Use associations and outlandish examples to help remember lists and concepts.** In order to learn and remember a new idea, your brain must associate it with something you already know. Acronyms can help. HOMES gives you a mental association list to remember the Great Lakes—**H**uron, **O**ntario, **M**ichigan, **E**rie, and **S**uperior. Mental pictures can direct your brain where to look—picture a group of HOMES floating around on a great lake in order to remember the acronym you have selected. When someone asks you the names of the Great Lakes, the mental picture of the floating homes reminds you of the acronym, and you rattle them off brilliantly. The more absurd the mental picture or association, the easier your brain will have remembering it.

- **Use as many modalities as possible when you study or learn material.** In addition to our visual and auditory modalities, we also learn things by touching, moving, or even by smell or taste. Smell is one of our strongest memory triggers. Certain smells from your childhood can bring back very vivid memories and feelings. Music also has a very strong memory bank. Think of all the songs that you can remember word for word. When you are studying, use visual clues, write out important material, say things out loud, and put actions or images to what you are trying to remember. Think of ways to help your stronger modalities compensate for weaker ones.

- **Relax, focus, and think positively.** You can reduce the stress that may interfere with your memory by physically relaxing. Get a good night's sleep before an important test or assignment. Eat a good meal, avoiding sugar and caffeine. These stimulants may make you feel more alert without providing the real fuel your brain needs to perform. Remember that your brain is a physical organ and will perform at its best when it is rested and well fed. A short period of aerobic exercise before a test or performance will literally clear your brain of the chemical sludge of worry and anxiety so that you can think more clearly. Deep, focused breathing will supply important oxygen to your brain to help you calm down, stay focused, and think efficiently. If you start to panic, close your eyes, take three slow, deep breaths, and begin again. Try to go into the test with positive expectations and confidence. If you are convinced you are going to fail, your anxiety will interfere with your performance and become a self-fulfilling prophecy. Take care of yourself and organize your studies so that you can approach each task with a clear and confident brain.

Learning Styles and Learning Disabilities

With all the possible connections in the human brain, no two brains are wired exactly the same. Genetic factors influence brain structure in the same way they may determine height or eye color. Birth trauma, injuries, or physical conditions may impact the structure and functioning of the brain. Environmental factors, such as diet, pollution, drug use, or even sunlight, can physically change the brain. The brain is a muscle and can also be affected by use and training. For a variety of reasons, each brain will function a little differently. Individual brains usually process information in a very specific and characteristic way. Some brains have a photographic memory while others may have an incredible gift for recognizing and ordering sounds. Some brains organize information in a linear, orderly fashion while others are more scattered and creative. Some brains have difficulty putting ideas into words, but can express complicated thoughts through art or mathematical concepts or car mechanics. Some brains function best in uninterrupted silence while others thrive in activity and chaos. Some brains can translate thoughts into brilliant, lyrical writing while others cannot seem to master the basic skills of handwriting.

None of these styles or strengths is directly related to intelligence. Certain individuals with a very low IQ may have a photographic memory or an amazing talent in music or art. Other individuals who are labeled with a genius IQ may have dramatic weaknesses or disabilities in one or more area of brain processing. A learning disability is a problem in the way your brain processes information, not a factor of intelligence. However, when a normally intelligent individual can't process information in a situation where everyone else seems to be learning effortlessly, it is easy to feel stupid. If everyone could be taught in the way he or she processes information best, we could all work around our weaknesses and capitalize on our strengths. And, whenever possible, we do. Both consciously and unconsciously, you have learned the methods and circumstances by which you learn best. A weakness in one area of processing is like having a column standing in the middle of a basketball court—as long as you know it is there, you can work around it. If you cannot see or understand it, you will keep running into it.

Schools tend to teach best to auditory, linear learners with good visual processing skills. Lectures and the scientific method are most easily processed by individuals who remember what they hear and whose brain structure has an orderly, traditional retrieval system. Reading and writing require strong visual processing skills and hand-eye coordination. Classroom learning requires physical restraint and freedom from distractibility. Any student who has a processing weakness in one or more of these areas may experience difficulty learning in school. This same individual might learn quite efficiently in a different setting. What we call a "learning disability" simply describes a learning style that does not process information in the ways most commonly required in school. Some learning disabled (LD) students will never completely master skills in a specific area while others can learn these skills in a nontraditional way or with additional time and study.

Schools may provide programs and services to help LD students compensate for processing problems, but you will also have to be your own advocate and researcher. Trust your instincts and pay attention to the methods and skills that are most effective and efficient for you. Ask your teachers to provide information in different ways or to measure you in ways that you can demonstrate how much you actually know. You may need specific testing results and a professional learning specialist to back you up and help you articulate what you need. Coaching and specialized study techniques can make it easier.

Most important, don't get discouraged. For every processing weakness, there is invariably an area of unusual strength. In the same way a blind person develops extremely acute hearing and sense of touch, a difficulty in one area of the brain may actually develop or result from a valuable strength in another area. Albert Einstein did not talk until he was four or read until he was nine. He had great difficulty learning math in the traditional schools and was thought to be backward and limited by his early teachers. Leonardo da Vinci was a brilliant artist, inventor, and scholar, yet his notes were unreadable until it was discovered that they were written backward in mirror image, a common symptom of dyslexia. Thomas Edison failed in school but still managed to invent the light bulb; and Benjamin Franklin used his distractibility and lack of a fixed focus to come up with more than 500 inventions, numerous books, and a cascade of projects that contributed in many ways to the foundation of our democratic system.

Actress and singer Cher will not audition for a part without having the script ahead of time—she is dyslexic and reads slowly and with some difficulty. Luckily, her brain has compensated; after she has read a script once, she practically knows it by heart.

School was difficult. I never read when I was in school—I read my first book when I was eighteen or nineteen. I learned almost everything by listening. I just couldn't keep up. You can be intelligent, but if you don't have a way of letting people know, you seem stupid. My grades were sporadic. I got D's and F's in some classes and A's and B's in others. My mother just couldn't understand why I could do so well in one class one semester and fail the next. I couldn't understand it either. Eventually I left school—the second week of eleventh grade. I was sitting there one day and I just got up and said, "I'm not coming back."

Tom Cruise, Whoopi Goldberg, Winston Churchill, Woodrow Wilson, Nelson Rockefeller, Hans Christian Anderson, Auguste Rodin, and General George Patton are just a few of the many famous and talented individuals who have worked with and around their learning disability to contribute to society.

Managing A.D.D.

Attention deficit disorder is a chemical brain disorder that affects 3–5 percent of the students in the U.S. Individuals with A.D.D. have difficulty getting organized and may feel lost in a sea of misplaced items, missed appointments, unfinished projects, and boundless plans and schemes. Quickly bored, A.D.D. individuals can be energetic and creative, but easily frustrated and impatient with details. Often hampered by their distractibility and impulsivity, many struggle with an underlying sense of underachievement, misunderstanding, and anxiety. These same individuals can be remarkably creative and productive, much loved for their passionate energy and resilient, in spite of it all. Like a wild pony or a high-powered Porsche, this frisky version of a brain takes some skill and experience to control.

- Make sure you get plenty of sleep on a regular basis—eight to nine hours each night.

- Break tasks down into manageable parts and deal with just one at a time. Don't do all the fun things first.

- *Do it now.* Delaying a task or putting it in a pile is a sure way to forget it. Then you will worry and feel guilty trying to remember what it was.

- Clean up and put things away as you go along and thus avoid the overwhelming chaos and mess that can accumulate.

- Invest in Post-its. Keep them handy and post them around to remind you of things you need to do—or as notes of encouragement.

- Watch your diet—avoid foods that drain your focusing power such as sugar, alcohol, and junk food.

- Exercise regularly to reduce stress and improve your ability to concentrate.

- When you get in a bind, try not to make excuses, lie, or get angry—these defenses just make things worse.

- Use lists and planners; keep your workplace simple and uncluttered.

- Try earplugs or Mozart in the background to mask out distracting noises while you study.

- Establish a routine and an assigned, convenient place for the things you are always losing.

A.D.D. may help explain why you have difficulty with certain types of tasks, but it is not an excuse, nor will everything improve just because you now understand the problem. Persevere, do your best, and admit when you make a mistake. Try not to get defensive or discouraged when you slip up. You can apologize for the *results* of your behavior even if your *intent* was innocent. An apology will clear the air and help you learn from your mistakes. Find a friend, counselor, teacher, or parent with whom you can laugh and commiserate without censure, advice, or tedious explanations. Monitor your own tasks whenever possible so that you can schedule them to best fit your habits, moods, and attention level. Celebrate your successes, large and small.

Quandary: *Is There More to Our Mind Than a Brain?*[4]

As we explore and locate different human responses within the neural structure of the brain, we are faced with the very human question, "Is that all there is?" Are our personality, emotions, thoughts, individuality, and spirit just the sum total of a bunch of neurons firing through nerve endings in the brain? Do we have a soul or central consciousness that is somehow distinct and individual, a subjective state of being? Are we more than the sum total of our brain's biology?

The **Materialists** insist that the idea of a separate, subjective mind is an illusion. In his book *Consciousness Explained*, philosopher/scientist Daniel Dennett states, "The mind is somehow nothing but a physical phenomenon. In short, the mind is the brain." Marvin Minsky at MIT goes further to say, "The brain is just hundreds of different machines—connected to each other by bundles of nerve fibers, but not everything is connected to everything else. There isn't any you."

The **Mysterians** agree that the mind is a function of the brain, but insist that there are processes at work that we cannot understand or identify. Philosopher Jerry Fodor invokes the analogy of the caterpillar and the butterfly—we know that one evolves from the other, but we can't begin to imagine how it happens. In his book, *Minds, Brains and Science*, John Searle criticizes the Materialist point of view as attempting to explain away what we do not understand. "I think it is madness to suppose that everything is understandable by us."

Consider what you know about the brain. Think about cases of brain damage or disease that drastically change the personality or awareness of a person. Where is the soul or self of someone who shows no brain activity, but survives in a coma or life-support system? What happens when someone has amnesia and forgets who he is? Who is the self that operates under the influence of external chemicals put into the brain? And where is your unaltered self at that time? Are there parts of your experience, thought processes, emotions, or identity that cannot be explained or altered by the brain?

USES OF DRUGS

Historical and Medical Uses

Fascination and involvement with drugs and their mind-altering capabilities have been a part of the human experience since the beginning of recorded time. Homer described an opium plant brewed as tea and served to welcome travelers. Ancient Aztec stone carvings, dating back 3,500 years, show the ritual eating of hallucinogenic mushrooms. The use of marijuana for medicinal and religious purposes is documented in China, India, and Africa as early as 2,500 B.C. Coca leaves have been chewed by the Indians of South America for increased energy and adjustment to high altitudes. Whiskey, rum, and tobacco were the major cash crops that established the economic health of the newly formed United States. Even animals show an interest in mind-altering drugs—cats to catnip, cows to locoweed—and once addicted, experimental rats will choose their addiction over all other life-preserving drives until they drop dead.

Historically, the European countries tended toward alcohol as the drug of choice while Asia, Africa, and India preferred hashish and opium. In the Western world, tobacco and hallucinogens, such as peyote and mescaline, were the commonly used drugs in Native American rituals and religion. By the early fifteen century, international travel and trade began to blur these boundaries. Columbus brought the new drug, tobacco, to the Old World and, within fifty years, it was being grown and used all over the world. Nicotine's highly addictive nature and the introduction of smoking, a new way to ingest drugs, created instant markets for tobacco. By 1617, it was the primary cash export of the new colonies. In exchange, the European traders introduced alcohol to the Native Americans. Very different from the introspective, ceremonial drugs the Indians were used to, alcohol quickly addicted and devastated entire nations of Native Americans, facilitating their near annihilation at the hands of the hard-drinking Europeans.

Alcohol was a common factor in early American life. It was used medicinally for many ailments, was an essential part of most religious events, and was offered as refreshment for tired shoppers, workers, and men awaiting a haircut. In spite of a growing problem of drunkenness and alcoholism, it wasn't until the 1800s that alcohol acquired a bad name. Many well-known persons, Abe Lincoln, Horace Greeley, Walt Whitman, Susan B. Anthony, Thoreau, Emerson, and Longfellow among them, and a tough group of militant women decried the drunken state of affairs. They worked to ban alcohol as a means to reform and civilize a harsh, aggressive new nation. After almost one hundred years of crusading, Prohibition was enacted as the 18th Amendment and put into practice through the Volsted Act of 1919. It was a dismal failure. Difficult and unpopular to enforce, the prohibition of alcohol created a large-scale disregard for the law and introduced the beginnings of organized crime in the United States. Coming at the end of World War I, Prohibition also created an awkward social position for the United States as a newly recognized world power. Fourteen years after the passage, Congress ratified the 21st Amendment, revoking the 18th Amendment.

Marijuana, as a species of the hemp plant, was also brought to the colonies and became second only to tobacco as a primary cash crop. Hemp was used in rope and sails for its strong fiber. It was also used for a wide range of medicinal purposes (childbirth, gout, rheumatism, cholera, hysteria, migraines), and was marketed by all the leading pharmaceutical companies as an over-the-counter drug. Marijuana cigarettes were brought across the Mexican border by migrant workers, but since marijuana grew wild all over the southwest, they were considered a low-grade, cheap cigarette. There appeared to be little interest in marijuana as a recreational, mind-altering drug. These uses were well known in other parts of the world. There are references to marijuana in the *Iliad, Arabian Nights,* and the Old Testament. It was frequently used in Africa for both medicinal and ceremonial purposes. In India, bhang, ganja, and charas (forms of marijuana) were used in cooking and teas.

During Prohibition, there was a new interest in the still legal marijuana. It became popular in jazz circles in New Orleans and soon attracted adverse publicity in the press. Sensationalist, mostly unfounded, reports of violent crime and depravity swept the country. When Prohibition ended, the newly formed Federal Narcotics Bureau, under the direction of Harry Anslinger, began a nationwide campaign against marijuana. Within five years, forty-six of the forty-eight states had laws against marijuana.

At the same time, opium had become a major source of trade from Great Britain to China, the largest export market in the world. Several New England family fortunes, including the Delanos, were also made transporting opium from Turkey to China. China attempted to stop this trade which was draining its economy and was soundly defeated by England in the Opium Wars of 1839. Drugs were an ideal market because once an addiction was established, the market renewed and perpetuated itself. Drugs were cheap to produce and their price could be set at whatever the market would bear.

Opium was probably brought to the United States as early as the pilgrims in the form of laudanum, a popular medication during that time. The tonics and elixirs of the pioneer days were mostly forms of opium. It was not until the mid-nineteenth century that it became widely used for recreational purposes. The Chinese railroad workers brought the tradition of smoking opium for pleasure to the U.S. and opium dens began to surface in the larger cities. In 1806, morphine became recognized as an extremely effective pain killer. When the syringe was invented in 1853, it allowed morphine to be injected. This was a much more effective and addicting way of ingesting the drug. The Civil War was the first widespread use of morphine and over 200,000 soldiers became addicted. This was the first time that doctors recognized addiction as a medical problem and it was called the "soldier's disease."

By 1890, of a population of 90,000,000 it is estimated that some 1,500,000 were addicted to some form of opium. An international Hague Confer-

American Teen Drug Use
Released 12/18/98[5]

After a five-year study of drug use trends in a survey of over 50,000 eighth, tenth, and twelfth grade students, the U.S. Department of Health and Human Services released the following statistics:

- All three grades have shown significant decline in the numbers of students reporting use of any illicit drug during the last year.

- **Marijuana** use declined in all three grades, but was still widespread. Twenty-two percent of the eighth graders had tried marijuana and 49 percent of the twelfth graders said they had done so. Personal disapproval and concern over risk factors increased, particularly among eighth graders.

- **Stimulant** (amphetamine) use decreased among both eighth and tenth graders and leveled off for twelfth graders. Concern among twelfth graders about the dangers of trying amphetamines even once or twice rose from 29 percent in 1995 to 35 percent in 1998.

- Use of **hallucinogens,** specifically LSD and Ecstasy, was moderately down in all three grades.

- **Inhalants** continued a pattern of gradual decline over the past three years of the study. There was a sharp jump in the number of students who saw inhalant use as dangerous.

- **Heroin**—After a rise during the early 1990s, heroin use leveled off, and there was an increased concern about the dangers related to heroin.

- **Cocaine**—The use of both cocaine and crack rose gradually throughout the 1990s and continued to rise slightly, particularly in the lower grades.

- Use of **tranquilizers** slowed down among eighth graders, but continued to increase gradually among tenth and twelfth graders.

- **Alcohol** continued to be the drug of choice, increasing gradually, with some decline in binge drinking in eighth and tenth grade. The perceived risk associated with binge drinking began to rise among eighth and tenth graders, but 33 percent of all high school seniors reported being drunk at least once in the month before the survey.

ence in 1911 attempted to regulate the opium trade and was the first to identify opium addiction as a "high moral crime." In the United States, the Harrison Act imposed a tax on the import and production of opium and its new derivative, heroin. Heroin was developed in Germany to replace morphine as a pain killer and cure morphine addiction. It was used for fifteen years before it was discovered that it too was extremely addicting. When nonmedicinal use of opium became illegal, heroin became the primary drug of choice for the black market because in its powder form it was easy to transport and hide. Twenty-five dollars of opium processed as heroin could be sold on the black market for $200,000.

Amphetamines did not enter the drug market until the late 1800s and gained widespread use during World War II. Soldiers were given a free supply of Benzedrine pills ("bennies") to help them stay alert and cope with the stresses of war. Loved ones and workers back home also began to pop bennies to ease the stresses of a wartime economy and fears. After the war, they continued to be used by truck drivers, workers, students, and housewives for energy, weight control, and nasal decongestion. Barbiturates also entered the scene around the time of Prohibition, as a sedative replacement for alcohol.

All of these drugs became a part of the social rebellion of the 1960s. Laws strictly prohibited the use of the opiates, marijuana, and other street drugs, but television broadly advertised nicotine, alcohol, and a wide range of pills. When the Surgeon General released his report in 1964 that cigarette smoking caused lung cancer and other fatal diseases, sales dropped for two months, then resumed and continued to increase in spite of the health warnings, ban on TV advertising, and a 40 percent tax.

The civil rights movement and a wave of drug-advocating entertainers and writers created a new climate of experimentation and resistance to legal and moral drug prohibition. Interest in the much maligned Native American cultures popularized the use of hallucinogens for spiritual and personal enlightenment. Dr. Timothy Leary, a clinical psychologist at Harvard, began experimenting with LSD, an extremely powerful derivative of ergot, a parasitic fungus that grows on rye and other grains. Fired from Harvard, Leary continued to publicize the mind-expanding properties of this "miracle drug." Marijuana and LSD became the drugs of choice for the "flower children" in their efforts to "drop out, turn on, tune in." Soldiers returning from an unpopular war in Vietnam brought to the United States a strain of marijuana that was six to ten times more powerful than the local or Mexican varieties. Ironically, as several states moved to decriminalize the possession of small amounts of marijuana in the mid 1970s, the actual strength of the drug was much greater than it had been when the penalty of a first-offense possession had ranged from two years to life imprisonment.

Teenagers today have unprecedented access to a stronger and wider range of drugs. Virtually no teenager, urban or rural, rich or poor, will go through high school without being faced with very immediate decisions about drug use. One study of a high school class in 1984 showed that about 60 percent of marijuana users had their first experience with drugs between sixth and ninth grade.[7] Accidents related to alcohol remain the leading cause of death to those under age twenty-one. Estimates indicate that almost one-third of all teens smoke tobacco, and two-thirds have tried it. Domestic marijuana is available now that is ten to fifteen times more potent than the marijuana smoked in the '60s. A smokable and highly addictive form of cocaine, called "crack," hit the streets in the '80s for the low, introductory price of $5.00. LSD, mushrooms, and mescaline enjoy periodic surges of popularity. Other laboratory derivatives of amphetamines, barbiturates, or opiates periodically hit the streets as the newest "designer drugs."

Today's teens are also more educated about drug use. Many have witnessed the painful problems of friends or family members and steadfastly choose not to use drugs. Others have read and seen enough not to risk their minds and bodies experimenting with drugs. Many high school students who have tried marijuana discontinue its use before they get out of high school. Students have taken the lead in responsible efforts to stop drunk driving and many regularly appoint a designated driver and will not let their friends drive drunk. After crack's initial ap-

> *Children grew up in a world where magic potions could cure everything from obesity to fatigue. No need to be tired, homely, listless, tense, hyperactive, sleepless, full, fat or skinny—swallow a pill and get FAST! FAST! FAST! relief.[6]*
> —*John Rublowsky*

pearance on the drug market, most teenagers today realize its immediate danger and will have nothing to do with it. Both in the cities and in the suburbs, teenagers are beginning to question their role as an easy market for adult drug trafficking.

Recreational and Personal Use

People, teenagers or adults, do not use drugs because they want to kill off brain cells or spent time in jail, or increase their chances of developing cancer or AIDS. Historically, spiritually and medically people use drugs to change their mood or experience. An aspirin will affect your brain chemistry so that you do not feel the pain that is in your body. Tranquilizers can make you relax when you are under stress. Cocaine can make you feel alert and energetic when you are tired and bored. Alcohol can temporarily quiet your fears and insecurities enabling you to be more carefree and spontaneous.

MAGIC. No fuss, no muss, no pain, no limits. To be alive, our bodies and minds are always somewhere on a continuum between total pain and total pleasure.

PAIN ← ☺ → PLEASURE

Most of the time, we are somewhere in the middle—the standard "OK" response to "how ya' doing?" The flu, breaking up with your girlfriend, or failing at an important task can drag us down to the pain side of the continuum. Winning a game, relaxing in front of a warm, cozy fire, or spending a laughter-filled evening with good friends tend to make us feel much better than OK. Almost everything that we care about in our lives has the potential to make us feel pleasure and pain. If you love to play soccer, you may experience the thrill of victory or a game well played. You may also know the pain of missing a crucial kick or an injury that puts you out for the season. At different times, a close friend can make you feel either terrific or terrible. Nothing makes us feel good all the time, no matter how great it is.

Each person has his own safe place—running, painting, swimming, fishing, weaving, gardening. The activity itself is less important than the act of drawing on your own resources.

—Barbara Gordon

EXCEPT MAGIC. Drugs promise us magic and that is exactly what they deliver. Webster defines magic as "the art of producing illusions."[8] You still have a headache, but aspirin provides you with the illusion that you feel fine. That can be a pretty handy illusion unless, of course, the headache pain is a warning of a more serious problem that needs your attention. Experiencing the illusion of calm when you are under stress can be helpful if it helps you function more effectively to reduce the stress. It can also be counterproductive if you use the illusion to deny or avoid the problem that created the stress in the first place. One of the most intriguing drug illusions was demonstrated by Ben Johnson. He lost his Olympic gold medal and world record in the 100-meter run because of his use of steroids. After a two-year suspension, Johnson tried to reclaim his record without the help of steroids only to come in seventh, almost a full second below his steroid-induced, world-record time.

Drugs offer us the illusion of control. By using a drug, you can control and improve how you feel. You don't need anyone else to help you out or be nice to you or give you permission. You can alter your own feelings and mood. Without any pain or exercise or personal changes, you can feel better, happier, stronger, more confident, and more relaxed. And unlike more natural mood swings, most drugs produce a pretty consistent, dependable change.

The less real power you have in other areas of your life, the more likely you will use drugs as a source of control. This is where teenagers may be particularly vulnerable to the abuse of drugs. As our world has become more complex, teenagers, in spite of their adult bodies and drives, usually have a very limited range of power. They are not children (and

---

Controlling Bad Moods and Feelings

Everyone has bad days and uncomfortable feelings. We also have many resources to control and comfort ourselves—without the risks involved with chemicals.

Pick **two** feelings that are especially uncomfortable or difficult for you to deal with. Then make a list of things *you* can do that make yourself feel better during those times.

NEGATIVE FEELINGS LIST: *angry, left out, embarrassed, sad, inadequate, abandoned, afraid, alienated, anxious, bad, betrayed, jealous, helpless, hurt, bored, depressed, lonely, misunderstood, odd, disappointed, shy, grief-stricken, guilty, insecure, pressured, trapped, uptight, impatient, incompetent, inferior, paranoid, sorry for self, stupid, intimidated, rejected, tense.*

POSSIBLE ANTIDOTES: *Exercise, listening to music, a hot bath, reading, yelling, crying, talking to a friend, writing a letter, writing in a journal, playing an instrument, hiking, taking a walk, going to a movie, running, meditation, a favorite food, buying something special, yoga, talking with a parent, calling an old friend, spending time with a pet, helping someone out, making something, drawing, confronting the problem, laughing, etc.* Think of your own.

Negative feeling: _____

Antidotes that work for me: _____

_____

_____

_____

_____

Negative feeling: _____

Antidotes that work for me: _____

_____

_____

_____

_____

expected not to act like them!), but they are also denied most adult freedoms and power. Confined by financial, legal, and parental restrictions, teens have a limited number of ways to control and change their lives.

Adolescence is also a time of transition—learning new skills, trying new things, and taking on new responsibilities. These changes involve a certain amount of pain or discomfort as individuals experience the natural insecurity and mistakes of personal development. With increased pressures and a limited amount of power, it is not surprising that drugs can become the central focus of power and entertainment for many adolescents.

Some people use drugs to increase pleasure—to feel higher, smarter, stronger, or more confident. Drugs are also used to avoid pain, to help resolve conflicts or feelings of inadequacy. "Bottled courage" may ease the nervousness of an important date. Many people use alcohol or other drugs to quiet their internal conflict about sexual decisions or activity. Steroids numb the pain of excessive workouts and marijuana can block out the pressures to achieve in an academically and socially competitive culture. The opiates may provide relief and pleasure in lives otherwise shadowed by poverty and racism.

> *Long before a girl or a boy picks up a cigarette or a beer, he or she has been primed by advertising to expect transformation via a product. From infancy on, we get a seductive and incessant message from ads—products are magical, can fulfill our dreams. . . . We are primed from birth to believe that magical products can make our lives extraordinary.*
>
> *—Jean Kilbourne*

As with any illusion, however, the situation or personal characteristics have not changed. Things just temporarily feel differently. This creates three major obstacles to growing and becoming more competent.

1. **We don't learn how to handle normal life stresses on our own.** While drugs may make us feel less inhibited and more confident at the moment, they hinder learning and deny us the experience and satisfaction of accomplishing a difficult task on our own. A twenty-two-year-old who has never gone on a date straight will be just as nervous and awkward without drugs as a thirteen-year-old on her first date. With practice and experience, we overcome our insecurities and learn valuable social skills. With drugs, we avoid both our feelings and our own maturation.

2. **We become intolerant of even minor discomfort and need to have our needs met immediately.** Life is full of conflicts, challenges, and frustrations which we must resolve or cope with. For many reasons, we live in a time that seems to promise life without all of these inconveniences. The media and advertising suggest that life should be easy and, if it isn't, we need to buy something or ingest something to solve our problems. You too can lose weight without dieting or exercise. Is your life boring? Fly off to Club Med or buy a new car or drink the right beer.

   Becoming an adult requires a growing ability to *delay gratification*—that is, to put up with temporary inconvenience or discomfort in order to achieve a more distant goal. Children can't do it. They want what they want and they want it NOW. Waiting or saving or working for long periods of time is very difficult. As adults, we put up with some things in order to accomplish more important things. We can wait until the cookie dough is cooked before eating it (most of the time); we can choose to spend time studying now in order to get into the college we want to attend in the future; we can work at a not-so-enjoyable job and save our money to buy the new stereo system that we want. Drugs offer instant relief, instant results, and can make us impatient with the longer, more demanding work of building toward our goals.

3. **We become increasingly dependent on chemicals to regulate our moods and solve our problems.** Ironically, control, the initial promise of drugs, may be the very price they exact of us in the long run. Any chemical that increases pleasure and reduces pain is psychologically addictive and most are physiologically addictive as well. As we use drugs to regulate our lives, our normal responses and coping mechanisms become dulled and inefficient. Our brain does not function efficiently because external chemicals have replaced or blocked its normal patterns. We do not learn the social and personal skills we need to confidently cope with the problems and pressures in our lives. We begin to need drugs just to feel normal. Once the solution, drugs can easily become the problem.

Quandary: **It's Tough to Break the Grip of that Wonderful Stuff that Kills**

"Let's clear up one misconception right here at the start—cocaine is wonderful. Doctors who heal the lives it fractures will tell you as much. Cocaine is a rocket launch. You're the rocket. It is also a soft June moon or a Bob Dylan concert or a flight in a glider or hot apple strudel or a stolen kiss in the dark, depending. That's the sad truth.

"Cocaine is also the stranger's car your momma told you never to get into. But, hell, it's long and low and sleek and the pipes have an Indy car's burble and it's only a short ride and everyone knows how it's fun to go fast.

"I'm convinced the reason Len Bias and Don Rogers are dead, the reason John Lucas isn't playing pro basketball and Steve Howe isn't pitching in the bigs and Mercury Morris went to jail, the reason Alan Wiggins is an Oriole instead of a Padre and Vida Blue never plans his life more than 24 hours ahead anymore, is that nobody levels with the youth of America.

"We righteously say drugs will take you to hell and make your hair grow in green and drive you crazy and give you pimples . . . but then they try them and find out they're wonderful, and so they think they've been conned, and then they do them some more.

"Which can get you dead, we've been reminded in recent weeks.

"Cocaine is euphoric. Everything's right. There's a feeling of power. You feel no fatigue. That's the truth of the matter. It's wonderful stuff.

"That's the problem. As good as it makes you feel in the beginning, after a while that's how bad it makes you feel. And you know you could feel better if you could just take some more. . . . It's tough to get off this drug.

"A Len Bias or two may not make much of a dent. Rogers' death is evidence of that. People forget. Sometimes people want to forget. That's another sad truth."

written by Joe Hamelin, McClatch News Service, July 1, 1986

How can people be effectively warned and educated to deal with the risks and realities of drug use? What does a person need to know and think about in order to make safe, healthy decisions? Research has clearly shown that students are faced with these decisions in junior high and younger. What information and advice would you give a younger brother or sister who is thinking about drugs?

Everyone is faced with the ongoing decision, "Am I going to use drugs?" Whether you say "No" every time, "Yes" every time, or change your decision over your lifetime, you still will make this decision every time the opportunity presents itself. Each of us needs to understand as much as possible about what a drug actually does to our mind and body. We must examine any drug use in the context of our own personal development and our relationships with the people we care about. And we must also consider our values surrounding how we want to live our lives. How do drugs affect our independence and personal growth? What is the role of pain and pleasure in our lives? What are the legal, medical, and personal consequences of drug use?

> *When a person does something, he will try, if at all possible to convince himself (and others) that it was a logical, reasonable thing to do.*
> *—Elliot Aronson*

Weighing this decision is more complicated than it first appears. Everyone seems to have an opinion and set of values surrounding the use of drugs. This opinion is usually an emotional, gut-level response to upbringing, personal experience, political position, and some undefinable personal bias. Human beings also have an incredible ability to make facts fit whatever opinion they may hold. Leon Festinger, a social psychologist, has developed a theory which he calls *cognitive dissonance.* Cognitive dissonance is **"the discomfort that a person feels when he or she holds two mutually illogical beliefs or behaviors."**[9] We like to think of ourselves as logical, intelligent, and good people, so when we act illogically or immorally, we feel stupid. For instance, suppose that we know:

⇨   *Cigarette smoking is dangerous to my health.*

AND   ⇨   *I smoke cigarettes.*

The logical response is to stop smoking, but if we don't want to or are addicted and find it very difficult to quit, we experience *dissonance.* When this happens, we unconsciously need to either:

1. change one of the beliefs (*I don't really smoke that much, the dangers are really overrated, I am in excellent health, it won't affect me*)

OR   2. form a bridging belief (*Everybody has to die someday, I like living dangerously, I'm going to quit as soon as exams are over, Uncle Joe smokes two packs a day and he is 99*)

Studies done after the Surgeon General's report on smoking came out showed that people did just that. Ten percent of the nonsmokers did not believe the report, while 40 percent of the smokers didn't believe it. Smokers consistently underestimated how much they smoked and 60 percent who smoked one to two packs a day considered themselves moderate smokers.[10]

> *Get your facts first, then you can distort them as you please.*
> *—Mark Twain*

Decision making creates dissonance because we have to choose one alternative and give up another. Rarely are our decisions all good or all bad, so when we are forced to choose, we give up the good things of the choice not taken and take on the bad things of the choice that we took. Quickly,

I have every sympathy with the American who was so horrified by what they had read of the effects of smoking that they gave up reading.
—Harry G. Strauss

we downplay the disadvantages of the choice we have taken and the advantages of the choice we have given up. Suppose you have to decide between studying for an important test or going to a great movie with your friends. If you decide to study, you will most likely convince yourself that it wasn't that great a movie, you are a better person for studying, and the test will determine important things in your life. If you decide to go to the movie, you will probably come to think that the test is not all that important, life is too short to spend in just study, and if you don't know the material now, cramming is just a superficial form of learning. You may even convince yourself that you will wake up at 4:00 A.M. to go over the material. One study showed that car advertisements were most closely read by people who had just bought the car. The ads were a wonderful place to hear all the good things about the decision they had already made.

Even scientific studies have been shown to unconsciously bias the results or interpretation of their data to fit with preconceived notions or theory. When you read information about drugs, there are always two biases at work—the bias of the writer or researcher and the bias of the reader (that's you). Every book or study on drug use is filtered through a set of beliefs and values. NORML, a group lobbying for the legalization of marijuana, and the Partnership for Drugfree America will interpret and present the same information very differently. Most drug literature will not come right out and tell you what their bias is. You will have to read critically and try to evaluate their conclusions as objectively as possible.

Don't forget that you too bring your own bias to your reading. Your preconceived notions about drugs, either pro or con, will also color what you read and believe. One study on racial segregation[11] showed that people tend to remember the plausible arguments that agreed with their position and the ridiculous arguments opposing their viewpoint. Our own bias is often the most difficult to spot. This distortion is amusing to note in friends and thought-provoking as we attempt to sort through the information that is available to us. Cognitive dissonance becomes dangerous when it distorts information that is critical to our well-being. A smoker who consistently distorts either the dangers of smoking or her own habit is making important decisions that will affect her health and future. Accepting the dissonance between the facts and her behavior could help her to change her behavior and quit smoking.

The other problem in making decisions about drugs is that we can't really depend on personal experience. The way that we learn from experience is by carefully evaluating its pros and cons and consequences. To do that, we use our brain. Drugs complicate that process because they act on the very organ that we use to evaluate our experience. If you ask someone who is quite inebriated if they are capable of safely driving a car, he will most likely tell you that of course he is. His sober brain would disagree, but, at that point, his brain is not sober—it is not able to clearly evaluate the situation. Intravenous drug users don't want to get AIDS any more than you do, but their drug use makes their brain unable to dictate careful precautions. Heavy marijuana users are usually the last to see the changes in their own behavior because the THC in their brain has changed the way they think.

Another problem with judging by personal experience is that very often the negative consequences of drug use are very subtle or long-term. Brain cells have no feeling. A person can have a serious brain tumor without any pain. Therefore, when we kill brain cells, we have no immediate pain response to warn us of the damage. If you put your hand on a hot stove, you get burned, it hurts, and you don't do it again. If a drug is doing similar damage to your brain, you don't feel it. Similarly, long-term damage to your liver, heart, lungs, or reproductive organs does not show up in your immediate experience. The immediate high of cocaine experientially outweighs the potential threat of addiction or physical damage. Some drugs can be lethal or addicting from short-term experimental use and certain people seem to quickly lose control over their decision making about a drug. If you have a history of drug or alcohol abuse in your family or are in a physically or psychologically stressful time of life, you are at high risk for becoming drug dependent in a short amount of time. Most alcoholics take ten to fifteen years for the disease to fully develop, but recent studies have shown that young people at the start of puberty are developing full-blown alcoholism in two to three years.

Everybody Has a Message

As you start thinking and making decisions for yourself, you will notice that many forces around you are giving both spoken and unspoken messages about drug use. While spoken messages may be very direct, the unspoken messages may affect us more strongly because they are based on what others actually do and how they respond to our ideas and decisions. A parent may say that he does not want you using any drugs, but smokes or drinks himself. A friend may say that it is cool that you have chosen not to use drugs and then exclude you from the weekend parties that may include drug use. Rock stars in the '60s may have glamorized drug use with their music, but sent a different message by the number who died through overdose or accidents.

Think about each of the following influences in your life and try to identify both the spoken and unspoken messages each has given you about drugs.

MESSENGER	SPOKEN	UNSPOKEN
The Government or Law		
The Music You Enjoy		
TV and Movies You Watch		
Your School and Teachers		

Your Parents		
Your Brothers and Sisters		
Your Social Group		
Your Closest Friends		
Your Own Position		

Notice where these messages match and where they conflict. Which messages have most influenced your own position?

Drugs and the Law

The law varies from state to state and law enforcement may be handled differently under different jurisdictions. In order to act responsibly, it is important to know the exact law in your area. Here are some questions teenagers often ask about law enforcement and drug use.[13] You can have a police officer come to speak to your class or make an appointment to talk with someone at your local police department. Most departments have public relations personnel who would be happy to answer your questions.

Drugs and Law Enforcement

1. Is it legal for police to come into your backyard while you're having a party? Can they search your car/house/purse/person? What constitutes probable cause when there is suspicion about drug use at a party?

2. If a person is over 21 and is drinking with minors, can he be arrested for contributing to the delinquency of minors?

3. Can parents serve their kids and their kids' friends liquor in their own home?

4. If I was the designated driver after a party and had not been drinking, but was driving my inebriated friends home and was pulled over, what would happen to me? What if they were drinking in my car, but I wasn't?

5. What would happen if a minor was caught with a joint or two? A small amount of cocaine? A dose of LSD?

6. When cops take down the names of people at a party they have busted, what do they do with the names?

7. Is it illegal to buy, sell, or carry drug paraphernalia?

8. If a waitress in a restaurant offers me a drink and I take it (I am under 21), can she be arrested? Can I? Can the restaurant lose its license?

9. If I use a fake ID and get caught, what will happen?

10. Do officers ever work undercover at liquor stores to catch kids shoulder-tapping? Is the person who buys liquor for kids who have shoulder-tapped breaking the law? What happens to her? To the kids?

11. Drugs are so out in the open at concerts. Why aren't people who sell or use drugs there arrested? Can I be arrested for being high at a concert?

12. If I was taken to jail for an offense, what would happen?

13. If you are stopped for driving under the influence, do they test for other drugs or just alcohol?

What other questions do you have about drugs and law enforcement?

The role of law enforcement in drug use is quite controversial and changeable. Two of the most dangerous and addictive drugs in the world today—alcohol and nicotine—are legal. At one point in Spanish history, the use of caffeine was punishable by death. The outlawing of alcohol during Prohibition did little to reduce its use and created the beginnings of criminal drug trafficking. Heroin, Benzedrine, cocaine, LSD, and marijuana have all been legal at one point in U.S. history. Alcohol, tobacco, and hemp were all primary exports in the economic development of our country and today the underground drug market accounts for billions of dollars in the international market.

Some people believe the drug laws should be made stricter and more carefully enforced. In 1989, Congress put into effect a new law that would strip federal student grants and loans to people convicted of using or selling illegal drugs. The drinking age was raised to twenty-one throughout the United States and many states initiated legislation to restrict the driving privileges of teenagers convicted of any drug offense. Studies of the long-term effects of drugs are just beginning to provide evidence of permanent damage to the brain, liver, kidneys, and even the chromosomes through chronic use of certain drugs. Much is still unknown. Young people are especially vulnerable to drug damage because their bodies and brains are disrupted while they are still growing. Surveys show that drug use is often beginning in elementary and junior high schools, long before kids have the experience and wisdom to make good choices about the drugs offered them. Sixty to 70 percent of the rising rate of crime in the U.S. is drug-related. Drugs also account for more than 70 percent of the accidental deaths in this country. Many innocent people are affected by drug use—children, accident and crime victims, and families. These people believe that it is the right and responsibility of the government to protect the innocent and control the use of drugs.

Others believe that drug use is a medical and personal decision that should not be monitored by the government. They cite the inconsistency of drug laws as evidence that these laws are capricious and discriminatory. Alcohol and tobacco are at least as addicting and dangerous as any of the illegal drugs. Cigarettes kill 250,000 people each year while only 2,500 die of heroin-related causes. Many drug laws do not reflect the current attitudes and use, reducing the general respect for the law. Fifty to 80 percent of people in the U.S. today have used marijuana—a clear indication that laws don't stop people from using. Most drug-related crimes are a result of the fact that drugs are illegal. Price and quality is controlled by a profit-based black market. If drugs were legal, prices would drop, dangerous drug cutting would be controlled, and the government would have a lucrative tax base. Addicts would be able to get help without fear of prosecution. As it is, only small-time users and dealers are ever prosecuted. The real moneymakers are too politically and economically powerful to control.

Marijuana is particularly controversial because it is commonly available and its effects are subtle. In the 1960s, it became the drug of choice of the counterculture who saw it as much less addicting and detrimental than alcohol. The dramatic and mostly ungrounded claims of the press and

Federal Narcotics Bureau seemed blatantly ridiculous to anyone who had used marijuana. The research was initially quite mixed, often reflecting political bias more than scientific objectivity. Some studies indicated no serious long-term effects; others showed a variety of problems ranging from short-term memory loss to amotivational syndrome to increased infertility. The shortage of long-term studies and the subtle, pervasive nature of marijuana intoxication seemed to make it difficult to draw unbiased conclusions. Researching marijuana can be very frustrating because one book or study will completely contradict and ignore another. The most recent data does support the need for caution, particularly in the chronic use of marijuana. At the same time, the potency and general use of marijuana has increased.

Your Legal Liability

Every state has specific laws, liabilities, and consequences regarding the use, possession, and distribution of alcohol or drugs by minors. *You need to know what the laws are in your state and how these offenses are handled.* Some violations are considered a **misdemeanor**—an offense that carries a fine and possible jail time or probation. This violation is usually dropped from your record after a number of years or when you become an adult. Other violations are classified as a **felony,** which is a more serious legal status, usually requiring some jail time, a fine, and/or extended probation. A felony conviction may remain permanently on your record and can restrict your right to vote, travel, or take up certain professions. Some states erase this record when you become an adult, while other states may put you on trial as an adult even if you are still a minor. Penalties also vary from state to state and may include a substantial fine, restitution for damages, jail time, probation, and/or community service. Many states will revoke your driver's license for drug- or alcohol-related offenses even if the offense is not related to driving.

Criminal violations include the following:

- Forging an ID
- Purchase or possession of alcohol by a minor
- Purchasing or furnishing alcohol for a minor
- Drinking or possession of alcohol in a public place
- Driving while under the influence of alcohol or illegal drug
- Possession of controlled dangerous substance (illegal drug)
- Sale, gift, or distribution of controlled dangerous substance (illegal drug)
- Distribution to persons under 18
- Sale on school property or within 1000 feet of any school
- Transporting controlled dangerous substances across state lines

A parent who supplies alcohol or drugs to a minor, or who allows alcohol or drugs to be used by a minor when he or she is in a position to prevent that use, may be liable for damages or injuries resulting from the minor's impairment. For example, if someone is injured as a result of alcohol or drug use at a party at your house, your parents may be liable for civil or criminal damages. Some states hold the parent legally responsible even if he or she was not aware that the drinking or drug use was going on. The parent has the legal obligation to supervise and control the behavior of minors in his or her home. *Be careful not to put your parents in this position.*

Quandary: *Should Marijuana Be Legalized?*

One way to think about a difficult quandary is to force yourself to objectively consider all of the positions. For each of the statements below, develop a convincing argument both FOR and AGAINST that position. Watch your own bias and attempt to see both sides of the issue as clearly as possible.

A. *What we <u>do</u> know about the effects of marijuana is damaging enough to require legal constraints and there are still many unanswered and frightening questions about long-term chromosome damage that may significantly affect generations to come.*

B. *Marijuana should be legalized because it is demonstrably less addictive and dangerous than either alcohol or tobacco which are both legal.*

C. *Legalizing marijuana would only increase its availability and acceptance, particularly among young people who are physically more vulnerable to its negative effects.*

D. *Because marijuana is illegal, there is no way to control price or quality. Street drugs are often dangerously cut with speed or other addictive stimulants to increase demand and cut the cost for the seller. Legalizing it would make it safer and cheaper.*

The more you think about these issues objectively, the more complicated they tend to become. Most issues do not have just a good or bad side, but some of each. When we try to simplify our thoughts or reduce dissonance, we often gloss over important points that need to be considered.

Write down your own position on this issue, then note the factors that influenced your decision AND any reservations or questions that you still have.

My position _____

Determining factors _____

_____

_____

Reservations or unknowns _____

_____

_____

_____

_____

Medical Marijuana—A Medical or Political Issue?

On November 5, 1996, Californians passed Proposition 215, the Medical Marijuana Initiative, by a 56 percent to 44 percent vote, permitting seriously and terminally ill patients to use marijuana in their medical treatment. Marijuana has been used for the reduction of extreme nausea caused by cancer chemotherapy and AIDS treatment. It also reportedly increases appetite during these treatments, permitting more normal food intake and preventing dangerous weight loss. Marijuana has also been used to reduce eye pressure in glaucoma patients and to control muscle spasms, seizures, and chronic muscular pain in patients with epilepsy, multiple sclerosis, arthritis, or spinal cord injuries. Before it was made illegal by the Marijuana Tax Act of 1937, marijuana, or *Cannabis indica*, as it was known, was widely studied and used as an appetite stimulant, muscle relaxant, analgesic, hypnotic, and anticonvulsant.

By 2000, measures permitting the use of medical marijuana had been passed in Alaska, Arizona, California, Colorado, Hawaii, Maine, Nevada, Oregon, and Washington, but these state laws were still in conflict with the federal law that classified marijuana as a Schedule I Controlled Substance. The definition of a Schedule I drug is a drug with no accepted medical use in the United States, and a high potential for abuse. Schedule I substances include marijuana, heroin, some forms of morphine, and LSD. "We have never really had a situation like this before," said California Attorney General Lungren. "We now have a law in which the state says something is legal that is illegal under federal law."[13]

In August 2000, the Supreme Court struck down the state laws, citing that medical marijuana laws provided *"incentives for drug manufacturers and distributors to invoke the asserted needs of others as a justification for their drug trafficking,"* and that allowing the medicinal distribution of marijuana would *"promote disrespect and disregard for an act of Congress that is central to combating illicit drug trafficking and use by giving a judicial stamp of approval to the open and notorious distribution of (illegal) substances to potentially thousands of users without any of the strict controls required."*[14]

Opponents of medical marijuana believe that legalizing marijuana for medical uses will make it more available and acceptable for recreational use. The Drug Enforcement Administration states that *"there are over 10,000 scientific studies that prove marijuana is a harmful addictive drug and not one reliable study that demonstrates marijuana has any medical value."*[15] The DEA argues that marijuana is *"an unstable mixture of more than 425 chemicals which harmful consequences include, but are not limited to the following: premature cancer, addiction, coordination and perception impairment, a number of mental disorders, including depression, hostility and increased aggressiveness, general apathy, memory loss, reproductive disabilities, and impairment to the immune system."*[16] Given these serious side effects, the Department of Justice believes that the "compassionate" concerns for people suffering from cancer, AIDS, and glaucoma *"are being used unfairly by groups whose real agenda is to legalize marijuana."*[17] They note that no other medication has ever been prescribed by means of smoking and that THC is already legally available in capsule form, Marinol, for medical use. DEA states that the vast majority of health organizations, including the American Medical Association, the American Cancer Society, National Sclerosis Association, the American Glaucoma Association, American Academy of Ophthalmology, National Eye Institute, and the National Cancer Institute, have concluded that smoking marijuana is not a safe and effective medicine.

The Drug Enforcement Administration fears that lightening the restrictions on marijuana use in any way will contribute to increased use and a sense that marijuana is harmless, particularly among young people. *"Legalizing marijuana would add a third drug that combines some of the most serious risks of alcohol and tobacco. Marijuana offers both the intoxicating effects of alcohol and the long-term lung damage of tobacco."*[18]

On the other side, proponents of the use of medical marijuana insist that people can clearly distinguish between the medical use and the recreational use of marijuana. A 1999 Gallup poll reported that 73 percent of Americans support making marijuana legally available for doctors to prescribe.[19] NORML, the National Organization for the Reform of Marijuana Laws, cites the conclusion of the U.S. National Academy of Sciences, Institute of Medicine that says, *"Scientific data indicate the potential therapeutic value of cannabinoid drugs, primarily THC, for pain relief, control of nausea and vomiting, and appetite stimulation. . . . Except for the harms associated with smoking, the adverse effects of marijuana use are within the range tolerated for other medications."*[20] Medical marijuana advocates insist that many physicians pretend to ignore the fact that their patients with cancer, AIDS, or multiple sclerosis are smoking marijuana for relief; some quietly encourage them. In a 1990 survey, 44 percent of oncologists said they had suggested that a patient smoke marijuana for relief of the nausea induced by chemotherapy.[21] NORML lists over 100 medical and research organizations that support the use and/or study of medical marijuana.[22] Dr. Jerome Kassirer, editor, *New England Journal of Medicine*, January 30, 1997, said *"Federal authorities should rescind their prohibition of the medical use of marijuana for seriously ill patients and allow physicians to decide which patients to treat. The government should change marijuana's status from that of a Schedule I [prohibited] drug . . . to that of a Schedule II drug . . . and regulate accordingly."* Like DEA, NORML also has a strong nonmedical agenda regarding marijuana: *"There is nothing wrong with the responsible use of marijuana by adults and it should be of no interest or concern to the government."*[23] Political judgments of whether the *recreational* use of marijuana is dangerous or harmless significantly influence how individuals and agencies evaluate the *medial* use of marijuana.

The arguments given both for and against the medical use of marijuana are a good example of how confusing it can be to sort through both opinions and research. Knowledgeable, strong-minded individuals and organizations on both sides can present very convincing, yet conflicting evidence. Neither side may be intentionally misleading and both sides usually believe that their position imparts a moral or social imperative. *Remember, as you read information or opinions, you are most likely to remember the strong arguments for your own point of view and the ridiculous arguments for the position that you don't agree with.*[24] It is hard to keep an open mind and objectively evaluate the information that you hear. Be sure to determine the bias of a source, individual, or Web site so you can thoughtfully evaluate what you are told.

DRUG INFORMATION

Caffeine

Description

Legal in most countries, caffeine is possibly the most commonly used mind-altering drug. It occurs naturally in over sixty plants and is used in coffee, tea, cocoa, chocolate, headache remedies, weight control aids, diuretics, and soft drinks.

Physical and Psychological Effects

Depending on how much is consumed, caffeine temporarily increases heartbeat and metabolism, stomach acid secretion, and urine production. It dilates some blood vessels and constricts others. Caffeine reduces drowsiness, increases alertness, and shortens reaction time. This alertness may increase reading speed, but does not appear to improve more complex mental or physical performance.

How It Works on the Brain

Caffeine is one of a group of compounds called methylxanthines which act directly to stimulate certain neurotransmitters in the central nervous system.

Side Effects

Coffee drinking has been linked to heart disease, benign breast disease, cancer, and other health problems, but the most current studies do not confirm a cause and effect relationship. Coffee drinkers often smoke, have high-fat diets, and don't exercise often, which may be the real culprits.

Precautions

While the studies are not conclusive, most doctors recommend that people with heart problems, pregnant and nursing women, and young children abstain from coffee or restrict their use to 200 milligrams per day (approximately one to two cups of coffee, three to four cups of tea, or four sodas).

Addiction, Withdrawal, and Overdose

Caffeine is mildly addicting. Quitting or temporary nonuse may bring on some withdrawal symptoms about twelve to sixteen hours after the last dose—headache, irritability, drowsiness, mild depression, and nausea. Overdose, often known as "coffee nerves," may include trembling, nervousness, chronic muscle tension, irritability, throbbing headaches, disorientation, sluggishness, depression, and insomnia. The amount needed to bring on these effects varies widely, usually dependent on how accustomed an individual is to caffeine, his body weight, and general health.

Nicotine

Description	Nicotine is an oily liquid found in the tobacco plant. It is toxic, used as a pesticide in agriculture and to kill parasites in veterinary medicine. Nicotine can be ingested through the smoke of cigarettes, pipes, or cigars, sniffed in the form of snuff, or released through tobacco chew.
Physical and Psychological Effects	Nicotine is one of the most powerful of all known drugs. It would only take two or three drops placed on your tongue to kill you. Tobacco smoke contains only a minuscule amount. In this form, nicotine has an immediate stimulating effect on the brain followed by a longer period of mild sedation. It makes the heart beat faster and raises blood pressure. Nicotine reduces the blood flow to the surface of the body, dropping skin temperature particularly in the hands and feet. By stimulating the output of saliva, nicotine lessens hunger pains and reduces the secretion of gastric juices. In small doses, nicotine seems to increase concentration and learning, particularly under stressful circumstances.
How It Works on the Brain	Nicotine appears to fit into receptor sites in the brain that stimulate the release of acetylcholine which stimulates certain brain functions and sedates others. The stimulation effect is shorter-lived then the sedation, which can last as long as one hour.
Side Effects	The primary side effect of nicotine is that it is extremely addictive. Once a smoker is addicted, the tar and gases inhaled with the nicotine create serious health problems. Over two dozen gases, including carbon monoxide, are found in cigarette smoke. These gases penetrate the walls of the lungs and arteries causing respiratory diseases, heart attacks, strokes, and cancer. Tar, the residue of cigarette smoke, accounts for most of cigarette's cancer-causing agents. More than 350,000 deaths each year are attributed to smoking. Smoking also increases facial wrinkles and weakens bones.
Precautions	Nicotine passes through the placenta and can overstimulate the fetus, causing reduced birth weight and prematurity. Studies have also indicated that secondary smoke breathed in areas where cigarette smoke has been exhaled creates a level of nicotine in the blood of nonsmokers and can lead to respiratory problems.
Addiction, Withdrawal, and Overdose	Nicotine is highly addictive. Withdrawal is marked by a craving for cigarettes, tension, irritability, depression, difficulty concentrating, sleep disturbances, a drop in pulse rate and blood pressure, constipation, and jaw-clenching. The physical symptoms of withdrawal can last up to a week, but habitual dependencies may remain for a much longer time.

Alcohol

Description

Ethanol, the active ingredient in alcohol, is produced by the fermentation of certain fruits, grains, or vegetables. A 12-ounce bottle of beer contains the same amount of ethanol as 1.5 ounces of distilled spirits or 5 ounces of wine.

Physical and Psychological Effects

Most people experience an initial relaxation and loss of alertness, anxiety, and inhibition. In larger amounts, perception, speech, vision, and coordination become hampered. Reaction time slows and there is a loss of balance. The effects of alcohol depend on amount taken, body size, and when you last ate. Men have an enzyme in their stomach called alcohol dehydrogenase which destroys about 20 percent of the alcohol consumed. The female stomach breaks down almost no alcohol. Given the typical difference in body size between the two sexes, one drink puts about the same concentration of alcohol in the brains of women as two drinks does in men. It takes the body one to two hours to metabolize one drink.

How It Works on the Brain

New research has shown that alcohol does not simply depress the central nervous system; it works to rewire the way information is passed through the brain cells. On the first level, about a half a standard bar drink, the nervous system is actually stimulated. The left hemisphere functioning is blocked, temporarily giving more leeway to the spontaneous, fun-loving right hemisphere. After that, ethanol, the main ingredient, is embedded in the cell membrane and begins to interfere with learning and memory. At higher doses, ethanol begins to depress basic body functions resulting in sleepiness, blackouts, or even death.

Side Effects

Alcohol is responsible for 60 percent of all traffic fatalities because of the combined effect of reduced coordination and reaction time and a drinker's distorted perception of her own sobriety. Chronic use often leads to alcoholic dependence. Cirrhosis of the liver, peptic ulcers, pneumonia, heart disease, vitamin deficiencies, fetal alcohol syndrome, and gastritis can all result from excessive alcohol use.

Precautions:

Alcohol passes through the placenta to the fetus and women are advised not to drink during pregnancy. The effects of alcohol are more pronounced when combined with other drugs and should be carefully monitored. Prescription tranquilizers, sedatives, or narcotics combined with alcohol can result in accidental overdose.

Addiction, Withdrawal, and Overdose

The simplest form of alcohol overdose and withdrawal is the hangover—dry mouth, dizziness, nausea, exhaustion, and headache. Once addicted to alcohol, withdrawal may include more severe symptoms of tremors, vomiting, cramps, delirium, loss of appetite, stomach inflammation, and short-term memory loss.

Marijuana

Description

Marijuana is made from the leaves and seeds of the *Cannabis sativa* plant. It contains 421 active chemical ingredients, with delta-9-tetrahydro-cannabinol (THC) being responsible for the main, mind-altering effects. Most marijuana is smoked in joints or pipes, though the leaves may be used in cookies or teas for a delayed effect. Medically, it has been used to treat glaucoma and reduce nausea in cancer treatment.

Physical and Psychological Effects

The effects of marijuana vary by person and situation. Common effects are a heightened sense of awareness to music, light and sensory input, sedation, increased appetite, and euphoria. This marijuana "high" usually lasts from two to four hours. Short-term memory, hand-eye coordination, and reaction time are reduced. Because 40–50 percent of the chemicals in marijuana stay in the body and brain cells for around a week, these secondary effects may last longer than the high feelings.

How It Works on the Brain

The chemicals in marijuana settle in the fatty tissues of the cell membrane. This initially slows down the firing of the neurotransmitters, quieting brain activity and lowering brain energy. Senses, thoughts, and feelings are experienced in slow motion. Because the brain is running more slowly and on less energy, information is not learned or put into long-term memory. As cannabinoids are added faster than they can be cleared out (one week to four months), the cell membrane becomes clogged, blocking input and glucose. Once saturated, the cell dies.

Side Effects

Amotivational syndrome is common among chronic marijuana users. Apathy, low motivation, loss of attention span, poor judgment, lowered communication skills, and difficulty carrying out complicated plans or tasks are indicative of this syndrome. Chronic marijuana use has also been shown to lower fertility, reduce the efficiency of the body's immune system, and increase the occurrence of upper respiratory infections and lung cancer. Marijuana "burn out" includes reduced intellectual processing, problems with short-term memory and learning, depression, and anxiety.

Precautions

Marijuana is fat soluble, not water soluble, so it embeds in the limpid, or fatty tissues, lining the cell membranes. It takes six to eight days for the cell to get rid of these embedded chemicals. If more THC continues to be taken in before the cell membrane is cleaned out, these tissues become saturated—the cell can no longer get the protein and glucose through the cell walls that it needs. The cell then starves.

Addiction, Withdrawal, and Overdose

Marijuana use can easily become habitual and create real problems for chronic users. There does not appear to be a strong physiological withdrawal with marijuana, but psychological and social factors make it difficult for chronic users to stop. There are some indications of a genetic predisposition to marijuana addiction. With marijuana, overdosing is more likely to be an ongoing process than a single occurrence.

Cocaine

Description	Cocaine is one of fourteen alkaloids contained in the leaf of the coca plant which grows almost exclusively in South America. It can be sniffed, smoked, or injected. Prior to 1906, it was used medically and, in very mild doses, as a stimulant in Coca-Cola and other tonics.
Physical and Psychological Effects	Cocaine acts as a local anesthetic and a stimulant. The anesthetic qualities numb the membranes on contact. The cocaine rush, which lasts about ten to fifteen minutes, is caused by excessive stimulation of the central nervous system. Elevated heart rate, accelerated respiration, euphoria, talkativeness, a heightened sense of awareness, and heightened sex drive are common effects. Continued use may bring on cardiovascular and respiratory problems, depression, lowered sex drive, antisocial behavior, insomnia, and addiction.
How It Works on the Brain	Cocaine stimulates the release of the brain's natural stimulants, norepinephrine, dopamine, and epinephrine. These neurotransmitters normally regulate emotions and the experience of pain and pleasure. By overreleasing these chemicals, a person feels a rush of pleasure. This rapid release lowers the level of neurotransmitters in the brain so that subsequent use requires more cocaine in order to have the same feeling—this is called tolerance. Chronic use of cocaine depletes the body's natural painkillers, causing the depression and physical pain associated with cocaine cravings and withdrawal.
Side Effects	High blood pressure, stuffy nose, sweating, nausea, abdominal pain, dilated pupils, headache, loss of appetite, and vitamin and mineral depletion are common physical side effects of cocaine use. Heart irregularities, upper respiratory infections, hallucinations, paranoia, and an increase in violent behavior are often a problem with chronic cocaine users.
Precautions	Cocaine is a highly addictive and expensive habit. Smoking crack or free-basing cocaine dramatically increases the speed of addiction. Babies born to a mother who used cocaine during pregnancy are more likely to miscarry, have a higher rate of birth defects, and may be born addicted to the cocaine in the mother's system.
Addiction, Withdrawal, and Overdose	The neurological action of cocaine sets up a very strong tolerance and addiction pattern—cocaine addiction has the lowest recovery rate of any drug. Since cocaine depletes the body's natural pain reducers, it is required in increasing amounts just to feel normal. The euphoric, but short-lived effect of this drug, followed by a *decreased* sense of well-being once it has worn off, leads many people to use more and more of the drug. Anxiety, depression, headache, confusion, dry throat, dizziness, and fainting are the initial signs of overdose. Profuse perspiration, unconsciousness, and a weak, irregular pulse may be followed by respiratory or cardiac arrest.

Hallucinogens

Description	A group of drugs that changes visual and mental perceptions of internal and external realities. Drugs commonly included in this category include LSD (lysergic acid diethylamide), mescaline, peyote, psilocybin, DMT, STP, and Ecstasy.
Physical and Psychological Effects	Hallucinogens produce abnormal sensory feelings which are usually experienced visually in hallucinations or visual distortions. A "psychedelic trip" may produce great euphoria or deep depression and paranoia depending on a person's mental state, environment, and the content of the drug.
How It Works on the Brain	The chemical structure of LSD is very similar to the naturally occurring neurotransmitter, serotonin. LSD is extremely potent and fits into the receptor sites established for serotonin. The serotonin system is not well understood at this time, but it appears to have an important role in body temperature and sleep and waking. LSD may have some connection to a dream state.
Side Effects	Hallucinogens do not appear to be addictive, but their potency and distortion of reality can be very frightening. Most people who have experienced a "bad trip" are not anxious to use the drug again. Physical and emotional circumstances can result in accidents or suicide. Some LSD users have had a psychotic break while under the drug's influence or a more gradual development of schizophrenic symptoms.
Precautions	Panic attacks and flashbacks are not uncommon with the use of hallucinogens. A panic attack resembles temporary psychosis complete with hallucinations, delusions, and a high level of anxiety. A flashback is usually a visual image from a psychedelic trip that is reabsorbed and processed by the neuron long after the drug experience. This can be understandably unsettling.
Addiction, Withdrawal, and Overdose	There is no record of addiction or lethal overdose with hallucinogens. The panic attack described above is a form of overdose.

Club Drugs/Designer Drugs

Club or designer drugs are a variety of drugs that include stimulants, depressants, and/or hallucinogens often used at parties or clubs to heighten experience or interaction. The drugs included in this category are, by definition, trendy and changing. All-night dance parties, or "raves," may center on a particular drug. *Ecstasy* and *Rohypnol* are two current examples.

Ecstasy, or XTC, is a form of stimulant and hallucinogen that can produce an agitated state of awareness and pleasure. A form of methylphenidate, Ecstasy creates a rush of alertness and heightened senses. Less pleasant side effects may include mental confusion, insomnia, and paranoia. Ecstasy is usually taken in tablet or capsule form and can be slipped into beverages by individuals who want to intoxicate others—with or without their knowledge. *Liquid Ecstasy,* or GBH, may actually relax or sedate an individual and can also be secretly slipped into drinks to influence a person's mental state.

Rohypnol, or *roofies,* is a form of tranquilizer that can impair a person for eight to twelve hours, causing amnesia and low blood pressure. This is referred to as the "date rape drug" or "forget-me pill" for its ability to make an unsuspecting girl semiconscious, sexually compliant, and unable to remember what has happened to her. Rohypnol can also cause critical heart failure. The tasteless pill can be slipped into a drink at a bar or party, without any awareness of what the individual may already have in her system, or what her body can tolerate.

The existence of these colorless, tasteless, and odorless drugs, and the apparent willingness of some people to use them on others, makes it extremely important to party safely and remain alert and aware of your surroundings.

- *Know the people that you party with. Be cautious with strangers.*

- *Never put your drink or soda can down; hold on to it or throw it away.*

- *Have a buddy or good friend who will keep an eye on you and notice any unusual or suspicious behavior. Do the same for your friend.*

- *At clubs, concerts, or parties, never accept an opened drink from a stranger or even an acquaintance who you do not totally trust. Occasionally, even a friend may get intoxicated or high, and behave in ways you would not normally expect.*

Opiates

Description	The opiate drugs, primarily codeine, opium, morphine, and heroin, have been used for centuries to control pain, diarrhea, and coughing. The opium poppy is the natural source of opiates. Heroin is no longer legal in the U.S., but morphine and codeine are still used for medicinal purposes.
Physical and Psychological Effects	Heroin and the other opiates create an intense rush of euphoria and physical pleasure, though some initial users experience such extreme nausea and vomiting that they never want to use the drug again. After the initial rush, users "nod off" into a state of relaxation and dreamlike feelings of warmth, well-being, and peacefulness. Sensitivity to pain is reduced, breathing becomes shallow, and pupils of the eyes dilate.
How It Works on the Brain	The major active ingredient of the opiates is morphine. The morphine molecule closely resembles naturally occurring brain opiates which regulate our perception of pain and pleasure. Under stress, these endorphins are released into the bloodstream to help counter pain and suffering created by the stress. Opiates fit the receptor sites of the natural opiates and stimulate the release of these endorphins.
Side Effects	The drop in respiration, blood pressure, and temperature is a frequent cause of overdose and death among occasional users. Heroin users are much more prone to malnutrition, hepatitis, tuberculosis, and sexual infections because of the lifestyle often associated with heroin addiction.
Precautions	Opiates are highly addictive and pass through the placenta to the fetus. Babies born to addicted mothers experience similar addiction and withdrawal. Heroin addicts are the fastest growing group of new AIDS cases; the drug is most often taken intravenously under unsanitary conditions.
Addiction, Withdrawal, and Overdose	Tolerance for opiates develops quickly and withdrawal can be quite unpleasant, beginning as soon as eight to twelve hours after the drug-dependent person's last dose. The body quickly needs more and more of the drug in order to feel normal. Symptoms of withdrawal include restlessness, insomnia, chills, nausea, vomiting, and muscular aches. While not life-threatening, withdrawal can be extremely painful and go on for seven to ten days. Heroin addiction is difficult to kick, but current programs using Methadone (a less sedating replacement drug) and Naltrexone (an opiate-blocking drug) have been much more successful than previous efforts.

Prescription Drugs

Descriptions	Drugs used for medical purposes sometimes have mind-altering characteristics, may be addicting and, if used in excess, may cause a lethal overdose. These drugs, called *psychoactive drugs,* are regulated by a doctor's prescription and supervision, but may be misused or gotten illegally for nonmedical purposes. There are six categories of psychoactive drugs that are frequently abused: **Sedatives**—*Mebaral, Nebutal Sodium, Phenobarbital, Placidyl, Doriden* **Narcotics**—*Codeine, Darvon, Demerol, Percodan, Methadone, Morphine, Fiorinal* **Stimulants**—*Dexedrine, Ritalin, Cylert, Preludin, Fastin, Desoxyn, Biphetamine, Aderall* **Tranquilizers**—*Valium, Librium, Miltown, Xanax, Dalmane, Equanil, Tranxene* **Antidepressants**—*Elavil, Tofanil, Norpramin, Endep, Ludiomil, Vivactil* **Antipsychotics**—*Thorazine, Prolixin, Haldol, Tindal, Serentil, Stelazine*
Physical and Psychological Effects	Sedatives—relieve tension and stress, help sleep Narcotics—analgesic relief of pain, also sedative effects Stimulants—increase energy and alertness Tranquilizers—relieve minor tension and anxiety Antidepressants—relieve depression and anxiety Antipsychotics—control major mental illness
How It Works on the Brain	All of the psychoactive drugs work by either blocking certain receptor sites in the brain or overstimulating the release of natural neurotransmitters. Some drugs replace or enhance the endorphins in the brain to balance or alter brain chemistry.
Side Effects	Sedatives—drowsiness, skin rashes, lethargy, mild allergic-like reactions Narcotics—light-headedness, nausea, sweating Stimulants—nervousness, insomnia, dizziness, loss of appetite, restlessness Tranquilizers—drowsiness, dizziness, weakness, difficult concentrating Antidepressants—drowsiness, blurred vision, dry mouth, changes in heart rate Antipsychotics—drowsiness, dizziness, changes in blood pressure
Precautions:	Sedatives—do not mix with alcohol, antihistamines, or depressants, don't drive Narcotics—do not mix with alcohol or other sedatives, caution if you have respiratory problems Stimulants—don't use if heart disease, hypertension, hypothyroid, glaucoma Tranquilizers—do not mix with alcohol or other sedatives, don't drive Antidepressants—do not combine with alcohol or other sedatives Antipsychotics—do not mix with alcohol or other depressants, do not use if you have low blood pressure, or liver, heart, kidney, or Parkinson's disease.
Addiction, Withdrawal, and Overdose	**The biggest danger of prescription drugs is a false sense of safety because they are legally prescribed by a doctor.** These are powerful drugs that can interact with other drugs in lethal ways—combining tranquilizers with alcohol is the most common form of fatal overdose. <u>Adverse reactions to drug mixing or overdose should be treated at a hospital immediately</u>. All psychoactive drugs are also potentially addictive, particularly the tranquilizers, sedatives, narcotics, and stimulants.

Steroids

Description

Anabolic steroids are synthetic versions of testosterone. They can be taken either in pill form or by injection. There are many brand names for steroids and, since November 1990, they are legally available only by prescription for starvation or burn victims.

Physical and Psychological Effects

Steroids reduce muscle fatigue, increasing the amount of work muscles can do before breaking down. With exercise, muscles become bigger and stronger in just a few months. There is a sharp increase in aggressiveness and self-confidence combined with a quick temper, often known as "roid rage." In males, normal testosterone production is shut down. The testicles shrink and there is often noticeable breast growth. In females, the vocal cords thicken, breasts shrink, the clitoris becomes enlarged, and menstruation may stop. Acne, baldness, and increased facial hair is common in both males and females. Sexual energy is initially increased, but then falls to a gradual disinterest in sex.

How It Works on the Brain

Steroids bind to certain receptors in the brain. Flooded with these testosteronelike chemicals, the brain shuts down normal testosterone production. It also stops the growth of long bones, which in children and teenagers can permanently reduce final height.

Side Effects

Steroids have been shown to have some serious side effects. Strokes, heart and liver diseases, sexual dysfunction, high blood pressure, and aggressive, even violent, behavior have all been associated with steroid use. Chronic use has been shown to lower the immune system and reduce sperm count by an average of 73 percent. *Megarexia* is also common. Like anorexia, this is a distorted body image when a person thinks he looks "wimpy" no matter how much muscle he puts on. He can't get big enough and is plagued by fears of not being strong enough, often increasing his steroid use and exercise to the point of collapse.

Precautions

Like all intravenous drug use, individuals run the risk of AIDS if they use or share unclean needles.

Addiction, Withdrawal, and Overdose

It is still uncertain whether steroids are physically addictive, but people clearly get hooked on having a "superbody" and go through a difficult withdrawal period when they stop using steroids. Anxiety, irritability, loss of confidence, and serious depression are common.

USE AND ABUSE

Where's the Line?

Sometimes children from alcoholic homes think that alcoholism won't happen to them. They think they're going to be smarter than their parents and have enough will power and self-control to control their drinking. Becoming an alcoholic doesn't have anything to do with willpower or self-control. Becoming an alcoholic occurs when one has a physiological change in the body's tolerance for alcohol.

—Claudia Black

For many people, the line between use and abuse is very simple—any use at all is abuse. This is true of individuals who find drug use spiritually, medically, philosophically, or ethically inappropriate. Christian Scientists do not use any form of drug, including medicines, because they believe that chemicals interfere with a higher human consciousness and Spirit. Other religions believe that recreational drug use blunts the moral and spiritual fiber of a community, creating false gods and powers. Many doctors and biologists feel that the ingestion of any foreign chemicals is not healthy or wise. Other people prefer to live naturally, coping with problems and enjoying their life without the artificial aid of chemicals.

Alcoholics and other drug addicts know that for them, any use will quickly lead to abuse. They are not able to control their drug use because their body has a physical craving that will override any rational, social, or ethical decisions they might otherwise make. Children from alcoholic or drug-dependent families might wisely decide that the genetic risk is too high for them to experiment with drugs. Often, the damage and pain caused by the drug use of someone that they love is enough to make them choose a drug-free life.

While some people may use drugs without knowing the negative aspects of drug use, most people who do choose to use a drug attempt to weigh the pros and cons and use in moderation. As we have seen, however, it is sometimes difficult to personally recognize the difference between moderate social use and abuse or dependency. One of the primary defense mechanisms involved in drug use is ***denial.*** This is the process by which we protect ourselves from something by blocking it out of our awareness. Denial is automatic; it is done subconsciously. It operates below our level of awareness so we don't really know that we are denying anything. When we are in denial, we aren't lying to ourselves and others; we really don't believe something to be true. Denial presents itself in several ways:[25]

1. Simple Denial: *believing that something is not true which is indeed a fact and obvious to important others.*

2. Minimizing: *admitting to superficial aspects of the problem, but not willing to see it as serious.*

3. Blaming: *denying responsibility for behavior or drug use; fixing the blame on someone or something else.*

4. Rationalizing: *giving alibis, excuses, justifications, or other explanations for behavior.*

5. <u>Intellectualizing</u>: *theorizing or generalizing about the problem to avoid emotional, personal awareness.*

6. <u>Diversion</u>: *changing the subject to avoid discussing the problem.*

7. <u>Hostility</u>: *becoming angry or irritable to force the challenger to back off from the problem.*

It is very difficult to see these patterns in ourselves because, at the time, our defenses seem reasonable and true. You can probably think of a friend or family member who has used one or more of these forms of denial when confronted with their abuse of drugs. Denial is very useful in reducing the cognitive dissonance that we talked about earlier.

So, how can you know when you or a friend has passed the line between moderate social use and serious trouble? This is very tricky indeed. Serious trouble with drugs can come from *misuse, overuse,* or *addiction.*

Misuse includes any use of a drug at the wrong time or place for unhealthy reasons. *Do you have to sneak around and lie about your drug use? Do you break family, school, or legal rules in order to get and use drugs? Have you gotten into trouble with your family, friends, or authorities because of your drug use? Have you ever driven a car under the influence of a drug? Have drugs ever interfered with your ability or interest in other things you care about? Have drugs begun to dictate who you like to be with? Do you use drugs to avoid dealing with tough situations or feelings? Do you need drugs to relax and have a good time? Have drugs become your primary source of recreation and social interaction?*

Overuse includes both how often and how much of a drug you are using. Daily or regular weekend use of drugs can easily set up lifetime habits of psychological or physical dependency. Ingesting too much of any chemical can be lethal even to a first-time user. *Do you find that drugs are a regular part of your daily or weekly routine? Do you always include drugs in any social or recreational activity? Do you often use more than you intended? When was the last time you said no when offered a drug? When you do use a drug, do you tend to get "loaded"? Does it seem to take more of a drug to get you high than it used to? How much of your money do you spend on drugs? Have you ever been so intoxicated that you could not control yourself? Have you ever had a "blackout" or been unable to remember what you did when you were high? Have you ever had sex while under the influence that you later regretted or were embarrassed about? Has anyone ever taken advantage of you sexually while you were under the influence? Have you ever been involved in an accident or near accident because of your drug use?*

Addiction or *chemical dependency* is a physiological disease—a physical craving for a particular drug that will outweigh almost every other consideration. Alcoholics and drug addicts frequently choose their drug over health, common sense, success, their values, and the people that they love. Some people appear to be more prone to addiction than oth-

Cocaine is God's way of telling someone they make too much money.
—Robin Williams

Addiction is a physical problem no different from diarrhea. It's a compulsion you cannot control. Will power has nothing to do with it.
—Dr. Michael Stone

ers. Like an allergy, some people simply cannot take a drink or use drugs without craving more. It tends to run in families and can be generalized from one drug to another. Stress, poor communication skills, and low self-esteem appear to contribute to a person's vulnerability.

Chemical dependency is a chronic and progressive disease. That means that it develops slowly over a period of time and gets worse and worse. As people have begun using drugs at an earlier age, it has been discovered that young people, during the time that their bodies are growing and changing, actually develop addictions at a much faster rate than adults. Teenagers can become full-blown alcoholics in two or three years when it generally takes ten to fifteen years in an adult. Cocaine addiction takes an average of four to four and a half years in an adult, but only fifteen and a half months for a teenager. Once a body develops an addiction, it appears to remain a part of its chemical makeup whether a person is using or not. Smokers, alcoholics, or other drug addicts tend to pick up right where they left off even after years of abstinence. Once addicted, an individual can never use that drug without reexperiencing the previous level of addiction.

Some signs of a developing chemical dependency are:

- *Unexplained mood swings*

- *Lying or denial of drug problem if confronted*

- *Change in values or interests*

- *Strain on intimate relationships—family or friends*

- *Increased irritation and agitation*

- *Increased defensiveness*

- *Increase in erratic or socially inappropriate behavior*

- *Increased absences of dropping out of activities*

- *Increased forgetfulness and disorganization*

- *Preoccupation with drug use and availability*

Alcoholism stunted my growth, both musically and in a human way. My ability to deal with close relationships is severely limited by the fact that I spent all my formative years completely anesthetized.
—*Eric Clapton*

The problem with the signs of chemical dependency is that the chemical dependent is usually the last to recognize them. He can deny or explain away any symptom in his own behavior. To acknowledge that there is a problem suggests a need to do something about it. That is why in meetings of Alcoholics Anonymous, speakers begin by identifying themselves as an alcoholic—"I'm Mary. I'm an alcoholic." This is recognition of the critical need to overcome denial. If a person is physically or psychologically addicted to a drug, she will avoid anything that may interfere with her use of that drug—her body needs it and she wants it, no matter what. As the disease progresses and the need becomes stronger, this avoidance of the problem becomes greater. While it is easiest to treat an addiction when it first begins, most addicts tend to "hit bottom" or get to the point where their life is such a mess that they can no longer deny the problem.

Looking at Myself[26]

One of the ways that you can look at your own drug use and evaluate its role in your life is to look at its consequences in your day-to-day life. Subtle changes may have occurred without your noticing. Putting it all together may help you see a pattern that is not what you had intended. Try to respond to this inventory as honestly as you can. Your responses are confidential and their interpretation is up to you. You may want to share your answers with a good friend to see if he agrees with your assessment. If you don't use at all, just skip over this exercise!

_____   I tend to hang out with other users.

_____   I am more comfortable socially when I am using.

_____   One of my close friends thinks I use too much.

_____   Some people at school think I'm a "druggie."

_____   At least one friend has dropped me because of my use.

_____   I've let friends down because I was under the influence.

_____   Most of my friends don't know how much I use.

_____   I use as much or more than most of my friends.

_____   Almost all of my social activities involve drugs.

_____   I am not as interested in sports or hobbies since I started using.

_____   I have the most fun when I am high.

_____   I seem to have more friends and acceptance since I started using.

_____   I have changed my regular routines to fit my drug use.

_____   I have broken promises I have made regarding my drug use.

_____   Most of my money goes to drug-related activities.

_____   I am usually broke because most of my money goes to drugs.

_____   I owe people money or favors for drugs.

_____   I sometimes have to scrounge for money to get the drugs I want.

_____   I have taken advantage of my friends or family in order to get drugs.

_____   I have stolen from my family to get drug money.

_____   I have sold drugs to friends in order to get money for my own.

_____   I have done things while using that I am ashamed of.

_____   I have lied to my parents or friends about my drug use.

_____   I have hurt my parents or friends with my drug use.

_____   My relationship with my parents has gotten worse since I started using.

_____   My parents don't seem to trust me now that I use drugs.

_____   My parents have no idea how much I use.

_____   I don't enjoy being with my family much since I started using.

_____   My parents are always worried or nagging about my drug use.

_____   My brother or sister is worried about my drug use.

_____   My family doesn't seem to understand me much since I started using.

_____   I have been in trouble at school because of my drug use.

_____   My grades have gotten worse since I started using.

_____   I have gone to class or taken a test while high.

_____   An adult at school is concerned about my drug use.

_____   At least one person has suggested that I should get help for my chemical use.

_____   I sometimes get really depressed.

_____   I have considered suicide once or more during or after my drug use.

_____   I have gotten really angry or violent with friends or family when I was high.

_____   I am tired of people bugging me about my drug use.

_____   I tend to get pretty angry and defensive about my drug use.

_____   Sometimes I do worry about my own use.

_____   I seem to be using more and enjoying it less.

_____   I have been in trouble with the law because of my drug use.

_____   I don't use any more than anybody else, but I always seem to get busted.

_____   My memory isn't as good as it was before I started using.

_____   I have been in an accident as a result of my drug use.

_____   I seem to be more accident-prone since I started using.

_____   I have been really sick or hung over as a result of my drug use.

_____   I seem to get sick more often since I have been using.

_____   I have driven when under the influence of drugs.

_____   I have scared myself by some things I have done while using.

_____   I sometimes worry that I might accidentally overdose.

_____   I sometimes use before I go to a party or meet my friends.

_____   I have used before or during school.

_____   I sometimes mix drugs in order to get high.

_____   I am always willing to try a new drug even if I don't know much about it.

_____   I have used one drug to come down from another.

Alcoholism and other drug addictions are physical diseases which usually require both medical and psychological intervention. You may be able to quit on your own before the disease gets too advanced, but full-blown addictions are difficult to treat even with professional help. There are many good treatment centers that help teenagers and adults live with sobriety. Most programs include regular participation in support groups such as Alcoholics Anonymous (AA) or Narcotics Anonymous (NA).

The AA preamble states *"Alcoholics Anonymous is a fellowship of men and women who share their experience, strength and hope with each other that they may solve their common problem and help others to recover from alcoholism. The only requirement for membership is a desire to stop drinking."* First started in 1935 in Akron, Ohio, there are now chapters of Alcoholics Anonymous throughout the world with many meetings every day of the week. The groups share leadership, are fully self-supporting, and never endorse, finance, or lend their name to any outside enterprise. There are small, closed meetings which are open only to persons who are personally dealing with addictions. There are also larger speaker meetings which anyone may attend. Most colleges have a chapter of AA or NA. Attending an AA meeting is a good way to better understand the personal side of chemical dependency and perhaps evaluate your own use. You can get a listing of local chapters and meeting times by calling the AA office listed in the phone book or classified ads.

Breaking an Addiction—Ways to Quit Smoking

Smoking is one of the most dangerous and difficult drugs to be addicted to. It is legal, available, and easily becomes an habitual part of your everyday life. Smoking is the leading cause of lung cancer, emphysema, and other lung diseases, but it is a hard addiction to break. Here are some suggestions from the American Lung Association.[27]

- Figure out why you smoke—for stimulation, something to do with your hands, pleasurable relaxation, psychological addiction, habit.

- Ask yourself why you want to quit—health reasons, to have more energy, to feel more in control, has become socially awkward, better sense of taste and smell, get rid of smoker's cough, feel stronger, etc.

- Buy only one pack at a time. Don't buy a new one until you are completely out.

- Keep a record of each cigarette you smoke. Notice what triggers your craving.

- Avoid situations that trigger your smoking craving.

- Try slow, deep breathing whenever you want a cigarette. It reduces tension and will give you something to do until the craving passes.

- Find alternatives to smoking. When you have a craving, doodle, take a walk, chew on carrots or celery, stretch, exercise, work on a hobby, play solitaire, work on a project, exercise with handgrippers, drink water, chew gum, or find something else you can do to keep busy until the craving passes.

- Make smoking difficult for yourself. Smoke with your other hand or put your cigarettes in an inconvenient place.

- Start exercising regularly. It will reduce tension, keep extra weight off, and make you feel better.

- Begin to visualize yourself free of smoking—think of yourself as a nonsmoker.

- Brush your teeth after every meal—it's a great substitute for smoking.

- Reward yourself for not smoking. Think of things you would like to have or do and reward yourself with them when you successfully go without smoking. Make the rewards in proportion to what you achieve—a special bubble bath at the end of a cigarette-free day or a day of skiing as a reward for a whole week without smoking.

- Be prepared for some withdrawal symptoms and know you can get through them. Some things you might experience include: increased coughing (your lungs are cleaning themselves), constipation, lack of concentration, fatigue, headache, slight sore throat, nervousness, trouble sleeping. All these annoyances will pass. Remember, *it only takes a week to get the nicotine out of your system.*

- Change brands—switch to a brand lower in tar and nicotine. Keep switching lower and lower.

- Figure out how much you will save in a year by not smoking.

- Start smoking less of each cigarette.

- Start a butt jar—save all your cigarette butts in a large glass jar and keep it where you can see it as a reminder of what an ugly habit you are getting rid of. If you need more evidence, open it and take a whiff now and then.

- Delay five minutes before having a cigarette—you may change your mind. The urge passes whether you smoke or not.

- Stop carrying matches and lighters. Make yourself really scrounge around for a light.

- Get rid of any smoking accessories.

- Don't empty your ashtrays so often—keep them as a reminder of how much you have been smoking.

- Don't do anything else when you smoke—no TV, reading, drinking coffee, talking with friends. Go off on your own and have your smoke.

- Drink a lot of water and juices to flush the nicotine out of your system faster.

- Take things one day at a time. Don't worry about not smoking tomorrow, just get through today.

- Remember, just one cigarette will hurt. It can undo all your hard work. Once addicted, one cigarette will start the craving all over again.

- Review your reasons for quitting and reward yourself for your progress.

- Try going to places where you can't smoke; get together with nonsmoking friends.

- Start banking your savings. Put your old cigarette money in a jar and plan for something you want to buy with it at the end of one year.

Drugs and Driving

More people have died in drug-related automobile accidents in the United States than died in all of the U.S. wars since 1775. Alcohol-related accidents are the major cause of death for people under twenty-one years of age, and many innocent bystanders or passengers are killed by drunk drivers every year. Through organizations such as Students Against Drunk Drivers, teenagers have been one of the leading forces against drunk driving in the United States.

The difficulty with drinking and trying to decide if one is capable of driving is that under the influence, we are "high" and sure we can perform well when, in fact, we have cerebral and motor impairment.
—Dr. Joseph Zuska

It is important to realize that not only alcohol, but other drugs, including prescription and some over-the-counter drugs, can seriously impair driving ability—particularly when combined with alcohol. Cold, sinus, or hay fever medications can cause drowsiness which can seriously slow your reaction time and thinking abilities. Marijuana interferes with perception and attention processes—two very important skills in driving. Combined with alcohol, marijuana sharply reduces judgment and performance. Since the THC remains in the brain for days, even weeks, studies have shown that intoxication can return for no apparent reason long after the initial high. This makes the effects of marijuana on driving quite unpredictable.

Impairment of motor skills and increased reaction time occurs at alcohol levels slightly above .05 before there are any visible danger signs. Above this level, your vigilance and accuracy are reduced, your reaction time is significantly shortened, and your short-term memory is impaired. Long before your physical skills are affected, your ability to process complex images and information and make quick decisions is significantly weakened.

Each individual will respond differently to the same level of alcohol in different situations. In general, it takes your body one hour to process one drink. One drink is the equivalent to 12 oz. of beer, 3 oz. of wine, or 1.5 oz. of whiskey. While the amount you drink is certainly a factor, your level of intoxication will also depend on how quickly you drink, your body weight and height, and the amount and kinds of food you have eaten. Milk, cheese, or fatty food will slow down the time it takes for alcohol to get into your blood. Remember too that females do not naturally have the alcohol absorption enzyme, alcohol dehydrogenase, in their stomachs so that more alcohol will reach their bloodstream. Anger appears to heighten alcohol's debilitating effects. Studies have shown that drunk-driving accidents often follow stressful arguments and that individuals who are quick to anger when intoxicated are more likely to have driving accidents.

Drinking coffee, eating, deep breathing, exercise, cold showers, or taking a stimulant will *not* make you sober even though you may *feel* more alert. **You need to wait at least one hour per drink after your last drink before you are ready to drive.** Better yet, don't drink at all if you need to drive or have a designated driver who does not drink. Make a deal with your parents that they will pick you up if you are ever in an unsafe situation and that you will do the same for them. Also, don't forget if you have taken any prescription drugs. Their effect when combined with alcohol will be much stronger than either drug alone.

In most states, it is illegal to have a bottle of alcohol which has been opened, its seal broken, or contents partially removed in a moving vehicle unless it is in the trunk. Any adult who serves a minor or allows alcohol to be served to minors in their home, *whether they know it or not*, can be charged with contribution to the delinquency of minors and held responsible for any death or damage incurred.

CODEPENDENCY AND ENABLING

Love and Addictions

By the time someone becomes addicted to a drug, her perception of the problem is distorted by the drug and her physical need to continue. In the beginning, it is often the people who love her the most who are affected. Her behavior often becomes erratic and undependable; she may seem irritable and preoccupied. A beautiful, loving mother may become a sloppy, abusive drunk. A much admired older brother may become aloof and always in trouble. A best friend may start preferring other company and become undependable and hostile. To the child or friend, it becomes painfully apparent that the drug has become more important than their relationship.

> *We estimate that there are twelve to fifteen million children under eighteen living in alcoholic homes today.*
> —Claudia Black

Most of us try to hang on to the relationship in spite of the pain and rejection. Chemically dependent people make a lot of promises and we believe them. *It won't happen again. Dad is just having a bad day. If you would just stop hassling me, I'd want to spend more time with you.* We try to be nicer, more understanding, less worried, stronger, and more lovable. Sometimes, we even start using with them. Afraid that the chemically dependent person will get angry and actually leave us, we start denying our own feelings and pain. *I'm sure he didn't mean to hurt my feelings. It doesn't really matter. It's just a phase. She doesn't really drink more than anyone else and who can blame her anyway?* It is very difficult to think of someone we know and love as "AN ALCOHOLIC" or "DRUG ADDICT." Those are labels that apply to people in movies or strangers or bums on the street, not to someone we know. Like the chemical dependent, we begin to deny, distort, avoid, and rationalize the problem. And perhaps even more than the chemical dependent who has his drug to medicate the discomfort, we are in a lot of pain.

Children and loved ones of chemical dependents develop a set of unhealthy defenses to protect themselves from this pain and rejection. Because the chemical makes his parent, sibling, friend, or lover emotionally unavailable and unpredictable, he develops a "crazy" set of beliefs about himself and relationships. By lying and denying his own feelings, he becomes what is often called *codependent.* Some of the rules learned in this type of dysfunctional relationship are:

> *You're codependent for sure when you wake up in the morning and say to your family: Good morning, How am I?*
> —Jann Mitchell

- *Don't feel or talk about your feelings.*

- *Don't think, figure things out, or make decisions—you don't know what you want or what is best for you.*

- *Don't identify or mention problems—it is not OK to have them.*

- *Be good, right, perfect, and strong.*

- *Don't be who you are because that is not good enough.*

- *Don't be selfish—always take care of others, never hurt their feelings or make them angry.*

- *Don't have fun, be silly, or enjoy life—it costs money, makes noise, or isn't necessary.*

- *Don't trust yourself, others, or your Higher Power.*

- *Don't be open, honest, or direct—hint, manipulate, get others to talk for you, guess what others want and need, and expect them to do the same for you.*

- *Don't get too close to people—it isn't safe.*

- *Don't disrupt things by growing or changing.*

Alcoholism and the Family

Alateen is an organization that supports teenagers who have an alcoholic family member or close friend. It is sometimes hard to realize that the alcoholic's behavior has affected your own life and stability—family members often experience the same type of denial that alcoholics assume. Here are some questions that Alateen suggests to think about in evaluating your relationships and well-being.[28]

1. Do you have a parent or sibling whose alcohol use is upsetting you?

2. Does it seem like every holiday or family outing is spoiled by someone's drinking?

3. Do you tell lies to cover up for someone's drinking or what is happening in your home?

4. Are you afraid or embarrassed to bring your friends home?

5. Do you ever feel that if this person really loved you, he would stop drinking?

6. Do you ever feel that if you were just better, smarter, better behaved this person would stop drinking?

7. Does this person sometimes break promises to you or let you down?

8. Are you afraid to upset this person for fear it will make her drink more?

9. Do you cover up your feelings by pretending that you don't care?

10. Do you often feel depressed or down on yourself?

11. Do you often feel confused and worried about what is happening in your family?

12. Have you ever feared for your own safety or the safety of other members of your family?

13. Do you often feel guilty or apologetic?

14. Do you ever feel that alcohol is more important to this person than you are?

15. Have you ever tried to control this person's drinking by hiding the car keys, pouring liquor down the drain, watering down the liquor, etc.?

Every family has its problems, but healthy families work together openly to talk and work things out. It is OK to talk about feelings and problems in an atmosphere where each member is emotionally connected and respected. When alcohol or drug use threatens these basic love relationships, there are lots of secrets and unspoken feelings. **One of the things that we do is to try to protect the person we love from the negative consequences of his use.**

We try not to get upset with him when he lies or disappoints us. We even try to believe him when we know he is lying or will not follow through on what he says. We may cover up for his use by hiding the evidence or making excuses for him or protecting him from getting into trouble. Most of all, we silently agree not to talk about the problem and convince ourselves that everything is really OK when we know it is not. This is called *enabling*. It is usually done out of love or a desire to protect someone we love or out of a fear of losing or annoying the user. In effect, however, it enables the user to continue to use without feeling the negative consequences of her use and thereby learning and changing her behavior.

In families where a chemical dependency is well established, there is usually a set of roles that different individuals assume in order to keep the dysfunctional family afloat. People may shift roles from time to time and, in smaller families, individuals may take on more than one role depending on the circumstances. Everyone is unconsciously doing her part to try to keep the family from falling apart.

One of the most deceptive roles in the family is the **family hero.** His job is to make everything look OK. He is very hardworking and successful. He takes charge and makes sure that everyone is taken care of. If Mom is too drunk to fix dinner, he does it. If his younger sister is getting into trouble with the law or at school, he is on the honor roll and the star quarterback. He goes to the best schools, works at the best jobs, and is always in control. *See, we couldn't have a drug problem in the family, look at Johnny!* Underneath, Johnny feels confused and inadequate. No matter how wonderful he tries to be, the problem doesn't really go away. He often feels hurt, lonely, and never really happy no matter what he accomplishes.

Since there is no way to compete with the glory of the family hero, the second child often becomes the **family scapegoat.** Her job is to draw the fire and explain away all of the tension in the family. She is angry, withdrawn, defiant, and always in trouble. The black sheep of the family, she breaks rules, challenges authority, may be sexually promiscuous, and often becomes a drug user herself. *If it weren't for Susie, everything would be just fine. She's the problem if there is one!* Underneath, Susie feels hurt, rejected, and afraid. She tries to find comfort outside of the family and is usually misunderstood and punished or treated as *the* problem.

Another role that usually occurs amidst this uproar is the **lost child.** This person just hides and causes no trouble. His job is to give everyone a break from the action. He is the perfect example of *denial*—he doesn't see anything, hear anything, or feel anything. He often stays to himself, alone in his room or with his books or a favorite pet. He may be overweight and prone to minor illness. He tends to be quiet, independent, and a loner—in fact, people tend to forget he is even around. *Oh yeah, where is Billy anyway?* Underneath, he is extremely lonely, angry, and hurt with no way to express these feelings. He often has difficulty forming relationships inside or outside the family.

The youngest child is often adopted as the **family pet.** Her job is to keep everyone laughing and avoiding the problem. She's cute, funny, and too

> *The problem with denial is that everyone has the same answer. If you DO have a drug problem, you will probably deny it and say you don't. If you DON'T have a drug problem, you will probably deny it and say you don't. It is often very hard to tell the difference.*

fragile, young, or innocent to know what's really going on. Everyone tries to protect her and hide things from her, so she has all of the underlying feelings and none of the facts. She will do anything for attention and is often hyperactive. She can be delightful, but no one tends to take her very seriously. *Oh, Mary Belle, what a silly little lady you are! Just run along and play now.* Underneath, Mary Belle feels scared, confused, and lonely. She doesn't know what will happen to her if everyone stops laughing.

So what can *you* do if you believe that someone you love is developing a serious problem with their drug use?

Well, you can't make them stop and, most likely, you won't be able to simply reason with them. They probably don't see the problem and will get angry or lie if you try to interfere. The first thing you can do is to **STOP ENABLING.** Don't cover up or make excuses for her behavior. Don't lend him money for drugs or take over his responsibilities while he is using. Let him clean up his own messes. Tell her that you are worried about her and that you think she has a problem. Don't believe his lies and do let him know when he has hurt or disappointed you.

If your friend or relative thanks you and stops using, that's wonderful, but don't hold your breath. **BE PREPARED FOR DENIAL** and be ready to put up with some abuse. The person will probably tell you that you are crazy and offer a wide range of excuses and promises. Don't buy it. Stick to your guns, citing specific incidents and concerns. Don't let that person redefine your perceptions or tell you how you feel. She may get angry and blame you for the problem. You may even lose the friendship for a while. Addiction is a disease and usually requires professional treatment or intervention. Your goal is to stop enabling and help get your loved one to treatment. When a parent, sibling, or friend gets hostile at your confrontation, it is difficult to keep trying and keep caring. Remember, you are fighting a powerful addiction. **Once in recovery, people often cite the concern and honesty of one brave friend that started them thinking.** It may take a while to sink in, but don't let your concerns go unspoken.

> *God, grant me the serenity to accept the things I cannot change, courage to change the things I can, and wisdom to know the difference.*
> —Serenity Prayer

If a friend or relative has undergone treatment for her addiction, she will need you more than ever to remain drug free—a difficult task in today's alcohol and drug using society. **RECOGNIZE AND SUPPORT YOUR FRIEND'S EFFORTS TO CONTROL HER ADDICTION.** Attend an AA or NA meeting with her to help you better understand the struggle. Know that *any* use will quickly lead to abuse and support her efforts not to use at all. Avoid places with your friend where others will be using drugs. Join her in drug-free activities. If you are going to a concert where you know there will be use, join her in abstaining for the evening. At Grateful Dead concerts there was an AA group called the Wharf Rats for alcoholics who want to enjoy the music without using drugs. Help your friend rebuild nondrug-using friendships and explore drug-free ways of having fun, relaxing, and finding meaning in life. Your friendship may help you evaluate and think about the role of drugs in your own life.

The last thing that you can do is to **TAKE CARE OF YOURSELF.** It is painful and confusing to love someone who is chemically dependent, especially if it is a parent or sibling. You may convince yourself that you don't care or aren't really affected by it, but the damage usually goes much deeper. Children of alcoholics tend to marry alcoholics and many become alcoholics themselves. The unspoken fears and insecurities of loving an addict can unconsciously affect your future relationships and your deeper feelings about yourself. Groups such as Alateen and Adult Children of Alcoholics meet to help break some of the cycles of codependency and addiction.

Do-It-Yourself Quandary

Identify an important dilemma related to the brain or chemicals in our culture today that was not discussed in this chapter.

- *What factors make this issue particularly complicated or difficult to resolve?*

- *What values or ethical considerations are involved?*

- *What solutions or choices are available?*

Dear Quandary Master . . .

Here are some letters asking for advice and information about some drug-related situations. Make your answers as realistic and helpful as possible. Be sure to include any relevant information or resources that might be helpful.

#1.

Dear Quandary Master,

Please take this letter seriously because I am really in a bind. A good friend of mine has been pretty heavy into drugs for over a year now—mostly pot, but some downers and some coke. It has put a strain on our friendship, but I figure that it's his life and he has to make his own decisions. We've been friends for a long time and have an unspoken pact that we respect each other's differences. Yesterday, we went surfing together and as I was getting my stuff out of his trunk, I knocked over his backpack and a bag full of pills and another bag of white powder fell out— way more than he could use. To make a long story short, he admitted that he is dealing the stuff. He says he's not dealing at school because he doesn't want to get into trouble, but he has a few connections just to make some extra cash. One of his "connections" is at the junior high. Maybe I am old-fashioned, but I think what he is doing is wrong. He got pretty mad at me and said if they didn't buy it from him, they'd buy it from someone else; at least he made sure they got clean stuff. When I talked to my girlfriend about it last night, she told me it was none of my business and I'd better stay out of it. I know what she means, but it just doesn't feel right. What should I do?

Signed, Frantic Friend

#2.

Dear Quandary Master,

Help! My parents are all excited about throwing a big sweet-sixteen party for me at our beach house. They have hired a great band and are going to a lot of trouble to provide lots of food and have agreed to let several of my friends spend the night. The two rules they set down are no booze and no crashers. I only told a couple of my close friends, but by the time I got to school, people were coming up to me saying they'd heard about the great party. When I tried to tell them it was just a private party with no alcohol, they winked and said "No problem, we'll bring our own." My friends are cool, but at this point, half the state seems to be psyched for this party. The whole thing is out of control. I am dreading the party and my parents can't figure out why I'm not more excited. They have gone to a lot of trouble and expense for me. What can I do?

Signed, Party Patsy

#3.

Dear Quandary Master,

In spite of what most adults seem to think, there really isn't any peer pressure to use drugs at my school. Sure, a lot of kids do, but nobody twists your arm to join them and everyone respects your decision if you choose not to. I am not interested in drinking or taking any other drugs and that is cool with my friends. I was elected class president, am a decent athlete, and have lots of friends. In spite of all this, my decision does put me in a bind sometimes. Most of the parties do involve drinking and sometimes I am not invited because my friends know I'm not into that. When I do go, I usually have a good time and am quite popular as a designated driver.

To tell you the truth, though, it does get pretty boring being around a bunch of wasted people. Their jokes aren't very funny and they do some pretty stupid things. I really like these guys when they are sober, but it is just not much fun being with them when they are drinking. There are other guys who don't drink, but they aren't really my close friends. I don't know whether to just stay home and feel left out or go to the parties and feel out of it. Maybe I should loosen up and have a drink, but I really don't want to do that either. Any suggestions?

Signed, Straight Stanley

#4.

Dear Quandary Master,

My parents have laid down the law that I am not to go to any party where there are drugs or alcohol until I am out of high school. They don't seem to realize that they are condemning me to social isolation for the next three years. My friends are not druggies, but there really isn't any such thing as a drug-free party at my school. There are plenty that don't serve alcohol, but everyone brings their own. I drink a little bit, but I can control myself and don't have any trouble dealing with the party scene.

The trouble is that my older brother screwed up big time with drugs when he was in high school and my parents think they can protect me by being extra strict. In fact, it is just making me feel more rebellious. I have to lie to them just to be with my friends. I know that they are worried about me, but I'm not my brother and I can handle myself. They are not being realistic and it is not fair that I should pay for my brother's mistakes. If I try to reason with them and tell them what things are really like today, they will ground me forever. Help! I hate lying to them, but what else can I do?

Signed, Jailed Jenny

#5.

Dear Quandary Master,

My problem isn't really mine—it's my mom. She's a great lady . . . when she's sober. As a kid, I was so proud of her. She was always the best mom. She's really beautiful and funny and so easy to talk to. She was always there for me whether it was a school play or homemade cookies when I got home from school or just to talk to when I felt hurt or lonely. Then she and Dad got divorced, and she started drinking a lot more. I felt bad for her at first. Then I would be embarrassed when she showed up at school or a game drunk. I felt hurt and angry when she would forget to pick me up from a friend's house and I would have to make all kinds of excuses. Last year, she completely forgot my birthday.

Now I am just worried. She stays away for days at a time and I don't know if she is dead or alive. One time my dad had to pick her up at the police station for a DWI. I have actually taken parts out of the car motor so that she won't be able to drive. I hide her booze and drain it down the toilet, but she always finds more. My dad has tried to get her into treatment, but she won't go. He says that I should come live with him until she gets help, but I can't leave her alone. I am all she has left. What if she falls down the stairs again and there is no one there to help her? She was always there for me when I was little. I've got to be here for her now. But I don't know what to do. I just want my old mom back.

Signed, Desperate David

#6.

Dear Quandary Master,

Nobody would believe this letter is from me. Everyone thinks that I am totally carefree and spacey, not a worry in the world. I get into trouble a lot, but nothing big, just lots of little stuff—late papers, forgot my assignment, lost my book, missed a class, late for practice. My grades are all over the place—I'll ace a test one day and totally blow it the next. Some classes, I'll do fine on the test, but get a C because I forgot to turn in my homework. My teachers don't think it is so funny, but my friends just think I'm an airhead. I get in trouble with them too, when I forget to pick somebody up or I say something stupid without thinking, but they just roll their eyes like "what can you expect?" I laugh, but I am tired of looking like such an idiot. I am <u>not</u> stupid, but I can't seem to stick to one thing at a time or finish anything I start. I get all excited about Save the Whales and then the next week, I am taking up rock climbing and forget the poor whales. Sometimes I just sit and stare at my homework and can't get started, or I'll be reading a book and realize I have no idea what I read for the last five pages.

I try to act like none of this bothers me, but I am constantly worried about what I am going to screw up next. I am not a bad guy, but sometimes I get really depressed about it cause I just don't know what to do. Don't tell me to get organized—believe me, I've tried and it doesn't work.

Signed, Absentminded Al

#7.

Dear Quandary Master,

I'm not a teenager, but I definitely have a quandary. I am forty years old and my oldest daughter, Violet, is sixteen. She is bright and talented, and her mom and I are very proud of her. But something seems wrong. Violet is usually pretty easygoing, but over the last three or four months, she seems to flair up over any little thing. Her grades are still good, but she has started complaining about her teachers, and seems to have dropped all the activities at school that she used to love. When I ask, she just says they are lame, and she wants more time to practice her guitar and study. She has a boyfriend that I worry about too. Nice enough guy, but he is two years older, is a skinhead, plays in a band, and just waves from his SUV with that gangster rap playing when he comes to pick her up. I've told her to ask him over, but she just makes this face and says he's real busy.

I've tried to sit down and talk with her, but it seems she is pretty busy, too. This morning, her mom was doing the laundry and came across a small hash pipe in Violet's jacket pocket. She called me right away, and the two of us don't know what to do next. Obviously, we will talk to her, but she will probably say she was holding it for a friend or something. I would like to believe that, but I think I have known better for a while—I just didn't want to face up to it. We love her so much. I hate it when she gets angry and shuts me out, but I am worried and feel like I need to do something. What can I do that won't drive her even further away? How can I help?

Signed, Scared Dad

WEB SITES

Alcohol

www.health.org

www.casacolumbia.org

www.samhsa.gov/csap

www.edc.org/hec

www.jointogether.org

www.madd.org

www.alcoholics-anonymous.org/index.html

www.al-anon-alateen.org

www.health.org/nacoa

www.askpri.org

The Brain

www.mindtools.com

http://faculty.washington.edu/chudler/facts.html

www.epub.org.br/cm

www.exploratorium.edu/memory/index.html

www.dana.org

www.nimh.nih.gov

www.findarticles.com/m1511/n8 v19/20979819/p1/article.jhtml

www.sfn.org/briefings/estrogen.html

www.neuroskills.com/index.html?main=tbi/brain.html

www.omnimag.com/live science
www.abcnews.go.com/sections/science/DailyNews/einstein990617.html

Drugs

www.health.org/index.htm
www.nida.nih.gov
www.DrugAbuseStatistics.samhsa.gov
http://content.health.msn.com/drugs
www.drugfreeamerica.org
www.tfy.drugsense.org/think.htm
www.habitsmart.com
www.ojp.usdoj.gov/bjs/drugs.htm
www.onlinerecovery.org/na
www.dancesafe.org/sideshow
www.dpf.org

Learning Disabilities/ADHD

www.adhd.kids.tripod.com
www.chadd.org
www.ncld.org
www.add.org/index.html
www.addvance.com *(women and girls)*
www.allkindsofminds.org

Marijuana

www.commonlink.com/~olsen/MEDICAL/journals.html
www.marijuana-anonymous.org/index.shtml
www.newscientist.com/nsplus/insight/drugs/marijuana/
www.healthcentral.com/Centers/OneCenter.cfm?Center=Marijuana

Smoking

www.cancer.org
www.cancernet.nci.hih.gov
www.infact.org
www.stat.org
www.kickbutt.org
www.cdc.gov/tobacco/tips4youth.htm

---

[1]Ornstein, R., and R. Thompson. *The Amazing Brain.* Boston: Houghton Mifflin Company, 1984, p. 21.

[2]Ibid., p. 166.

[3]BBC News Online, Friday, June 18, 1999. Published at 12:23 GMT 13:23 UK.

[4]Adapted from *Is the Mind an Illusion? Newsweek* magazine, April 20, 1992, p. 71.

[5]Department of Health and Human Services, University of Michigan's Survey Research Center, December 1998.

[6]Rublowsky, John. *The Stoned Age: A History of Drugs in America.* New York: G. P. Putnam's Sons, 1974.

[7]Gold, Mark S., M.D. *The Facts About Drugs and Alcohol.* New York: Bantam Books, 1988.

[8]*Webster's College Dictionary,* Random House, 1991.

[9]Aronson, Elliot. *The Social Animal.* San Francisco: W.H. Freeman and Company, 1972.

[10]Ibid., p. 90.

[11]Jones and Kohler. The effects of plausibility on the learning of controversial statements. *Journal of Abnormal and Social Psychology*, 1958.

[12]Questions compiled from Human Development students at Cate School, Carpinteria, California, 1990.

[13]News release from Attorney General Dan Lungren, California Department of Justice, December 3, 1996.

[14]U.S. v. Oakland Cannabis Buyers' Cooperative, A-145.

[15]www.usdoj.gov/dea/pubs/savit/myths.htm. Talking Points for Challenging the Medical Use of Marijuana Argument.

[16]Ibid., The Medical and Scientific Evidence.

[17]Ibid., The Medical and Scientific Evidence.

[18]Social and Cultural Issues.

[19]Gallup Poll News Service, conducted March 21, 1999, as reported in the National Journal, April 10, 1999.

[20]Statement on the Medical Use of Marijuana in Support of Maryland Senate Bill 705, NORML.

[21]From the Department of Psychiatry, Harvard Medical School, and the Massachusetts Mental Health Center, Boston, JAMA, June 21, 1995, Vol. 273, No. 23, 1875.

[22]www.norml.org/laws/statement_md_2001_app_a.shtml; Appendix A: Partial List of Organizations Supporting "Supervised Access" to Medical Marijuana.

[23]Stated underlying premise for the NORML 2001 Conference, Washington, D.C., April 9–21, 2001.

[24]Jones and Kohler, The effects of plausibility on the learning of controversial statements. Journal of Abnormal and Social Psychology, 1958.

[25]Adapted from the Hazelden Foundation.

[26]Adapted from items included in the Insight program developed by Community Intervention, Minneapolis, 1985.

[27]Adapted from *Freedom from Smoking in 20 Days* © American Lung Association, 1740 Broadway, New York, NY 10019.

[28]Adapted from *Alateen, Is it for You?* © 1981 by Al-Anon Family Group Headquarters, Inc. Reprinted by permission of Al-Anon Family Group Headquarters, Inc..

Chapter 4

Relationships

Much of the joy, despair, laughter, tears, happiness, grief, compassion, jealousy, confusion, comfort, and substance of our lives comes from our relationships with others. As infants we are completely dependent on others to meet our basic survival needs. Even as we learn to take care of ourselves, we still turn to others for companionship, comfort, assistance, and love. Families, friendships, communities, nations, school and religious groups, gangs, clubs, cults, twelve-step programs, bowling groups, music, sports or hobby fans all provide a network of groups that support and enrich our lives.

BUT . . . as everyone knows, other people are not always easy to live with. Nor are we. Communication, cooperation, and the resolution of conflict are lifelong skills that tax the full extent of our human development. Human history is a history of our moments of success and of our tragic failures in our relationship with others. Our own lives are marked by personal growth and frustration as we learn to connect and coexist with the people who are important to us. Ironically, our ability to understand, respect, and get along with others all stems from the basic respect and esteem that we have for ourselves.

Today we are faced with the preeminent fact that, if civilization is to survive, we must cultivate the science of human relationships—the ability of all peoples, of all kinds, to live together, in the same world, at peace.

—Franklin D. Roosevelt

SELF-ESTEEM

"Appreciating my own worth and importance and having the character to be accountable for myself and to act responsibly toward others." This was the official definition of self-esteem used by the California Task

Force to Promote Self-Esteem and Personal and Social Responsibility established in 1990. This three-year task force of twenty-five men and women, representing a multicultural assortment of professional and community leaders, set out to determine the connection between self-esteem and the problems of school dropouts, teenage pregnancy, domestic violence, drug and alcohol addiction, crime, and violence. The task force found an inseparable connection between each of these problems and how an individual views and values himself. A girl who values herself and her future makes sexual decisions that protect her body and birth-giving potential. A pregnant fifteen-year-old is often faced with decisions and realities that undermine her confidence and sense of worth. Drug use often robs a person of the skills and independence that create a positive sense of self, and individuals with a high sense of self-esteem seem able to resist the attraction of a quick fix that drugs may offer. It is a catch-22: the more self-esteem you have, the more likely you are to take positive risks, reach out to other people, protect yourself from self-destructive activities, and be successful. This, in turn, builds more self-esteem. When you feel insecure, incompetent, or unlovable, you are less likely to take the steps necessary for your own development and protection—you just don't value yourself enough.

The Bucket Theory of Self-Esteem

One way of thinking about self-esteem is to imagine that as a baby, everyone is given a solid metal bucket to carry their confidence, self-respect, and good feelings about themselves. As a baby, you came into the world with the basic survival instinct to value and protect yourself. You cried when you were hungry or hurt, you grabbed for what you needed, and you thought you were pretty important and special. Most babies get their bucket filled as they grow and are loved by their parents. Most parents do their best to protect their baby's bucket of self-worth and esteem.

What kinds of things might fill a baby's self-esteem needs? What things did you get as a baby that filled your bucket?

Sometimes things happen when we are very little that permanently damage or dent our buckets. A certain number of these things happen to all of us because:

- **the world does not center on our individual needs**

- **parents are human and often inexperienced at parenting—they make mistakes and can only parent as well as they are able**

- **life includes accidents and misunderstandings**

- **children see themselves as much more powerful than they are—they may feel responsible for events that are really beyond their control**

- **social circumstances, prejudices, and restraints may limit or denigrate an individual child**

What are some of the things that might be a part of a child's life that would damage or weaken the self-esteem bucket? What parts of your childhood may have weakened your bucket?

Some Thoughts on Self-Esteem

Failure is an event, not a person.
—William D. Brown

♥

Cherish forever what makes you unique 'cause you're really a yawn when it goes.
—Bette Midler

♥

I don't know the key to success, but the key to failure is trying to please everybody.
—Bill Cosby

♥

Nobody can make you feel inferior without your consent.
—Eleanor Roosevelt

♥

Don't compromise yourself. You are all you've got.
—Janis Joplin

♥

You grow up the day you have your first real laugh at yourself.
—Ethel Barrymore

♥

They say such nice things about people at their funerals that it makes me sad to realize that I'm going to miss mine by just a few days.
—Garrison Keillor

So, we all arrive at any given time with bucket in hand, somewhat bumped and bruised, perhaps, but full of the support and nurturing that we need to be happy and successful. When your bucket is low, much of your energy and attention becomes focused on survival—on protecting and thinking about yourself. As you proceed through your life, different experiences, relationships, and attitudes add to or dip into your level of self-esteem.

ACHIEVEMENT: grades, sports, talents, awards, accomplishments

+   successes, praise, accomplishments, winning, personal strengths

–   failure, criticism, losing, personal weaknesses

RELATIONSHIPS: friends, family, teachers, social groups, beaus

+   acceptance, love, encouragement, belonging, respect, feeling needed, intimacy, receiving praise, loving and helping others

–   rejection, isolation, ridicule, loss, feeling unneeded and unloved, hurting others

SELF-ACTUALIZATION: inner strength and acceptance

+   believing in yourself, working toward personal goals, standing up for what you believe in, positive risk taking, making decisions that keep you healthy and strong, thinking for yourself, respecting your uniqueness and inner wisdom

–   self-destructive behavior, valuing others' opinions above your own, expecting others to be responsible for you, putting yourself down, negative risk taking, violating your personal beliefs and values

If you have collected a couple of holes in your bucket, you may find that you need more esteem than others since it is always leaking out even if nothing happens that takes esteem away from you. You need to realize that you do need more esteem. Counseling and other healing relationships—good friends, mentors, spiritual advisers, family members—may help you to understand and repair your leaks. You also need to understand that you are bringing these leaks from old relationships or events; the people around you now may be confused or resent being asked to keep filling up your bucket. When people really care about you, they will try to understand and respect your needs, but you also need to strengthen your own self-actualizing ways of improving your esteem.

Here are some things that you can do to keep your bucket filled:

* *Don't throw away compliments or belittle your accomplishments.* Be proud of who you are and behave in ways that you can be proud of.

* *Ask for what you need.* Don't expect others to read your mind and automatically know what you need or how you feel. Be honest and direct.

* *Don't be overly concerned or influenced by others' opinions.* Learn to think for yourself and weigh others' opinions objectively.

* *Face challenges with confidence and determination.* Challenge yourself to do and be your best. Don't compromise your values or possi-

> *Perhaps the most important single cause of a person's success or failure has to do with the question of what he believes about himself.*
> —Arthur Combs

> *Shine the light you are.*
> *You are a shining star.*
> *Don't follow leaders.*
> *Just be who you are.*
> *Butterfly, butterfly,*
> *Wake up and fly . . .*
> —Jason

bilities. Stand up to your fears and self-doubts, to the opinions and pressures of others.

> *To be nobody but yourself in a world which is doing its best, night and day, to make you everybody else, means to fight the hardest battle which any human can fight and never stop fighting.*
>
> — *e.e. cummings*

- **Don't give up on yourself.** Push through the difficult spots and keep trying. Allow yourself to take risks and make mistakes—that is how you learn and grow. Evaluate yourself in terms of your own goals and progress, not anyone else's.

- **Get to know yourself; respect your strengths and your limitations.** Don't expect yourself to be perfect or to do everything well the first time you try. Accept your imperfections and know which ones you can work on and which ones you will need to learn to live with.

- **Form nourishing, supportive relationships with people who like and respect you.** Don't keep trying to win over people who are critical and destructive to your self-esteem. Let people get to know the real you, complete with imperfections, fears, and inadequacies. If a person loves you for who are *pretending* to be, you will know that you are not truly loved.

- **Give yourself the same consideration and support you would give a good friend.** We all grow strongest and happiest when treated with kindness, respect, and understanding. **Treat yourself accordingly.**

What Do Your Parents Respect and Appreciate About You?

Much of your initial self-esteem comes from the messages you have received from your parents about yourself, but often in the day-to-day business of family life, those messages get confused or buried. It is important for you to know what your parents respect and appreciate about you. For this exercise, ask each of your parents to write a list of qualities that they especially value in you. Ask them to be specific, perhaps citing examples or instances when they have been particularly aware of your strengths.

Before they return their list to you, write your own list of what you think they will write. You might also want to write a list of the qualities that you especially respect and appreciate about them.

Here's What *I* Like About Me . . .

Use this space to fill in words, pictures, or reminders of what you especially like about yourself. Write small so you can get a lot in and add to your montage when you accomplish something you are proud of or recognize a new talent or skill. On one of those days when your self-esteem is feeling a little shaky, take a look back at this page to help keep things in perspective!

What's So Great About Me?

I am me.
In all the world there is no one else exactly like me.
There are persons who have some parts like me, but no one adds up exactly like me. . . .
I own everything about me—my body, . . . my mind, . . . my eyes, . . .
my feelings . . . my mouth, . . . my voice . . .
and all my actions whether they be to others or to myself.
I own my own fantasies, my dreams, my hopes, my fears.
I own all my triumphs and successes, all my failures and mistakes. . . .
I know there are aspects about myself that puzzle me and other parts that I do not know.
But as long as I am friendly and loving to myself, I
can courageously and hopefully look for the solutions to the puzzles. . . .
I have the tools to survive, to be close to others, to be productive,
to make sense and order out of the world of people and things outside of me.
I own me and therefore I can engineer me.
I am me and I am okay.

by Virginia Satir[1]

In small groups of three or four, take turns answering each of the following questions. Be sure to listen carefully and supportively to each other.

1. What was one accomplishment or instance in which you were really proud of yourself before the age of twelve?

2. Who is one person in your life who has made you feel special and valued? What does that person like about you?

3. What is one factor, person, or experience in your life which has helped your self-esteem?

4. What is one factor, person, or experience in your life which has hurt your self-esteem?

5. What is one thing that you can usually do to help when you are feeling down on yourself?

6. What is something that you do particularly well?

7. Who is one person in your life to whom you have been particularly valuable or helpful?

8. What is something that you are getting better at?

9. What is something that you can do now that you couldn't do last year?

10. What is something that you have a difficult time dealing with?

11. What is one of your goals to change about yourself?

12. **FEEDBACK:** After you have answered all the questions, have each person tell you one thing that they especially like or respect about you.

PSYCHOLOGICAL SELF-DEFENSE

No matter how strong your self-esteem is or how carefully you work to stay balanced, things happen to all of us that attack our sense of self-worth and confidence. Mistakes, accidents, or misunderstandings can temporarily leave us feeling inadequate or foolish. Everyone has times when he is embarrassed or ashamed of the way he has behaved. Other people may intentionally or unintentionally be cruel or inconsiderate to you. We all experience bad days, stupid mistakes, frustrating weaknesses, and difficult relationships. In response to these normal frustrations, everyone, at least occasionally, uses *defense mechanisms* to soften her disappointment, reduce feelings of guilt or embarrassment, and protect her self-image.

Defense mechanisms are ways that people think or things that people do that keep them from dealing with unpleasant thoughts, seeing unpleasant things in themselves, or making changes that are difficult or frightening. Sometimes these defenses are completely conscious—you know full well that you didn't study well enough for a test, but you complain about the teacher's bias to justify your low grade. At other times, a defense mechanism may be unconscious—you are not consciously aware that you are defending yourself or avoiding your real feelings. For instance, if you were bullied or teased by a group at school, you may get angry and take it out on your best friend for some minor inconvenience that you would normally overlook. When he asks you what your problem is, you are completely convinced that the problem is his behavior.

Defense mechanisms are normal and, from time to time, help you through a tough spot. If used too much, however, they can keep you from facing up to problems, learning from your mistakes and resolving conflicts in your relationships. Sometimes, they just make a bad day or situation worse. Defense mechanisms can keep you from being really honest with yourself and are usually irritating or frustrating to others. Ironically, the very things that we do to try to make ourselves look better are often the things that others do not like about us. Think about how much nicer it is when a friend admits she has made a mistake than when she tries to blame it on you or some other innocent party. Think of how much closer you feel to someone who can openly admit to feeling anxious or inadequate rather than pretending to be tough or indifferent. It takes personal courage to face up to your imperfections and admit your mistakes, but it usually gains you respect and peace of mind in the long run.

Some of the ways that people typically defend themselves are:

- **RATIONALIZATION:** unconsciously giving questionable reasons to justify behavior or relieve disappointment. *I don't really want to go to that party because I have a lot of studying to do and most of the people there are losers anyway.*

- **BLAMING:** placing the blame on someone else who is related to the situation in some way rather than accepting personal responsibility for a mistake or error. *If our team had a decent pitcher, the other team wouldn't be hitting all those balls where I can't get to them in time.*

- **PROJECTION:** projecting unacceptable or uncomfortable feelings onto someone else. *I don't know what you are talking about—I'm in a perfectly good mood, but you sure are oversensitive this afternoon.*

- **DISPLACEMENT:** giving vent to anger or tension through someone or something not directly connected with the source of frustration. *After getting yelled at by my math teacher for not having my assignment completed, I got a personal foul in the soccer game for illegally attacking the girl who was guarding me too closely.*

- **REPRESSION:** unconsciously blocking painful, threatening, or disturbing thoughts, experiences, or impulses from your mind. *When I think back, I can't remember anything between the ages of nine and eleven when my parents were getting divorced.*

- **COMPENSATION:** attempts to develop strength in one area to make up for real or imagined weaknesses in another. *I was never any good in sports and was always the last one picked for a team, so I spent a lot of time perfecting my artwork.*

- **OVERCOMPENSATION:** a direct attack on a perceived weakness until it becomes a strength. *Steroids help me work out and develop serious muscles so nobody pushes me around anymore.*

- **INTELLECTUALIZATION:** developing a logical but usually irrelevant justification for a desired decision or behavior. *I figure that if stores are going to put small, valuable items right near the door, they are just asking for someone to take them.*

- **REGRESSION:** a return to a less mature form of behavior. *I was so hurt and upset that I completely lost my temper and burst into tears.*

- **SUBLIMATION:** converting a desire to engage in socially unacceptable behavior into an act that is more socially accepted. *When I feel angry or frustrated, I just go in my room and play heavy metal music VERY loudly.*

- **REACTION FORMATION:** condemning or attacking others for behaviors which you unconsciously find enticing. *When I was secretly bingeing and purging, the sight of overweight people was disgusting to me.*

- **FANTASIZING:** escape into daydreams to relieve boredom or feel more worthy and competent. *Instead of practicing my backhand, I would lie around for hours imagining my critical coach's amazement when I became the unchallenged champion at Wimbledon.*

Avoiding or minimizing a problem, putting others on the defensive, stalling, focusing on the problems of others rather than your own, insisting that you don't really care about the problem or its consequences, or denying your own power or responsibility for the problem are all popular subsets of the defenses listed above. Whenever you notice that you or someone else is acting defensively, you can be sure that, in some way, that person's self-esteem is feeling threatened.

Coping with Conflict

1. Deal with <u>yourself first</u>, the <u>person next</u>, and the <u>situation last</u>.

    a. <u>Distance</u> yourself from the problem or the person until you have had a chance to calm down and think.

    b. Listen to the other person's side without judging or blaming.

    c. Attack the problem, not the person. Don't look for winners or losers, just a solution.

2. Confront the person or situation privately and give everyone an opportunity to save face.

3. Be respectful. Avoid name-calling or accusations. Use language that will contribute to a solution, not escalate the conflict.

4. Tell the other person about your concerns. Start your sentences with "I," not "you." "I" sentences tend to express your thoughts and feelings; "you" sentences often blame or attack.

5. Focus on the future solution, not past complaints.

6. Be willing to admit to your mistakes and recognize ways that you have contributed to the conflict.

7. State the problem objectively after hearing both sides. Make sure you both agree what the problem really is.

8. Know what you want to come out of the resolution:

    a. What are your own needs?

    b. What do you want the other person to do?

    c. How do you want the situation to change?

9. Understand what the other person wants to come out of the resolution.

10. Keep listening and work together. Know what your most important concerns are and be ready to compromise on the rest.

Developing a Counterattack

Which defenses do you tend to use most often? What areas of your life or personality tend to make you most defensive? Pick one situation in which you usually get defensive. Notice what triggers you (a certain person, topic, incident) and how you usually respond. Identify the underlying feelings that are making you uncomfortable. On your own, or with a good friend or partner that you trust, try to imagine what it would be like not to react defensively, but to face the situation honestly and directly. Once you have come up with an honest alternative, practice it with your partner. Have him gradually increase the threat as you become more comfortable with your new, more confident response.

Favorite defenses:

Situations/people that get me every time:

Trigger situation:

Usual, defensive response:

Underlying feelings:

Revised response:

EMOTIONS AND EMOTIONAL PROBLEMS

From a screaming, laughing baby who reacts instantly to his feelings to a quiet old woman who experiences a wide range of feelings without a blink of her eye, we are all emotional creatures. Our emotions provide the joys and sorrows of our lives, the heights and the depths of being fully human. Emotions are a natural, instinctive part of our mind/body design, but, as usual, our upbringing, culture, and ability to think about ourselves complicate and define our emotions. We learn that some emotions are "good" and some are "bad." We learn that some can be shared freely and others should be hidden away. Certain emotions are acceptable for males and others for females; some considered normal and healthy in the United States are culturally unacceptable in Japan. Some provoke destructive behavior and always seem to get us into trouble; others inspire us to act in productive and compassionate ways. Some people feel controlled by their emotions while others insist that emotions can and should be controlled by reason and self-restraint.

Emotions, in and of themselves, are natural, psychological responses to our environment. Like physiological responses, they let us know when we are in danger, unhealthy, or when we are effectively meeting our psychological needs. Like a fever or a rosy complexion, emotions are not inherently good or bad although they may reflect a state of health or discomfort. Properly understood and expressed, our emotions can provide a valuable key to self-understanding and personal growth. Repressing or denying our feelings is not mentally or physically healthy. Acting out our feelings without any reflection or personal control is often not very productive either. ***We do not choose our feelings, but we do choose how to interpret and act upon them.***

Suppose that your girlfriend drops you cold and begins dating your biggest rival from the water polo team. You may feel hurt, sad, jealous, rejected, angry, lonely, embarrassed, incredulous, foolish, vindictive, and manipulated. The first thing that you will do is to unconsciously decide which of those emotions you are most comfortable feeling. This decision will be based on a long personal history of what emotions are acceptable to your self-image, culture, family, and personality. You may be perfectly comfortable feeling like the lovesick victim who sings the blues, but cringe at the anger or vindictive feelings you have toward your lost love. Or you may delight in getting revenge and channeling all of your feelings into self-righteous outrage, but shudder at the thought of feeling betrayed or socially embarrassed.

Sometimes we use one feeling to cover another feeling that is too painful or inconsistent with the way that we like to think about ourselves. In our culture, it is more "manly" to get angry and punish somebody than to cry and express sad, vulnerable feelings. As one particularly astute young man put it, "No matter what I feel, I get mad." Girls, on the other hand, are often taught that anger is "unladylike" and may repress their angry feelings and express only their more sensitive, nurturing emotions. Both males and females experience a full range of emotions, but after a normal course of social upbringing, each may actually lose touch with their socially unacceptable feelings. This is not only confusing, but blocks off part of your emotional awareness. The repressed feelings don't go away, but are usually expressed in disguised ways—physical problems, dreams, or unconsciously motivated behavior. You may insist that you are not really angry at your former girlfriend, but accidentally ram into her car in the parking lot. Or you may insist that her defection doesn't really bother you at all, but get an upset stomach every time the water polo team has a game or find yourself silently crying at sad movies. Unidentified anger or sadness can be turned inward, and you may become unaccountably depressed or down on yourself.

Surprisingly, most of the trouble that we have with our feelings occurs when we repress them or make judgments about them. ***Emotions are temporary and valueless.*** If you are hurt or sad, a good cry or a comforting talk with a friend will usually make you feel much better. If you define anger as a normal, temporary reaction to frustration or disappointment, you can blow off steam and cool down to rectify or accept the situation. Once you are aware of your guilt feelings, you can examine the situation to see what you can change in order to feel better about yourself. Repressing or denying your feelings restricts your ability to learn from them and distorts your self-awareness. When you hide your emotions from yourself, your friends or family may be more aware of what you are feeling than you are. Have you ever found yourself shouting "I am NOT upset!" to a friend or family member's concern? Feelings don't just "go away"—they go underground, often reemerging at the most inconvenient and inappropriate times.

While emotions may be normal psychological responses to your environment, the interpretation and expression of your feelings is learned and well within your control. You can experience sadness as catastrophic and threatening, or as the rich underside of love. You do not *have* to punch someone if you are angry, even if you feel like it. You do not have to run around acting out your feelings in order to acknowledge and experience them. If you are worried and frustrated about environmental issues, you can channel your fears and outrage into productive social or political action or you can angrily attack someone who you feel is partially responsible or you can quietly sink into a depression and do nothing. **You are responsible for choosing what you do with the feelings you have.** Feelings do not automatically cause us to behave in certain ways.

The old advice of counting to ten before you express your anger may help you acknowledge your feelings as well as decide the best way to act on them. You may want to confront the situation directly and immediately. Or you may decide to take some time to cool off before you can express yourself coherently. You may just want to rant and rave and get it out of your system or you may want to go for a walk or hit a tennis ball around or listen to some music to respond to your anger. You may want to talk about how you are feeling or you may be able to meditate or think privately about what you are feeling and what you want to do with those feelings. Often your anger is a cover-up for feelings of hurt or disappointment or fear. Communication and resolution will proceed more smoothly if you can identify these underlying feelings instead of just getting mad.

Albert Ellis developed a theory called *rational emotive psychotherapy* which is based on the assumption that thought and emotion significantly overlap in many respects. Therefore, unsettling feelings can be controlled or changed by changing your thinking about them. Ellis theorized that we develop major illogical ideas or philosophies which encourage us to be unhappy and dissatisfied.

"Good" and "Bad" Feelings

Each of us has our own personal inventory of emotional comfort that we have learned from our upbringing, culture, and peers. Rate each of the following emotions based on your own comfort zone.

1 = Easy to deal with   2 = Uncomfortable but manageable   3 = Difficult for me   4 = Rarely feel it

_____ fear	_____ anger	_____ sadness/depression
_____ jealousy	_____ anxiety	_____ rejection
_____ inadequacy	_____ embarrassment	_____ insecurity
_____ loneliness	_____ guilt	_____ disappointment
_____ dependency	_____ high-pressure	_____ exclusion
_____ pride	_____ playfulness	_____ confidence
_____ compassion	_____ empathy	_____ openness
_____ enthusiasm	_____ closeness	_____ independence
_____ courage	_____ patience	_____ happiness

For each of the emotions that you rated either 3 or 4, think about the judgments that you learned about these feelings while you were growing up or from your peers. Think of how you usually respond to these feelings and alternate ways that might be more comfortable or productive. Rarely feeling a particular emotion may mean that it is so easy that you barely notice it or that it is so difficult that you don't even allow yourself to be aware of it. Complete the following sentences several times for each of the feelings that you have some difficulty with.

When I feel _____ , I usually _____ .

When my dad felt _____ , he usually _____ .

When my mom felt _____ , she usually _____ .

When my friends feel _____ , they usually _____ .

If I just allowed myself to feel _____ , I'm afraid I would _____ .

A better way to deal with my _____ might be to _____ .

Here are some of the assumptions that Ellis believes create neurotic and self-defeating behavior:

ILLOGICAL	RATIONAL
• It is a dire necessity for a person to be loved or approved of by everyone for everything she does.	• It is important to like and respect yourself; to concentrate on loving rather than being loved.
• It is terrible, horrible, and catastrophic when things are not as you want them to be.	• It is too bad when things don't work out the way you want, but you need to accept problems as an inevitable and valuable part of life.
• Unhappiness is caused by external factors, events, and people.	• Almost all human unhappiness is caused or sustained by the view one takes rather than the event itself.
• If something is dangerous or fearsome, you should be terribly concerned about it.	• Many things are dangerous or scary—we need to face them, render them as safe as possible, and not obsess on how difficult things are.
• If at all possible, you should avoid life's difficulties.	• It is best in the long run to face difficulties directly and honestly.
• You should be thoroughly competent, adequate, intelligent, and achieving in all possible respects.	• You should try to do your best, but accept the fact that you are imperfect with general human limitations and fallibility.
• It is vitally important what other people do and say and you need to do your best to control and change them.	• Other people's problems and ideas are their own and you have very little power or ability to change them.
• Once something has affected you or been difficult for you, it will always be painful and difficult.	• You are capable of learning and changing throughout your life, mastering new skills and personal strengths.

Depression and Suicide

One of the more difficult and disabling emotions is **depression.** Everyone has bad days and bad moods—life is not always easy—but occasionally we get stuck in a period of time when nothing seems to break the cycle of depression. Most depression is related to loss and change, and there are plenty of both during adolescence. It is not surprising that adolescents may be particularly vulnerable. Clinical depression is described by the American Psychiatric Association as *fairly prominent and persistent loss of pleasure and interest in usual activities and pursuits; feelings of sadness, hopelessness, and discouragement.* Some common symptoms of adolescent depression are:

- *Sadness*

- *Change in eating/sleeping habits; weight gain or loss; sleep disturbances, difficulty getting up in the morning*

- *Isolation and withdrawal*

- *Fluctuations between indifference and being extremely talkative*

- *Anger and rage often expressed in sarcasm, irritability, and indiscriminate attacks on friends, authorities, or social injustice*

- *Restlessness and agitation*

- *Poor self-esteem, feelings of inadequacy, helplessness, and hopelessness*

- *Feelings of emptiness in life, pessimism about the future, thinking about death and suicide*

- *Increased use of drugs and alcohol*

- *Defiance and rebellious refusal to work or cooperate with others*

Psychologists categorize depression as either *reactive* or *chronic.* **Reactive depression** is a response to a life event such as a death, divorce, disappointment, or other identifiable loss or change. It can be very debilitating and may last one to two years, but it is specific and not likely to reoccur without further trauma. **Chronic depression** is less specific and may occur periodically without any identifiable cause. Current opinion believes that chronic depression is probably the result of early child abuse or a chemical imbalance in the brain. Research strongly suggests that this type of depression runs in families and is closely related to alcoholism, eating disorders, and obsessive/compulsive behavior.

Noble deeds and hot baths are the best cures for depression.
—Dodie Smith

Some people who experience chronic depression also experience periods of manic behavior. They are unable to sleep, have wide mood swings, and may find it difficult to control their impulses and behavior. This combination is called **manic-depression.** Chronic depression and manic-depression are often successfully treated with antidepressants and antipsychotic drugs. This biological base of depression can be confusing and frightening because it is very difficult to predict and control without professional assistance. This may be because it appears to be a physical rather than strictly psychological problem.

Another category of depression that is very common during adolescence is **masked depression.** This occurs when a person is psychologically depressed, but masks the common signs of sadness and lethargy with anger, acting out, or drug use. This form of depression often goes undetected and untreated because the person's hostile behavior tends to push everyone away. Teenagers with masked depression often get into trouble instead of getting help. Sometimes, even the individual is not consciously aware of her own feelings of sadness and hopelessness. By blocking these feelings out and alienating most sources of support and help, these individuals are at high risk for suicide attempts. Reckless driving, careless risk taking, eating disorders, and other forms of self-destructive behavior may be masked forms of a suicidal behavior.

Coping with Depression

Life presents us with many challenges, losses, and changes and we all must learn how to cope with the sadness and fears that accompany these natural life stresses. In a small group, read over the suggestions listed below and then come up with a more extensive list of activities or responses that help you cope with difficult times.

1. *Go for a long walk or hike by yourself.*

2. *Listen to your favorite music.*

3. *Sing or chant or dance or scream.*

4. *Make a list of your strengths. Spend at least an hour concentrating on fully appreciating yourself.*

5. *Consult a nutrition book and consider what you might add to your diet for pep and vitality.*

6. *Exercise. While you may not feel like it at first, it will rouse your body and improve your spirits.*

7. *Get together with a good friend and talk, laugh, and ask for support.*

8. *Make a list of things you are feeling guilty about. Consider how you might make amends, do it, and burn the list.*

9. *Clean up something.*

OTHERS:

One of the most distressing results of serious depression, of course, is suicide. Suicide is the second most common cause of death among adolescents and that rate has risen over 200 percent since the 1960s. In the United States, at least 5,000 adolescents currently take their own lives each year. Girls are three times more likely to attempt suicide than boys, but because they tend to use guns and more violent methods, boys are actually successful at killing themselves three times as often. Gay and lesbian teens are two to three times more likely to attempt suicide and may account for as many as one-third of successful teen suicides. Surveys indicate that about 11 percent of high school students have made at least one suicide attempt and 40 percent have thought about it to the extent of actually having a plan. There are over one hundred suicide attempts for every successful suicide—most teenagers do not really want to die, but want help or escape from the problems that are troubling them.

Suicidal ideation (thinking about and planning possible suicide) can begin with a serious life crisis or disappointment. Death, divorce or remarriage within the family, pregnancy, serious illness or injury, moving, a romantic breakup, or school pressures may all precipitate depressed, suicidal thinking. Family pressures and lack of communication, poor social and coping skills, losses suffered or anticipated, social and personal isolation, lack of emotional support, and untreated chronic depression are the underlying causes. Some signs to be concerned about in yourself or in a friend include:

- *Sudden changes in physical appearance, personality, or behavior.*

- *Depression and unpredictable mood swings and emotional outbursts; tearfulness, fatigue, loss of appetite, changes in sleep patterns.*

- *Preoccupation with death and suicide; making threats or offhanded comments about wanting to end it all; giving away prized possessions; previous suicide attempts.*

- *Poor grades, truancy, disciplinary problems, excessive use of drugs or alcohol.*

What can you do to help if you are concerned about a friend, family member, or just someone that you have noticed exhibiting these warning signs?

While you cannot change or unconditionally protect the people that you love, most people feel frightened and guilt-ridden when a friend or family member attempts suicide. Here are some suggestions on what you can do to recognize and respond to the danger of suicide in someone that you care about:

1. **Be aware of suicidal tendencies and depression.** Don't ignore a friend's persistent talk about suicide, even if it is in jest. Confront it directly and with genuine concern: *I am worried about you—you seem to be talking about death and suicide a lot lately. Is something bothering you?* You may need to directly ask *"Are you considering suicide?"* Don't just brush off his behavior as a faze or attention getting. It is better to overreact honestly and directly, than to tragically underreact.

2. **Listen.** Just listen to his feelings and listen without judgment or advice. It is very tempting to try to solve the problem or make your friend feel better. If he is seriously depressed, however, saying "cheer up" or trying to divert his attention won't help and may make him feel more isolated and misunderstood. Take the time to really listen and try to understand how he is feeling.

3. **Be honest.** If a person is struggling with a life-and-death depression, trite niceties and fake sympathy just won't cut it. It is critical that you are genuine and sincere in your response—this will help her to be honest with you. You can say "I feel really scared by what you are telling me," or "I don't know exactly what I can do to be your friend right now—please help me." Just let her know that you care about her, that you don't want her to hurt herself, and that you will be there for her no matter what. Don't be afraid that you will put ideas into her head if you talk openly about suicide. Talking about them may bring these scary ideas out into the open where they can be dealt with more effectively.

4. **Share your feelings.** Don't try to gloss over the problems or feelings with phony optimism or philosophy. Some of life really is tough, and there are times when we all feel discouraged and hopeless. You can share times when you have felt sad, hurt, or despairing. Your friend needs to know that he is not alone, that we all struggle with difficult experiences and feelings and that, in some ways, you can understand how he is feeling.

5. **Get help.** This is not always easy and may seem like a violation of trust with your friend, but suicidal depression is serious. You cannot handle the responsibility for protecting and caring for your friend alone—this could cost her life. You need to talk to a parent, clergy, teacher, or counselor for guidance and support. It is easiest if you can get your friend to agree to seek help and you may be able to go along to provide moral support. But even if your friend objects and gets angry at you, you must insist that someone share this information. If your friend suddenly decides that everything is really fine and flatteringly says that talking to you has made her feel all better, still insist that she talk with a professional or trained person so that you will feel better. If the person is actively suicidal, do not leave her alone.

> *A normal person is just someone that you don't know very well.*
>
> —*J. Houston*

What Is Counseling?

People have a lot of different ideas about what counseling is. Some think that it is a powerful form of mind reading or mind control while others think that it is just a bunch of hocus-pocus that doesn't really help anyone. Some think that counselors coddle or feel sorry for their clients while others fear that counselors callously force their clients to face deep, dark, scary things about themselves. Some people believe that seeing a counselor is a sign of personal weakness, modern narcissism, or an indication that someone thinks you are crazy. While, like any profession, there are good and bad counselors, skillful counseling is none of these things.

The healthy and strong individual is one who asks for help when he needs it—whether he's got an abscess on his knee or in his soul.

—Rona Barrett

Counseling is an objective, professional relationship which can provide you with a "time out" space to think through the problems and connections you are dealing with in your life. A counselor or therapist is trained to recognize the patterns and responses that may keep you from resolving important life issues and relationships. A good counselor will offer you the questions, honesty, and unconditional acceptance that you need to keep getting stronger. She is someone that you trust and don't need to impress or encounter in your everyday life. While many of us have friends or family members that we can always turn to for support and encouragement, it is sometimes nice to have a stranger to confide in that you don't have to face outside of the counseling relationship. Within this safe, isolated relationship, you can confront your fears, feelings, and weaknesses without fear of rejection or retribution.

Seriously disturbed or psychotic individuals do need extensive psychiatric help, but most people who see counselors are dealing with normal problems or changes in their lives. It may be a recurring problem that you just can't seem to resolve on your own or unusual circumstances that you don't know how to deal with. You may be dealing with difficult changes or loss in your life and could benefit from some extra support and guidance as you figure out how to manage. There are very few individuals whose lives are so uncomplicated and easy that they could never use the support of an objective resource and support person. Sometimes it may just take one or two sessions; other times you may want to spend some concentrated time unraveling old patterns and confusion.

You are the best judge of when and what kind of counseling you might gain from. You should give a counselor the benefit of the doubt and time enough to get to know his approach, but you should always retain the right to judge whether or not the time is helpful to you. Talk to people that you respect to see if they can recommend a good counselor. Counselors and therapists have many different styles, personalities, and philosophical orientations. Find one that is a good match for you. This does not mean that the process will always be comfortable or easy, but you will know when you can trust and respect the person that you are working with.

Out of every crisis comes the chance to be reborn, to reconceive ourselves as individuals, to choose the kind of change that will help us grow, and to fulfill ourselves more completely.

—Nena O'Neill

Respect your own evaluation and then get ready to work! Counselors can provide some helpful observations, questions, and support, but therapy is the process of taking more effective control of your own life. That is hard work no matter how good your counselor is. It requires courage, honesty, and determination. Don't worry, you will only confront what you are ready and able to confront—your unconscious brain is incredibly protective. Life will keep throwing you the same difficult "opportunities" until you finally get it right. Some problems will consistently get easier and others you will resolve over and over again. Be kind and patient with yourself. Accept your problems as opportunities to learn something important about yourself and your life. Celebrate your victories and progress as you stretch and confront your insecurities. You alone are responsible for your character, judgments, and development, but reaching out for help when you need it is a sign of strength and maturity. You must do the actual maturing, but you don't always have to do it alone.

GENDER ROLES

A man and his son were driving down the highway and had a collision with a Mack truck. The man was killed instantly and the son was rushed to the hospital in an ambulance. The doctor in the emergency room took one look at the boy and said "I cannot operate on this boy. He is my son." **How could this be?**

(Not too long ago, most people couldn't figure out the answer to this riddle. Has that changed? If so, why?)

Part of our self-image comes from a variety of social roles or expectations that other people have of us because of some physical, personal, or cultural characteristic. People may expect certain behavior or attributes of you because you are tall or Mexican or deaf or attractive or make good grades or like to surf or are a boy. These expectations are called *stereotypes.* Sometimes these stereotypes may fit who you really are and sometimes they are totally inappropriate and misleading. In all cases, it is a mistake to assume that every individual in a particular group is alike. Individual members may have some interests, values, or qualities in common, but each person is a unique combination of many personal characteristics and social roles. Stereotypes can be positive or negative, but they are always a superficial description of a multifaceted human being. Think of some of the stereotypes that you have about the following groups:

truck drivers	*secretaries*	*corporate executives*
surfers	*rock musicians*	*WASPs*
doctors	*football players*	*ballet dancers*
Asian students	*homosexuals*	*Dead Heads*
blacks	*psychiatrists*	*beauty contestants*
plumbers	*nurses*	*preppies*
feminists	*alcoholics*	*computer nerds*

Some of your stereotypes may be very specific, while others allow for some variety. How many of your stereotypes included a gender expectation? How many of your mental descriptions included a racial component? Most of our stereotypes and expectations are *nonconscious*—we pick them up from our experiences and the attitudes of the people around us without really realizing it. Psychologists call this assortment of underlying assumptions and expectations a ***nonconscious ideology.*** Nonconscious ideology is *"a set of beliefs that we accept implicitly but of which we are unaware because we cannot even conceive of an alternative view of the world."*[2]

What color is a "flesh-colored" Band-Aid? If you are black, you know that it is a sort of tannish color. If you are Caucasian, you may have assumed that it is the color of "flesh"—-your flesh. If you are waiting to see a new doctor, you may be surprised if she is a female or if a male nurse comes in first to take your temperature. It may surprise you to learn that a football player is gay or a National Merit Scholar. If a Dead Head says that she doesn't use drugs or a beauty contestant insists that his or her talent be taken seriously, we tend to smile skeptically. It is difficult to rethink our prejudices because we think of them as facts, not opinions.

One group that everyone in the world belongs to is a gender group. You are either a male or a female, and there are many different expectations that go along with each of these roles. The first thing that we want to

Boys learn how to make 16 kinds of kites, a water telescope, hunting apparatus, puppets, various and diverse whirligigs; how to stock a marine aquarium, choose a dog, build a snow fort. . . . Girls learn how to make a hammock, corn husk and flower dolls, fans, a lawn-tennis net; how to organize a walking club, preserve wild-flowers, paint in water colors, observe the holidays the old-fashioned way.
—Advertisement from a merchandise catalogue

know about a little baby is the gender. Observation and research have shown that we then begin immediately to treat her differently. We actually tend to hold boy and girl babies differently and use words like *pretty* and *strong* according to their gender. We surround baby girls with pink and yellow, colors that may actually stimulate verbal development. We tend to give boys action toys that encourage high activity and competition while girls receive dolls and homemaking toys that encourage nurturing and caretaking. Parents expect boys to be more active and aggressive and unconsciously tolerate more noise and competition from their sons than from their daughters. They are more likely to help their daughters when asked and encourage their sons to try harder and do it for themselves.[3] Parents tend to tolerate more "tomboy" behavior in girls, but react strongly to "sissy" behavior in boys.[4] By age five, children have already developed clearly defined notions of what is appropriate behavior for women and for men.[5]

In school, teachers, peers, and the curriculum tend to reinforce these basic stereotypes. Girls and boys watch their peers and are quick to mimic gender-appropriate play and activity and are likely to be teased and isolated if they don't. Teachers tend to reward girls for being well-behaved, neat, and cooperative. Teachers also praise boys more, give boys more specific feedback and academic help, and encourage their comments during class discussion. They are twice as likely to give boys detailed instructions on how to do things for themselves and simply complete the project for girls. Nonconsciously, boys learn to be independent and girls learn to be dependent.[6] Throughout elementary and secondary school, the curriculum tends to be male-oriented. History, literature, math, and science all tend to consciously and nonconsciously reflect masculine interests and accomplishments.

Looking at Advantages and Disadvantages

Have the boys and girls meet separately for ten to fifteen minutes. Each group should write down a list of the advantages and disadvantages they believe the **other** gender has—boys come up with the advantages and disadvantages of being a girl and vice versa. Be sure to list each advantage or disadvantage clearly so that the other group can understand what you mean without any further explanation.

When the boys and girls get back together, the group that is going first should sit in a circle in the middle of the room. The other group forms a circle around the outside. The inner circle is then given the list of advantages and disadvantages the other group has come up with. The outer circle may not speak or contribute in any way. One person may be appointed to clarify any confusion about the list, but the inner circle should forget that the outer circle is there as much as possible. The inner circle then reads and reacts to the list of advantages and disadvantages. Their task is not to judge or criticize the other group's list, but to talk about how they feel about the other gender's perceptions. They may also add any advantages or disadvantages that they believe exist that are not on the list.

The groups then switch places and the second group repeats the process. After both groups have had a chance to respond, open up the discussion to the full group. *What surprises or misunderstandings surfaced during the discussions? Who do you think has it easier in this society—females or males? How many boys think girls have it easier? How many girls think boys have it easier? How many people wish they could switch places?*

> *I am the woman who holds up the sky. The rainbow runs through my eyes. The sun makes a path to my womb. My thoughts are in the shape of clouds. But my words are yet to come.*
>
> —*Poem of the Ute Indians*

It is difficult even to be aware of the messages that we learn about being male or female because they are so ingrained in our social environment and upbringing. When a group of teachers was told that they responded differently to girls and boys, they flatly denied it. Even watching a video of their teaching, they could not see the bias until they actually counted the interactions and responses. It is difficult to realize that our curriculums focus almost exclusively on the white, male perspective because that is the way it always has been. Because we don't include female and minority voices, we subsequently devalue them and don't believe that they are important enough to study.

"Masculine" and "Feminine" in Your Daily Life

Think about the messages that you get about being a female or male every day. How would your day, experiences, relationships, and self-concept be different if you were the other gender?

- Go through your daily routine and think about how it would be different if you were a member of the opposite gender.

- In the classroom, notice who talks and how the teacher responds according to gender. Does the gender of the teacher make any difference? (Studies suggest that it doesn't.)

- Look at what you study in school. How much of the literature you read is written by men? How is the female experience included in your study of history? What subtle role does gender play in your other courses?

- How are your relationships with other people influenced by your gender? Would your parents treat you any differently if you were of the other gender? How would your friendships change? Would teachers, coaches, construction workers, police, or total strangers treat you differently?

- How has your gender influenced your personal interests and activities? What activities do you enjoy that would be more difficult to continue if you were a member of the other gender? What do you dislike now that you could stop doing?

- How does the media—advertising, movies, TV, music—typify your gender? What are the subtle and not-so-subtle messages the media portrays about your body, your social role, and your sexuality?

- What parts of your personality might change if you were a member of the other gender? How would the way you express your feelings and opinions change?

- How would your sexual identity, concerns, and behavior change if you were a member of the other sex?

- How would your plans for your future change?

While we tend to think of sexism as exclusively a problem for women, rigid gender stereotyping is detrimental to any individual. Males and females can be caught by the prejudices and expectations of gender roles which specify and limit how they feel, what they do, or who they may become. Sexism is not strictly a matter of power, but also of personal freedom and expression. In the long run, the price that men pay for power in a patriarchal society may be as debilitating as the loss of personal power is to women. Both the women's movement and the

Quandary: *What Makes Boys Masculine and Girls Feminine?*

It is an ongoing, fascinating debate whether the noticeable differences between masculine and feminine behavior are biological or learned. We know that males and females have distinctive physical differences, that we can visually tell the difference between a male and female brain, and that men and women have different proportions of hormones racing through their bodies. We also know that males and females are treated quite differently from birth—talked to and held differently, surrounded by different colors and toys, and expected to behave differently. Do we treat males and females differently because they are different or do males and females behave differently because we treat them differently? Here are some the conflicting research and opinions.

- Gender is determined by the twenty-third set of chromosomes which in females is XX and in males is XY. Seven weeks into pregnancy, the Y chromosome in males stimulates the production of testosterone which directs the ovaries to become testes and the clitoris to become a penis.

- Testosterone injections in pregnant laboratory animals have created female offspring which are more aggressive than noninjected females.

- Baby boys sleep an average of one to two hours less per day. As a consequence, mothers spend more time holding them and encouraging them to reach, grasp, and stand, further increasing their activity and interest in manipulating their environment.

- Baby girls make more babbling and cooing noises as infants which encourages parents to talk more to their baby girls. This interaction encourages the female's earlier development of verbal skills.

- In her anthropological studies, Margaret Mead found three South Pacific societies in which cultural gender roles were quite different, contradicting any biological basis for these roles. In the Arapesh, both men and women were cooperative and nonaggressive, sharing equally the characteristics which we call feminine. The Mundugumor men and women were equally aggressive and competitive. In the Tchambuli tribe, the traditional gender roles were reversed. The men take care of the children and create beautiful artwork, while the women fish, trade, and are domineering and independent.

- While there are some exceptions, most societies follow the traditional division of labor with men doing the hunting and fighting and women creating the home and taking care of the children.

- Women's biological role as childbearers extended naturally into the area of housekeeping and emotional nurturance. Since women are busy with caring for the children and physically more vulnerable when pregnant, men naturally took on the role of protector and food provider which required more physical strength and aggressiveness.

- While in the United States only 13.4 percent of the doctors and 4.3 percent of the dentists are women, in the Soviet Union 80 percent of the doctors and 87 percent of the dentists are women, suggesting cultural training rather than biological predisposition.

- Rough, aggressive play is expected and tolerated much more from young boys.

- Male and female brains are physically different. The female brain has a larger corpus collosum between the two hemispheres, which seems to facilitate greater communication between the left and right hemispheres. Research has shown that women tend to use their left and right hemispheres about equally, while men tend to specialize in the use of the linear left hemisphere.

- In spite of the commonly noted differences between men and women, there are countless exceptions to each stereotype. Some girls are more active, competitive, and linear thinking than some boys and some boys are more verbal, sensitive, and intuitive than some girls. Few individuals perfectly fit the cultural gender roles.

- Carl Jung believed that all human beings have both feminine and masculine archetypes within them that shade and balance the personality—the anima (feminine) and the animus (masculine). Culture encourages or represses different aspects of these archetypes, but developing and understanding both parts of your personality allows you to understand and respond to members of the other gender.

Similarities and Differences

List ways that you think females and males are:

ALIKE	DIFFERENT

Which differences do you think are biological and which differences are learned?

How do these differences and similarities help and hinder relationships between men and women?

What can men and women learn or gain from each others' differences?

men's movement are attempting to help men and women be conscious of the limitations of rigid sex roles and envision more flexible ways of being and relating to each other.

Women's Issues

What Is Feminism?

For many people, feminism is the "F" word, conjuring up visions of emasculating females, radical politics, and antimale sentiment. Quite simply, Webster's College Dictionary defines feminism as *"a doctrine advocating social, political, and economic rights for women equal to those of men."* Many men as well as women are feminists. Some people may be strong feminists without realizing it. Ask some people that you know the following two questions:

1. *Do you think that women should have social, political, and economic rights equal to those of men?*

2. *Are you a feminist?*

Why might the answers to these two questions differ?

• **Role Limitations and Self-Esteem:** In our society, most men *and* women grow up unconsciously learning that women are inferior to men. Most positions of power are held by men and traditional women's roles tend to be paid less and valued less. Like boys, girls tend to internalize these expectations and see themselves as less intelligent, capable, and powerful. In one study of third graders,[7] boys and girls were given a simple puzzle to complete. Both boys and girls finished it quickly and when asked how they did so well, boys responded that they were quite good at puzzles and girls responded that it was an easy puzzle or that they had been lucky. The same children were then given a very difficult puzzle which most could not complete. When asked why they had not been able to do it, boys responded that it was a stupid puzzle and girls responded that they must not be very good at puzzles. Even at this early age, girls tended to brush off success and internalize failure while boys did the opposite.

• **Economic:** Even with recent advances of professional women, as of 1999 employed women still earned only 72.2 percent of their male counterparts. Specifically, according to the Department of Labor, in 1999 the median annual earnings for year-round full-time working women was $26,324 while the median annual earnings for a comparable working man was $36,476.[8] The average female college graduate continues to earn less than a man who has only a high school diploma. While some women are paid less for the same job, this discrepancy also reflects the number of low-paying jobs that are traditionally reserved for women and the "invisible ceiling" which keeps women from advancing to the highest-paying jobs. Women make up less than 1 percent of corporate officers and directors of 4,000 Fortune 500 companies; over half of these companies do not have even one female board member.

• **Body Image:** As a sexual object, women have always been coached and pressured into measuring up to an ideal female image. A woman must paint her face, shave her legs and armpits, disguise her body odor, wear restrictive and often uncomfortable clothing and, usually, lose weight in order to be "attractive" and catch a man. The underlying message is that "you are not OK the way you are" and most women buy it. A majority of women report that they do not like their own bodies, and about 150,000 talented, intelligent young women starve themselves to death through anorexia each year.

• **Sexual Harassment and Assault:** The rate of sexual violence against women has more than doubled since the early 1970s, at a rate of nearly twice that of all other violent crimes. One in five adult women have been sexually assaulted and one in three college women will have to deal with some form of date rape during their four years of higher education. Sex-related murders rose 160 percent between 1976 and 1984 with at least one-third of these women being murdered by their husband or boyfriend. Official complaints of sexual or gender harassment on the job have more than doubled since 1970.

- **Political Power and Representation:** Women were only granted the right to vote in 1920. Until then, men made the political, and often all the economic, decisions relating to family as well as society. While women in the United States have made significant political strides since then, the only woman ever to have been nominated for either the presidency or vice-presidency by a major party was Geraldine Ferraro, whom Democratic presidential nominee Walter Mondale nominated to be his running mate in 1984. Historically, 203 women have served in the United States of Representatives, twenty-five have served in the Senate, and six have served in both chambers. In the current Congress, thirteen of the 100 senators and fifty-nine of the 435 representatives in the House are women. While this is the largest number of women to have served at the same time, they still account for only approximately 13 percent of all members. As of 2000, only 20.6 percent of all federal judges are women. Women's political issues such as equal job opportunity, reproductive rights, child care, sexual harassment and assault, and low-income assistance are typically decided by a predominantly male legislative and judicial system.[9]

Men's Issues

- **Male Identification:** Most children spend the majority of their time around women—mothers, child-care workers, elementary school teachers. For boys, this provides little day-to-day observation of what it is to be a man. Boys are forced to rely on cultural and media stereotypes as role models. Fathers often come home tired from a long work-day and may be cast in the role of disciplinarian—"Just wait until your father gets home." While more and more fathers are taking an active role in raising their children, work, divorce, and their own masculine upbringing may limit their ability to relate to their sons. Many men are learning to form close, personal friendships with each other, but some are still uncomfortable expressing their feelings, fears, and weaknesses to other men. They either keep them hidden or talk to women.

- **Health:** The "macho" sex role would certainly appear to be detrimental to men's health. From birth to death, the male mortality rate is at least twice as high as that of females. Today, the female life expectancy is seven years higher than that of the male—if this rate continues, the ratio of women to men over sixty-five will approach 3:2. A male is encouraged to take more physical risks, encounters more disabling hazards on the job, and is trained from an early age to disregard his body's signals of disease and discomfort. Men seek a doctor's help and are hospitalized less often than women, but this delay is often critical. Men are four times more likely to die from respiratory diseases and twice as likely to die from cardiovascular and liver diseases. Men die from hypertension 40 percent more often, pneumonia and influenza 64 percent more often, and arteriosclerosis 20 percent more often.

- **Body Image:** From an early age, boys are expected to be stronger, faster, and more athletic than girls. Before puberty, there are very few physical differences in male and female strength and speed, so this macho expectation is usually maintained through more aggressive male behavior and socialized compliance on the part of little girls. After puberty, the nonathletic male may question his masculinity and ability to attract girls, and compensate through excessive workouts, steroid use, or other risk-taking behavior. Men, like women, come in many body types that may or may not fit the masculine stereotype. The media and advertising have increased the pressure on men to measure up to the "ideal" male body.

- **Burden of Responsibility:** From asking a girl out on a date to providing for a family, men are often placed in a position of unquestioned responsibility. They are often expected to make the first move, know how to fix things when they break, solve any problem that comes up, lift heavy things, stay calm in a crisis, make a lot of money, and never need help. These expectations are often internalized by men themselves—they expect themselves to be responsible for everything and may feel less than a man if they can't or don't.

- **Repression of Feelings:** While women are expected to be emotional and express their feelings, men are usually restricted to feeling strong or angry. Boys are taught not to cry when they are hurt, not to be a "sissy" when they are afraid, and to slap someone on the back when they feel close or affectionate. Channeling such a wide range of human emotions into calm or anger often gets males into trouble. Boys are much more likely to get into trouble at school and with the law for aggressive or antisocial behavior. Men are six times more likely to be arrested on narcotics charges, thirteen times more likely to be arrested for drunkenness, fourteen times more likely to be arrested for weapons offenses, and three times more likely to be arrested for involvement in a motor vehicle accident. (Men usually account for approximately 80 percent of all murder victims as well.)

- **Performance Anxiety:** If women are expected to be subhuman, men are often expected to be superhuman. Men are expected to maintain a competitive edge in business, sports, muscles, finances, sex, cars, women, politics, war—you name it, if you're not winning, you are losing. This pressure to compete and overpower others can easily undermine male self-esteem and relationships. Males are three or four times more likely to be treated at child guidance clinics and adult males outnumber adult females requiring psychiatric services by 20 percent. The male rate of suicide is over three times the female rate.

RACISM

Another way in which we often group and stereotype individuals is by race or ethnic background. When someone combines a racial stereotype with the belief that one race is superior to another, it is called *racism.* The word *prejudice* comes from the idea to prejudge or assume that all members of a given group share the same personality or social traits regardless of the facts. *Discrimination* is differential treatment based on these prejudices and stereotypes.

Without the influence of adults, children are rarely innately prejudiced, but racism has been a common factor in adult societies throughout history. Prejudice is sometimes viewed as the result of economic and political forces. When jobs, money, or resources are limited, discrimination protects these resources for the dominant group and may even allow them to feel entitled to their advantages. Discrimination and prejudice tends to increase in hard economic times. When the Chinese first migrated to the northwest, they were seen as "depraved and vicious" competitors in the rush for gold. Ten years later when they were willing to undertake the difficult, dangerous work of building the railroads, they were regarded as "sober, industrious and law-abiding." After the Civil War, when returning soldiers put a new pressure on the job market, the Chinese were again redefined as "criminal . . . conniving . . . crafty and stupid."[10] Economic and social competition tends to breed prejudice.

A related theory of prejudice is called *scapegoating.* A *scapegoat* is a relatively powerless bystander who is made to take the blame for something that is not really her fault. If you are angry at your teacher, but fear for your grade, you may take it out on a younger student or your dog. In Nazi Germany, the Jews were the scapegoats for the general frustrations of a depressed economy. In a study by Hovland and Sears,[11] it was found that between 1882 and 1930 the number of black lynchings in the United States was directly related to the price of cotton during that year. As the price of cotton dropped and people experienced economic hardship, the number of lynchings increased. Another study demonstrated that simple personal frustrations, such as being unfairly treated or foiled in what you would like to do, tend to increase whatever racial prejudices you may have.[12]

There is also evidence that some personality types may be more predisposed to prejudice than others. Adorno and his associates[13] identified an *authoritarian personality* type that showed a consistently high degree of prejudice against all minority groups. Authoritarian personalities tend to:

- *be very rigid in what they believe*

- *follow "conventional" rules*

- *be intolerant of weakness in themselves and others*

- *be highly punitive and suspicious of others*

- *be unusually respectful and unquestioning of authority*

Most authoritarian adults were raised by strict, harsh parents who were also quite prejudiced, so this personality pattern may simply be the result of upbringing and conformity to family and social values. Some social theorists believe that although economic competition, frustration, and personality may explain some prejudice, most prejudiced behavior is simply conformity to social norms. We all were raised with a set of prejudices that consciously and unconsciously creep into our attitudes and behavior. No matter what racial group you belong to, you have expectations and fears that influence the assumptions you make about groups and people that you do not know.

I have a dream that my four little children will one day live in a nation where they will not be judged by the color of their skin but by the content of their character.
—*Martin Luther King, Jr.*

Of all the injuries inflicted by racism on people of color, the most corrosive is the wound within, the internalized racism that leads some victims, at unspeakable cost to their own sense of self, to embrace the values of their oppressors.
—*H. Jack Geiger*

Quandary: *The Invisible Knapsack*

In her work on women's studies at Wellesley College, Peggy McIntosh identified a "knapsack" of unearned privileges which a racial majority member unknowingly enjoys. "A white skin in the United States opens many doors for whites whether or not we approve of the way dominance has been conferred on us." Some of the invisible privileges that McIntosh discovered in her own life by contrast with the African-American women in her office:

1. *I can turn on the television or open to the front page of the paper and see people of my race widely and positively represented.*

2. *When I am told about our national heritage or about "civilization," I am shown that people of my color made it what it is.*

3. *I can be sure that my children will be given curricular materials that testify to the existence of their race.*

4. *I can go into a supermarket and find the staple foods which fit my cultural traditions, into a hairdresser's shop and find someone who can cut my hair.*

5. *I can swear or dress in secondhand clothes or not answer letters without having people attribute these choices to the bad morals, the poverty, or the illiteracy of my race.*

6. *I can do well in a challenging situation without being called a credit to my race.*

7. *I am never asked to speak for all the people of my racial group.*

8. *I can easily buy posters, postcards, picture books, greeting cards, dolls, and children's magazines featuring people of my race.*

9. *I can choose blemish cover or Band-Aids in "flesh" color and have them more or less match my skin.*

10. *I can go shopping alone most of the time, pretty well assured that I will not be followed or harassed by store detectives.*

11. *I can if I wish arrange to be in the company of people of my race most of the time.*

12. *Whether I use checks, credit cards, or cash, I can count on my skin color not to work against the appearance of financial responsibility.*

13. *I can be pretty sure that if I ask to talk to "the person in charge," I will be facing a person of my race.*

14. *If a traffic cop pulls me over or if the IRS audits my tax return, I can be sure I haven't been singled out because of my race.*

15. *I can go home from most meetings of groups I belong to feeling somewhat tied in, rather than isolated, out of place, outnumbered, unheard, held at a distance, or feared.*

16. *I can take a job with an affirmative action employer without having co-workers on the job suspect that I got it because of my race.*

17. *If my day, week, or year is going badly, I need not ask of each negative episode or situation whether it has racial overtones.*

"Many, perhaps most, of our white students in the U.S. think that racism doesn't affect them because they are not people of color; they do not see 'whiteness' as a racial identity. In my class and place, I did not see myself as a racist because I was taught to recognize racism only as individual acts of meanness by members of my group, never in invisible systems conferring unsought racial dominance on my group from birth."[14]

How has your racial identity unconsciously affected who you are? What unearned advantages and disadvantages do you have?

Resolving Conflict Situations

Great Spirit, help me never to judge another until I have walked in his moccasins for two weeks.
—*Sioux Indian Prayer*

One of the problems of communication between different groups of people is the difficulty we have genuinely empathizing with others whose experience and social learning is very different from our own. Divide the class into seven small groups. Each group is assigned one of the following conflict situations. After reading the description, discuss in your small group:

1. How would you feel in this situation?
2. What are the conflicts?
3. What would be the best way to resolve these conflicts?

Each group will then report back to the class on what they have discussed and decided.

#1. Tony is a successful, black businessman who is refused membership at an all-white, private country club where many important business contacts and deals are made. He can easily afford the membership, enjoys playing golf and tennis, and would like to belong for both business and social reasons.

#2. Li Ann's parents made many sacrifices to move to the United States so that she could have a good American education and be successful, but she finds that her schooling has taken her further and further from the Chinese culture, traditions, and values that her parents hold most dear. Her parents try not to show it, but they are confused and hurt by her changes.

#3. Miguel is a Mexican-American student who overhears some of his Anglo friends making racist, derogatory comments about the Mexican workers at his school. His friends assure Miguel that he is "different" and they weren't talking about him when they referred to the "Mexicans."

#4. Sophie is a bright, talented minority student who has worked hard to get into a top college. When she is accepted, several of her classmates are angry and openly claim that she only got in because she is a minority.

#5. Richard is an Orthodox Jewish student whose parents have strongly discouraged him from dating the girl that he seriously cares about because she is not Jewish. They fear that he will abandon important family values if he becomes seriously involved with someone who does not share his religion and traditions.

#6. Deborah is a Native American student who is studying U.S. history from a primarily white, European point of view in which Native Americans are typically portrayed as heathens or drunks. Occasionally, she is singled out and asked to present the "Indian point of view."

#7. Timothy is a wealthy, somewhat sheltered Anglo student whose parents are quite prejudiced against many minority groups. He adamantly disagrees with them, but has had no personal experience with anyone of a different race or background. When he tries to get to know some of the minority students at school, he is awkward and nervous. They dismiss him as a "rich, white boy."

FAMILIES

Families are the training ground for all of our relationships. It is in your family that you learn the rules of culture and society. You learn to love, to share, to express your feelings and ideas, and to resolve conflict. It is the mirror of your family that gives you your first look at yourself. This

> *The family is the cornerstone of our society. More than any other force it shapes the attitudes, the hopes, the ambitions, the values of the child.*
>
> —*Lyndon B. Johnson*

mirror reflects your self-image, your body image, and your sense of importance and competence. Your family also lays the foundation for your values, social behavior, and worldview. As your primary social and emotional base, your family will provide much of the security, love, laughter, direction, frustration, challenge, pain, and joy in your life. If you are lucky, your family will teach you how to be an effective, cooperative member of a group, and it will also teach you how to be independent and unique.

Much attention has been paid to the idea of *functional* and *dysfunctional* families. While no family is completely healthy and functional all the time, there appears to be some underlying family characteristics that allow some families to weather the inevitable storms of life and provide each family member with a strong set of personal and social skills.

FUNCTIONAL FAMILIES:	DYSFUNCTIONAL FAMILIES:
Feel free to talk about comfortable and uncomfortable personal feelings	*Have lots of secrets and subjects that are forbidden to talk about*
Value the people in the family more than how well they perform	*Place conditions and expectations—good and bad—on family members*
Accept and value individual differences in the family	*Have rigid and codependent individual roles*
Have clear, but flexible rules	*Have unclear, inconsistent, and rigid rules*
Confront and work through family stress and problems	*Deny problems and avoid dealing with family and personal issues*
Nurture high self-esteem and independence	*Inhibit self-esteem, personal growth, and independence*
Have a strong parental partnership	*Form combative subgroups within the family*
Have a generally relaxed atmosphere of love, joy, and good humor	*Have a tense atmosphere that is full of anger, stress, and fear*
Are honest and supportive of each other	*Are unreliable and critical of each other*

One of the more difficult tasks for you, and for families in general, is the continual development of individuals from childish dependency to adult independence. Most parents are overwhelmed by the responsibility of caring for a newborn baby. It is only strong maternal and paternal love that changes a freewheeling, independent young adult into a nurturing, protective, and somewhat frantic twenty-four-hour caretaker. After assuming such awesome, time-consuming, and powerful responsibility for another human being, parents must gradually and supportively let go. At the same time, a totally dependent, hapless, inexperienced, fearless baby begins to learn the skills and information that she will need to proudly and competently take care of herself.

This is a normal, healthy transfer of authority, but human beings being what they are, it does not always go smoothly and easily. Parents often panic at the prospect of losing the ability to control and protect their precious offspring. Cocky precious offspring often panic at the enormous

Family faces are mirrors. Looking at people who belong to us, we see the past, present, and future.

—Gail Lumet Buckley

responsibility for actually protecting and taking care of themselves. Most of this process of *separation* and *individuation* is an emotional tug of war between dependence and independence. For both parents and children, the closer that each gets to forming new adult roles and relationships, the stronger the urge to retreat and go back to the safety of the way things used to be. For most people in our society, this transition is not a straight line, but rather one of starts and stops, excitement and misgivings, courage and hesitation. Finally, at some point, the family loses a child and gains another adult. In our culture, this usually involves moving out of the family home, becoming financially self-supporting, relating to other members of the family as an adult and, perhaps, starting a second family of your own.

Family Interviews

You can learn a lot about your family and upbringing from your parents. Find a time when one of your parents can sit down and be "interviewed" about your family. Your job is to ask the questions and make sure that you understand your parent's answers. Try to delay your own responses or reactions until after your parent has had his say.

1. *How is our family different from the family you were raised in?*

2. *What are the most important things that you gained from your family?*

3. *What was the hardest thing for you to learn when you were growing up?*

4. *What was your relationship with your parents like when you were my age?*

5. *How was your family upbringing different from Mom's/Dad's?*

6. *When you first became a parent, what was the most difficult thing to adjust to? What else was going on in your life at that time?*

7. *What was your (or Mom's) pregnancy and delivery of me like?*

8. *What was I like as a little baby?*

9. *What characteristics of yourself and Mom/Dad do you see in me?*

10. *What are the most important things that you have tried to teach me?*

11. *What has been the hardest part of parenting me?*

12. *What has been the most rewarding part of parenting me?*

13. *What is the hardest part of seeing me grow up?*

14. *What are you most looking forward to when I am an adult?*

15. *What do you think makes our family unique?*

16. *What issues do you think our family has the hardest time talking about or handling effectively?*

Use your listening skills—try to genuinely understand how the parent you are interviewing thinks and feels about your family. What surprises you about your parent's answers? What did you learn about yourself? What did you learn about him or her? How were your parent's families different from each other's?

Negotiating with Your Parents

As you grow and change, your relationship with your parents will undergo significant changes as well. You will spend less time with your family and more time with your friends. You have many things on your mind and many new responsibilities that do not include your parents. Once aware of everything in your life, your parents now know much less about your daily life, challenges, and relationships. Some parents understand and accept these changes; others panic and try to regain some control. For all parents, your growing independence changes the way they feel about themselves and their relationship to you, and these changes are not always easy or comfortable. Family rules and expectations need to change as you become more responsible for yourself, but this shift may be new and scary for the adults who have been responsible for your safety for the last fourteen to eighteen years. When you make a mistake or break their trust, reestablishing their confidence may be a slow, exasperating task. Most parents want to let you grow and establish your own life, but they aren't always sure how.

You can help by trying to view the situation from your parents' point of view and help them understand your needs and concerns. Adolescence is a time of so many dramatic changes and parents inevitably feel ambivalent. They are excited to see you grow and mature, and they probably enjoy the freedom your independence has given them. But they also probably miss you and are nostalgic for the time when they could understand and protect you from everything bad in the world. Arguments and strong differences of opinion are inevitable, but your parents may feel that you are rejecting their values, or even them personally. As you experiment with different clothing, looks, or hairstyles, your parents may remember fondly when you wore what they suggested; when you seemed so anxious to please them. Some parents worry that they have failed to teach or impart the lessons and values they believe will help you in life. Others lament the fact that the very person who used to admire them and follow them around now thinks they haven't had an intelligent thought or insight in several years. Most parents miss feeling needed and included in your life. Parents sometimes have a strange way of showing their emotions. When they are proud of you, they may make a scene and embarrass you in public. When they are scared that something terrible has happened to you, they may yell at you when they find that you are safe. When they miss having you around, they may ground you and make you more anxious to get out of the house. Be patient, and know that your parents are trying to love you in the best way they know how.

Here are some ways you can help your parents learn how to reconnect and build a new, more adult relationship with you.

1. **Take the first step by respecting their role as your parents.** Address them politely and honor the time, money, and care that they have given you. They aren't perfect; but, if you stop to think, you probably

could do a lot worse and have many things for which to be grateful. Your respect, which means a lot to them, will dramatically increase their willingness to listen and see things your way too.

2. **Discuss rules and consequences in a calm, mature way.** Explain how you feel, and suggest possible solutions and compromises. Respect their opinions and be prepared to give and take. Complaining and slamming doors will just convince them that you are still a child. When you notice that you are about to blow up, back off and regroup. Even if you don't win the battle, you will gain big points for self-control and maturity that will pay off in the long run.

3. **Always be honest.** Even a small lie can undermine your parents' trust. If you make a mistake, own up to it and apologize. If you disagree with a rule or decision, talk it out; don't just sneak around it. You may get away with a lie, but the dishonesty will work away at the trust and communication in your relationship. In the long run, you can lose your parents' confidence and respect.

4. **Avoid the power struggle whenever possible.** It may be difficult for your parents to accept how little power they now have to protect and control you. They can try to make you study, but you are the one who ultimately chooses how hard you will work. They can establish expectations, but you are the one who will make the daily decisions about your behavior. Not being able to control or protect you makes them very nervous. Respect their authority. Letting them have the last word may actually make them more able to hear your point of view.

5. **Discover what they fear.** Rules and restrictions usually evolve in some way out of your parents' fears. Ask your parents to identify and explain what they worry about. This conversation may help you *both* understand which concerns are realistic and what you can do to make everyone more comfortable.

6. **Try to fit them into your schedule from time to time.** Busy schedules sometimes prohibit families from having much time together. A recent study found that parents and teens in the United States spend, on the average, thirty minutes a week together—most of it shopping. If you can reserve some time every week to do something together that you will both enjoy, you will see your relationship improve significantly. Dinner or breakfast together every day keeps communication open and makes it easier to talk about difficult things when they arise. Your parents will come to know and respect you as a young adult. Playing a game, taking a walk, going to a movie, going on a camping trip, discussing the news, volunteering at a homeless shelter together, attending a concert or play, or working together on a project will all begin to lay the foundation for a healthy, lifelong, adult relationship with your parents.

Making It On Your Own

How does it feel to be on your own, like a rolling stone? —Bob Dylan

As you grow and take over more responsibility for yourself, there are many questions and feelings to be aware of. You may do the following exercise on your own, either aloud or in writing, or with a good friend or partner. Give three or four different endings to each sentence. Try not to think too hard about each sentence or censor your thoughts—your first, spontaneous responses will be the most informative. If you are working with a partner, take turns giving several endings to each sentence.

One of the things I value most about my childhood is _____.

When I was a kid, my mother always _____.

When I was a kid, my father always _____.

One of the things I appreciate most about my mom is _____.

One of the things I appreciate most about my dad is _____.

To me, growing up means _____.

One of the hard things about growing up is _____.

Sometimes when things get rough, I wish I could still _____.

One of the things I worry about is _____.

One of the things I am looking forward to is _____.

It drives me crazy when my mother _____.

It drives me crazy when my father _____.

I wish my mother could _____.

I wish my father could _____.

If I become a parent I hope I can _____.

One of the things I need to learn before I become an adult is _____.

MARRIAGE

Your family of origin inevitably has its share of difficulties, squabbles, rivalries, and frustrations and you all share a very close genetic makeup, values, experiences, and upbringing. Marriage brings together two people from different backgrounds and different genders with at least subtly different values and expectations. The challenge to communicate, resolve differences, compromise, stay committed to the relationship, and continue to love and respect your mate is probably the most difficult form of human relationship. Almost 50 percent of today's marriages end in divorce. The average marriage today lasts only 9.4 years. In spite of the odds and the pain involved in ending a marriage, 95 percent of all men and women in the United States will marry at some time and of those marriages that end in divorce, 95 percent will try again with a second or third marriage.

In its ideal form, marriage is a loving and cooperative union of two people, working and playing together to enrich each other's lives. It respects the individuality, personalities, and needs of each person, but is also able to compromise and make sacrifices for the partnership. It is a team that works together toward a home, financial stability, and a family. It is a secure base for raising children and meeting whatever crises life may issue. It nourishes the basis for a trusting, caring sexual relationship that recognizes the needs and desires of both partners. The ideal marriage establishes a lifelong basis of shared experience, memory, and friendship that can provide joy, comfort, and companionship in old age.

Ideal, indeed! The depth and complexities of a long-term, committed relationship require a very mature type of love generously complemented by patience, honesty, tolerance, flexibility, humor, empathy, and compatibility. Some partnerships start out with better odds than others, but all marriages require lifelong nurturing and negotiation. Marrying to escape an unhappy family life or the loneliness of being single, for convenience or social expectations, or exclusively because of sexual attraction are not likely to support the day-to-day pragmatic and emotional demands of a long-term relationship. Friendship, individual maturity, and a shared sense of humor are much more likely to weather the inevitable storms.

My Ideal Marriage Requirements

*Check off or fill in the following requirements that you believe will help you form an ideal marriage. Put an **X** by any requirement that you think is absolutely essential and a ✓ by those which you think would be nice but negotiable. Leave blank any that you don't feel are that important and cross out any that you absolutely do not want in your marriage. Add or edit any requirements that are important to you.*

Things I need to accomplish before I marry:

❑ finish college   ❑ establish my career   ❑ be financially independent
❑ travel   ❑ sow some wild oats   ❑ live on my own
❑ have two or three serious relationships   ❑ establish my independence
❑ resolve my relationship with my parents   ❑ come to terms with myself
❑ feel pretty secure in my own individuality   ❑ establish a group of friends
❑ be at least _____ years old   ❑ live with my mate for awhile
❑ come to terms with _____
❑ something I've always wanted to do before I get married: _____

Qualities of the mate that I marry:

❑ attractive   ❑ ambitious   ❑ good cook   ❑ good with kids
❑ has money   ❑ good listener   ❑ intelligent   ❑ loves the outdoors
❑ loves music   ❑ sensitive   ❑ good sense of humor   ❑ good with finances
❑ honest   ❑ well-mannered   ❑ neat and clean   ❑ sociable
❑ likes sports   ❑ same religion   ❑ same racial group   ❑ good dancer
❑ sexy   ❑ quiet   ❑ same socioeconomic background   ❑ playful
❑ understanding   ❑ even-tempered   ❑ responsible   ❑ self-confident
❑ romantic   ❑ talkative   ❑ thoughtful about special occasions
❑ adventurous   ❑ political   ❑ has lots of friends   ❑ good body
❑ punctual   ❑ emotional   ❑ respected by others   ❑ liked by my parents
❑ affectionate   ❑ faithful   ❑ physically fit   ❑ a good lover
❑ _____   ❑ _____   ❑ _____

Things that we need to agree on:

❑ gender roles in marriage   ❑ woman's last name   ❑ children's last names
❑ to have children or not   ❑ number of children   ❑ how soon to have children
❑ who will care for kids when young   ❑ who will work when children are young
❑ division of household responsibilities   ❑ who will work outside of home
❑ career moves   ❑ political views   ❑ frequency and role of sex in our relationship
❑ sexual commitment   ❑ how kids should be disciplined   ❑ who makes financial decisions
❑ budget   ❑ how money is allocated   ❑ like same kinds of foods
❑ shared religious beliefs   ❑ importance of religion in our life   ❑ recreation
❑ leisure activities   ❑ sleeping routines   ❑ type of vacations we enjoy
❑ role of separate friends and activities   ❑ type and location of home   ❑ privacy and time apart
❑ _____   ❑ _____   ❑ _____

Family values and routines that are important to me:

❑ having a clean house   ❑ having a neat yard and gardens   ❑ personal hygiene
❑ traditional holiday celebrations   ❑ attending church regularly   ❑ personal privacy
❑ inclusion of extended family ❑ being on time   ❑ mealtime rituals
❑ treatment of older family members   ❑ role of children   ❑ pets
❑ use of alcohol or drugs   ❑ ethnic or religious traditions   ❑ politically active
❑ special cultural or athletic interests   ❑ hiking or camping   ❑ physical fitness
❑ amount of extended family interaction   ❑ attitudes about death and grieving   ❑ expression of feelings
❑ _____   ❑ _____   ❑ _____

Keep this list and note how your requirements change over time or when you are seriously interested in a possible mate.

Values that Keep a Marriage Alive

In a marital stability survey of 351 couples who were married fifteen years or more, these are some of the reasons they gave for having a successful marriage. Rank these statements according to what you think would be important in your marriage. Rank the statements 1 (most important) to 12 (least important).[15]

_____   We agree on aims and goals.

_____   We laugh together.

_____   Marriage is sacred.

_____   My spouse is my best friend.

_____   Marriage is a long-term commitment.

_____   We agree on our sex life.

_____   We agree on a philosophy of life.

_____   An enduring marriage is important to social stability.

_____   I like my spouse as a person.

_____   I want the relationship to succeed.

_____   We have a stimulating exchange of ideas.

_____   My spouse continues to grow more interesting.

Divorce

Marriage is a serious commitment forming the basis of family and security for children, but it does not always work out. Many children and teens today have to come to terms with the disillusionment of a failed marriage. A young child may not understand what is happening and feel personally rejected or responsible when one parent leaves the home. Teenagers may be surprised by the depth and confusion of their own feelings. It is more expensive to operate two houses and finances may become a big problem. It is easy to feel pressured to take sides in parental disagreements, and some parents unknowingly place their children in an awkward position as messenger or negotiator. In an especially messy divorce, children are sometimes used to blackmail or get back at an angry parent. At some point, children of divorce may have to adjust to their parents' dating, remarriage, and stepfamilies. None of this is particularly easy for anyone.

For most children, the most difficult part of a divorce is the subtle, or at times, not so subtle, *deprivation of parenting.* Both parents tend to go through a very difficult adjustment following the dissolution of their marriage which can take two-and-one-half to three-and-one-half years to heal. During this time, it is very difficult for them to be emotionally available for their children. Most parents go through some form of depression and may be irritable, tearful, or distracted. Some throw themselves into their work, new relationships, alcohol, or other distractions to keep from thinking about the pain of their marital problems. Many are too overwhelmed by social, emotional, legal, and financial pressures to respond effectively to their children's emotional needs.

Faced with the emotional vulnerability of one or both of his parents, a child may attempt to avoid his own feelings while taking care of his parents. Some are able to do this successfully for quite a while. Then, sometimes years later, they experience all of the feelings that were repressed as they attempted to "parent" their parents. Others just become numb and imagine that they can live without love, sorrow, anger, worry, or pain. Some teenagers start using drugs or alcohol to medicate their feelings. They may become cynical, angry, and antisocial. They may dramatically change their appearance, interests, and social groups. No matter how common or uneventful divorce has become, it still entails a confusing range of feelings and fears if it happens to you. These family changes inevitably create feelings of impermanence and a shaky state of insecurity.

When a child experiences her parents' divorce, she will inevitably go through painful but normal feelings of loss and grief. The loss seems to affect the past, present, and future. Happy memories of her parents and family during more pleasant times may temporarily be painful to remember. The present seems like a bad dream; it is hard to concentrate or think about anything but the divorce. Suddenly, all of those unquestioned assumptions about the future and whom it would include are permanently changed and lost. Most children go through periods of denial, pleading, anger, and sadness before they are able to begin to heal and put their lives back together. These are not easy feelings, but it is much healthier to deal with them directly and work through them.

What Can Parents Do to Make a Divorce Easier?

Judith Wallerstein has studied the effects of divorce on children since 1971.[16] While over 50 percent have some serious difficulties adjusting to the divorce, parents can help this adjustment.

- *Keep the lines of communication and honesty open.*
- *Keep the kids included in new life changes. Get involved in new family activities.*
- *Keep the post-divorce hostility under control.*
- *Both parents need to maintain an emotional relationship with the children.*
- *Set limits and maintain a family routine that begins to rebuild a sense of security.*
- *Seek counseling or a support group when things get rough.*

If you or a friend are going through a parental divorce, remember:

- *You are not to blame if your parents get divorced.*
- *It is quite natural to feel sad, angry, afraid, confused, ashamed, guilty, relieved, and worried. These feelings won't last forever!*
- *If you are confused or scared, tell your parents how you feel and ask questions.*
- *Don't keep your feelings all bottled up—talk to someone.*
- *Tell your parents you won't take sides, carry messages, or listen to bad things about either of them.*
- *You may want to help out more, but you are not responsible for taking care of your parents.*
- *Be honest—tell your parents how you feel and what you need from them.*

When a Family Changes . . .

Divorce is **always** the result of an inability of the parents to resolve their differences, but it usually creates special problems for the children involved as well. Each family and individual situation will be different and require different solutions. Try to come up with some good responses or solutions to the following problems that children sometimes have to confront. Discuss your responses in small groups, carefully listening to the advice and experience of members who may have encountered similar situations.

- *Your parents are fighting over custody and the judge asks you who you would like to live with.*

- *Your mother tells you to bug your father about his child-support payment.*

- *Your father interrogates you for information about the man that your mother is dating.*

- *Your mother refuses to come to your graduation if your father's new wife is there.*

- *Each of your parents is pressuring you to spend Christmas day with them, but they live too far apart for you to be with both.*

- *Since the divorce, neither of your parents seems to be able to afford the extras that you have been accustomed to. Your father is always complaining about expenses and your mother barely seems to be able to make ends meet.*

- *One parent is constantly criticizing and blaming the other.*

- *After your mother got custody, your father sort of disappeared from your life. The only time you hear from him is Christmas and your birthday—if he remembers.*

- *Both parents seem preoccupied with their own problems and haven't had much time or attention for you.*

- *Your younger brother is acting out and getting into trouble, but your parents don't seem to notice or just get angry with him. You know he is upset about the divorce, but nobody seems to be helping.*

- *You know your parents have enough problems of their own, but you are feeling pretty depressed, helpless, lethargic, and even a little suicidal since the divorce was finalized.*

- *You can't stand the person that your father is dating—and it looks like it is getting serious.*

- *Your mother's new husband is OK, but his children are impossible and are taking over the house.*

Quandary: *Why Do Many Marriages Fail?*

With almost one in every two marriages ending in divorce, social scientists, religious leaders, politicians, and almost everyone else has an opinion on why marriages are not working out as often as they used to. Listed below are some of the theories about modern marriage and divorce. Read and discuss them carefully, then come up with your own theory and recommendations.

- Marriages are no less fragile or unhappy than before. Relaxed laws and social expectations about divorce merely allow people to get out of unhappy marriages that they would have suffered through before.

- People are alive and active for a longer time than anytime before in the history of marriage. While a typical marriage may have lasted twenty to thirty years before, men and women now face fifty to sixty years together.

- Modern men and women expect marriage to be easy and romantic and are quick to give up when normal conflicts and drudgery invade their relationships. They don't have the patience or gumption to work things through.

- The nuclear family has become too insulated, isolating husbands and wives from a wider range of extended family, friends, and community to support their individual and family needs. This creates an unrealistic strain on a marital relationship as two people try to meet all of these needs.

- Modern career pressures have taken men and women out of the family, providing less stability and commitment to each other and the family unit. Professional contacts between men and women provide more opportunities to fall in love or become sexually involved outside of marriage.

- The breakdown in traditional gender roles have left families without "Mom" as a stabilizing, stay-at-home force to create a comfortable, nurturing environment. "Dad" no longer has a traditional role to play, so the family and husband/wife relationship becomes disoriented and fragile.

- People are still committed to marriage, but have developed a more realistic, fulfilling form of serial monogamy—single, committed relationships that last for a while until each partner moves on to another single, committed relationship.

- The sexual revolution and the constant message from advertising suggest that you CAN have it all! This has created an immature dissatisfaction with anything or anyone for very long. There are too many choices, "new, improved products," and a general feeling that you will be missing out on something if you don't keep shopping around.

- Modern individuals are narcissistic and demand instant gratification. They think primarily about themselves and their immediate desires and are unwilling to make sacrifices for their marriage, mate, or long-term objectives. Traditional sanctions about fidelity, commitment, and the family have given way to more self-centered values.

What is your theory about modern marriage and families? Do you think that the trend is negative or merely a natural evolution of family patterns? What are the drawbacks of "serial monogamy" and divorce? Do you intend to get married? Do you expect to get divorced? What plans and protections do you intend to make in order to have the kind of marriage you would like?

FRIENDSHIP

One of the most enduring, rewarding kinds of love is called friendship. Human beings are basically social animals. We prefer to live, work, play, and contemplate our lives together. We are also solitary, unique creatures who will be born, experience our thoughts and feelings, and die alone. Friendship provides a bridge between these two realities. Sigmund Freud believed that this basic ambivalence between independence and dependence is one of the primary conflicts that motivates human behavior. We do not want to be swallowed up by other people, but we do not want to drift off separately on our own. We crave both the love, comfort, and companionship of others and the expression of our own rich, independent spirit.

There are as many different forms of friendship as there are people and relationships. Some friendships are short and intense. You may meet someone on an Outward Bound trip with whom you share your fears, hopes, tears, laughter, and many experiences you will never forget— and never see that person again. Or you may have a friend with whom you have grown up, who has always been there for the important times in your life, and will share your old age. Some friendships are quiet, comfortable relationships while others are full of disagreements, conflicts, and making up. Some friends are very much like you and some seem to be your exact opposite. Some are female and some are male. You may even end up marrying one of your best friends. Different friends may play different roles in your life—you may turn to one friend

Qualities of a Friend

As a group, pick six qualities that you agree are most important in a friend. You can pick qualities from the list below or think up others on your own. Once you have settled on six (or seven if the group insists!), assign each quality a particular spot in the room. You can write them on pieces of paper or a blackboard to help people remember. Everyone then thinks for himself which one of these qualities he believes is the most important. When a signal is given, each person should get up and stand by the quality she has selected. (If, by some chance, you should all pick the same one, proceed to the second most important.) Each group is then given a chance to explain and defend its choice. Switching is allowed at any point, but you must briefly state the reason why you have changed your mind.

loyalty	*shared interests*	*shared values*
fun to be with	*sense of humor*	*respect*
sensitivity	*acceptance*	*understanding*
support	*trust*	*honesty*
generosity	*unconditional positive regard*	*reliability*

You can also do this exercise on your own, picking out the twelve qualities that you think are most important and ranking them from the most important to the least important.

> *A lot of people have become more responsible than they thought they could because someone else thought they could.*
>
> *—Gene Bedley*

when you need someone to talk to, another when you want to go rock climbing, and another when you just want to relax and pass the time.

While most of us worry about *having* **friends, the real trick is** *being* **a good friend.** You don't have much control over another person's behavior or affections, but with time and practice, you can become a good friend yourself. And not coincidentally, people who know how to *be* a good friend usually *have* a lot of good friends. Some of the things that you can do to be a good friend include:

- **Be honest.** Share your own honest opinions, feelings, and thoughts with your friends. Share your good side as well as your imperfections, insecurities, and questions. The more you are willing and able to share of yourself, the more your friend will know and understand you.

- **Be respectful and sensitive to your friend's ideas and feelings.** Respect her right to be different from you and to have her own beliefs, imperfections, and opinions. Listen and try to understand and accept your friend just as she is.

- **Appreciate and enjoy your friend.** Let him know that you value his friendship and the time that you share. Allow both your friend and the friendship to evolve and grow so that it stays healthy and satisfying to you both.

- **Know that your friend will disappoint you from time to time.** Don't expect that your friend will always understand you or do what you would like her to do. Stick by your friend and work together to resolve your differences. Remember that everyone has bad days, misunderstandings, and personal weaknesses. Learn to apologize when you have violated the friendship.

- **Share your secrets, hopes, and dreams with your friend.** By disclosing the things that are important to you and listening to the things that are important to him, you gradually build up a special trust with your friend.

- **Be loyal, generous, tolerant, and considerate of your friend.** Don't make promises that you can't keep. Stand by your friend and respect her feelings, needs, and ideas. Allow your friend the time and space to pursue other friendships and interests. Jealousy and possessiveness can undermine even the best friendship.

- **Be there, if possible, when your friend needs you and reach out for his help when you need it.** Healthy friendships are reciprocal and involve a mutual amount of give and take. If one person is always in control or dependent, the relationship will become unbalanced and burdensome.

- **Respect, appreciate, and nurture your relationships—friendships don't just happen.** Let your friend know that you value her friendship. Make an effort to plan activities or spend time together. Resolve conflicts honestly when they occur. Share the good times as well as the bad times.

> *I do my thing and you do yours.*
> *I am not in this world to live up to your expectations,*
> *And you are not in this world to live up to mine.*
> *I am I and you are you.*
> *If by chance we find each other,*
> *It's beautiful.*
> *If not,*
> *It can't be helped.*
>
> *—Fritz Perls*

> *The highest compact we can make with our fellow man is, let there be truth between us two forevermore.*
>
> *—Ralph Waldo Emerson*

What Would a Friend Do?

Listed below are a series of problems that sometimes come up in friendships. In pairs or small groups, select or assign one or two of the problem situations and figure out what would be the best response for a friend to make. Report your solutions back to the larger group for their feedback. Be sure to be realistic and true to your values of friendship.

- *You are in a larger group that begins to make fun of your friend. (Imagine responses both as if your friend is or isn't present.)*

- *Your parents disapprove of one of your good friends and have forbidden you to see him.*

- *Your friend has gotten herself into some trouble and has asked you to lie to cover for her.*

- *Your friend insists that you are still "best friends," but is spending more and more time with some other friends in a group that you are not very comfortable with.*

- *You have just found out that your friend has told someone else a confidential secret that you had entrusted to her.*

- *Your friend's parents are getting a divorce and he has been depressed, angry, and no fun to be with lately, but doesn't want to talk about it.*

- *Your friend is really great when the two of you are together, but in a group, she shows off and doesn't really act like herself.*

- *You are at a party with your friend and he begins to drink a lot and starts making a fool of himself.*

- *Your friend tells you that she thinks she is pregnant.*

- *Your friend confides that his father drinks too much and has been physically threatening his mother and siblings.*

- *Your friend tells you that she thinks she might be gay.*

- *Your friend is pressuring you to do something that violates your values.*

- *Two of your good friends hate each other, want you to take sides, and are jealous of the time that you spend with the other one.*

- *Your best friend has been seriously losing weight—she is always talking about food, but rarely eats much and you suspect that she throws up what she does eat. She is very defensive and angry if you bring it up with her.*

UNCONDITIONAL POSITIVE REGARD

UNCONDITIONAL POSITIVE REGARD MEANS THAT A PERSON ACCEPTS AND RESPECTS YOU SIMPLY FOR WHO YOU ARE. YOU DO NOT HAVE TO IMPRESS, PRETEND, OR PLEASE HER OR BE ON YOUR GUARD WITH HER—YOU NEED ONLY BE YOURSELF. HE UNDERSTANDS YOU AND ACCEPTS YOUR IMPERFECTIONS, VANITIES, MEANNESS, AND SILLINESS. SHE KNOWS THAT YOU ARE UNIQUE AND WORTHY JUST THE WAY YOU ARE, SHARING YOUR LAUGHTER, TEARS, FEARS, ANGER, AND TENDERNESS WITHOUT THREAT OR JUDGMENT.

Four Friends

Friendships enrich our lives, provide us with laughter, comfort, and camaraderie and give us an opportunity to develop our own best qualities. Often, however, friends are so comfortable and reliable that we take them for granted. Take some time to think about four of your best friends and what they have contributed to your life. Try to have at least one of these friends be someone of the other gender.

My friend's name _____

We've been friends from _____

to _____.

A time when s/he really helped me out:

Qualities I really admire in this friend:

I can always depend on this friend to:

Ways that I contribute to our friendship:

My friend's name _____

We've been friends from _____

to _____.

A time when s/he really helped me out:

Qualities I really admire in this friend:

I can always depend on this friend to:

Ways that I contribute to our friendship:

My friend's name _____

We've been friends from _____

to _____.

A time when s/he really helped me out:

Qualities I really admire in this friend:

I can always depend on this friend to:

Ways that I contribute to our friendship:

My friend's name _____

We've been friends from _____

to _____.

A time when s/he really helped me out:

Qualities I really admire in this friend:

I can always depend on this friend to:

Ways that I contribute to our friendship:

Quandary: What Is More Important than Friendship?

Friendship creates a rich and supportive network for our lives, but occasionally it may conflict with our own values or beliefs. We find ourselves in a position of having to choose between our friendship and what we believe in. This can often be a very difficult choice. In each of the following situations, decide what you would do. Cross your arms across your chest if you would do nothing or raise your hand in the air if you would take some personal action against your friend's behavior. This may involve authorities, the police, parents, a counselor, a teacher, or your friend directly, but its end result must be to stop your friend or the situation—whatever it takes. Put a thumbs down if this would probably end your friendship with this person.

- Your friend is shoplifting.

- Your friend is stealing from another friend of yours.

- Your friend is stealing large sums of money from her parents.

- Your friend is stealing from you.

- Your friend is using a stolen calling-card number.

- Your friend has plagiarized a major term paper.

- Your friend has cheated off your paper for a major test.

- Your friend wants you to help her get a copy of the upcoming test.

- Your friend is selling drugs at the local elementary school.

- Your friend is using illegal drugs.

- You believe that your friend is developing a serious alcohol problem.

- Your friend insists on driving home when she is obviously inebriated.

- Your friend is responsible for a violation that another student is about to get kicked out of school for.

- Your friend has been bullying and physically harassing some younger students.

- Your friend has been involved in secret threats and harassment of a minority student.

- Your friend is sexually harassing a member of the other gender.

- Your friend is planning a prank that is potentially dangerous.

- Your friend was driving and left the scene of an accident where someone was seriously injured.

- Your friend has told you that she is seriously thinking about committing suicide, but insists that you not tell anyone.

- Your friend has been beaten and threatened by a parent, but he begs you not to tell anyone.

In what situations are your personal values more important than your friendship? What do you value more than friendship? What would destroy the friendship that you felt for someone?

Popularity

One thing that begins to develop in middle childhood and is usually in full bloom by adolescence is a sense of *social consciousness*—an awareness of where you stand in relation to significant groups in your life. As you grow up, your identity gradually shifts from being exclusively a member of a family to more immediately being a member of a larger, less homogeneous peer group. Gradually that shift will continue until you actually become an independent, adult member of both your family and your peer group. In the meantime, establishing your role and identity with people your own age takes on increasing importance. Friendships, social status, and popularity help you define your new identity outside of the family.

This is not a particularly simple or confidence-producing process, however. Not only are you probably feeling occasionally anxious and inadequate, so is everyone else. Confidence and security breed compassion, openness, and tolerance, but insecurity tends to breed defensiveness and discrimination. Until people get their feet on the ground and establish the confidence and social skills to interact assuredly, adolescent groups can be quite competitive, exclusionary, and judgmental. Small groups may form which become closed to people not directly associated with the group. Individuals may be judged by what they wear, who they hang around with, and their physical appearance or social behavior rather than their personal qualities. There is safety in numbers, so many people spend their time trying to blend in or be the person that they think everyone else would approve.

Of course, everyone else is doing the same thing, so it is very difficult to know exactly who is approving of whom and who is setting the expectations. The best approach is obvious and everyone is quick to tell you— BE YOURSELF! But when you are in the middle of the process of defining who you are, what you want to be, what clothes, music, activities you really like, "being yourself" is easier said than done. Most teenagers would be delighted to just be themselves, but the problem is, they are constantly changing. Adolescence is a time of routine physical, social, and emotional change. Your peers, and the social acceptance and rejection they offer, will probably be more important to you during high school and early college than at any other time of your life.

You will learn a lot from your peers and will share many common questions, predicaments, and experiences. In time, you will be able to easily recognize how you are like your friends and how you are different. Your self-esteem will come out of self-respect rather than fitting a popular model of other people's expectations. Being true to yourself will serve you much better in the long run than any popularity contest. Friends are better counted by loyalty and kindness than by number. The stronger you become as an individual, the less social status and initiations will matter to you. Ironically, when this happens, you will most likely find that your peers like and accept you more than ever.

Measuring the Climate of a Group

On a separate piece of paper, write two columns of numbers listed from one to ten in one column and one to ten in the other. Mark each of the following statements according to how you feel as a member of a particular group—your class, your social group, any group that will be completing this survey with you. Each statement should be marked:

5 = *strongly agree*   **4** = *agree*   **3** = *mixed feelings or unsure*   **2** = *disagree*   **1** = *strongly disagree*

After you have completed both columns, fold your sheet and turn it in to your teacher or teaching assistant. Do not put your name on it—your answers should all remain anonymous. As a group, you may decide that you want to indicate whether you are male or female to determine if there are any differences between the way boys and girls perceive your group. After the scores have all been tabulated, discuss the results as a group. What are your strengths and weaknesses as a group? What do you think accounts for your group's strengths? What can the group do to address its weaknesses?

Column One: How I Feel in This Group

1. I feel that most people in this group know me for who I really am.

2. I enjoy participating in group activities and meetings.

3. This group makes it comfortable for me to just be myself.

4. I feel that I am a valued and respected member of this group.

5. There is always someone in this group that I can go to if I have a problem.

6. I am comfortable joining in with any of the smaller groups within this group.

7. I feel included in most things that go on in this group.

8. I usually feel comfortable speaking my mind honestly in this group.

9. I like most of the people in this group.

10. When people disagree or criticize me in this group, I know they still like and respect me.

Column Two: My Perception of the Group

1. Most people are proud to be a part of this group.

2. Individual talents and diversity are encouraged in this group.

3. There is a feeling of unity and loyalty in this group.

4. Group members are usually kind and accepting of each other.

5. Leadership and ideas are contributed by many people, not just a few.

6. All group members are respected and included in group activities.

7. This group works well together to get things done.

8. Everyone has a chance to speak up and be listened to in this group.

9. Most people in this group say what they really think and feel.

10. Conflicts and disagreements are handled openly and fairly in this group.

What Is in Vogue at Your School?

One of the ways to identify and strengthen your own preferences, values, and differences is to become more aware of the social climate and norms of your peer group. A *norm* is an unspoken social expectation or preference that is commonly accepted as the proper or desirable way to behave—behavior that we tend to think of as "in" or "cool." Some norms are temporary fads that change from season to season while others are basic, nonconscious principles of all our social interaction. Some norms will coincide with your own personal preferences. Others will disagree in either minor or critically important ways.

Go through each of the behaviors and values listed below and put a check (✔) in the boxes of all the ones that are generally considered desirable in your peer group. If a behavior doesn't have any special value in your group, just leave it blank. If it has a negative value, put an ✗ in its box. Complete the lists in a small group so that you can check out your own perceptions with others. Fill in things that are popular or "in" at your school in the blanks at the bottom. Then privately, check off your own personal preferences in the second column. Take some time to carefully evaluate where you agree with your peer group and where you are different. How do you respond to situations where your preferences conflict with your group's? What preferences are you willing to compromise? On which preferences do you need to stand alone?

Group	Mine		Group	Mine	
❏	◯	being a jock	❏	◯	making good grades
❏	◯	arts and drama	❏	◯	being a school leader
❏	◯	close family relationships	❏	◯	having a job
❏	◯	having a lot of money	❏	◯	_____ cars
❏	◯	neat clothing/appearance	❏	◯	running or exercising
❏	◯	being thin (girls)	❏	◯	being muscular (boys)
❏	◯	smoking tobacco	❏	◯	being in the party crowd
❏	◯	marijuana	❏	◯	cocaine
❏	◯	drinking	❏	◯	LSD
❏	◯	being a virgin (boy)	❏	◯	being a virgin (girl)
❏	◯	cheating in school	❏	◯	_____ music
❏	◯	_____	❏	◯	_____
❏	◯	_____	❏	◯	_____
❏	◯	_____	❏	◯	_____
❏	◯	_____	❏	◯	_____
❏	◯	_____	❏	◯	_____
❏	◯	_____	❏	◯	_____

WHAT'S LOVE GOT TO DO WITH IT?

There is probably no type of feeling or relationship that provokes more attention, praise, despondency, or desire than love. All of the major religions of the world are based on some type of love. Patriotism and group loyalty are built on a widespread love of the principles and members of a certain group. Families survive incredible catastrophes and internal conflict through their basic connection of love for each other. Children fail to thrive and develop into competent, healthy adults without love. Friendship thrives or dissolves on the basis of love. Pets seem to be able to give love unconditionally—their love can foster comfort and companionship and cause incredible sadness when they die. There is no end to songs about romantic love and heartbreak. A good part of your life will be spent seeking, nurturing, and trying to understand a love relationship with one special individual with whom you have chosen to share your life, sorrows, pleasures, body, children, hopes, and fears.

In spite of this universal preoccupation with love, it is a hard concept to define. We use love in many different contexts without the least bit of question. Nobody doubts that you can love God, your dog, surfing, music, the earth, pickles, freedom, Jacuzzis, your mom, the color blue, thunderstorms, and sleeping late on Saturday morning. A lover might be anyone from a sexual partner to an aficionado of some activity (art lover, sports lover). Movies, plays, literature, and popular music present many different pictures of love—erotic love, infatuation, young love, jealous love, addictive love, and, of course, unrequited love. Sometimes our expectations and hopes for love are extravagant and unrealistic. Sometimes our fear of intimacy blocks our ability to truly give and receive any love at all. We can't seem to live happily without love, but most of us have some difficulty recognizing, protecting, appreciating, and reciprocating the love in our lives.

Carefully read the quotes about love and complete the exercises following them.

What They Say About Love . . .

There is a single magic, a single power, a single salvation and a single happiness, and that is called loving. —Herman Hesse

We cannot really love anybody with whom we never laugh. —Agnes Repplier

Love does not consist of gazing at each other, but in looking together in the same direction. —Antoine de Saint-Exupéry

Love doesn't just sit there like a stone. It has to be made like bread, remade all the time, made new. —Ursula Leguin

Love's a disease, but curable. —Rose Macaulay

Love is a rose but you better not pick it, it only grows when it's on the vine. —Neil Young

To love at all is to be vulnerable. Love anything and your heart will certainly be wrung and possibly be broken. If you want to make sure of keeping it intact, you must give your heart to no one, not even to an animal. —C. S. Lewis

A Love Montage

Fill in the space below with all of the people, things, activities, events, or qualities that you love. Don't edit; just include anything that you would easily say that you love; persons, sunsets, cheesecake, rock climbing, chipmunks, whatever. Write them large or small, at any angle or place on the page, creating your own artistic picture of love.

I Love:

Being Loved . . .

Think of someone in your life who has loved you in a particularly remarkable way. What does that person do or say that makes you feel loved? What qualities does he have that make him so loving? How do you know that you can trust her love? How does he respond to you when you are scared? angry? hurt? disappointed? mean? silly? demanding? happy? discouraged? How has her love affected you as a person? What have you done to deserve such a special love? Try to write a portrait of that person and his love for you.

Types of Love

In a small group, share your lists of things that you love and some of the main characteristics of your experience of being loved. Try to come up with a list of all the different types of love that you can think of. For each category, identify or define the qualities that embody that type of love. In the next section, pick out the more universal qualities of love that each type has in common—why we call them all LOVE.

Types of love:

Qualities that they have in common:

Now, as a group, try to come up with your best definition of what love is:

Romantic love is perhaps the most exciting, mystifying, exhilarating, and short-lived kind of love there is. It is an irresistible combination of bliss, sexual attraction, possessiveness, intense highs, and devastating lows. Your heart beats faster, it is hard to concentrate, and you inevitably say something stupid or can't say anything at all. Romantic love may be the beginning of a richer, long-lasting love or a fanciful physical attraction or a painful, unrequited love. It may break your heart, make you feel on top of the world, get you pregnant, or spice up an otherwise boring or difficult period in your life. In any case, it is a wonderful, terrible, inevitable part of being human.

"Everybody plays the fool, sometime. There's no exception to the rule . . ."

Romantic love is well known for its ability to wreak havoc for everyone at one time or another in his life. Divide into small groups of two to three persons. Each group will have two minutes to come up with its best response to each of the romantic dilemmas listed below. After each group has responded to all of the situations, the responses will be judged from 1 (weak response, think again) to 5 (perfect reaction!) in each of the following categories:

Realism	*Realistic and believable given the situation*
Effectiveness	*Would work and produce desirable results*
Self-affirmation	*Respects your values and integrity, would leave you feeling good about yourself and probably gain the respect of important others*

You can judge the responses individually, as a class, or pick a panel of judges to give their scores. The important thing is to hear a lot of different responses to the same situation, evaluate their pros and cons, and consider which responses would work for you.

---

1. *The person that your best friend has a mad crush on has indicated that he is not interested in her, but would like to get to know you better.*

_____ Realism _____ Effectiveness _____ Self-affirmation

2. *You are very interested in someone who doesn't seem to know you are alive and don't know how to get her attention.*

_____ Realism _____ Effectiveness _____ Self-affirmation

3. *You hear from a pretty reliable source that your boyfriend has been secretly seeing another girl on the side.*

_____ Realism   _____ Effectiveness   _____ Self-affirmation

4. *You and your girlfriend strongly disagree about the place of sex in your relationship.*

_____ Realism   _____ Effectiveness   _____ Self-affirmation

5. *You really like your boyfriend, but he is monopolizing your time to the extent that you don't have any time left for other friends or doing things on your own.*

_____ Realism   _____ Effectiveness   _____ Self-affirmation

LOSS

Loss is an inevitable, ongoing element of life. Life involves constant changes and each change brings about minor or important losses. One of the skills of healthy adulthood is the ability to acknowledge, accept, and adjust to the various losses in our lives. By the time a person has finished high school, 50 percent will have experienced the divorce of their parents and 20 percent will have experienced the death of a parent or sibling. Many others will have gone through the losses involved in moving, changing schools, the death of a loved pet, abortion, a lost friendship, or a physical disability or accident. All of us go through the loss of childhood innocence and dependence as we "put away childish things" and take on the more complicated responsibilities and realities of adulthood.

Some of these losses are minor and short-lived. Others seem to scar our self-esteem and ability to move on with our lives. Eighty percent of the children experiencing substantial losses carry the unresolved pain and memory into adulthood with them. Traumatizing loss is complex because it usually involves many associated losses. When parents divorce, a child loses much more than the family unit or the daily physical presence of one of his parents. The imagined future and shared family history is lost. Financial changes may bring about a loss of financial security, physical possessions, social status, or even the family home. Children of a divorce may lose trust in their relationships, in their parents, and in the institution of marriage. Many children feel a loss of control and confidence in themselves and others. Adjustment to a loss takes place faster when *all* the losses are recognized and addressed.

Some of the losses people experience include:

Death of a parent, sibling, or friend	*Change in family financial status*
Divorce or separation of parents	*Love relationship breakup*
Serious illness or injury	*Brother/sister leaving home*
Rape	*Trouble with school or the police*
Remarriage of parent	*Physical and appearance changes*
Unwanted pregnancy or abortion	*Loss of good friend*
New home or new school	*Lost opportunity or position*

> *There is no such thing as a problem without a gift for you in its hands.*
> —Richard Bach

When we experience both traumatic and not-so-obvious losses in our lives, we go through different levels of grief. You may not experience these levels in any certain order and may return to one level over and over again until it is resolved or you are ready to deal with the other levels. Since any major loss also involves many smaller losses, you may be dealing with separate losses on different levels at the same time. This can be confusing, frightening, and exhausting.

The different levels or responses to loss are:

Denial This can range from emotional numbness to a more irrational blocking of information or reality. Almost everyone has an immediate "No, it can't be" response to loss. Most teenagers who have lost a parent report having no feelings during the funeral or time immediately following the death. They often "forget" that the parent has died periodically during the first year of mourning. Children going through a divorce or extended illness may deny that there is anything really wrong and convince themselves that everything will soon return to normal. During this phase, people avoid talking about the problem, keep busy, and may look fine on the surface. At the same time, they may begin to withdraw from other people and activities, be less able to concentrate, become argumentative and fearful, and have trouble eating and sleeping.

Anger

Anger is a tough phase of grieving because it feels irrational even to the person who is experiencing it. It also tends to alienate the people around you. The loss seems unfair and we want someone or something to blame. A person may feel angry at the lost person for abandoning her, at friends for not being able to comfort her, at teachers for expecting too much from her, at peers for still having two parents (and maybe not appreciating them), at her remaining parent for being alone, at herself for having to cope with this loss, or at God for not protecting her from such pain and loneliness. She usually recognizes how irrational these angers are and may end up displacing her angry feelings onto petty, unrelated events. This can be confusing to innocent bystanders and make the person dealing with the loss feel stupid and out of control. Anger is a cry for help and comfort. Some people stay angry to avoid the pain and depression of accepting their loss.

Bargaining

When denial and anger don't work to resolve our losses, most of us make at least some attempt at bargaining with life. Like little children trying to win over a stern parent, we try to be *so* good or *so* helpful or *so* successful or *so* cooperative that the lost object or person will reappear. When this doesn't work, we may try threats, sickness, guilt, tantrums, trouble, or any other form of blackmail that we can think of.

Depression

Sooner or later, most people's defenses give way and they are ready to face the sadness and grief of their loss. This is a painful, difficult time when an individual usually feels isolated, sad, and lonely. His self-esteem is usually low and it seems hard to imagine ever feeling whole and happy again. He may become passive, listless, and unable to control his frequent tears. It is a time of pain and fearfulness, but it is also the beginning of healing. Internalizing the grief in self-blame or self-pity or externalizing the grief by striking out at others are not true expressions of sadness and will prolong the process of healing. Until an individual has honestly experienced his sadness, he has great difficulty accepting and recovering from his loss.

Acceptance

With grief comes gradual healing and acceptance. While the lost person or circumstances are not forgotten, the grieving individual is no longer preoccupied with the loss and her feelings of anger or depression. She realizes that she cannot always control or prevent unpleasant things in her life. She learns to cope with her feelings and her loss and develop a renewed sense of trust and self-esteem. Memories become less painful and loss becomes an accepted part of the full pattern of life and love.

Everyone grieves in his own way. Some people are visibly engulfed in depression as they wade through their feelings and grief. Others need to keep busy until they are able to cope with their grief in a more private, quiet way. A minor loss may be quickly forgotten while a significant loss may take years from which to fully recover. If you are faced with a significant loss, be patient and accepting of yourself. Recognize the various dimensions of your loss and try not to block out the many different feelings that you may have. Reach out to others and ask for the support and help that you need. Recovery is not a smooth, even process; it is more

---

Hospice

Hospice is a professional organization that deals with death and dying. Trained counselors, nurses, and doctors are available to help family members and dying individuals with loss issues both before and after a death. Hospice usually offers individual, family, and group counseling on a sliding fee scale. Most areas have a hospice chapter—the phone number will be listed in the phone book.

like a roller coaster of stops and starts, progress and regression. It takes time to heal. Allow yourself the time that you need and don't lose faith that "this too will pass." Take good care of yourself and turn to friends, family, religious advisers, or counselors for the love and support that you need.

How to Help a Friend

It can also be confusing and frightening if you have a good friend who has recently experienced a traumatic loss. Your friendship, patience, and understanding can be very helpful, but at times you may feel helpless, uneasy, unappreciated, impatient, and sad yourself.

- **Recognize your own feelings about loss or death or divorce.** Understand the levels of grief and what to expect from your friend. It may be helpful for you to talk with a parent, teacher, or counselor about how *you* are feeling so that you don't get overwhelmed by your friend's grief. Other people's loss inevitably stirs up our own worries and sense of vulnerability. We may unconsciously not want to deal with our friend's feelings so that we don't have to face our own fears.

- **Be honest with your friend.** Don't ignore the fact that something has happened. Many people feel so awkward that they avoid the person or act as if nothing had happened. Let your friend know honestly how you are feeling for him and that you are available to listen when he would like to talk about it. It is OK to say "I feel so bad about your dad that I don't know what to say" or "It's still hard for me to believe that your parents split up—would you like to talk about it?" By honestly expressing your own feelings, you give your friend permission to talk honestly when he is ready.

- **Listen without judgment or a "mission."** It is not your job to rescue your friend or cheer her up. She just needs for you to be there with her. Try to understand the loss from your friend's perspective and be sensitive to her emotional needs and changes. Establish yourself as someone who can be trusted to listen and accept the emotional confusion she is feeling.

- **Be alert to your friend's despair and cries for help.** If you find yourself overly concerned about his safety or stability, talk him into getting some professional help from a counselor, the hospice group, or religious adviser. If he doesn't respond, but you are still concerned, go talk with someone yourself. Grieving individuals can be suicidal.

- **Be patient.** Grieving individuals can be illogical, repetitive, aggravating, and depressing. He may misplace some of his anger at you because you are a trusted ally. You will inevitably tire of his grieving long before he is ready to let go of it. Take a break, talk to someone about how *you* are feeling, and try to keep your impatience in perspective. Recommend professional counselor or support if his demands are seriously jeopardizing your relationship.

- **Don't just ask if there is something you can do.** Most grieving people are not collected and confident enough to ask for something specific. Think of some helpful gesture or gift on your own. A friend dealing with a significant loss is likely to feel disoriented and tired. Give her a break by helping out with basic tasks and thoughtful extras.

It is important to recognize that grief comes in many forms and can take a long time to resolve. You can be of special help by sticking with your friend after the newness and shock wear off—that is when she will really need you.

SPIRITUAL RELATIONSHIPS

The question of our place in the larger scheme of things, the cosmic universe, is an integral part of the human quandary and your individual quest. The greatest world religions, philosophy, art, and literature have this question at their core and each questing individual will ask these questions.

Out, out, brief candle! Life's but a walking shadow,
a poor player that struts and frets his hour upon the stage
and then is heard no more: it is a tale told by an idiot,
full of sound and fury, signifying nothing.[17]

Like Shakespeare's character, Macbeth, at some point we all question our own importance and significance.

Human consciousness of life and death raises questions of purpose and triggers a spiritual connection to something that is larger than our own human experience. Are we merely a biochemical coincidence in an indifferent universe? Does it matter if we strive to be ethical and kind, or is life just a matter of personal advantage and transient pleasure or suffering? What should we aim to accomplish in our lifetime? Why were we born? What will our life signify after we die? Why does a God or higher power allow human suffering and depravity? Should we strive to become better people or just hang on and try to enjoy the ride?

Religion provides a focus for these questions for many young people, but the cynicism of our times has left others without the structure or vocabulary to explore these mysteries. We live in a time when it is difficult to believe in things. Many families and marriages have fallen apart. High-ranking politicians, sports heroes, and religious leaders have disappointed us and acted badly. Advertising manipulates us, the media bombards us with casual sex and violence, and we mock ourselves for expecting better. And yet the questions remain. Why are young people bringing guns to school and killing their classmates? Why is suicide the second highest cause of adolescent death? Why are teenagers, who have more privilege and opportunity than ever before, cutting themselves or starving themselves or binge drinking on a regular basis? Why do many young people engage in reckless, impersonal sexual behavior that leaves them feeling lonely and violated? Why is there a dramatic increase in ulcers, migraines, and depression among teens and even young children? Why are so many children and young adults on some kind of psychoactive medication to get through the day?

Most teenagers wonder and worry about these things but don't find them terribly surprising. While most manage personally to avoid serious problems, almost everyone has a friend or acquaintance who has struggled with one or more of these issues. We live in an upside-down world in which very often the adults are the naive ones requiring protection or education. Perhaps this role-reversal has always been true to one degree or another, but today it has left young people without wise elders or heroes or even boundaries to question. A sense of spiritual connectedness or foundation is essential to making sense of any of these questions. If there are no values, no higher objectives, no connection to anything larger than the moment, nothing makes much sense, and the solutions are beyond our grasp. In his book *Connections*,[18] Ned Hallowell states

> *If we look past the deceptions that have been committed so often in the name of God and consider spiritual connectedness as the genuine human concern that it is, we see there is an undisputed mystery that surrounds our lives on this planet.... How we engage this mystery defines our spiritual connectedness. Whether we do it alone or in a group, whether we do it under a banner or without formal ties, whether we do it systematically and at a scheduled time or spontaneously when we are so moved, whether we do it out of fear or obligation or love or curiosity or out of hunger, whether we do it with full faith or full of skepticism, whether or not we know what we're doing when we do it, we all engage somehow at some time with the mystery of life.... Though unseen and unprovable, this connection can be felt as the surest connection we have.*

Take some time to think quietly about the questions in this section and what you believe. Write in your journal about your spiritual quandaries and beliefs. How do those questions and beliefs shape and affect the way you choose to live your life? You may want to pursue the questions with your parents, a close friend, or a religious advisor. Some people like to visit a variety of religious services to study what different faiths believe in. Some schools offer courses in religious and spiritual thought, and there are many outstanding books that can help you think through these questions. With time, you will discover that your spirituality, whether it is formal or very personal, will form the basis of your health, relationships, decisions, and life goals.

Do-It-Yourself Quandary

Identify an important dilemma related to relationships in our culture today that was not discussed in this chapter.

- *What factors make this issue particularly complicated or difficult to resolve?*

- *What values or ethical considerations are involved?*

- *What solutions or choices are available?*

Dear Quandary Master . . .

Here are some letters asking for advice and information about some relationship problems. Make your answers as realistic and helpful as possible. Be sure to include any relevant information or resources that might be helpful.

#1.

Dear Quandary Master,

This is a really stupid problem, but it's really dragging me down. I fake it at school, but deep down inside, I don't really have much confidence in myself. Things seem to come naturally to others, but no matter how hard I try, I never seem to say the right thing or look right or be comfortable in a group. I have some friends, but if they really knew me, they'd probably think I was a jerk too. I try not to care what other people think, but I don't want to be a social reject. The popular kids at school act as if I didn't exist. Don't tell me to just be myself because that definitely would not work. I've been trying so hard not to make a fool of myself that I don't really know who I am anymore.

Signed, Larry the Loser

#2.

Dear Quandary Master,

I am really worried about a good friend of mine. He's a nice guy, but he's always down on himself. He is never satisfied no matter how well he does, and he shrugs off any compliments or support I try to give him. I try to ignore all his put-downs, but lately he seems really depressed. He never wants to do anything, sleeps a lot and, to be honest, he's not looking too great. It's like nothing matters to him. He hasn't actually talked about suicide, but he seems real morbid—always noticing stuff about death and real pessimistic about everything. I can't put my finger on it, but he's kind of scaring me. I'm not his mom or anything, but I can't help thinking something is really wrong. Am I overreacting? Is he just trying to get attention? What should I do?

Signed, Concerned Cathy

#3.

Dear Quandary Master,

Don't get me wrong; my parents are very nice people and I do love them, but they are definitely losing it. They cannot accept the fact that I am fifteen years old and have my own life to lead. My mother always wants to know exactly where I am, who I am with, and I have to be home by 11:00, even on weekends. My parents won't let me ride with any of my friends who have their license because they aren't "experienced drivers." If I am going to a party, they insist on speaking with the parent to be sure there is adequate supervision. I am only allowed to go to a concert if my dad takes us and picks us up. Every Sunday is "family day" and I am expected to spend the whole day doing dumb things with my family. When I say that I want some time with my friends, my mom just says I can invite them to join us. They just don't get it. I feel like a six-year-old. How can I get them to realize that they've got to let me grow up?

Signed, Apron-strings Adelaide

#4.

Dear Quandary Master,

You probably get a lot of letters like this, but I never thought I would be writing one. We have the "perfect" family—a great house, three kids, active, nice parents who come to all our games and are always there when we need them—and last week, they told us that they are getting a divorce. They took us out to our favorite restaurant (I will NEVER go there again) and explained all reasonably like that they just couldn't live together anymore and they still loved us and it wasn't our fault and all that grown-up BS. My brother said he knew it was coming, but I was clueless. My little sister just started to cry. I don't know what to do. I just feel angry and sick to my stomach. I don't want anyone to know, but I feel so lonely and confused. I keep hoping they will get back together or that this is just a bad dream. I know they fought sometimes, but it wasn't that bad. I could help out more and they could see a counselor or something. How can I make them see that we can work it out if we just stick together as a family?

Signed, Another Divorce Statistic?

#5.

Dear Quandary Master,

Barbara and I have been going together for almost two years now. We are young, but it really seems like we were made for each other. We enjoy the same sports and activities and never seem to run out of things to talk about. We are in love, but she is also my best friend. I can tell her anything and she understands. We both want to wait to have intercourse, but we do have a pretty terrific physical relationship. The problem is that I graduate this year and Barbara still has another year of high school. I have been accepted at a good college, but it is over two thousand miles away. I can't imagine not having her around. I guess I am also a little worried about what will happen to our relationship—it is too important to me to risk losing it. I have thought about maybe going to the local college for a year or taking a year off to work nearby. My parents like Barbara, but they are worried that we are too young to be so serious. They don't seem to realize that she is more important to me than college or "expanding my horizons." Barbara says she will wait, but I don't want to. What should we do?

Signed, Lovesick Louie

#6.

Dear Quandary Master,

I'm discouraged. I go to church with my folks every week, but lately, that just seems to raise more questions than it answers for me. If God is so wise and all-knowing, why are we in such a mess these days? Why are little kids starving and supposedly mature adults dropping bombs on each other, and kids my age blowing each other away at school? Big companies pollute the environment or cheat their workers just to make a profit. I look around and it seems that nice guys do finish last and some real jerks get away with murder. If you cheat on a paper, it may be wrong, but, if you don't get caught, you'll probably get a better grade. Even with my group of friends, who are pretty nice girls, being sarcastic and catty gets you a lot more attention than doing something nice—or, God forbid, taking an unpopular stand because you think it is "right."

I was babysitting for my six-year-old niece last week and told her to say her prayers before she went to sleep. She got real quiet and then asked, "What if there really isn't a God?" She was worried because she didn't think God should let her friend at school pick on her, but her question really stuck with me. What if all the things I believe in are just a joke? Are there answers or just a lot of confusing questions? Most of my friends don't talk about this stuff and my parents say I just need to have faith. Arghh. This is important to me. What do I do?

Signed, Disillusioned Delilah

WEB SITES

Counseling and Help Lines
www.nrscrisisline.org *(runaways)*
www.TheTeenLine.org
www.1000deaths.com/lists.html
www.feminist.org/911/crisis.html
www.1800hithome.com
www.ndvh.org *(domestic violence)*

Death and Grieving
www.growthhouse.org
www.willowgreen.com
www.compassionatefriends.org
www.hospicefoundation.org/virtual html/lwg.htm
www.euthanasia.com
http://web.lwc.edu/administrative/library/suiweb.htm
   (Web sites pro and con on euthanasia)
www.rights.org/deathnet/KevorkianFile.html

Depression and Mood Disorders
www.nimh.nih.gov/publicat/depressionmenu.cfm
http://panicdisorder.about.com/health/panicdisorder
www.nimh.nih.gov/anxiety/anxiety/ptsd/index.htm

www.geocities.com/HotSprings/3628/index2.html

www.have-a-heart.com

Families

www.family.org/cforum/research

www.ibiblio.org/gaylaw/issue6/Mcneill.htm

http://families-first.com/index.htm

www.stanford.edu/~trigon/clh

Gender Roles

www.stanford.edu/group/IRWG

www.wkap.nl/aims scope.htm/0360-0025
   (research journal on sex roles)

www.fordham.edu/halsall/sbook1v.html *(in history)*

http://ucs.orst.edu/~huj/512

www.chebucto.ns.ca/CommunitySupport/Men4Change/index.htm

www.nomas.org

www.razzberry.chickclick.com/theworld/prejudice/sexism

www.un.org/womenwatch

www.encyberpedia.com/women.htm

www.tnom.com *(men)*

http://63.111.42.146/home *(women)*

Multiculturism and Racism

http://phylogeny.arizona.edu/tree/phylogeny.html

http://kumo.swcp.com/biz/theedge

www.magenta.nl/crosspoint

www.webcom.com/intvoice

www.splcenter.org

www.splcenter.org/teaachingtolerance/tt-index.html

www.adl.org

www.igc.org/igc/gateway/index.html

Suicide Prevention

http://suicidehotlines.com

ftp://rtfm.mit.edu/pub/usenet/news.answers/suicide/info

---

[1]Satir, Virginia. *Self-Esteem.* Celestial Arts, 1975.

[2]Aronson, Elliot. *The Social Animal.* San Francisco: W.H. Freeman and Company, 1972.

[3]Fagot, B. I. The influence of sex of child on parental reactions to toddler children. *Child Development,* 1978.

[4]Lansky, L. M., Crandall, Kagan, and Baker. Sex differences in aggression and its correlates in middle class adolescents. *Child Development*, 1961.

[5]Hartley, Ruth. Children's concepts of male and female roles. *Scientific American*, 226 (1) 1972.

[6]Sadker, Myra, and David. Sexism in the schoolroom of the 1980s. *Psychology Today*, March, 1985.

[7]Nichols, John. Causal attributions and other achievement-related cognitions: Effects of task outcome, attainment value and sex. *Journal of Personality and Social Psychology*, 31, 1975.

[8]U.S. Bureau of the Census, Current Population Reports, Series p-60, U.S. Bureau of Labor Statistics, Consumer Price Index, http://www.census.gov/prod/2000pubs/p60-209.pdf. and http://www.census.gov/hhes/income/histinc/p.38.html.

[9]Employee Relations Office, U.S. Courts, "The Judiciary Fair Employment Practices Report," Fiscal Year 1999 and the Federal Judicial Center, History Office, as of February 24, 1997 in http:www.gendergap.com/governme.html.

[10]Jacobs and Landau. *To Serve the Devil*. Vol 2. New York: Vintage Books, 1971.

[11]Hovland and Sears. Minor studies of aggression: Correlation of lynching with economic indices. *Journal of Psychology*, 9, 1940.

[12]Miller and Bulgaski. Minor studies in aggression: The influence of frustrations imposed by the in-group on attitudes expressed by the out-group. *Journal of Psychology*, 25, 1948.

[13]Adorno, Frenkel-Brunswick, Levinson, and Sanford. *The Authoritarian Personality*. New York: Harper, 1950.

[14]McIntosh, Peggy. White privilege: Unpacking the invisible knapsack. *Peace and Freedom Journal*, July/August, 1989.

[15]Men answered in this order (5, 9, 4, 1, 3, 12, 11, 8, 2, 7, -, 6). Women answered in this order (5, 8, 4, 1, 3, -, 9, 11, 2, 7, 12, 6).

[16]Wallerstein, Judith S. *Second Chances: Men, Women and Children a Decade After Divorce*. Technor and Fields, 1989.

[17]Shakespeare. *Macbeth*, Act V, Scene 5.

[18]Hallowell, Ned. *Connections*.

Chapter 5

Sexuality

TALKING ABOUT SEX

We live in a society and time that is preoccupied with sex. MTV, movies, the news, advertising, and our daily conversations use sex to impress, shock, amuse, titillate, attract, entertain, or sell a product. But rarely do any of these media or most people talk honestly and personally about sexuality. We tell jokes, smile suggestively, and generally say what we think others would like to hear. What we seldom do is honestly express our questions, needs, or concerns. If we admit that we don't know something or don't like something, our sexuality or maturity seems to be called into question. Few families include sexual feelings or behavior in their comfortable dinner table conversations. Even sexually intimate couples may have a difficult time openly discussing their sexual feelings and interests.

Talking about sex in a group has its own set of advantages and disadvantages. The discussion will inevitably be less personal. There will probably be fewer implications about your personal behavior and relationships. If there is someone in the group that you do have a personal relationship with, you may discover that the more formal group setting may help you discuss some important issues that were difficult to bring up on your own.

It will take a while to establish real honesty and trust in a group. Take some time with your group to establish the ground rules that you can all agree upon. Be sure to address issues of confidentiality, decision making, communication, and how you will expect to be treated in the group.

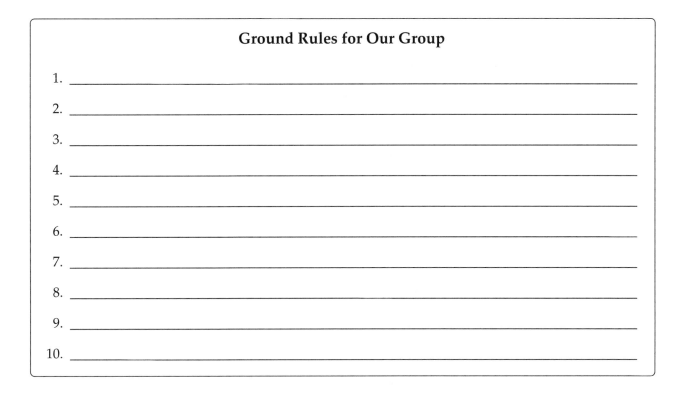

Ground Rules for Our Group

1. _____

2. _____

3. _____

4. _____

5. _____

6. _____

7. _____

8. _____

9. _____

10. _____

While it is important that everyone contributes to and agrees upon these rules, be patient. There will be a time of testing and trust building before everyone is comfortable. Every group has its own personality and timetable. Rebuilding a broken trust is always difficult, so go slowly and pay attention to the guidelines and relationships that need work.

Asking Questions and Saying "I Don't Know"

In spite of what romance, most movies, and common bravado would lead us to believe, talking honestly and directly about sex is important. Many girls have gotten pregnant because they were too embarrassed to talk about birth control. Many boys have become teenage fathers because they "assumed" that she was on the pill and were not comfortable talking it over. Your personal protection against AIDS includes knowing your partner's sexual background and openly discussing your sexual activity and the use of condoms. On the more positive side, open communication with your sexual partner increases the intimacy, pleasure, and strength of your relationship. Mind reading, making assumptions, or faking it inevitably weaken a relationship and can lead to real trouble.

With all these good reasons for communicating honestly, why don't we do it more often?

- Fear of rejection or ridicule—*What if I say something really dumb?* Laugh. We all have dumb questions and inaccurate information. We just don't know what they are until we ask and get things straightened out.

- Fear that you are the only one who doesn't know something—*Everyone else looks like they already know all this stuff.* That's because they are trying to look as cool and sophisticated as you are trying to look. The reason so much sexual talk is pretense is that nobody wants to risk looking stupid. Even if others laugh, you can be sure there is at least one other person out there who appreciates your courage. And anyway, now you know the answer.

- Fear of bringing doubt or question on your own sexuality—*What will people think if I ask about that?* Everyone wonders and worries about their own sexuality at one time or another. Did I do it right? Am I supposed to feel this way? Am I normal? All these feelings ARE normal. The more comfortable you become with your sexuality, the more honest you can be about your questions, doubts, and worries.

- Fear that the confidentiality can't be trusted—*What if the person I am talking to judges me or tells other people what I have said?* That is a reasonable fear and you shouldn't talk intimately with people that you don't trust. You also shouldn't have sex with them.

- Desire to look more OR less experienced than you really are—*My thoughts, feelings, and experiences are* **not** *OK; I want to appear differently than I am.* This either means that you are worried about how other people are judging you or that *you* are not really comfortable with what you are doing. Both of these possibilities are important to think about.

- Embarrassment—*I just can't say those words or talk about how I think or feel about sex.* It **is** difficult to overcome years of giggling or embarrassment. Overcoming this unease is an important part of growing up and becoming ready for a mature sexual relationship.

- Fear that talk will destroy the romance or spontaneity of sex—*Don't dissect and intellectualize so much; just relax and cut loose!* Actually, talking about sex can be very sexy and romantic. Once you know and trust your partner, make careful decisions that you both feel good about, and are protected from unwanted consequences, you are much freer to relax and enjoy yourself.

- Fear that talk will encourage action and promiscuity—*If you start letting teenagers talk about sex, they are going to start thinking about sex, and that will just lead to more sexual activity and problems.* As you already know, nobody needs to give teenagers a reason to think about sex. It is all around you. Sexual hormones are changing the way you look, think, and feel. Research has shown that the comfort level and communication around sexuality actually reduces unwanted pregnancies and STDs. In many cases, people also become more comfortable saying no.

- Sex is a personal and private subject—*It is nobody else's business what I do and think about sex.* Masturbation is a personal and private subject. An intimate sexual encounter with another person requires honesty, trust, communication, and respect.

Talking with Your Parents

Sex is one area of your life where your focus will shift dramatically from parents and family to your peers. It can still be helpful to be able to turn to your parents for guidance and support when you need it. The following interview may give you a better idea of your parents' background and ideas about sex and may make it easier for the three of you to talk about sexual issues.

Interviewing Your Parents

Find a time when one or both of your parents can sit down and be "interviewed." Your job is to ask the questions and make sure that you understand your parents' answers. Try to delay your own responses or reactions until after your parents have had their say.

1. How do you think things have changed sexually for teenagers since you were in high school?

2. How did you learn about sex? What were the messages, spoken and unspoken, that you received about sex from friends, parents, school, church, media, etc?

3. What was the availability of birth control and abortion when you were a teenager?

4. Was there a sexual double standard for boys and girls when you were growing up?

5. A study of college students in 1965 showed that 35 percent of the boys and 61 percent of the girls believed that sex before marriage was wrong. How have you seen that change? If so, why do you think it has changed?

6. When do you think it is appropriate for two people to have sexual intercourse?

7. How do you feel about abortion?

8. How do you think you would respond if I got into an unplanned pregnancy situation?

9. What is the most difficult part of parenting a teenager today? What worries you most about me sexually?

10. What is the most important piece of advice you would give me about sex?

Use your listening skills—try to genuinely understand how your parents think and feel about these issues.

➡ How was it different to grow up when they were teenagers?

➡ What is it like to parent a teenager today?

➡ What are their expectations, questions, and fears for you?

➡ How well do your parents understand the sexual climate in which you are growing up?

➡ In what areas do you and your parents agree?

➡ In what areas do you and your parents disagree?

➡ What surprised you about your parents' answers?

Listening to a Different Point of View

Physically and socially, boys and girls experience their sexuality in different ways. Our bodies and sexual responses are different. Pregnancy affects girls and boys differently. There are different social expectations and pressures surrounding masculinity and femininity. Boys have no firsthand experience with a menstrual cycle or the female sexual anatomy or a girl's fear of rape. Girls may not understand locker-room bantering, the burden of making the first move, or a boy's concern about having an erection at the appropriate—or inappropriate—time. Both girls and boys often wonder what is attractive to the opposite sex and what they are looking for in a steady relationship. And both genders have strange, puzzling behaviors that make no sense whatsoever to their sexual counterparts.

For sex, love, marriage, parenting, and coexistence in general to be cooperative and satisfying, we must all work to understand the different experience, concerns, and expectations of being a man or a woman. The following exercise gives you a chance to be a fly on the wall while members of the opposite sex answer the questions that you have.

Fishbowl

To prepare for the Fishbowl, boys and girls must meet separately for twenty-five to forty-five minutes to come up with the questions you would like to hear members of the opposite sex discuss. Brainstorm for a while until you come up with four or five questions that you think would make an interesting discussion.

Your questions should be written on separate index cards. When boys and girls get back together, the group that is going first should sit in a circle in the middle of the room. The other group forms a circle around the outside. The inner circle is then given the stack of questions from the other group. The outer circle may not speak or contribute in any way. One person may be appointed to clarify any confusion about a question, but the inner circle should forget that the outer circle is there as much as possible.

After the allotted time (twenty to thirty minutes, depending on the group and number of questions), the outer circle may react to what they have heard. This is not a time for agreeing or disagreeing, but for responding to what you learned from the discussion. The emphasis is on increased understanding and awareness of what it is like to be in the other group.

The inner circle may want to talk about how they felt during the discussion knowing that the outer circle was listening. What pressure did you feel to say or not say certain things? How would the discussion have been different if it had not been observed?

The groups then switch and repeat the process.

> *Sometimes I wonder if men and women really suit each other. Perhaps they should live next door and just visit now and then.*
>
> —Katherine Hepburn

> **Good ground rules for questions are:**
>
> 1. *Check your motivation—what is really confusing to you about the behavior or attitudes of the opposite sex?*
>
> 2. *Would you feel comfortable answering the same question?*
>
> 3. *Phrase your questions so that no one is put on the spot—say "Do boys ever . . ." rather than "Do you ever . . ."*

SEXUAL MATURATION

One of the major changes during puberty, of course, is the development of sexual characteristics and the ability to create children. Your body changes shape. Estrogen and testosterone are released into your hormonal system. Internally, the male testes begin to make sperm and the female ovaries begin to release the ovum or eggs in a regular, monthly cycle.

Before we go any further, take some time individually or as a class to write down a list of reasons why it is important to understand sexual anatomy and physiology. Sex is certainly much more than biology, but biology does play a rather significant role. You can engage in sexual behavior without knowing what is what, but think about how biological knowledge might make your sex life safer and more satisfying.[1]

1. _____

2. _____

3. _____

4. _____

5. _____

6. _____

Researching Your Sexual Anatomy/Physiology

Listed below are a number of questions about how your anatomy and physiology affect your sexuality.[2] Assign one or two questions to each class member and spend a class session teaching each other the answers. There is space after each question to jot down some pertinent information you learn about each question. Some good reference sources are listed at the end of this chapter.

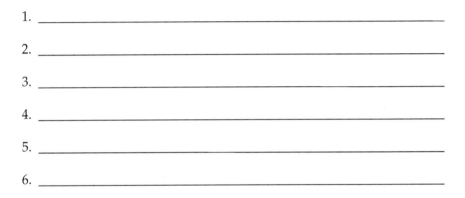

1. When does a fetus become male or female? When do reproductive genitals develop?

2. Do both males and females have a "refractory period" after orgasm, a period of time during which one is not able to have another orgasm regardless of the stimulation?

3. How do male and female orgasms differ? Do both require about the same amount of time to achieve orgasm?

4. How long can sperm stay alive inside the female body? Outside in the air?

5. How much blood does a girl lose during her period? Does it affect her strength or health?

6. Can a male urinate during ejaculation?

7. Can a girl get pregnant before she has had her first period?

8. What happens to a male if he is sexually aroused, has an erection, but does not have an orgasm? Do women have the same experience?

9. What erotic zones do males and females have in common?

10. What is the function of the clitoris?

11. How do alcohol and other drugs affect sexual arousal and performance?

12. Do males have a stronger sex drive than females?

13. Do all virgin females have a hymen?

14. What causes wet dreams for males? Do females have wet dreams?

15. How is the size of a penis related to sexual performance?

16. Can a girl get pregnant without having penis-vagina intercourse? Can she get pregnant if the boy does not ejaculate? (Not including artificial insemination.)

17. How long can an unfertilized egg live?

18. How many sperm are in the average male ejaculation? How big are sperm?

19. Must a female have an orgasm in order to conceive?

20. How early can a woman know she is pregnant? What are some of the first signs?

21. How reliable are home pregnancy tests? Are some brands more reliable than others?

22. Is it harmful to have intercourse while menstruating? Can you get pregnant at that time?

23. Can a woman safely have sex while she is pregnant?

24. How is the sex of a baby determined? Is there a better chance of having a boy or a girl?

25. Can twins have different fathers?

26. How medically dangerous is an abortion? What factors affect the level of safety? Does it hurt?

27. How does an abortion affect a woman's future chances of becoming pregnant?

28. Is there any way to tell if a girl is faking an orgasm?

29. What is "simultaneous orgasm" and how common is it?

30. When is intercourse painful for a girl? What if she bleeds during her first intercourse?

31. Are boys and girls "turned on" by different things?

32. Why are some people gay?

33. What is statutory rape?

Your Turn

Now it is your turn to ask the questions. *Everybody* has questions about sex. They may be biological questions or "how-to" questions or questions about sexual feelings, behavior, decisions, or values. It is not always easy to ask these questions, so this exercise gives you the chance to ask anonymously. Write down two or three questions you have on index cards, one question per card. Then turn these questions in as instructed. Your teacher, teaching assistants, and class members can then use these questions to address the various concerns that you have.

Male and Female Reproductive Systems

For this next exercise, you need to pair up with a member of the opposite sex. On a separate sheet of paper, you and your partner are to draw the male and female reproductive systems, labeling all of the parts that are listed on the next two pages. If you get stuck, ask around or find a detailed diagram in your resource library, but do as much as you can on your own. Make sure that you've got everything in the right place.

Male Reproductive Anatomy

A. PENIS — Center of sexual excitement in a man. Contains sponge-like tissue which fills with blood when stimulated. Also used for intercourse and urinating.

B. SCROTUM — Pouch of skin in the male that contains the testes. Protects the testes from injury and keeps them about 1–5 degrees cooler than the rest of the body.

C. TESTES — Testosterone is made in the testes. Sperm are made and stored in the testes.

D. EPIDIDYMIS — Approximately twenty feet of very thin tightly rolled tubing. It carries sperm to the vas deferens.

E. VAS DEFERENS — The long narrow tube is connected to the end of each epididymis and travels over the back of the bladder carrying sperm to the ejaculatory tubes.

F. SEMINAL VESICLES — An organ that produces a thick liquid which is part of the male semen. The semen nourishes the sperm and helps it travel.

G. PROSTATE — This organ produces a thin milky liquid which mixes with the sperm and liquid from the seminal vesicles. It protects the sperm from acids in the vagina.

H. URETHRA — A tube which carries the urine away from the bladder and carries semen during sexual excitement and ejaculation.

I. COWPER'S GLANDS — Produce a mucous liquid at the onset of sexual excitement which removes traces of urine from the urethra.

Also draw in the bladder, pubic hair, and anus.

Female Reproductive Anatomy

A. UTERUS

A hollow muscular organ in the female in which the fetus develops during pregnancy.

B. URETHRA

Urinary duct opening for the passage of urine. Approximately one inch below the clitoris.

C. CLITORIS

Female genital which has tissue similar to that of the penis. It is the center of sexual arousal in the female. Approximately one inch long, it is covered by a semicircular hood, so only about one-eighth inch is visible.

D. FALLOPIAN TUBES

Two tubes, about five inches long, which carry the egg from the ovaries to the uterus. Each tube contains cilia and is rimmed with finger-like fringes.

E. VAGINA

A female sex organ, approximately four to five inches long, that receives the penis during sexual intercourse and acts as a birth canal for the delivery of a baby.

F. CERVIX

The lower part or mouth of the uterus. Expands during labor to deliver a baby.

G. LABIA MAJORA

Folds of tissue that cover and protect the clitoris, urethra, and vagina.

H. LABIA MINORA

Smaller folds of tissue that secrete moisture upon sexual stimulation.

I. OVARIES

Glands that contain thousands of follicles that produce estrogen and progesterone. These hormones are responsible for thickening and maintaining the lining of the uterus. The follicles also contain immature eggs which they release once a month.

Also draw in the bladder, pubic hair, and anus.

Quandary: *What Should Be Taught in Sex Education Classes?*

There is a lot of controversy about what should be taught in sex education classes or if sex education should be taught in schools at all. Many people believe that sex is a personal, family matter that should be discussed within the privacy and values of each family. Many educators agree and believe that teaching about sex is beyond the responsibility of schools. Others see sexuality as a biological function that should not be avoided by schools simply because it has social and ethical components. Other educators and parents insist that sex is an essential part of human development that must be addressed realistically and directly by both families and schools. Others believe that schools must educate about sexuality because most families don't.

Once a school community decides to include sex education in its offerings, many questions arise. *Should students be required to take such a course or be able to opt out? Should values be discussed and included and, if so, whose? How explicit should teaching and materials be? At what age should different topics be taught? How should controversial topics such as abortion and homosexuality be included?*

Central to many of these questions is the issue of **abstinence.** While research statistics and teenage pregnancies make it clear that many teenagers are sexually active, most adults, agencies, churches, and schools believe that abstinence is the safest, most developmentally appropriate choice for teenagers. Some believe that to teach about birth control or safe sex is to condone and maybe even encourage sexual behavior. This sends a dangerous message to young people and may actually pressure some to become more sexually active than they would have chosen to be without such information. Some believe that these sex education courses become just one more pressure on teenagers to grow up too quickly and behave in sexually inappropriate and dangerous ways.

Others who agree that abstinence is the best choice also believe that it is unrealistic not to provide information and protection for teenagers who do not make this choice. They believe that sex education must educate students to understand their sexuality and to act responsibly when and if they decide to become sexually active. AIDS has raised the stakes on sexual ignorance and many adults believe that it is irresponsible not to provide teenagers with the facts and protection they need.

Some others believe that abstinence is an ideal which has never really worked with teenagers, or adults for that matter, and that we must separate biology, relationships, and ethics if we hope to understand what is really going on. Regardless of what adults believe or say, teenagers will and have always made their own decisions about sex. While valueless education is impossible and undesirable, students need information, honesty, and realism to make safe, responsible decisions.

What do you think should be taught in a sex education course? In what ways might such a course create pressure on students to be sexually active? How should the issue of abstinence and sexual activity be dealt with? What do you need and want to know from this type of course?

The Menstrual Cycle

The menstrual cycle is an important component of female sexuality and a critical factor in creating—or not creating—a baby. Fertility and certain forms of birth control depend on controlling or being aware of this cycle, so it is important for both females and males to understand how it works. This cycle is wonderfully complex and takes some careful thought to understand how everything works together.

Technically a woman can only get pregnant during the four days of her cycle between the time the egg is released from the ovaries and when it exits through the vagina. The difficulty is knowing exactly which four days the egg is on its journey. This is particularly true for adolescent girls whose cycle may not have completely stabilized. Mood swings, diet, stress, and exercise can affect the regular cycle from month to month. Even in adult females, the ovaries sometimes get off cue and release two eggs at different times—that is how fraternal twins are conceived. That is also how it is possible to get pregnant from intercourse during your menstrual flow. One of the ovaries prematurely released a second egg.

The Female Menstrual Cycle

This whole amazing process is orchestrated by the **pituitary gland**, that "master gland" which is located in the base of the brain, just below the hypothalamus. The cycle is approximately twenty-eight days long, but an individual woman's regular cycle may be longer or shorter. Day one of the cycle is generally counted from the first day of the menstrual blood flow.

This "blood" is actually **endometrium**, a combination of blood, mucus, and cells that have been built up to nourish a growing fetus. If the egg has not been fertilized, it disintegrates and the uterus sheds the endometrium lining. This takes about three to seven days and is called the **menstrual period** or **menstruation**.

During this time, the levels of estrogen and progesterone have dropped, body temperature returns to normal, and most women experience a relief from any premenstrual symptoms. Some women do have mild to painful cramps, lower back pain, and a lower energy level during their periods.

By about the fourth day of the cycle, the pituitary gland starts the whole process over again by sending a **FSH** (follicle-stimulating hormone) to the ovaries which causes the ovaries to produce more **estrogen**. This increased level of estrogen starts to build the endometrium lining in the uterus.

It also sends the message for one of the **follicles**, which contain the tiny premature **ovum** or egg, to start getting ready. The estrogen also stimulates the production of cervical mucus around the cervix, which can assist and nourish the sperm on its journey. The estrogen level reaches its first peak by about day fourteen.

At this point, the pituitary gland adds **LH** (luteinizing hormone) to the bloodstream. LH causes the now mature egg to burst out of the follicle and begin its three- to four-day journey through the fallopian tubes. This is called **ovulation** and is the most obviously fertile time of the menstrual cycle. It is also a time of high energy and productivity for most females though some women experience some cramping or lower back pain at the time of ovulation.

At the time of ovulation, the morning body temperature usually drops about 1 degree. LH also takes the leftover cells from the follicle and forms a new structure called **corpus luteum**. Stimulated by the LH, the corpus luteum produces **progesterone** and more estrogen, which further enrich the uterine lining in preparation for the care and feeding of a fertilized egg.

By the twentieth day of the cycle, estrogen and progesterone are at their highest levels and the endometrium lining is rich and full. During this time, a female may experience some water retention and sensitivity of the breast and genitalia and the body temperature usually fluctuates about 1 degree above normal.

If the egg has not been fertilized, the levels of estrogen and progesterone in the blood go into overload and the pituitary gland stops sending out FSH and LH. Without these hormones, the corpus luteum cannot produce estrogen or progesterone, so it just withers away.

During the week before menstruation, many women experience a variety of premenstrual symptoms ranging from a mild sense of fullness and irritation to severe headaches and mood swings. Estrogen and progesterone levels drop, the egg disintegrates, and the endometrium draws away from the uterus taking us back to the menstrual period and the beginning of the cycle.

Whew. Got all that?

Read the description of the menstrual cycle on page 237. Then graph what each factor is doing during the cycle so that you can see when and how all of these components interact. Try to use all of the **boldface** terms in your graph.

Now, put all of that information into a more visual format. Starting with DAY ONE, graph or describe what is going on in each part of the female's body and experience.

	PROLIFERATIVE PHASE				SECRETORY PHASE		
	1	5	10	14	20	25	28
Days of Cycle							
Hormones secreted Function:							
Estrogen level							
Progesterone level							
Body temperature							
Ovaries/ovum							
Uterus/cervix							
Physical/emotional reactions							
	1	5	10	14	20	25	28
Days of Cycle							

Quandary: *How Did You Learn About Menstruation?*

If you are a girl, how were you prepared for your first period? Who did you tell? How did they react? What misinformation or confusion did you have? How do you feel about menstruation?

If you are a boy, how did you learn that girls menstruate? What situations surrounding menstruation do you find embarrassing or confusing? How do you feel about a girl if you know she is having her period?

As any female can tell you, however, the menstrual cycle is more than just a biological event. Throughout the history of womankind and mankind, there has always been a wide range of feelings, attitudes, and values associated with menstruation. In some cultures, it is a mark of shame and embarrassment; in others, it is publicly celebrated as a rite of passage into womanhood. In our society, menstruation tends to be a well-known secret surrounded by embarrassment and misinformation. Many boys learn about menstruation through bits of overheard conversation or television ads about "those days." Some girls experience their first period without any advance information or preparation. This lack of open communication often creates a variety of confusing and sometimes amusing myths about menstruation.

Check out the following statements and make sure you've got the facts straight.

> ***Synchronous Menstruation***
>
> *When a group of women live together, their menstrual cycles begin to coincide. Researchers believe that this is the result of a scent or pheromone that triggers the brain.*

T   F   Women should not do any strenuous exercise during their period.
FACT:

T   F   Women who live together or spend a lot of time together often get their period at the same time.
FACT:

T   F   Virgins cannot use tampons because their hymen is not broken.
FACT:

T   F   Girls can get anemia from the loss of blood during their period.
FACT:

T   F   You can't get pregnant from intercourse during your period.
FACT:

T   F   It is unsafe and sometimes painful to have intercourse during your period.
FACT:

T   F   Many girls complain of premenstrual symptoms, but there are no biological grounds for these problems.
FACT:

T   F   A woman should not drink coffee or alcohol or eat chocolate during her period.
FACT:

T   F   If a girl misses her period, she is either pregnant or sick.
FACT:

T   F   If you use tampons, you can get toxic shock syndrome, which can be fatal.
FACT:

T   F   Only a small number of women get menstrual cramps.
FACT:

T   F   Women should use douches and hygiene spray during and after their period.
FACT:

Some Problems Related to Menstruation

Premenstrual Syndrome

While about 10 percent of all women never experience any changes or discomfort from their menstrual cycle, about 80 percent experience mild to moderate difficulties and 10 percent have symptoms which are extremely uncomfortable and debilitating.

Medical doctors are not sure exactly what causes this cluster of symptoms, but most agree that it is related to the fluctuating levels of estro-

PMS Check Chart

Rate each symptom
0 = none
1 = mild, doesn't interfere with activities
2 = moderate, interferes with activities
3 = severe, disabling, can't function normally

CIRCLE THE DAYS OF YOUR MENSTRUAL FLOW.

DAY OF CYCLE	1	2	3	4	5	6	7	8	9	10	11	12	13	14	15	16	17	18	19	20	21	22	23	24	25	26	27	28
Tension																												
Mood swings																												
Anxiety																												
Irritability																												
Weight gain																												
Breast tenderness																												
Bloating																												
Headache																												
Food cravings																												
Fatigue																												
Dizziness																												
Depression																												
Crying																												
Insomnia																												
Backache																												
Cramps																												
Diarrhea																												
Disorientation																												
Panic feelings																												
Restlessness																												
Muscle spasms																												
Low self-esteem																												

BOYS:

Luckily, you do not have to worry about these problems personally, but don't skip this section. The chances are pretty good that someone you love does—a mother, sister, girl-friend, or future wife. Your understanding and awareness of these problems will be greatly appreciated.

gen and progesterone and the chemically related prostaglandins. Symptoms of PMS vary, but the most common ones are:

Tension	*Mood swings*	*Irritability*
Feelings of panic	*Weight gain*	*Depression*
Headaches	*Restlessness*	*Clumsiness*
Dizziness	*Lethargy*	*Anxiety*
Backaches	*Crying spells*	*Muscle spasms*
Nausea	*Bloating*	*Food cravings*
Fatigue	*Insomnia*	*Disorientation*
Breast tenderness	*Difficulty concentrating*	*Increased appetite*

The best way to determine if PMS is affecting your body or mind is to keep a careful record over a period of three to four months and note any patterns that you observe. Many of these changes are subtle and you may not connect them with your menstrual cycle until you notice that they always come at a certain time of the month. Once you are aware of this pattern, you can begin to have more control over your symptoms and take care of yourself.

Taking Care of Yourself

If you believe that PMS is negatively affecting your moods and behavior, there are some concrete ways to manage it.

1. Take extra care with your diet. Avoid the sweets and caffeine that you may crave—the changes in progesterone in your body can create a temporary hypoglycemia. Blood sugar and insulin levels fluctuate, bringing on depression, fatigue, irritability, and headaches.

2. Avoid salty foods. Estrogen retains salt, producing symptoms such as bloating, headaches, and general irritability and tension.

3. The drop in hormone levels right before your period seems to create a decreased tolerance for alcohol.

4. Eat fresh foods that contain vitamins B_6, B, C, D, and E. Calcium, magnesium, and iron are also important. Juices, fresh fruit, fresh vegetables, yogurt, milk, eggs, unsalted cereals, bread, pasta, and rice are good. Avoid red meat during this time.

5. Five or six light meals rather than three big meals may be better for you during this period. This pattern tends to keep your blood sugar level more balanced.

6. Regular exercise is believed to regulate your hormonal levels and decrease the amount of fatty tissue where estrogen is stored.

7. Stress interferes with the pituitary gland's ability to release hormones effectively. Think ahead and reduce the stresses in your life during the times you have difficulty with PMS. Organize your commitments, prioritize, and find time to relax and have fun.

8. Account for PMS as you react to things in your life—remind yourself that you *will* get your energy back and things will probably look a lot better in a few days.

9. If your symptoms are still interfering with your life, consult your doctor. There are prescriptions and over-the-counter medicines that can help regulate the hormones that may be upsetting your balance.

Dysmenorrhea

This is the fancy name for menstrual cramps. These cramps can range from a dull ache in the lower abdomen or back to extremely painful contractions accompanied by chills, shaking, and nausea. While most women experience some cramping at some point in their lives, only about 10 percent will have to put up with the more incapacitating symptoms of dysmenorrhea.

Dysmenorrhea is thought to be caused by an overproduction of prostaglandins which regulate the action of the body's involuntary muscles. Cramps tend to more often affect younger women and are stronger during the first two days of the menstrual period.

If your cramping is severe and prolonged, there are several over-the-counter and prescriptions drugs that may provide relief. Anti-prostaglandin medication and ibuprofen help many women. A doctor can prescribe stronger versions of these medications if necessary.

Diet and exercise can be used to help prevent strong cramping. The dietary suggestions given for PMS also tend to relieve cramps, especially fresh orange juice and ripe bananas. Calcium and vitamin C starting a week before your period work for a lot of women. Aerobic exercise, like running, swimming, or cycling, releases endorphins which reduce cramping in many women. Slow, deep breathing, yoga, meditation, progressive relaxation, and a nice cup of chamomile and mint tea may each help you relax and gain control over this uncomfortable problem. If you can afford it, treat yourself to a monthly massage! (See chapter 3 on Stress Reduction.)

Toxic Shock Syndrome (TSS)

Toxic shock syndrome is extremely rare (five to ten cases out of 100,000 people), but you should know its symptoms because it can be fatal if not diagnosed quickly. It is caused by a bacteria called *Staphylococcus aureus*. It can occur in anyone because of infected wounds or skin abrasions, but most reported cases are of young, menstruating women.

The symptoms occur abruptly and require immediate medical attention. These symptoms include:

sudden fever over 101°F
headache
diarrhea and vomiting
sore throat
dizziness
muscle aches
rash over hands and feet

With prompt medical diagnosis and treatment, the fatality rate of TSS has sharply diminished over the past ten years. It can have other serious side effects, however, such as gangrene, amnesia, lung and kidney damage, heart problems, and partial paralysis.

The incidence of TSS seems to be primarily related to the use of superabsorbent tampons. In some cases, the superabsorbent fibers actually dried out the uterine wall, making it more vulnerable to tears and infections. Women tended to change these tampons less frequently, creating a breeding ground for the *Staphylococcus aureus*. The diaphragm and contraceptive sponge also have created similar problems when not used correctly. Be sure to consult with your doctor or read the package instructions carefully.

You can safely use tampons if you change them frequently, at least every three or four hours. Using a pad rather than a tampon while you are sleeping may be a safer choice. Avoid superabsorbent tampons and tampons with plastic containers which may scratch or irritate your vagina.

If you are using a tampon, diaphragm, or contraceptive sponge and come down with any of the symptoms listed above, call your doctor immediately.

Endometriosis

Endometriosis occurs when the endometrium tissue that normally grows on the uterine wall during the menstrual cycle begins to grow in other places in your abdomen. This results in painful cramping and longer, heavier periods. This problem is much more common among twenty- to thirty-year-olds than teens.

It is a serious, progressive disorder which is not only painful, but can result in infertility. If your periods become longer and increasingly incapacitating, you should check with a doctor. The diagnosis and treatment of this disease is still somewhat controversial, so do some research and get a second opinion before committing yourself to any plan of treatment.

Menopause

Menopause is not a disorder, and for many women it is not a problem at all. Menopause is the natural stopping of the menstrual cycle when a woman is past childbearing age, usually sometime between forty-eight and fifty-two years of age. That is a long way off and may be difficult to imagine as your menstrual cycle is just getting established. But it is a natural and healthy part of the reproductive cycle that you should be aware of.

> I am 60 years old and they say you never get too old to enjoy sex. I know because once I asked my grandma when you stop liking it and she was 80. She said "Child, you'll have to ask someone older than me."
> —Helda D.[3]

Biologically, the eggs in the ovary are depleted or unresponsive to the messages from the pituitary gland to ovulate, so the whole cycle begins to shut down. Estrogen and progestin are still produced, but at a lower level similar to that before menarche. The production of estrogen switches from the ovaries to the adrenal glands, located just above the kidneys. Some women's periods just stop or gradually become lighter and shorter until they stop completely. Most women go through a *premenopausal* stage when their periods become irregular. They may have a period without ovulation, skip a period, or even ovulate without having a period. (A woman may still be ovulating, therefore be able to become pregnant, up to a year after her last period!)

During the five or more years before and after menopause, most women experience some changes as their body adjusts to the new levels and functioning of hormones. Many women have mild to severe hot flashes that last two to three minutes. Some women have them once or twice a month, others as often as hourly. The pituitary gland seems to deregulate the body's thermostat, responding to normal body heat with sweating and flushing that can be uncomfortable and interrupt sleep. We don't really understand exactly how or why these flashes occur, but negative stresses, alcohol, caffeine, smoking, blood sugar, and spicy, salty foods appear to trigger them in some women. Vitamin E, serotonin, vitamin C, and a regular pattern of exercise reduce the occurrence and severity of hot flashes in many.

Menopause can also bring about sexual and emotional changes in some women. Following menopause, the walls of the uterus and the vagina thin somewhat and may take longer to lubricate during sexual intercourse. The vagina, labia, and clitoral hood shrink slightly, but do not lose any sensitivity. In fact, for many women, sexual desire and response is increased. They may be the result of psychological factors as well as a proportional increase in testosterone as estrogen levels lower.

While for most, menopause passes uneventfully, some women do experience strong emotional swings. These may be related to the water retention which is regulated by estrogen and can set off feelings of depression, anxiety, and nervousness. These symptoms can usually be helped by reducing salt and sugar intake, increasing water intake, vitamin B_6, potassium, a healthy diet, and exercise.

For some women, a hormone therapy program may be advisable. Estrogen replacement therapy (ERT) is still controversial. While it can reduce some of the physical discomfort associated with menopause, there are some physical risks and its long-term safety is being questioned. By the time you are approaching menopause, these questions will most likely be answered, but, like any medical decision, ERT should be approached with an educated understanding of the benefits and risks for you personally.

WHAT IS SEX?

If there is no real emotional tie, I'd rather play tennis.
—*Bianca Jaggar*

While everyone seems to know what sex is, it is difficult to come up with a commonly agreed-upon definition. The birds and the bees just "do it," but human beings think about it, fantasize about it, sing about it, sell it, study it, moralize about it, connect it to love, and use it for violence. We use it to sell cars, beer, perfume, blue jeans, movies, music, and steak sauce. We attach a list of stereotypes, social roles, and political values to both gender and sexual orientation. Some people think sex includes only sexual intercourse while others believe that sex is a wide range of sensual pleasures, behaviors, and feelings. Freud shocked the Victorian world by insisting that even babies were driven by sexual energy and interests.

Obviously, human and animal sexuality exist to create babies. Its biological function is *reproduction*. Some churches and many individuals believe that this is the only legitimate function of sexuality. Sexual pleasure is an evolutionary come-on to ensure the survival of the

Cybersex

Most people now have access to sexual information, sex talk, and pornography in the privacy of their own computer. One advantage is that you can actually find answers to questions you would never dare ask out loud, and there are a lot of good, honest Web sites out there. Misinformation and exploitation are out there too, so check your sources and be sure you are getting accurate information. The pornography and cybersex sites are a more controversial matter. Sexual curiosity is a normal part of human nature, but you may get more than you bargained for on some Web sites. Pornography and cybersex rooms are usually set up and frequented by adults on the not-so-normal end of the spectrum. Having a sexual encounter via computer speaks to the loneliness and disconnectedness of our age. Don't let it define sexuality for you. Sex is confusing enough without learning about it from a bunch of adults who can't be in the same room with the person they are having sex with!

Sex is hardly ever just about sex.
   —*Shirley McLaine*

species, but in excess or for its own sake it leads to moral, personal, and social corrosion.

Others believe that sexual behavior can and should be a form of ***love-making***, with or without the desire to create a baby. The intimacy, vulnerability, and pleasure giving of a sexual relationship deepens and strengthens the emotional attachment between two individuals who love and care for each other. Some insist that this must be a long-term, monogamous relationship. Other believe that two relative strangers can have a temporary, but loving sexual encounter. Both would agree that sex without mutual respect and love is a form of narcissistic masturbation and possible sexual abuse.

Some people believe that while sex with love is very nice, sex without love can be pretty good too. This focus is on the ***physical pleasure*** and release created during sexual play, not the relationship. Casual sex can include personal want ads, prostitution, "scamming" or one-night stands, group sex, or just general promiscuity. Monogamous, long-term relationships can also value the playful, pleasure-seeking aspects of sex. As Magic Johnson sadly demonstrated, however, the more promiscuous type of casual sex has become a dangerous option in the age of AIDS.

Sex can also be viewed as ***fantasy*** or pornography—movies, pictures, literature, phone lines, or strip joints that are sexually arousing. Some people see this as a personal extension of the pleasure principle. Others see at least some forms of sexual fantasy as obscene and destructive. The Supreme Court has given up attempting to define legal "obscenity" and has left it to the discretion of local communities. The banning of a wide variety of books, movies, and music across the United States has demonstrated the range of opinion about what is obscene.

One case against pornography is that it often exploits the sexual fantasy of sex as ***power***, particularly against women. When the vulnerability and intimacy of sexual intercourse is used by one partner against another, sex becomes an act of violence and intimidation. In male prisons, forced sodomy becomes a means of imposing the power structure among inmates. Child molestation uses adult status and physique to control and coerce a relatively powerless partner. Both date and stranger rape of women or men are based on the power to humiliate and force someone else to submit.

Historically, sex has always been an important issue, but the social and religious rules have changed considerably. In ancient Greece, women were dominant in male/female relationships until property laws established that property would be passed on through the male heirs. A man then had to protect his inheritance by making sure that his wife's children were really his. Wives became isolated and their sexuality was carefully limited to childbearing within the marriage. Men, however, were not so sexually restricted and a second class of women, prostitutes, emerged for the enjoyment of sexual pleasure and social life. The good wife would be at home with the children tending the estate, while the good husband would be attending the opera with his legitimate prostitute. Men and prostitutes were quite sexually active, both heterosexually and homosexually.

In Rome, the situation was very similar, but wives were somewhat less constrained. They could leave the house with their husband's permission and share some of the social life with their husband. Men were usually married by age fifteen or sixteen and women by twelve or thirteen. Marriage and sex were legal arrangements for the purposes of building an estate and creating male heirs.

During the Middle Ages, Christianity changed many of the rules about sex, but did not provide much relief for women. Early Christians believed that sex and sin were synonymous, distracting men from the spiritual life. Women were a sexual temptation for men and therefore shameful. Even in marriage, sex was thought to be unhealthy, unclean, and wicked and was only allowed on certain days. Babies were conceived and born in original sin. Sex was a biological necessity and had no legitimate connection to love or pleasure.

When chivalry arrived in the Middle Ages, women were raised out of their bed of sin, but only if they were chaste and noble. This was the time of romantic love, not sexual love. Marriage was still an arrangement of legal convenience. Gradually sex and love became linked, but not exclusively. During the Reformation, Luther married a nun and acknowledged male and female sexual needs—his radical proposals included an allowance for married men and women to have sex twice a week.

By the nineteenth century in England, there was both strict repression of sexuality and a growing rebellion against these values. During these Victorian times, sex, even the body itself, was taboo. If a woman was pregnant, eyes dropped; she was fleetingly referred to as being in an "interesting condition" and everyone tried not to think about how she got that way. It was considered a "vile aspersion to suggest that a woman was capable of feeling sexual desire." Since almost one in four women would eventually die in childbirth, it is easy to understand why women might be less than excited about sex. At the same time, however, the feminist movement was being born and began pressing for legal and reproductive rights for women. In 1898, *The Adult*, the first journal of sex, was published—and banned.

In North America, survival was people's main concern. There wasn't much time or energy left for sex. Pioneer hardships naturally developed a more cooperative male/female relationship and marriage became a practical partnership. Sexual standards were still strict, but people married between thirteen and seventeen years of age so the restrictions did not have to confront active teenage sexuality.

Sexual Intercourse

Sexual intercourse is usually the "IT" that people are referring to when they talk about sex. *Have you done "it"? How was "it"? I don't think I'm ready for "it" yet.* Even on a purely physical level, sex includes much more than the act of intercourse, but, under the right circumstances, IT can be one of the highlights. When both partners are able to communicate and be responsive to each other's sexual needs, intercourse can be extremely pleasurable, both physically and emotionally. It is a private act of trust and vulnerability which can enhance or destroy a relationship. It can be an expression of love and intimacy between two people. It is also very relaxing, can reduce migraine headaches and premenstrual symptoms, and students love to claim it is an effective means of losing weight—unless, of course, you get pregnant. (Actually, an average "workout" of sexual intercourse lasts about ten to fifteen minutes and burns about 250 calories—the same as a quick walk around the block.)

Sexual intercourse is also how you make babies and how STDs are spread. Having intercourse against your will or even against your better judgment can be an extremely painful and damaging experience. It is not uncommon for a couple who is not communicating honestly about their feelings and wishes to break up almost immediately after they have had intercourse. This can leave one or both partners feeling used and abandoned.

Relaxed, mutually satisfying, and pleasurable sexual intercourse requires:

- *a healthy level of self-esteem and comfort with your body.*

- *the ability to communicate your sexual needs, feelings, and questions honestly and comfortably.*

- *a sensitive level of trust and respect between both partners.*

- *freedom from worries about pregnancy, STDs, being "caught," or how having intercourse will affect the relationship.*

- *an ability to respond sensitively to another person's body, feelings, vulnerability, and desires.*

- *a carefully considered decision that **you have made for yourself** for reasons that respect your own readiness, safety, feelings, and values.*

You can participate in the physical act of intercourse without all or any of these characteristics, but you will probably find that you are distracted or left with an empty, lonely feeling. The intensity and hoopla associated with a mature sexual relationship is much more than two bodies and an orgasm.

First let's look at what happens physically and biologically. While this will not account for all the mystique, controversy, or rave reviews about sex, it can be very helpful to understand how your body works and responds during sexual intercourse. It is also particularly important for males and females to understand how each other responds because we are indeed different and it can be difficult to understand these differences.

Phase One: Excitement

This can build over weeks (months? years?) of seeing and thinking about someone who is sexually appealing to you. It can include flirting, fantasy,

I should say that the majority of women (happily for society) are not very much troubled with sexual feeling of any kind.
—Dr. William Action, 1857

romance, dancing, dreams, pictures, books, movies, talk, and smiles as well as touching and kissing. Your heartbeat, blood pressure, and breathing rate increase. Your skin may become flushed and your body temperature rises. It may or may not lead to phases two, three, or four, but is generally pleasurable and provocative in its own right.

FEMALE	MALE
While females can be very excited by touch and visual stimuli, they are often sexually excited by the more social and romantic components of sex. Female sexual fantasies tend to involve relationships more than body parts. When aroused, the vagina becomes lubricated and the clitoris lengthens to about one inch. The labia and vagina swell slightly and breast nipples become erect and sensitive.	Stereotypically, males tend to be more aroused by visual and physical stimuli, but many are incurable romantics which can greatly endear them to their female counterparts. Excitement is usually accompanied by an erection of the penis and muscular contractions which pull the testes in closer to the body. It make take as little as ten seconds for the penis to become fully erect.

Phase Two: Plateau

This phase usually occurs during intercourse itself. The genitals are stimulated manually, orally, or through insertion of the penis into the vagina. Rhythmic motions "thrusting" in and out of the vagina stimulate the nerve endings on the head of the penis and on the clitoris. The penis is stimulated directly, but, remember, the clitoris is outside and above the action. While the act of insertion and body movement may be enough to stimulate the clitoris, manual stimulation may be important for the woman to reach orgasm. When both partners are relaxed and comfortable, this phase can be an extended period of pleasurable touching and stimulation.

FEMALE	MALE
Because of the location of the clitoris, it may take the female longer to reach full arousal. During this nonetheless pleasurable process, the uterus lifts and the clitoris pulls back under its protective hood, becoming more erect within the body. The labia swell further and may turn from pink to bright red.	The testes are drawn closer to the body and the penis swells to 50–100 percent of its original size and may become reddish purple. The direct stimulation of the glands and penis shaft through penetration may lead to a shorter plateau period for the male.

Phase Three: Orgasm

During the process of stimulation, the blood vessels in the male and female have become engorged with blood which is what causes them to become erect and sensitive. This is called *vasocongestion.* Somewhat more slowly, the involuntary muscular system has become flexed and tense, called *myotonia.* When both genital and muscular systems are fully aroused, heart rate, blood pressure, and breathing rate may increase as much as two and a half times. A nervous impulse, similar neurologically to that of a sneeze, releases the tension and blood pressure.

FEMALE	MALE
Breathing becomes fast and shallow. The vagina and uterus contract rhythmically. The clitoris remains erect and can be painfully sensitive to touch. The labia have become fully engorged and the breasts remain engorged and erect.	The muscles around the urethra and sphincter contract quickly and repeatedly, forcing semen out of the penis and creating a final burst of tension and relaxation throughout the body. The testicles are fully elevated next to the body. The penis ejaculates about a teaspoonful of semen which typically contains about 100,000 sperm.

Phase Four: Resolution

After orgasm, the genitals and body begin to return to normal. Breathing rate, heartbeat, and body temperature lower. Muscular tension is usually completely relaxed and engorged genitals gradually return to normal size and color.

FEMALE	MALE
The labia and breast nipples return to normal size. The clitoris reemerges and gradually resumes its unstimulated size. The female does not have any refractory period and can experience multiple orgasms during sexual intercourse.	The penis becomes soft and returns to normal size. The scrotum relaxes to normal size and position. The male genitals are usually painfully sensitive to touch after orgasm. A male has a refractory period which varies from minutes to hours before he can be physically aroused again.

All of this can take anywhere from five minutes to over an hour, depending on the comfort and skill of the partners. Ten to fifteen minutes is probably average.

Masturbation

Even in this more sexually explicit time of X-rated movies, MTV, and relaxed sexual standards, for most teenagers masturbation still remains a controversial and uncomfortable topic. When so many areas of sexuality have become publicly flaunted, it is interesting to wonder why we still blush, stammer, and play dumb when it comes to talking about masturbation. It is safe—no pregnancies, STDs, or AIDS. It doesn't violate or mislead another person. It can reduce stress, insomnia, head-

WHO MASTURBATES?

In 1948, Alfred C. Kinsey and his associates at the Institute for Sexual Research shocked, surprised, and changed the assumptions of a whole generation of Americans by publishing the first systematic studies of male and female sexuality. In this sample of 5,940 females and 5,300 males (all white, incidentally), 58 percent of the females and 92 percent of the males had masturbated to orgasm at least once. Almost 90 percent of the males has started masturbating between the age of ten and fifteen. Only about 20 percent of the females had tried masturbation at that age, but the percentages rose steadily until about forty years old. Teenage boys in this study reported masturbating on the average of twice a week. The average frequency for female masturbation was once every two or three weeks. In Kinsey's study, the more highly educated the person, the more likely he, or especially she, was to masturbate. Almost all of the college-educated males and two-thirds of the college-educated females reported masturbating at some point. **What variables do you think might account for this finding?**

aches, or PMS without drugs or side effects. It has been effectively used to cure *frigidity* (inability to have an orgasm), *impotence* (inability to have an erection), and *premature ejaculation* (having an orgasm too quickly). And it feels good. So what's the problem?

At one point, masturbation was blamed for an endless variety of physical and mental illness—insanity, epilepsy, deafness, headaches, asthma, "masturbation heart" (heart murmurs), and acne, to name a few. There is no medical evidence to support any of these accusations. Many world religions condemn masturbation as heathenish self-pleasuring or "self-abuse," though while reports of masturbation have existed in all cultures and throughout human history, it actually appears to be less prevalent in primitive societies and then approved of mainly for adolescents who are not otherwise sexually active.

Masturbation is "the stimulation or manipulation of one's own genitals, especially to orgasm."[4] Most mammals masturbate rather matter of factly. Babies and young children are delighted to discover their genitals. Touching or rubbing the genitals is pleasurable and comforting. Outside of an adult sexual context, this exploratory self-pleasuring is much like thumb sucking, scratching an itch, or massaging a tight muscle. It feels good and brings comfort and relief. In Italy, mothers will often stroke the genitals of a baby who is suffering from teething or other discomfort. By age four or five, this exploration usually extends to other children where curiosity and natural sensual feelings initiate games of showing and touching each other's bodies. Wrestling, playing doctor, or activities involving nakedness, both with other children of the same sex and the opposite sex, are common expressions of sexual curiosity.

But all this touching and albeit innocent expression of sexuality tends to make most parents nervous and uncomfortable. With or without words, explanations, threats, or condemnation, most children are taught not to touch "down there." Peers often pick up the message and tease each other mercilessly if suspected of or caught masturbating. Sometimes family or religious values specifically prohibit this aspect of sexuality. As you grow up, the natural, sensual act of touching your own body develops social and moral implications.

Some people masturbate regularly and enjoy it. Some people have a fulfilling, active sex life without ever masturbating. Others masturbate only at times when other sexual outlets are not available to them. Some people have no interest in masturbation or find it disgusting; others find it easier to have an orgasm than with sexual intercourse. Some believe that masturbation is a healthy, pleasurable part of their sexuality; others believe that it is a narcissistic and immoral distortion of sexual pleasure. Almost everyone today believes that masturbation will not hurt you physically. Its psychological and moral impact will depend greatly on your values, beliefs, and experiences. Masturbation can be a pleasurable, enhancing part of your sexuality or a source of guilt or obsession.

Take yourself seriously. Consider and respect your own feelings and values.

SEXUAL ORIENTATION

TERMS RELATED TO SEXUAL ORIENTATION

- *Bisexual*—persons who are attracted to and have sex with members of both sexes at some time during their adult life
- *Closet*—being homosexual in a state of secrecy or carefully guarded privacy
- *Coming out*—to become open about a homosexual orientation and lifestyle
- *Gay*—a code name originally used within the gay community, now commonly accepted, usually for gay men
- *Gay basher*—an individual who openly harasses or attacks homosexuals
- *Heterosexual*—a person who is predominantly attracted to the other gender
- *Homophobia*—unreasoning fear or hatred toward homosexuals
- *Homosexual*—a person who is predominantly attracted to the same gender
- *Lesbian*—a female homosexual
- *Straight*—a heterosexual person or group

One of the most emotional-laden and confusing aspects of sexuality is a person's sexual orientation. Throughout recorded history and in every society, some people have been sexually attracted to members of the same gender. In Kinsey's study, only 4 percent of males and 2 percent of females in the United States were exclusively homosexual, but also only 63 percent of males and 72 percent of females were exclusively heterosexual. The other one-third of males and one-quarter of females were somewhere on a bisexual continuum between homosexuals who had some heterosexual feelings or activity and heterosexuals who had some homosexual feelings or activity. Most researchers today agree that approximately 10 percent of the people in the world have a predominantly homosexual orientation. Homosexual individuals, both known and *closeted*, have contributed significantly to every area of human endeavor—Dag Hammershold, Tennessee Williams, Gertrude Stein, Alexander the Great, Tchaikovsky, John Maynard Keynes, Leonardo da Vinci, Elton John, Willa Cather, David Kopay, among many others.

Many gay men and women, however, have chosen to *stay in the closet* or hide their sexual orientation because of the strong and sometimes violent reactions from the *straight* community. The derogatory label of "faggot" comes from the old English action of tying homosexuals together and burning them at the stake like faggots of wood. Homosexuals were one of the first groups rounded up for extermination in Nazi Germany. Even today, *gay bashers* may violently attack gay bars or gay individuals, and homosexuals may be discriminated against in jobs, housing, and public facilities. Harvey Milk, the first openly gay city official in the United States, was assassinated during his first term of office. As many as one-third of all teenage suicide attempts are by gay or lesbian adolescents. It can be very lonely and frightening to have homosexual feelings in a world that is so fiercely heterosexual.

Prior to 1973, homosexuality was viewed as a mental illness, though there is no reported instance of a person being "cured" of homosexuality through therapy or treatment. In 1973, the American Psychiatric Association wrote:

> *Whereas homosexuality per se implies no impairment in judgment, stability, reliability or general social or vocational capabilities, therefore, be it resolved that the American Psychiatric Association deplores all public and private discrimination against homosexuals in such areas as employment, housing, public accommodation and licensing . . .*

The American Psychological Association added:

> *The American Psychological Association urges all mental health professionals to take the lead in removing the stigma of mental illness that has long been associated with homosexual orientation.*

Many world religions have also changed their positions on homosexuality. The National Council of Churches, the Roman Catholic Federation of Priests Council, and the Central Conference of American Rabbis have all gone on record in support of civil rights protection for gay people. The Roman Catholic Church still condemns homosexuality as sinful and some other religions agree, citing passages from the Bible that claim that homosexuality is unnatural and immoral. Some homosexuals attend a Metropolitan Community Church, a gay religious affiliation.

WHAT WE DO AND DON'T KNOW ABOUT HOMOSEXUALITY:

? *How is homosexuality determined?*
This question is still unanswered. The most recent Kinsey report found that early relationships with parents, childhood friendships, youthful sexual and emotional feelings, and traumatic sexual incidents had little or no effect on eventual sexual preference. Researchers at the Salk Institute have found that a section of the hypothalamus related to sexual behavior appears to be much smaller in homosexual men. A study at Boston University of identical twins found that if one identical twin was gay, the other was almost three times more likely to be gay than if the twins were fraternal—but there were many twins who did not follow this pattern. More research is needed to answer the questions raised by these new studies.

? *Is homosexuality a choice or a predisposition?*
Most gays will tell you that they discovered, not chose, their sexual orientation. They do not believe that they either chose or can change the sexual or emotional attraction they have for the same gender any more than heterosexuals can change their attraction for the other gender. Given the harassment of gays in this society, it is hard to imagine why anyone would freely choose such a difficult lifestyle, but we still don't know exactly what predisposes a person to be either gay or straight.

? *What causes homophobia?*
It is difficult to know for sure why some people feel so angry toward homosexuals. Different people relate their dislike of gays to religious or social taboos, but anti-gay feelings can become very obsessive and even violent. Some people who are homophobic tend to also have prejudicial feelings toward other minority groups or people who are different. This seems based on a fear or antipathy toward any lifestyle or group that changes a person's values or ideas. During childhood and adolescence when experimental, same-gender sex play and love are very common for both heterosexual and homosexual persons, jokes, ridicule, and personal fears may raise some doubts about one's own sexual orientation. Frequently people with the most violent reactions to homosexuality are those who are most uncomfortable with their own sexual feelings.

? *Do gay people molest children or try to recruit straight people?*
Ninety percent of all children who are sexually molested are females molested by an adult male. Of the remaining 10 percent, many of the molesters are not technically homosexual—they are more interested in children than members of their own gender, molesting both boys and girls. Most gays are very careful about approaching any potential partner. Like anyone, they would rather avoid the pain of rejection and possible abuse.

? *Should gay people come out?*
While it is always unfortunate for any of us to have to hide or feel threatened by a part of who we are, the question of coming out is really up to each individual. Some gay activists believe that if more gay people came out, homosexuality would become more accepted and comfortable for everyone. Many gay people resent "living a lie," and find that the fear and deception eats away

at their self-esteem and dignity. Other gay people believe that important jobs or relationships would be threatened if they were to come out. Some gays feel that their sex life is private and should be no one else's business. Homosexuality is just a small part of a person's identity, but for some people, when it is known, it may overshadow other qualities or relationships. Coming out, like any act of independence and self-affirmation, requires personal strength and courage. The unconditional love and support of families and friends can make this decision much easier.

? *Can you tell someone is gay by how they look or act?*
Contrary to popular stereotypes, only about 15 percent of gay men and 5 percent of lesbians are recognizable as such to most people. Gay men and lesbians may pick up more subtle cues in dress or references, but the truth is that most homosexuals look and act like anyone else. Many effeminate men and masculine-appearing women are heterosexual. Transvestites, usually men who use feminine clothes and gestures, may be either gay or straight.

??? **To try to understand these questions better, go back over the preceding questions and substitute the words *heterosexual* or *straight* for *homosexual* or *gay*. Do the questions make sense? How would you feel to have your sexual orientation questioned, judged, and analyzed?**

SEXUAL DECISION MAKING

Sex is often thought of as a romantic, spontaneous part of a relationship. Real intimacy, however, includes open communication and honest respect for the feelings, wishes, and values of both people in a relationship.

By yourself, or in small class groups, brainstorm all the possible considerations for making a decision about sexual behavior.

Good Reasons for **HAVING SEX** in a Relationship	Good Reasons for **NOT HAVING SEX** in a Relationship

After looking closely at your lists, come up with five basic considerations that each person should think about in deciding upon their sexual behavior in a relationship.

1. _____

2. _____

3. _____

4. _____

5. _____

Sexual Messages

Sex involves *your* body, *your* feelings, and *your* relationships, but everyone else has an opinion about what you should do. Before you can make a strong, independent decision that is right for you, you need to recognize the different messages that you are getting from others. Some will be quite direct (*"Have sex and your mother and I are cutting off your inheritance"*). Other messages are more subtle and indirect (*"If you aren't ready for a sexual relationship, maybe we should just date other people until you are"*).

Identify what messages each of these sources gives you about your sexual decisions.

PARENTS _____

CLOSE FRIENDS _____

BOYFRIEND/GIRLFRIEND _____

OTHER GUYS _____

OTHER GIRLS _____

CHURCH _____

SCHOOL _____

TV, MOVIES _____

MUSIC _____

ADVERTISING _____

INTERNET _____

SEXUAL VALUES

Decisions about your sexuality involve not only your physical readiness and factual information, but also your personal values, preferences, and the relationships that you choose. One of the main tasks of moving from childhood to adulthood is establishing your own set of values and making personal choices based on what **you** believe to be right and important. These beliefs will be shaped and informed by many things—the values your parents have taught you, religious beliefs, personal experiences, your friends, the media, and cultural ideology—but, in the end, they will be uniquely yours.

When you were a child, you probably accepted your parents' values as absolute. You may not have always liked their rules and discipline, but you had no reason to question their validity. You learned your basic values and rules of behavior from their teaching, admonitions, and actions. Studies have shown that this early training is very important—most people as adults believe in the same basic values as their parents.

Adolescence, however, is the time when you begin to evaluate and question things independently. You may end up agreeing with your parents, but you will no longer agree simply because they say so. You are capable and determined to think things through for yourself. This is a valuable and healthy turn of events, but it may catch your parents by surprise, particularly if you are the oldest child. Children are not always cooperative and obedient, but they rarely question the natural authority of their parents. Parents come to expect a certain degree of deference. When teenagers begin to challenge this authority and question family values, this can create quite a stir. It may also be disconcerting to you to discover that your parents are fallible human beings who make mistakes and don't have all the answers.

As in any new job, you are a beginner as you take over the task of establishing your own authority and values. Some teenagers wisely take on a little at a time and consult with their parents for advise and direction. Most of us, however, are excited and terrified by all the new possibilities, take a deep breath, and jump in—usually way over our heads. As you thrash around in this newfound independence, most people look to their peers who are grappling with the same feelings and frustrations that they are. This newly independent peer group provides new standards of behavior, ideas, music, clothes, and values to try on while you are formulating your own. While at times it may seem like the blind leading the blind, the camaraderie, understanding, and friendship that develops is an important and welcome source of strength as you let go of childhood dependencies. As you become more experienced and confident, you will question these peer values too until finally, you have become truly independent.

Teenagers sometimes run into trouble during this transition because they tend to believe that:

1. *There is no real peer pressure.*

2. *Anyone with any gumption can easily do and say what she believes.*

NEITHER OF THESE STATEMENTS IS TRUE. It is almost always difficult to disagree with a commonly accepted opinion or behavior. Today we celebrate Martin Luther King, but how did we treat him when he was alive? He was arrested over eighty-five times and, at age forty-three, was shot because he spoke out for what was, at that time, a controversial belief. Our history is full of men and women who have been chastised and alienated for unpopular values. The United States was established as a nation of nonconformists and outcasts. We theoretically value our independent spirit, but like any established group, we put pressure on our members to conform. We like people who conform and we ostracize those who don't.

In one study, Stanley Schacter observed a group that was asked to discuss what to do with John Rocco, a juvenile delinquent—give him a harsh or lenient sentence.[5] There were three *plants,* or participants who were actually working with the experimenters. One was a conformist—she was instructed to always go along with the opinion of the majority of the group. The next was wishy-washy—he was instructed to at first disagree, but then be swayed by the group opinion and agree. The last plant was instructed to politely, intelligently, but steadfastly remain independent, disagreeing with the majority group opinion. After the discussion, participants were asked to rate how much they liked the other participants in the group or might like to see them again. Almost everyone liked the conformist, saw great hope for the wishy-washy one, but didn't really like the one who disagreed. So establishing your own values and remaining independent may not be the best way to win friends and influence people!

In another experiment known as the Asch line experiment,[6] participants were asked to simply say which of a series of three lines was the same length as a fourth line that was held up separately. This was a simple visual task which people could answer with 100 percent accuracy. Only, in this experiment, all of the participants were plants except the last in the row who was the actual subject. The plants were instructed to all give the same wrong answer, much to the amazement and confusion of the poor, unknowing subject. Even in this situation of obvious visual information, 35 percent of the responses conformed to the wrong answer. And this was in a group of people that the subject did not know and presumably wouldn't care if they laughed or thought she was weird. Yet over a third of the time, people still conformed against what they knew to be true. We seem to have an almost instinctive desire not to stick out and, in the face of a unanimous group opinion, we may actually question our own perception. In a follow-up study where just one other person in the panel disagreed with the majority, conformity dropped to almost zero. It would seem that it just takes one brave soul to give others the permission to follow their own conscience.

Conformity is not always a bad thing. Imagine the traffic jams if everyone decided to drive independently and not stop at a red light just because everyone else did. Without rules and general conformity, games would become pretty ridiculous, many social interactions would become chaotic, and most group activities would become unmanageable. We conform to general expectations so that groups and societies can function smoothly.

But blind conformity and obedience can also violate your basic values and identity. In a dramatic and ingenious experiment, Stanley Milgram tried to find out how far people would violate their own values and sense of decency to conform to authority.[7] He set up an experiment ostensibly to test the effect of punishment on learning. He had two subjects—one to be the teacher and one the learner. A coin was flipped to determine which was which, and the learner was strapped into a chair that had electrodes placed on her skin. The teacher was then taken to another room with a control panel that would give different levels of shock to the learner whenever she made a mistake. The panel was labeled with the highest levels indicating extreme shock—indeed, the highest level was labeled in red, DANGER.

The teacher was given some nonsense syllables which he was asked to teach the learner to memorize. After the first couple of trials, the learner made a mistake and the teacher was instructed to give her a mild shock. For each subsequent mistake, the shock was increased. Soon the subject was making lots of mistakes and began to protest from the other room that she was in pain. If the teacher questioned going on, he was instructed to just continue the shock. Soon the learner cried out in pain and begged to be let out of the experiment. The teacher was instructed to pay no attention and continue the shocks. Finally there was no sound or response from the learner at all. The teacher was instructed that no response was an incorrect response and he must administer the next level of shock. Most teachers were very upset and begged to be let out of the experiment. They were worried about the learner and some were even in tears. But 65 percent of the participants continued administering the shock all the way through where it was marked danger. Sixty-five percent conformed to the demands of the experiment's authority, even when they believed that they were hurting, perhaps even killing, another human being.

Of course, the learner was part of the experiment. She was not being shocked at all and her responses were tape-recorded to be the same for each subject. The experiment was discontinued because it was too emotionally upsetting to the real subjects, the teachers. While they had not hurt anyone, they had to live with the fact that they had thought they were injuring another person and continued to conform anyway. Nazi Germany, Vietnam, Cambodia, and the Jonestown massacre provide all too real examples of how this can happen in real life.

It is extremely important to establish a clear sense of your own values and to know that it will not always be easy to follow them. The process of *values clarification* can help you to know and live by the values that you believe are just and true.

- First, you must *identify your values.* Think through the ethical considerations that determine what is good and just. Which are relative to you or a given situation, and which do you believe apply to all people in all situations? Are some values more valuable than others? Is there a core of universal values on which you can base all ethical decisions.

- Second, it is important to *voice your values.* This may just be to yourself so that you are clear about what you believe and stand for. It may also be more public, letting your friends, family, or other people know what you value. This may be when you are asked your opinion or when a joke or discussion violates your values. Speaking up when you see an injustice can be difficult, but it helps to clarify and strengthen your own sense of integrity.

- Finally, and over and over again throughout your life, you must summon up the courage to *act on your values.* As Spike Lee would say, *DO THE RIGHT THING.* Most real-life situations are complex and will contain both good and bad elements. Sometimes two values will conflict and you must choose which is more important to you. Sometimes the means and ends will conflict—you will be asked to violate your values for a good cause, or a just means will bring about an unjust end. You must not only determine what your values are, but how to implement them.

Questions to Ask Yourself

When and if you have sexual intercourse is one of your first really important adult decisions. You must decide for yourself if you are ready for this type of sexual intimacy. It is your body and your life. Having sex because other people think you should is not a good idea. Having sex because other people think you shouldn't is also not a good idea. This is an important time to think for yourself.

Here are some questions to consider as you decide what part sex is going to play in your life right now.

1. *How is my self-esteem?* Do I respect myself enough to make a caring, responsible decision about my well-being? Am I taking risks with myself that I wouldn't want to see a good friend take?

2. *Am I comfortable with my own body and nudity?* Do I like myself and my body?

3. *Do I trust and genuinely care about my partner?* Am I comfortable being myself around her? Am I comfortable with another person's body and nudity? Do I feel safe in this relationship?

4. *Can we talk openly and honestly about our sexual needs, feelings, and questions?* Do I often fake it or avoid talking about sex in our relationship? Can we laugh together and share our real feelings, fears, and silliness?

> *I discovered this very effective form of oral contraception. Last week I asked a girl to go to bed with me and she said no.*
> —Woody Allen

5. *Have we talked about birth control and AIDS?* Are we comfortable with the protection we have decided on? Can I be trusted to make sure we use it carefully and consistently?

6. *Do I have accurate information about sex, birth control, STDs, and AIDS?* Do I know enough to protect myself and be sensitive to the safety and sensitivities of my partner?

7. *Am I prepared and able to handle the consequences if something goes wrong?* How would I deal with an unplanned pregnancy, my partner's regret or rejection, or parental or school reaction if we are caught? Have I realistically evaluated my risk of contracting AIDS?

8. *What's my motivation?* Am I trying to rescue a relationship or succumb to some external pressure? Am I trying to prove something? Do I just want to avoid being the last virgin on the planet? Have I bought into the advertising notion that sex will solve my problems?

9. *Is this the way I want to remember my first time?* With this person? Under these circumstances? Will I feel good about the way I made this decision? Do I need alcohol or drugs to muster up my courage? (This question should hold true not just for the first time, but *every* time that you decide to have sex.)

10. *Will I respect myself in the morning?* Is my decision consistent with my important personal values? How would I feel about my parents' reaction if they knew? Does my decision feel right and good to me? If I stopped to really think about all of these questions, would I change my mind?

> *You can remember the second and the third and the fourth time, but there's no time like the first. It's always there.*
> —Shelagh Delany

Quandary: *It Takes Two to Tango . . .*

Once decided, the decision to be or not to be sexually active should be respected by both the individual and his or her partner. This is not a decision that you make once. It is a decision you make every time you are faced with the opportunity or desire to have sexual intercourse. Long after you have lost your virginity, you will still be making decisions about your sexuality. Each time and circumstance is a unique situation in which you have the right and responsibility to decide what to do. The circumstances might change slightly or your personal feelings or relationship might be different. New experience or information might give you a new perspective on your decision. Or you might just change your mind. You have the right to change and grow and reevaluate your thinking. Trust your instincts and respect yourself.

You must also respect the needs and wishes and decisions of your partner. This is not usually a problem if both partners agree in their decision—either yes or no. The difficulty comes when one person is ready to have sex and the other is not. Communication becomes both extremely important and extremely difficult at that time. The obvious response is that BOTH persons must be ready and comfortable with the decision.

How can two people discuss their feelings and wishes honestly without pressuring one another? How can you know that not only are you ready, but your partner is really ready as well? What are some signs that your relationship may or may not be ready to include sex?

CONCEPTION, PREGNANCY, AND CHILDBIRTH

Here is one biologist's description of the incredible "miracle of life" that begins with sexual intercourse and ends with the conception of a human embryo.[8]

If the timing is right and an egg has been released within 24–48 hours before intercourse, then there is a good chance that fertilization will occur. However, it is far from a sure thing. There are many obstacles for both the egg and the sperm to overcome. It is a veritable reenactment of Romeo and Juliet as outside forces conspire against our little gametes on their journey toward zygote-hood. Assuming that the egg has been released and no form of birth control is being used, here's how things should run their course:

1. About 200–400 million sperm are ejaculated out of the penis and into the vagina. The vagina has to protect itself from bacteria and fungi and other little organisms that are up to no good, so the interior is acidic. Many of the little troopers that just arrived will be wiped out almost immediately by this acidity (about 25–50 million). Not all of the sperm have got their act together so a bunch of them will wander off in the wrong direction never to be seen again.

2. By this time, the female body is hip to what's going on and the mucus plug that usually covers the cervix softens and lets the sperm swim toward the uterus. However (it couldn't be that easy!), there is a downward current in the uterus that is pushing against the direction of travel (about another 30–40 million sperm will buy the farm at this point).

3. Things have been pretty hard up to this point, but the toughest and most cunning male haploids have made it with flying colors. If this next part doesn't make life seem unfair, nothing will. There are two fallopian tubes, one going to each ovary. The sperm will divide into two groups and 50–100 million will swim with all their gusto up the wrong tube (a noble but useless maneuver).

4. Here we are with the 50–100 million of the best sperm of the lot swimming up the fallopian tube to find the egg. Many will go off course and try to fertilize a white blood cell or two. A bunch will just plain get tuckered out and give up.

5. In the great triathlon of conception, there can only be one winner, but there are about 40–100 finalists who reach the finish line and struggle to break the tape. The very tips of the sperm are covered with enzymes that become active when they reach the egg. The enzymes are designed to break the code of the egg's outermost layer. The first sperm to do so is let in. At this point, the sperm drops the tail and the egg changes the outer layer code so that none of the others may enter. No medals for second place. You should be comforted by knowing that half of your genetic information came from the most determined sperm cell of the bunch.

Some Early Signs of Pregnancy

- Missed menstrual period
- Breasts feel full and sensitive
- Ache or fullness in lower abdomen
- Fatigue or faintness
- Nausea or vomiting
- Frequent urination
- Increased vaginal secretion
- Positive pregnancy test

6. The egg will continue to travel down the fallopian tube and take about three days to reach the uterus. By this time, it will have divided into 100 cells and be looking for a place to settle down for nine months. About one week after it was fertilized and eight to nine days after it was released from the ovary (about Day 20 in the menstrual cycle), the egg will implant itself on the endometrium. Implantation is the official biological beginning to pregnancy.

7. If you look back at the menstrual cycle, you will see that at about this time, with no fertilized egg, everything is shutting down. However, the ball of cells called a blastocyst produces a hormone called HCG (human chorionic gonadotropin) that tells menstruation to cease and preserve the endometrium. HCG is the hormone that is detected by a pregnancy test and causes morning sickness. Pregnancy, therefore, may be detected as early as seven days after fertilization.

And this is only the beginning. Over the next nine months, this embryo will develop all the features and capabilities of a functioning human being. To put things into perspective, let's put this pregnancy into the context of a nine-month school year.

Time	*What's happening to MOM*	*What's happening to FETUS*
First day of school	• Sperm reaches egg • Conception occurs	• Blastocyst is created in fallopian tubes • After 30 minutes, cell begins dividing and multiplying
First school weekend	• HCG from placenta signals ovaries to keep producing estrogen and progesterone • Estrogen promotes growth of uterine lining • Progesterone relaxes muscles/cervix	• Embryo implants in uterine lining • Cell differentiation begins
End of September	• Period a week late	
First week in October	• Breasts swollen and sensitive • Some have morning sickness; feel tired and moody • Positive pregnancy test	• Embryo 4 weeks old, ¼-inch long • Heart and central nervous system form • Brain begins to develop • Heart begins beating by 25th day • Buds for arms and legs appear
Halloween	• Pregnancy detectable by physical exam • Feel very tired and need more sleep • May have morning sickness	• Embryo 8 weeks, now called a *fetus* • About 1 inch long, weight of aspirin • Arms, legs, fingers, and toes present • Still has a tail; head is very large
Thanksgiving	• Breasts enlarge and darken • Need to urinate more frequently • Mood swings; gain 2–4 lbs a month • Pregnancy doesn't really show yet • Start monthly doctor checkups	• Fetus 12 weeks old, 3–4 inches, 1 oz. • Responds to stimulation • Form recognizably human • Gender differentiated • Can suck, swallow, has facial expression

Christmas	• Pregnancy starts to visibly show • Fluttering movements may be felt • Morning sickness past; food cravings • Dreaming increases	• Fetus 16 weeks old, 6½ inches, 4 oz. • Sex organs distinct • Heartbeat strong
Semester Exams (in January)	• Quickening—you can feel fetus move • Heightened sense of creativity • Some skin blotches; nose or gums bleed easily; nipples begin producing colostrum • Gained 13–16 lbs	• Fetus 23 weeks old, 11 inches, 2 lbs. • Eyes begin to open • Eyelashes and eyebrows appear • Active and easily felt • Possible *viability* at 24 weeks
St. Patrick's Day	• Some indigestion or heartburn • Shortness of breath; uterus expanded to just below breastbone • Increased urination; stretch marks on abdomen and breasts	• Fetus 28 weeks old, 15 inches, 2½ lbs. • Eyes open • 75 percent chance of survival outside womb • Fatty tissue begins to grow
Mother's Day	• 85 percent of calcium and iron eaten go to fetus; feel awkward and tired • Braxton Hicks contractions prepare uterus; cervix begins to soften	• Fetus 36 weeks old • Gaining 2 lbs. per month • Fetus will drop into position
Last week in May— 266 days later . . .	• DUE DATE!!! (Be patient, first babies are usually late.) You will have gained 24–30 lbs. • Contractions begin; water breaks • Progressive dilation of cervix • Labor and delivery	• Fetus full term, 38 weeks old • Usually 6–10 lbs., 18–22 inches • Head still large for body • Ample body fat, lungs mature
Summer Vacation	Welcome to parenthood!	Newborn and ready to go!

And What's Happening to Dad?

The male obviously plays a critical role in conception, but may find his role during the next nine months somewhat confusing and ill-defined. This is particularly true in an unplanned, unmarried situation. In some situations, the father may not even be told and, in most cases, he does not have a legal say in decisions regarding the pregnancy. If the couple did not have a realistic plan about any failure of birth control, they may find themselves in unexpected disagreement. Even if they had agreed ahead of time, a real pregnancy may put their decision in a different light.

It can be very painful for a young man who strongly disapproves of abortion to have his sexual partner choose this way to deal with their embryo. It can also be unsettling for the father who thought that an abortion would be the best decision to find himself in part financially responsible for an unwanted baby. Emotionally, a teenage father has to deal with a wide range of contradictory feelings. It is his baby too, but he can physically escape this reality. He wants to do the right thing, but his partner has the final say in what that will be. He and his partner were jointly responsible for the acts that created this pregnancy, but he may feel guilty that she has to bear most of the burden. He wants to be supportive and caring, but as the pregnancy progresses it may become more and more difficult for him to identify with his partner's experience and feelings. The decisions, regrets, anger, and life changes are frequently too difficult for a young relationship to bear. Even the most conscientious young father may find himself feeling alienated and left out.

Talking about Pregnancy—Yes, It Could Happen to Us

In the following exercise, share your answers with a member of the opposite sex. (Or more than one—the "male" or "female" experience with pregnancy will vary greatly between individuals.) Write down your answers or notes before discussing them with your partner. Be as honest and realistic as possible. Try to gain a better understanding of how he or she might feel in the event of an unplanned pregnancy and how one might keep communication open and supportive between males and females.

Questions for Girls	Questions for Boys
• How would you feel if you found out that you were pregnant?	• How would you feel if you found out that you had gotten your partner pregnant?
• How would you like your partner to react to the news and to you?	
• What could your partner do that would make things easier for you?	
• How would you want to go about making a decision about the pregnancy?	
• During the pregnancy, what kind of support would you like from your partner?	• During the pregnancy, what role would you like to play?
• What do you think would help to keep your relationship open and supportive during the pregnancy?	
• During the birth, what kind of support would you like from your partner?	• During the birth, what role would you like to play?
• What responsibility and attachment would you feel to the newborn? How would you want to structure your long-term relationship with the baby and with your partner?	

Since a baby's entire body, brain, and nervous system is constructed from the nutrients provided by the mother's body, it is important for a pregnant woman to carefully monitor what she eats and drinks. Protein requirements increase about 60 percent. A pregnant woman needs about 66 percent more calcium than normal during the last three months when the teeth and bones of the fetus are forming. Blood volume increases by 50 percent during pregnancy, requiring extra iron. If you were to become pregnant as a teenager, you would have to eat especially well to nourish your baby and your own still-growing body.

Quandary: When Does "LIFE" Begin?

One of the central questions related to pregnancy and the termination of pregnancy is the biological and spiritual quandary of when this collection of cells embodies a human life. Some define human life in strictly biological terms; others equate it with viability or the ability to live outside of the mother's body; other talk about the inception of a human soul. This distinction is the basis of both ethical and legal opinions about abortion.

Here are some of the positions on this question:

1. Life begins at the moment of conception or 30 minutes later when cells begin to divide.

2. Life begins when the fertilized egg is implanted in the uterine lining (5–7 days after conception).

3. Life begins at the end of the third month, when the embryo becomes a fetus and begins to look human.

4. Life begins at "quickening," when the mother can feel the fetus move on its own (4.5–5 months).

5. Life begins at viability, when the fetus could possibly survive outside of the mother's body (approximately 24–28 weeks).

6. Life begins at birth.

Define what you mean by "life" and choose a position (or add your own) that you believe describes the true beginnings of life. Defend your position on both biological and ethical grounds.

Women are best advised to avoid tobacco, alcohol, caffeine, marijuana, aspirin, and most medications during pregnancy. All of these chemicals cross the placenta and enter the bloodstream that is feeding the developing fetus. Babies born to addicted mothers often go through a painful withdrawal period after birth and often show signs of brain damage and other birth defects. Insecticides, radiation, and extended use of a hot tub or sauna have also shown negative effects.

Childbirth

Many women and men today prepare themselves for childbirth by learning as much as possible about the birthing process and by training their bodies and minds to relax and work with the birth. Education and preparation reduce the fear and mystery often associated with childbirth in our culture. Many women prefer to be awake and alert during the birth of their baby—it is not often you get to see a baby born! Doctors are more likely to use limited and local anesthesia so that the mother and her body can naturally assist with the delivery. Many fathers today choose to be present during the birth of their baby, both to support their partner and to be a part of this incredible event.

Most couples decide to have their babies in a hospital where any complications can be handled quickly. Many hospitals have recognized that most deliveries do not require a surgical environment. Birthing rooms are often comfortably furnished and the mother-to-be and close family and friends can be together throughout labor and delivery. Birthing centers and assisted home deliveries may provide even more comfortable settings. The safety of both mother and baby should be carefully considered before deciding which to choose.

During the last month of pregnancy, the fetus settles into position with the head resting in the pelvic cradle. Most babies are delivered head first. If she is turned around, it is called a *breech birth* and may be more complicated. Progesterone has relaxed and thinned (*effaced*) the cervix. It has probably begun to *dilate* or open about one centimeter, about the size of a fingertip. During labor and delivery, the cervix will dilate to ten centimeters.

> *Making the decision to have a child—it's momentous. It is to decide forever to have your heart go walking around outside of your body.*
> —*Elizabeth Stone*

Labor is usually talked about in four stages and may take from two to twenty-four hours.

1. *First Stage—Dilation:* This is the waiting and working stage when the uterine contractions work to dilate the cervix. The contractions last from twenty to ninety seconds, increasing in intensity and length as you get closer to delivery. The mild, initial contractions begin with fifteen to twenty minute rests between contractions. By the end of labor, the contractions may be coming every two to three minutes. This is called the *transition phase.* It is the most difficult and frustrating part of labor, but it is short (usually only five to twenty contractions) and marks the end of the first stage and readiness for delivery.

2. *Second Stage—Expulsion:* The cervix is fully dilated and the baby begins to move down the *birth canal* (the expanded cervix and vagina). The contractions seem more manageable, your mood and energy are focused, everyone is getting pretty excited, and most women have a strong urge to push. With your doctor or midwife's guidance, you will use your strong uterine muscles to help guide the baby out. This stage usually takes from one-half to three hours. The baby is bluish-gray, covered with a white vernix coating and probably some blood. As he begins to breathe on his own, usually within fifteen to thirty seconds, he will begin to turn a more normal color.

3. *Third Stage—The Placenta:* After the baby is born, you must still deliver the *placenta*—the sack of nutrients that has been feeding your baby for nine months. The uterus continues to contract and the placenta is delivered easily and quickly (it is *much* smaller than a baby!), usually within ten to thirty minutes. In the meantime, you and your doctor or midwife will be checking out the baby and cutting the umbilical cord.

4. *Fourth Stage—Recovery:* For the next one to three hours, your body and uterus will begin to return to a more normal state. Milder contractions called *afterpains* will shrink the uterus and close off any open blood vessels. You may experience some trembling, chills, and swelling of the vaginal area. You will probably feel hungry, thirsty, and exhausted! Having a baby is a lot of work.

The Birth Experience

Giving birth is a memorable and personal experience. It is different for each woman and for each couple. The circumstances clearly dictate many of the emotions evoked. A planned, healthy baby coming into a stable, happy marriage will be a very different experience than an unwanted, premature baby delivered by an single, unsupported girl. Some women have short, easy deliveries. Others have longer, more difficult labors. Some men feel very needed and elated at being part of the birthing. Others find it very stressful.

Talk to three to five people about their birth experience.

1. Your mother or father—find out as much as you can about your own birth.

2. One or two women who have given birth in the last few years.

3. One or two fathers who have attended the delivery of their babies.

Ask them to describe what the birth experience was like for them. Think about what questions you would like to have answered. Most parents are happy to give you a blow-by-blow account and answer your questions.

Plans for an Unplanned Pregnancy

We maintain this incredible double standard with teenagers about sex. If you're swept away by passion, then you didn't do anything wrong. But if you went on a date after taking the pill or with a diaphragm, then you're bad. You were looking for sex and that's not permitted.
—Alice Radosh

There is no easy, comfortable solution to an unplanned, unwanted pregnancy. Each of your options has serious, often painful, drawbacks. Any girl or couple who has been faced with this situation knows that there are very difficult and soul-searching decisions to make. Even if a decision is made quickly and pragmatically, most people struggle with its implications for years, even for a lifetime. *What would I have done with my life if I had not had a child to care for at such a young age? What would my baby have looked like or become if I had not had an abortion? Where is the child that I put up for adoption—is she safe and well cared for?* These are difficult questions that must be faced and accepted.

Basically you have three options:

1. Keeping the Baby
One of the consequences of the sexual revolution is that it has become more commonly accepted for an unmarried teenager to keep and raise her baby. Many high schools and colleges have day-care centers and parenting classes for unwed mothers and fathers. Illegitimacy has lost some of its stigma of the past as movie stars and other public figures openly bear and raise children out of wedlock. Divorce has created many single-parent families, so it no longer seems unrealistic to raise a child outside of an established marriage. Faced with a pregnant daughter and an expensive cost of living, many parents today are willing to help out both financially and physically. The teenage birthrate in 1957 was actually higher than it is today, but that included a quarter of the eighteen- and nineteen-year-olds who were traditionally married. The number of out-of-wedlock births has doubled since the 1960s. Each year over one million teenage girls get pregnant in the United States and about half decide to keep their babies.

While it may be more commonplace today, it is probably not much easier. Babies are cute, cuddly, expensive, and a lot of work! Many fathers choose to be involved and help out, but over 75 percent choose not to get married. Those that do marry are two to three times more likely to enter into marriages that end in divorce. Day and night, the care of a baby drastically cuts into a young parent's finances, education, social life, and personal freedom. It is hard not to resent the intrusion when you are still growing up yourself and your friends, maybe even your partner, have relatively few responsibilities and demands. The romantic notions of baby clothes and toys, precious smiles, and material bonding quickly give way to the reality that parenthood is a twenty-four-hour-a-day, lifelong job.

2. Adoption

Before unwed parenting and abortion were accepted options to pregnant teenagers, you either got married or were sent off to a home for unwed mothers until you could put your baby up for adoption. In the 1960s over 35 percent of pregnant teens chose adoption; today only about 5 percent do. Giving up a baby that you have carried to term can be very difficult, but, in some cases, may be the only way to provide your baby with a stable home and family. There are many couples who are infertile, but very much want to love and care for children. An adoptive couple will sometimes pay for the many expenses involved in pregnancy and childbirth.

Only one in five girls under age fifteen receives any prenatal care at all during the vital first three months of pregnancy. Teenagers run twice the normal risk of delivering a low-birthweight baby, which puts the baby in danger of serious mental, physical, and developmental problems.

Adoptions can be arranged independently or through a licensed agency. Licensed agencies tend to provide a safer, more thorough procedure, carefully researching the background and suitability for the couple or individual wanting to adopt your baby. You can find an authorized adoption agency through your church, doctor, or social service department. Some antiabortion groups will manage and pay for your adoption. An independent adoption can be arranged through a doctor or lawyer. These adoptions may have fewer safeguards and less red tape, but often the prospective parents will pay anywhere from $3,000 to $20,000 to cover your expenses. The possibility of profit and financial pressure sometimes overrides the best interests of you and of your baby, so proceed with caution.

Adoption is a legal process in most states, terminating all parental rights and relinquishing the care and contact with your child to the adoptive couple or person. In most states, the adoptive and birth records are permanently sealed to everyone, including your child. Some adopted adult groups are protesting this procedure and insist that they have the right to know their genetic and parental background. More open, independent adoptions are sharing information and even contact between the child and both sets of parents. The birthfather's rights in the adoption procedure vary from state to state, but a 1972 Supreme Court ruling gave birthfathers the right to claim custody of their illegitimate children. Individual judges currently decide whether or not the adoption must have the birthfather's signed consent.

A legal adoption is granted only with the free consent of one or both birthparents. You will not sign the *relinquishment papers* until a week or two after the baby is born. You have the right to change your mind at any time before you sign these consent forms. The child is then placed in the adoptive home for the *interlocutory period* of about one year. Either of the birthparents can still petition the courts to have the child returned during this time. Once the court grants the final adoption decree, however, you no longer have any legal rights to the child.

3. Abortion

In the United States, about 30 percent of all abortions are performed on teenagers. Forty-five percent of all teenage pregnancies end in abortion. Abortions are most common among the affluent. At the cost of $200 to $1500, many poorer girls simply cannot afford this option. Federal funding for low-income abortions was barred by Congress in 1976 and is currently available in only nine states.

Abortion is the most controversial option for dealing with an unwanted pregnancy. Pro-life advocates decry the murder of a human life. Pro-choice marchers protest the government invasion of a woman's rights over her body. Congress and the Supreme Court grapple with the limits of legal decisions and personal rights. Churches take varying positions on the beginning of life and the morality of abortion.

Medically, abortion is a relatively simple and safe procedure if performed during the first trimester. Three methods are currently legal in the United States. All three can be done as an outpatient procedure.

Vacuum aspiration: A small tube is inserted into the uterus through the cervix. The tube is attached to a suction device that draws out the contents of the uterus including the lining and the embryonic or fetal tissue.

D&C (dilation and curettage): The cervix is dilated (enlarged) and a spoon-shaped instrument is inserted into the uterus. The lining and contents of the uterus are carefully scraped and removed.

Drug-induced abortion (RU-486): Newly legal in the United States, this type of abortion has been used safely in other parts of the world for some time. This procedure must be done in the first seven weeks and requires three office visits. During the first visit, the pregnancy is confirmed and the patient takes a pill containing 600 milligrams of mifepristone, the chemical name for RU-486. During a second visit, thirty-six to forty-eight hours later, the patient is given 400 micrograms of prostaglandin in a vaginal suppository and remains in the office for four hours. During this time, about two-thirds of patients spontaneously abort, though it may take up to twenty-four hours in others. A third visit, ten days later, determines if the abortion has been successful. If it has not, a vacuum abortion will be performed. Babies born after an unsuccessful drug-induced abortion have had a number of serious birth defects.

*A **saline abortion** is most commonly used after the first trimester. It usually requires a hospital stay, is more expensive, and raises serious legal and ethical questions for many people. The risk to the mother both physically and emotionally is considerably greater. A saline or hormonal solution is injected into the uterus. This fluid replaces the amniotic fluid and causes the death of the fetus. The uterus begins to contract and the fetus is then expelled through the birth canal.*

A study done by the Alan Guttmacher Institute at Princeton University found that the U.S. leads nearly all other developed nations in teenage pregnancies. American adolescents are no more sexually active than their British, Swedish, French, or Canadian counterparts, but they are many times more likely to get pregnant.

For girls, age fifteen to nineteen, the rates are:

Holland	14/1000
Sweden	35/1000
Franc	43/1000
England	44/1000
Canada	44/1000
U.S.	96/1000

Our teenage abortion rate is at least as high as the combined rates of abortion and birth in each of these countries. The study concluded that the countries with "the most easily accessible contraceptive services for teenagers and the most effective programs for sex education have the lowest rates of teenage pregnancy, abortion, and childbearing."

Abortion and the Law

Abortions were not legislated until the late 1800s. In many parts of the world, they were considered a medical procedure that was determined privately between doctor and patient. After 1880, abortion laws in the United States were decided by individual states. Most abortions were illegal by the late 1880s. Gradually, some states began to liberalize their laws in response to the women's movement and the tragedy of badly performed, illegal abortions. By 1973, some form of abortion was legal in fifteen states and the disparity between states brought the issue to the Supreme Court.

- **1973:** ROE vs. WADE
  In January of 1973, the Supreme Court found that the "right of privacy . . . founded on the Fourteenth Amendment's concept of personal liberty . . . is broad enough to encompass a woman's decision whether or not to terminate her pregnancy." This ruling overrode state laws prohibiting abortion.

- **1976:** HYDE AMENDMENT
  In July of 1976, Congress passed an amendment that banned Medicaid funding for abortions unless the mother's life was in danger. This severely limited access to a legal abortion by poor or underage women. Before this amendment, Medicaid funded one-third of all abortions in the U.S.

- **1988:** TITLE X
  Congress passed this federal regulation restricting any agency receiving federal funding to answer all abortion questions with the words *The project does not consider abortion an appropriate method of family planning.* The restriction was put on hold until the Supreme Court ruled on its legality.

- **1989:** HODGSON vs. MINNESOTA
  The Supreme Court upheld one of the strictest parental notification laws in the country. This decision led many states to enact stricter rules about restrictions on abortions for pregnant teenagers.

- **Late 1980s:** *Operation Rescue* initiated a nationwide strategy of civil disobedience by blocking clinics that offered abortions. Over 80 percent of all abortion clinics were picketed.

- **1991:** RUST vs. SULLIVAN
  Referred to as the *gag rule*, this Supreme Court decision upheld the Title X regulations, banning abortion discussion and referral in all federally-funded clinics.

- **1991:** Congress voted to reverse the Title X ban, but President Bush vetoed the reversal.

- **1992:** PENNSYLVANIA APPEAL
  The Supreme Court upheld a twenty-four-hour waiting period and a state sanctioned lecture on the pros and cons of abortion, but ruled that mandatory notification of the husband unfairly penalized women in abusive relationships.

- **1992:** Two abortion doctors and an escort at a clinic in Pensacola, Florida, were killed, followed by the murder of two female receptionists at clinics in Brookline, Massachusetts. Over 200 abortion clinics were bombed in the early 1990s.

- **1993:** President Clinton repealed the Title X gag rule.

- **2000:** At the turn of the century, abortion continues to be an emotionally laden political, ethical, and legal battle.
  * Only seventeen states currently fund abortion
  * Thirty-nine states require parent involvement and/or consent
  * Twenty-one states require state-directed counseling discouraging abortion
  * Twelve states enforce mandatory waiting periods before any abortion
  * Eighty-four percent of all counties in the U.S. have no abortion services

Quandary: The Moral Dilemma of Abortion

"Nothing like it has separated our society since the days of slavery" said Dr. C. Everett Koop, former Surgeon General of the United States. Abortion clinics have been bombed. Doctors performing abortions have been threatened and even murdered. Protesters on both sides have been threatened and attacked. Both those who regard abortion as murder of an unborn child and those who support the right of the individual woman to choose if she will bear a child feel very strongly and emotionally that their position is right and just. The true dilemma exists in the fact that both positions have valid moral grounds. Abortion does mean the destruction of a developing human life, yet there are circumstances when this would appear to be responsible, compassionate, and just.

Here are three questions that will help you think about your position on abortion:

1. **When does the developing mass of cells become a biological and/or psychological human life?**

2. **At what point does the unborn have rights that equal or supersede those of its mother?**

3. **What right and responsibility does the government have to determine these questions and impose a single viewpoint on all of its citizens?**

Think carefully about each of the positions presented below; then formulate your own position that you believe to be just and true. Be able to defend your position in terms of the three questions listed above.

A. *Abortion is murder. Under no circumstances can it be justified. The innocent fetus must not be killed just because it is the result of rape or incest. Even in cases where the mother's life is at risk, it is not fair to automatically sacrifice the life of the unborn child.*

B. *Abortion can only be justified when carrying the baby full-term would seriously endanger the mother's life. It is still murder, but is a kind of moral "self-defense."*

C. *Abortion is not necessary. There are many individuals who would love to adopt unwanted children. It is selfish and immoral for a woman to value nine months of inconvenience more than the full life of a human person.*

D. *Abortion can lead to unspeakable judgments on the value of an individual life. Aborting retarded or deformed fetuses is a step closer to doing away with a fetus because of its gender, race, social class, or star sign. Each human life is equally valuable and must be protected.*

E. *Abortion is not killing a human life until* (fill in the point at which you believe the cells become "human." What criteria do you use to make this decision?). *The ingredients do not equal the final product. Before this point, abortion is a morally justifiable means of preventing a human life that is unwanted.*

F. *Abortion is the lesser of two evils. Terminating a pregnancy is better than endangering the mother's life, scarring mother and child with the product of incest or rape, creating a child who will suffer physically and/or psychologically because of birth defects, or bringing into the world an unwanted child who will suffer neglect and abuse.*

G. *The fetus is an integral part of a woman's body and the woman alone has the absolute right to decide whether or not she will go through with the pregnancy. Government intervention in this decision is a gross violation of free choice and individual liberty.*

BIRTH CONTROL

- *Studies show that the average teen waits twelve months after first becoming sexually active before he or she seeks contraception.*
- *Forty-five percent of all teenage pregnancy occurs in the first six months of sexual activity; 36 percent occurs in the first three months.*

Technically, birth control is any technique or devise used to stop a sperm from fertilizing an egg or to stop the implantation of a fertilized egg in the uterine wall. Abortion, which actually terminates the development of an embryo after it has been implanted, is not a form of birth control. It may be an option some women choose to consider in their pregnancy, but it does not prevent conception, only childbirth. Methods of birth control range from not having sex (*abstinence or celibacy*) to natural methods (*rhythm method or withdrawal*) to keeping the sperm from meeting the egg (*barrier, chemical, or surgical methods*) to keeping an egg from being released or preventing implantation in the uterus (*hormonal or mechanical*).

Before we look at what is available in birth control today, take a minute to consider what you think would be the IDEAL BIRTH CONTROL method for sexually active males and females today. Consider effectiveness, side effects, comfort, expense, ease of use, and protection from STDs.

Qualities of the Ideal Method of Birth Control

1. _____

2. _____

3. _____

4. _____

5. _____

6. _____

Quandary: **The U.S. has the highest rate of teenage pregnancy of any developed nation.**

- Four out of every ten fifteen-year-old girls in the U.S. today will get pregnant before they are twenty.

- One out of every five girls will have an abortion before she is twenty.

- Forty-five percent of all teenage pregnancies occur within the first six months of sexual activity; 36 percent occur in the first three months.

- Twenty percent of fifteen-year-old girls, 33 percent of sixteen-year-old girls, and 43 percent of seventeen-year-old girls say they are sexually active—only 25 percent report using effective birth control regularly.

- Thirty-three percent of all girls requesting birth control do so because they are afraid they might be pregnant.

WHY DOES THIS HAPPEN?

List all the reasons that you can think of why people DO NOT use birth control.

1. _____

2. _____

3. _____

4. _____

5. _____

6. _____

Keep the qualities of an ideal birth control method in mind as you review the types of birth control that are available to-day. Either individually or in small groups, research the cost of each method. Then come up with the advantages and disadvantages for females and for males and write out what you think are the pros and cons of each approach to birth control.

METHOD:	*Sterilization* (EXAMPLE)

DESCRIPTION:
A onetime surgical technique that severs or clips the fallopian tubes in the female (TUBAL LIGATION) or the vas deferens in the male (VASECTOMY).

HOW IT WORKS:
Tubal ligation—prevents the egg from getting to the uterus
Vasectomy—prevents the sperm from getting to the urethra

EFFECTIVENESS RATE:
For Preventing Pregnancy: 99%
For Protecting Against STDs: 0%

SIDE EFFECTS OR PRECAUTIONS:
Procedure is usually irreversible.

HOW AND WHERE YOU CAN GET THIS METHOD:
Tubal ligation is performed in a hospital under general anesthesia.
Vasectomy can be done as outpatient surgery, in a doctor's office or clinic, usually with local anesthesia

HOW MUCH IT COSTS:
$500–$1,000 depending on age, sex, and health insurance

ADV/DISADVANTAGES FOR MALE	ADV/DISADVANTAGES FOR FEMALE
No mess, no fuss, no bother	No mess, no fuss, no bother
Very effective	Very effective
Tricky to reverse	Very difficult to reverse
Expensive	Very expensive, hospitalization
Some discomfort, localized pain	Quite uncomfortable, localized pain

RECOMMENDATIONS PRO AND CON FOR THIS METHOD:
An excellent, easy-to-use, effective, and very popular method for people who are sure that they do not want to have any more children. Most doctors will not perform it on teenagers or young adults. Not easily reversible. Some people have eggs or sperm saved and frozen for later implantation if they should change their mind. Some people are understandably squeamish about the idea of surgery on their reproductive organs. (Females DO continue to have their hormonal and menstrual cycle after tubal ligation.)

METHOD: *Abstinence* (no penis/vagina intercourse)

DESCRIPTION:

Abstinence includes refraining from any type of sexual contact as well as sexual contact that does not involve penetration, i.e., petting, mutual masturbation, or oral sex.

HOW IT WORKS:

Many young people choose to limit their sexual contact for a variety of personal and health reasons. Some believe that intercourse is the highest form of intimacy and commitment and do not want to have sex until they are in a permanent, mature relationship. Others know that they are not physically or emotionally ready to share their body in that way. Some teens do not want to take the risk of pregnancy or serious STDs. While some couples refrain from any type of genital touching, others may choose to touch and pleasure each other without penetration. It is important to remember that any exchange of bodily fluids, with or without penetration, may carry some risk of HIV infection.

EFFECTIVENESS RATE:

For Preventing Pregnancy: 100%

For Protecting Against STDs: varies with activity

SIDE EFFECTS OR PRECAUTIONS:

There are no negative side effects to abstinence. One precaution is that heavy petting may be physically arousing and override your self-control and good judgment. Couples who get excited may be tempted to have intercourse and have no protection or birth control at all.

HOW AND WHERE YOU CAN GET THIS METHOD:

No supplies necessary!

COST:

	Male	**Female**
ADVANTAGES		
DISADVANTAGES		
PROS		
CONS		

METHOD: *Condoms* (rubbers or prophylactics)

DESCRIPTION:

A condom is a thin, rubber latex sheath that fits over the erect penis. A condom comes rolled up in a small airtight package and is usually about seven to eight inches long and two inches wide when unrolled.

HOW IT WORKS:

The condom is a barrier method. It fits over an erect penis during intercourse to keep the semen from getting into the vagina. A small space must be left at the tip of the condom to collect the semen after ejaculation and prevent breaking. Care must be used to hold the condom in place during withdrawal so that it does not slip off.

EFFECTIVENESS RATE:

For Preventing Pregnancy: 86%
For Protecting Against STDs: 86%

SIDE EFFECTS OR PRECAUTIONS:

There are no physical side effects for condoms unless an individual is allergic to the latex used. User error results for about 11percent of condom failures. Check for an expiration date and store condoms away from heat and fluorescent light. Be sure the condom has not been damaged in any way; hold it at the base during withdrawal and use with a spermicidal foam or cream to increase effectiveness.

HOW AND WHERE YOU CAN GET THIS METHOD:

Available at drug store and many other places without prescription.

COST:

	Male	Female
ADVANTAGES		
DISADVANTAGES		
PROS		
CONS		

METHOD: *Spermicides*

DESCRIPTION:

Vaginal spermicides are designed for use with a diaphragm or condom to kill any sperm that may have gotten around that barrier method. Spermicides come in foams, jellies, and creams. Creams and jellies work best with the diaphragm, but foam is most effective with condoms.

HOW IT WORKS:

Spermicides are placed inside the diaphragm and around the edges before you insert the diaphragm. When used with a condom, the spermicide should be inserted into the vagina immediately before intercourse—not more than fifteen minutes. Additional spermicide must be inserted for each additional intercourse. The cream or foam must remain in the vagina for six to eight hours.

EFFECTIVENESS RATE:

For Preventing Pregnancy: 74% alone,
foam used with condoms may be 99% effective

For Protecting Against STDs: 0%

SIDE EFFECTS OR PRECAUTIONS:

May increase risk of yeast and urinary tract infections; frequent or prolonged use may irritate vaginal tissue and increase vulnerability to STDs.

HOW AND WHERE YOU CAN GET THIS METHOD:

Drugstore without prescription.

COST:

	Male	**Female**
ADVANTAGES		
DISADVANTAGES		
PROS		
CONS		

METHOD: *Diaphragm*

DESCRIPTION:

The diaphragm is a soft rubber cup with a flexible metal spring rim. It comes in sizes from two to four inches across and fits snugly over the cervix. The diaphragm is fitted by a doctor and should be replaced every three years. You may need a new size if you gain or lose more than ten pounds or after a pregnancy or miscarriage.

HOW IT WORKS:

The diaphragm is a barrier method. About one tablespoon of spermicidal cream or jelly is put in the diaphragm cup and around the edges before insertion. The diaphragm is inserted in the vagina so that it covers the cervix and rests above the pubic bone. You must leave the diaphragm in place for at least six hours, but not more than twenty-four.

EFFECTIVENESS RATE:

For Preventing Pregnancy:	94%
For Protecting Against STDs:	94%

SIDE EFFECTS OR PRECAUTIONS:

The diaphragm is very safe, is temporary, and has no side effects other than an occasional reaction to the spermicide. User error results from improper placement, slippage, or removing it too soon.

HOW AND WHERE YOU CAN GET THIS METHOD:

Available from a doctor or family-planning clinic.

COST:

	Male	Female
ADVANTAGES		
DISADVANTAGES		
PROS		
CONS		

METHOD: *Birth Control Pills* (oral contraceptives)

DESCRIPTION:
Birth control pills are some combination of estrogen and progestin, a synthetic form of the female hormone, progesterone, which interferes with normal ovulation, conception, or implantation.

HOW IT WORKS:
Birth control pills work primarily by inhibiting the release of the egg from the ovary. By raising the level of estrogen, the follicle-stimulating hormone, FSH, does not trigger the egg development. This is basically the same process that inhibits FSH during pregnancy. The progestin increases the thickness of the cervical fluid, slowing down sperm, and thins the uterine lining.

EFFECTIVENESS RATE:
For Preventing Pregnancy: 95% user error
For Protecting Against STDs: 0%

SIDE EFFECTS OR PRECAUTIONS:
Sometimes includes menstrual irregularities, headaches, acne, breast tenderness, weight gain, nausea or depression; should not be used by smokers or women prone to cardiovascular disease or with a history of breast cancer.

HOW AND WHERE YOU CAN GET THIS METHOD:
Must be obtained from a doctor's prescription; you will need an initial checkup and pelvic exam and should be rechecked once a year.

COST:

	Male	**Female**
ADVANTAGES		
DISADVANTAGES		
PROS		
CONS		

METHOD: *Norplant*

DESCRIPTION:

Norplant is a time-release hormone contraceptive implant. It consists of six match-size rubber capsules that contain progestin, a synthetic version of progesterone.

HOW IT WORKS:

The Norplant capsule sticks are inserted in the upper arm of the woman by a trained doctor. The hormone is released gradually through the walls of the capsules, which inhibits ovulation, thickens cervical fluids, and thins the endometrial lining. The capsules work for up to five years and should be professionally removed at that time or earlier.

EFFECTIVENESS RATE:

For Preventing Pregnancy: 99.5–96% over time

For Protecting Against STDs: 0%

SIDE EFFECTS OR PRECAUTIONS:

Norplant has the same general concerns as oral contraceptives, but has not been studied long enough to know what the long-term problems may be. It is expensive for the short run—$600–$700 for insertion and up to $150 per capsule ($900 for all six) for removal. Averaged over five years, the cost is about $300 a year—the same cost as birth control pills. If the capsules are removed earlier, the yearly cost would be significantly higher.

HOW AND WHERE YOU CAN GET THIS METHOD:

Available from doctors and family-planning clinics; make sure that your doctor has special training in how to insert Norplant.

COST:

	Male	Female
ADVANTAGES		
DISADVANTAGES		
PROS		
CONS		

METHOD: *Depo-Provera* (hormone injections)

DESCRIPTION:

Depot-methroxprogesterone acetate (DMPA) is a progestin hormone contraceptive. It is given as a 150-milligram injection every three months.

HOW IT WORKS:

DMPA works like other progesterone birth-control methods by preventing ovulation and thickening the cervical fluid. The first shot is given within a week after your menstrual period begins and is effective immediately for twelve to fourteen weeks. To continue using DMPA, you must get the shot every three months.

EFFECTIVENESS RATE:

For Preventing Pregnancy:	99.7%
For Protecting Against STDs:	0%

SIDE EFFECTS OR PRECAUTIONS:

Depo-Provera has the same general concerns as oral contraceptives, but has not been studied long enough to know what the long-term problems may be. There appears to be some weight gain with this method. There may also be a delay of six to twelve months after the last shot before a woman is fertile again. (Don't count the possibility of delay as birth control, but if you are trying to get pregnant, it may take longer.)

HOW AND WHERE YOU CAN GET THIS METHOD:

Available from a doctor or family-planning clinic.

COST:

	Male	Female
ADVANTAGES		
DISADVANTAGES		
PROS		
CONS		

METHOD: *Intrauterine Device* (IUD)

DESCRIPTION:

IUDs are small devices that fit inside the uterus. They come in various sizes and shapes, most containing either copper or progestin. The device has a plastic string that extends through the cervix to the vagina so that you can check to make sure it is still in place.

HOW IT WORKS:

IUDs are one of the oldest forms of birth control, but we are not absolutely sure how or why they work. Their presence in the uterus seems to prevent fertilization of the egg. Copper IUDs cause a mild inflammation of the uterine wall, producing white blood cells and enzymes that may attack the sperm. Progestin IUDs thicken the cervical mucus so the sperm cannot pass through.

EFFECTIVENESS RATE:

For Preventing Pregnancy: 99.2%
For Protecting Against STDs: 0%

SIDE EFFECTS OR PRECAUTIONS:

10% of all IUDs are spontaneously expelled during the first three months of use; this occurs more commonly among younger women and those with a heavy menstrual flow. There have been many documented health issues with the IUD, including pelvic infections, excessive bleeding and cramping, perforation of the uterus, and ectopic pregnancy. *IUDs may actually **increase** your risk of getting an STD (including HIV) because they alter and irritate the uterine lining.*

HOW AND WHERE YOU CAN GET THIS METHOD:

Available from your doctor or family-planning clinic.

COST:

	Male	Female
ADVANTAGES		
DISADVANTAGES		
PROS		
CONS		

METHOD: *Fertility Observation*

DESCRIPTION:

Fertility observation, or natural family planning, uses three fertility signs to determine when an egg has been ejected from the ovary (indicating the times of the month when you can or cannot get pregnant): the thickness of the cervical fluid, the basal body temperature, and the cervix shift.

HOW IT WORKS:

Unlike its older version, the rhythm method, which plotted fertility based on past cycles, the fertility observation method is based on what your body is doing at the present. You must be trained to gather and interpret the information that indicates ovulation. During a third of the month, you will be fertile and require abstinence or a barrier method if you do not want to get pregnant.

EFFECTIVENESS RATE:

For Preventing Pregnancy: 97%
For Protecting Against STDs: 0%

SIDE EFFECTS OR PRECAUTIONS:

There are no physical side effects for this method and you will be come more aware of your body cycles; you must keep a consistent record of your cycle and be prepared to exercise restraint and/or creativity during fertile periods.

HOW AND WHERE YOU CAN GET THIS METHOD:

Family-planning clinics and women's health centers usually offer classes or instruction in the method.

COST:

	Male	**Female**
ADVANTAGES		
DISADVANTAGES		
PROS		
CONS		

Each sexually active person must consider many things in order to make a responsible decision about his use of birth control. Listed below are some considerations that may influence a person's personal decision. While they are all important to one degree or another, sometimes they conflict or lead to different methods. Individually or with your class group, try to rank these considerations from the MOST IMPORTANT (#1) to LEAST IMPORTANT (#8 or #9)

What about Withdrawal?
Withdrawal is not a method of birth control—it is an emergency afterthought. There are sperm in the semen that are discharged BEFORE ejaculation, therefore before withdrawal—and remember it only takes one of those pesky little sperm to make a baby. **However**, *if you should somehow get yourself into an unprotected situation and come to your senses in time, by all means withdraw before ejaculation. It takes a lot of self-control and it may be too late, BUT it does lower the risk substantially.*

_____   **Ease of procurement**

_____   **Ease of use**

_____   **Immediate and long-term side effects**

_____   **Cost**

_____   **Protection against STDs**

_____   **Effectiveness**

_____   **Effect on spontaneity**

_____   **Effect on sexual pleasure**

_____   **Other:**_____

Quandary: What Method of Birth Control Would You Recommend For:

1. Someone who has never had sex, but is thinking about it possibly in the near future?
2. Someone who may have sex occasionally but not on any regular or predictable basis?
3. A couple who has a monogamous, serious relationship and has sex two to three times a month?
4. Someone who is sexually active with a variety of people?
5. A couple who is not comfortable discussing birth control with each other?
6. Someone who does not want to interrupt the spontaneity and momentum of her or his sexual activity?
7. Someone who is somewhat absentminded and carefree?
8. Someone who is worried about potential side effects?
9. Someone who is not comfortable with parents or other people knowing that he or she is having a sexual relationship?
10. All things considered, what method do you think is the best for a teenager who has chosen to be sexually active?

STDS AND AIDS

AIDS has given sexually transmitted diseases (STDs) new publicity and urgency, but STDs have been around as long as people have been having sex. As the name implies, STDs are diseases passed from one person to another through sexual contact. The intimate sexual contact combined with the warm, moist genital tract makes a perfect breeding ground for a variety of nasty organisms. With the exception of AIDS and genital herpes, they are all curable, but without treatment, they can cause considerable internal damage, even death. Syphilis goes underground after its initial symptoms, leaving you with the mistaken belief that everything is back to normal. Any genital sores or rashes should be checked out.

1. *Chlamydia:* The most common STD in the United States: an estimated 4 million each year, the majority of which are fifteen- to nineteen-year-olds.

   Symptoms: One in four men and one in two women experience NO initial symptoms at all. The most common symptom is an inflammation of the urethra causing painful urination and pus discharge. Some women experience pain in the lower abdomen. If you are sexually active with more than one partner, it is best to be tested annually for chlamydia.

   Effects: Untreated, chlamydia can cause sterility.

   Treatment: Medical evaluation, prescribed dosage of tetracycline.

2. *Gonorrhea:* The second most common STD with over 1.4 million cases reported a year.

   Symptoms: Gonococcus bacteria can settle in the mouth and throat as well as the rectum, uterus, and urinary tract. Symptoms of burning, itching, or yellowish discharge may show up after two to nine days. In females, these symptoms may be internal and not noticed, so it is extremely important that a male alert his partner if he has gonorrhea.

   Effects: Untreated, gonorrhea can cause sterility or complications during pregnancy.

   Treatment: Medical evaluation, prescribed antibiotics.

3. *Genital Warts:* A common strain of virus causing hard, fleshy bumps on the genitals, cervix, or vagina. An estimated 1 million cases develop each year.

   Symptoms: Cauliflower-shaped warts will appear on the genitals several months after exposure. The warts may be irritating and itchy. They may also develop inside the cervix of the female or urethra of the male.

   Effects: The warts themselves are not dangerous, but doctors are exploring the connection between genital warts and later development of cancers of the penis, vulva, and cervix.

   Treatment: Warts are treated in a doctor's office by burning with an electric needle or laser or freezing the warts with liquid nitrogen. Occasionally, surgery may be necessary.

4. *Genital Herpes:* Related to the virus that causes cold sores around the mouth, once infected with the herpes simplex virus, you carry it for life. An estimated 30 million adults in the U.S. currently have herpes and approximately 500,000 new cases are reported each year.

   Symptoms: Tiny clusters of fluid-filled and painful blisters on the genitals appear two to twenty days after infection. The sores disappear within one to three weeks and lie dormant until a period of illness or stress brings on another attack. The disease is only contagious when there is an active lesion.

Effects: The sores themselves are uncomfortable, but not dangerous to your health. Women with active herpes can infect their babies during childbirth, causing brain damage or death. Cesarean deliveries are often recommended.

Treatment: There is no cure for herpes, but acyclovir, an antiviral drug, is used to help control it.

5. *PID:* Pelvic inflammatory disease is the most frequent complication of STDs in women. The initial infection spreads to the fallopian tubes, causing scarring. PID affects nearly 11 percent of the childbearing-aged women in the U.S.

   Symptoms: The scarred tissue of the fallopian tubes blocks the passage of the fertilized egg, sometimes causing the egg to implant in the wall of the fallopian tube. Warning signs are swelling or tenderness in the cervix, uterus, or vagina.

   Effects: The scarring can create sterility or a tubal pregnancy which can endanger the female's life.

   Treatment: Diagnosis through a cervical pap smear or laparoscopy. Antibiotics can stop the disease, but must be taken by the female and her male partner in order to avoid reinfection.

6. *Syphilis:* One of the oldest STDs, syphilis was uncontrolled until the 1940s. Penicillin sharply reduced the incidence of syphilis, but the reported cases have doubled since 1984; currently 130,000 new cases reported a year.

   Symptoms: Genital lesions or chancres usually appear within six weeks of infection. They heal themselves. Within twelve weeks, the infection is back with a range of fever, aches, rashes, hair loss, and sores. These symptoms, too, will go away, but when the disease reappears it will invade the heart, eyes, brain, and other organs and is incurable.

   Effects: If untreated during the first two warning outbreaks, syphilis will cause blindness, insanity, and death. During pregnancy, the syphilis germ crosses the placenta causing meningitis, deformities, blindness, or stillbirth.

   Treatment: Antibiotics can stop the disease at any stage, but it cannot undo the damage that has been done. Blood tests can detect the antibodies to the disease after six weeks.

7. *Hepatitis B (HBV):* Hepatitis B is a viral infection that causes an inflammation of the liver and is very easily spread through sexual intercourse and other bodily fluids. Most people infected recover within a few months, but about 10 percent continue to carry the virus, infecting others, though they may have no further symptoms themselves. Three to 5 percent of people infected with hepatitis B develop life-threatening chronic hepatitis. This may be passed on to their babies, who become high risk for developing serious complications in later life.

Symptoms: The initial symptoms of HBV are like an intestinal flu—nausea, vomiting, headache, muscles aches, and a low-grade fever. These symptoms may be mild to severe; about a third of all infected people are asymptomatic.

Effects: Most people recover within four to eight weeks and develop a lifelong immunity to the virus. Ten percent continue to be carriers, and 3 to 5 percent of all infected individuals develop chronic hepatitis. This can progress to cirrhosis, liver cancer, liver failure, or death, and is responsible for about 9 percent of the deaths worldwide.

Treatment: There is no known cure or effective treatment for HBV at this time. Most infected individuals recover spontaneously. Infected individuals should avoid drinking alcohol, which can further damage the liver. Women who have contracted HBV should discontinue any hormonal birth control or estrogen treatment for the same reason. Pregnant women can transmit the virus to their unborn children and should take measures to lower that risk.

8. *HIV Infection and AIDS:* The AIDS epidemic was first identified in **1981** and named by the Centers for Disease Control in 1982 as a new disease that destroys the body's immune system—acquired immune deficiency syndrome.

   - In **1984,** scientists in France and the U.S. isolated the virus that causes AIDS—the human immunodeficiency virus or HIV. Documented cases of this new disease began springing up all over the world. By the end of 1984, 7,000 Americans had AIDS.

   - By **1985,** scientists had developed a blood test to detect the presence of HIV, but there was little hope of a vaccination or cure. Romantic-lead movie star, Rock Hudson, died of an AIDS-related illness.

   - In **1987,** President Kaunda of Zambia announced that his son had died of AIDS. In San Francisco, gay rights activist Cleve Jones made the first panel for the AIDS Memorial Quilt in memory of his friend, Marvin Feldman. Worldwide, by November 1987, 62,811 cases of AIDS had been officially reported to the World Health Organization (WHO) from 127 countries throughout the world.

   - In April of **1990,** Ryan White, a young hemophiliac infected with HIV through the use of infected blood products, died in the United States, at age nineteen. Ryan and his family had become well-known as a result of his difficult fight to be allowed to attend public school in the earlier stages of his disease. He had come to symbolize the nation's fears and prejudices about AIDS. A few months after Ryan White's death, Congress passed the Ryan White CARE Act, providing health care for people with AIDS who did not have adequate health insurance or other resources.

   - In **1991,** Earvin (Magic) Johnson announced that he had tested positive for HIV and was retiring from professional basketball. Two weeks later, Freddie Mercury, the lead singer of the rock group, Queen, died of an AIDS-related disease. More than 366,000 cases of full-blown AIDS were reported in 162 countries.

- In **1992,** tennis star, Arthur Ashe announced that he had been infected with HIV by a blood transfusion ten years earlier. He died one year later, only a month after acclaimed Russian ballet star, Rudolf Nureyev, died of the virus.

- In **1994,** AIDS had become the leading cause of death for Americans between the ages of twenty-five and forty-four. Over 400,000 had developed AIDS and over 250,000 had died.

- By **1997,** some progress was made in treating AIDS victims with protease inhibitors, but the treatment was expensive and limited. By the end of the year, the United Nations reported that the worldwide epidemic was worse than had been thought. It was now estimated that 30 million people around the world were infected, with 16,000 new infections occurring every day. While one in 100 individuals in the fifteen to forty-nine age group was thought to be infected, only one in ten were aware of their infection. It was estimated that 2.3 million people died of AIDS-related diseases in 1997—50 percent more than the year before. Half of these deaths were women and 460,000 were children under fifteen.

- In **1998,** the rate of new AIDS cases dropped for the first time since the epidemic began, but HIV was spreading more rapidly among teenagers and young adults than any other group in the United States.

- By the year **2000,** nineteen years after the first cases were reported, 33 million adults and 1.3 million children were infected worldwide—over 18.8 million people had died of AIDS-related diseases. Over 5.4 million people became newly infected in 1999, and 2.8 million people died that year. New infections in Western Europe appear to have leveled off, but Eastern Europe, which previously had a low recorded rate of HIV, began to show a steady increase. HIV infections in Russia doubled. HIV is a newer epidemic in most Asian countries—it varies greatly from country to country, but appears to be on the rise in China, India, and parts of Southeast Asia while recovering somewhat in hard-hit Thailand. The spread of HIV in Latin America is primarily through heterosexual contact and appears to be most prevalent among teens. Many of the Caribbean Islands struggle with HIV—5 percent of the adults in Haiti are currently affected. Close to 70 percent of the global total of HIV infections are in sub-Saharan Africa. The life expectancy rate there has dropped to forty-five years of age and UNAIDS has estimated that up to 40 percent of the people in sub-Saharan Africa could die of AIDS-related diseases in the next 20 years.[9] Heterosexual contact and intravenous drug use are the primary causes of infection. Homosexual transmission dropped significantly after the first decade of the epidemic, but appears to be on the rise again in the early years of the twenty-first century.

Half of all people who currently acquire HIV become infected before they turn twenty-five and typically die of AIDS-related complications before their thirty-fifth birthday. AIDS is the sixth leading cause of death among fifteen- to twenty-four-year-olds and the second leading cause of death among people twenty-five to forty-four. Girls account for

58 percent of the new cases in the younger age group, hitting African-American and Latino girls the hardest. The Kaiser Family Foundation's National Survey of Teens on HIV/AIDS[10] found that while most teens were concerned about AIDS and had a basic understanding of how it is transmitted, they had serious questions about how to protect themselves and how to go about getting tested.

1. One in six teens said they personally knew someone who had AIDS or had died of AIDS.

2. Most teens knew that sharing needles or having unprotected sex were high-risk behaviors; fewer knew that oral sex or having another STD increases one's risk for HIV.

3. Schools were the main source of information about HIV/AIDS, and seven out of ten older teens thought that schools should make condoms available.

4. Most teens wanted more information on how to get tested, but many also wanted more information on how to protect themselves and how to talk with their parents and partners about HIV/AIDS.

5. About a third of all sexually active teens wanted to know more about the proper use of condoms and other barrier methods of birth control.

6. Twenty-seven percent of the teens surveyed had been tested and another 16 percent had thought about it. Forty-eight percent of the students said that they would know where to go to get tested.

7. One third of the teens surveyed said that they had had sexual intercourse. Sixty-five percent of that group said that they used a condom all the time, 15 percent said most of the time, and 20 percent said sometimes or never.

How would you answer these questions from the survey?[11]

1. How serious a problem do you think AIDS is for people your age?
   Very serious   Somewhat serious
   Not too serious   Not at all serious

2. How concerned are you personally about becoming infected with AIDS?
   Very concerned   Somewhat concerned
   Not too concerned   Not at all concerned

3. There are drugs available to treat HIV, which can lengthen the life of a person infected.
   True   False   Don't know

4. There is no cure for AIDS.
   True   False   Don't know

5. Young people under eighteen need their parents' permission to get an HIV test.
   True   False   Don't know

6. Having another STD increases a person's risk of becoming infected.

    True   False   Don't know

7. Having intercourse without a condom increases a person's risk of becoming infected.

    True   False   Don't know

8. Sharing intravenous needles increases a person's risk of becoming infected.

    True   False   Don't know

9. You can become infected with HIV by having unprotected oral sex.

    True   False   Don't know

10. If you wanted to get tested for HIV do you:

    Know for sure where to go   Have some idea where to go
    Have no idea where to go

11. What topics would you like to have more information about:

    What AIDS is and how it is spread _____
    How to talk with your parents about HIV/AIDS _____
    How to talk with a partner about HIV/AIDS _____
    How to protect yourself from becoming infected with HIV _____
    Where to go to get tested for HIV _____
    The proper way to use condoms _____
    OTHER: _____

AIDS Statistics (from the World Health Organization)

	Currently infected	AIDS deaths	New cases in 1999
Sub-Sahara Africa	24,500,000	13,700,000	3,800,000
Southeast Asia	5,600,000	1,100,000	1,300,000
Latin America	1,300,000	520,000	150,000
North America	900,000	450,000	44,000
East Asia	530,000	40,000	120,000
Eastern Europe	420,000	17,000	95,000
Western Europe	520,000	210,000	30,000
North Africa	220,000		
Australia/New Zealand	15,000	8,000	500
TOTAL reported in 2000	36,000,000	21,800,000	5,400,000

In the United States: A total of 733,374 cases have been reported; 412,471 HIV-infected individuals are currently recorded. Estimates suggest that 650,000 to 900,000 individuals in the U.S. are now infected, with 40,000 new infections each year.

The states with the highest rate of HIV: *California, Nevada, Texas, Louisiana, Florida, New York, New Jersey, Connecticut, and Rhode Island.*

The states with the lowest rate of HIV: *Montana, Idaho, Wyoming, North Dakota, South Dakota, Minnesota, Wisconsin, Iowa, Maine, Vermont, and New Hampshire.*

Southern states currently have the largest increase in new cases.

AIDS in Africa: Twenty-three million Africans are currently infected; 1,700 new infections are reported every day. Botswana, where 36 percent of all adults are infected with HIV, has the highest rate of infection. Zimbabwe has an infection rate of 25 percent; in Zambia, 20 percent of the adults are infected. Ten percent of Ethiopian adults are infected, but it is estimated that 150,000 children under fifteen are also infected. **In some African nations, AIDS is expected to kill half of the teenagers in the country.**

In his research on ethical development cited in the first chapter, Kohlberg used a dilemma called *Henri's Dilemma* in which Henri must decide what to do when the druggist is selling the drug that will save the life of Henri's wife for ten times what it costs to make it. This dilemma is strikingly similar to the large-scale quandary facing our world as 95 percent of currently HIV-positive individuals, over 34 million people, cannot afford the anti-HIV drugs that could decrease suffering and extend their lives. Many international service organizations have challenged the large pharmaceutical company's profit motives and social responsibility in the face of this worldwide epidemic.

In 2001, a typical anti-HIV drug regimen in the United States cost around $15,000 a year. An Indian generic company offered a similar treatment for $600 a year. An American drug company sold anti-HIV drug, *stavudine*, for $6.10 per day in Uganda while it was being produced generically in Brazil for $.55. The major drug companies have protested that these pirated generics are violating the World Trade Organization patent agreements. Others contend that the ethical weight of a legal patent is indefensible when used to exploit and deny medical access to millions of HIV-infected people. Drug companies insist that the inflated prices of name-brand drugs include the cost of important research for new and better treatment. Without this revenue and profit incentives, advances in HIV medication and prevention would be severely limited. Generic companies are making a profit on the immediate production of anti-HIV drugs without contributing anything to future treatment breakthroughs.

The United Nations has suggested a "tiered pricing" or "equity pricing" scheme that would regulate the price of drugs according to a nation's ability to pay. In this way, wealthier nations would subsidize the cost of providing low-cost drugs to hard-hit Third World nations and drug companies would still be able to fund research and make a reasonable profit. The pharmaceutical companies worry that this price discrepancy would create a black market for the lower-cost drugs and advantaged nations would insist on comparably lower costs. Skeptics maintain that even at this reduced rate, most seriously affected nations still could not afford treatment. Julius Meme, permanent secretary of Kenya's Ministry of Health, "calculates that even with 85 percent discounts, Kenya would have to spend $12 billion yearly to treat its 2.2 million AIDS patients. 'The whole health budget is $9 billion.'"[12] The discounted drug cost of $400–$600 a year is more than many nation's average annual income.

An even more worrisome dynamic is that many Third World countries do not have the medical infrastructure to oversee and monitor the distribution of these anti-HIV drugs. If an anti-HIV treatment regimen is not taken regularly, without missing a day or discontinuing treatment, the HIV cells can create a virulent, drug-resistant strain of the virus that might then be spread worldwide. Even in medically sophisticated countries like the United States, about 10 percent of AIDS patients already harbor HIV strains resistant to AZT, the most common anti-HIV drug.[13] The economic, ethical, and logistical problems of Henri and his pharmacist become staggering when projected onto a global political and economic scale.

- *In what ways are the ethical considerations the same or similar? How are they different?*

- *Do seriously sick children and adults have a **right** to medical treatment regardless of where they live or their ability to pay?*

- *Do developed nations or multinational pharmaceutical companies have an **obligation** to share medical information and medication with people in less-developed countries?*

- *Is it ethical for companies to insist on making a profit in the face of such extensive human suffering? Without the profit motive, would companies have the interest and money to pursue new medical solutions?*

- *How have the global dynamics of an increasingly connected world influenced both the spread of AIDS and the demand for anti-HIV drugs? How do the ethnicity, economics, and remoteness of underdeveloped nations affect the way people think about this issue?*

Keeping Safe

The stakes for AIDS are high. It is fatal and, as far as we know, everyone who has been infected with HIV will eventually develop AIDS. At this time, the only way to protect yourself is not to get AIDS in the first place. *Luckily, that is not hard and involves simple actions completely within your control.*

1. **ABSTINENCE: The only 100 percent way to protect yourself from AIDS is to not have intercourse.** That may not seem like a very popular or realistic choice for some, but there are many pleasurable ways of being intimate and sexual that do not involve bodily fluids. Intimacy may include kissing, touching, or petting—what some people call "outercourse." If you want to add oral sex, you should use a condom or dental dam to be safe.

2. **USE A CONDOM:** A latex condom provides a barrier that keeps the semen away from the vagina and protects the penis from the vaginal secretions. The HIV germs can penetrate nonlatex condoms, so avoid the fancy lambskin types. If you use a lubricant, make sure it is water based. Vaseline and other oil-based lubricants break down on nonlatex fibers. Boys, practice using a condom so that it doesn't slip or break. Leave a small space or tip at the end of the condom to make

room for the ejaculated semen. Be sure to hold it in place when you pull out and discard it carefully. Girls, they are working on a female condom that will fit inside your vagina, but it is not available yet. In the meantime, you will have to depend on your partner. Don't have sex with anyone who is not using a condom.

3. **SPERMICIDES:** Most spermicides contain nonoxynol-9, a chemical which helps kill the HIV should the condom break or leak. Some condoms come with a spermicide coating. Bleach will kill the HIV outside the body. (Do NOT use bleach internally.)

4. **BE MONOGAMOUS:** If neither you nor your partner are having sex with anyone else, you are much safer, but either of you may be carrying the infection from a previous partner. It is good to talk openly about your sexual histories, but remember, many people who have the HIV infection don't know it. A study done in southern California found that half of the men and two-fifths of the women questioned said they would lie about how many people they had slept with. One man in five said he would lie about having been tested for the AIDS virus. To be really safe, both of you should be tested for HIV and then retested six months later before having unprotected sex.

5. **DON'T USE INJECTION DRUGS AND DON'T SHARE NEEDLES:** Injection drug users and their babies are the fastest growing group of AIDS patients in the United States. The mind-altering nature of drugs often increases the likelihood of risky sharing. Tattoo needles and even needles used to pierce your ears should not be shared. Doctors, hospitals, and dentists have become very careful. You have the right to expect a doctor or dentist to use gloves during any procedure that might involve blood.

6. **AVOID ANAL SEX:** The blood vessels in the anus and rectum easily rupture during anal intercourse, allowing direct entry into the bloodstream. Condoms provide protection, but you HAVE to use them because HIV can be transmitted so easily through anal sex.

The biggest danger of AIDS is not a lack of information or effective ways of preventing it. Like Magic Johnson, most people feel invincible— "Sometimes you're a little naive . . . you think it can never happen to you."[14] Most surveys show that information has not really changed people's sex behavior. About 98 percent of teens know how AIDS is transmitted, but only 1 percent consistently practice safe sex. Less than 20 percent of the college students surveyed reported using condoms more than half the time. The *more* sexual partners a person had, the *less* likely he or she was to use condoms. Passion and romance have never been particularly rational and in the heat of the moment, many of us throw caution to the wind. Some get away with it, some don't. The question you need to decide for yourself is, ***"Is it worth it?"***

> ## *Quandary:* *Talking to Your Partner About AIDS*
>
> It is not easy or fun to talk seriously about AIDS, but you need to know your partner to honestly assess the risk you are taking. It is also important that the two of you agree on the measures of safe sex you will use. High-risk behavior includes male homosexual contact, sexual contact with a prostitute, multiple sex partners, blood transfusions before 1985, or the use of injection drugs. Crack users are usually poor risks as well since crack tends to increase sexual desire and lower sexual judgment. Chronic marijuana use lowers the immune system and may make a person more susceptible to HIV if exposed. Recurring incidents of other STDs such as herpes, syphilis, and chlamydia may indicate a history of unprotected sex, and the lesions from these diseases provide direct access to the bloodstream for HIV. It is not always easy to ask about these things—or to get an honest answer. Even in all honesty, many people do not know they have been infected. It is best to play it safe, with "outercourse" or at least very safe sex. If your partner cares about you and about herself, she will agree.

SEXUAL ASSAULT

Sexual assault is one of the most unpleasant and difficult areas of sexuality for males and females to discuss unemotionally with each other. Each brings very different feelings, experiences, and perspectives to the discussion.

Most girls live with the reality of sexual assault from the beginning of their sexual awareness. They are warned not to walk alone at night and to avoid strange men and compromising situations. They are advised not to act, dress, or move in ways that might provoke sexual excitement or attack at the same time that they are encouraged to be sexually attractive and appealing to men. Most girls feel physically unable to fight off unwanted sexual contact and learn to rely on verbal or sexual manipulation to protect themselves. Girls learn to put up with jokes, whistles, name-calling, and touching that may make them feel uncomfortable, degraded, or threatened. Some girls feel frightened and helpless, some try to block the whole issue out of their consciousness and others feel angry and resentful. Most live with an underlying fear and sense of vulnerability.

Most boys are unaware of the fear and anger that the topic of sexual assault provokes in girls. Although one in nine boys is also sexually assaulted during his lifetime, most boys are not aware of this possibility and think of rape as another one of those female problems. Indeed, since boys in our culture are taught that they should always want and take advantage of any sexual opportunity, it may be hard to empathize with the threat of unwanted sex. Most boys have never felt degraded or victimized because of their sexuality. When the discussion turns to rape, boys may feel unjustly accused and stereotyped—why should males in general be held responsible for what a few men do? And what about the sexual and emotional teasing that men put up with from women?

Boys and girls need to understand and respect each other's feelings about sexual assault. Misunderstandings prevent males and females from working together to resolve and recover from extremely painful and damaging sexual experiences.

With a partner of the opposite sex, take turns answering the following questions. Focus on listening and genuinely understanding how the other person perceives and feels about the question. When one person has answered, the other may ask any questions that will help clarify the answer for him. BE CAREFUL THAT THESE QUESTIONS ARE INTENDED TO CLARIFY, NOT ATTACK, CHALLENGE, OR BELITTLE THE OTHER PERSON'S IDEAS OR FEELINGS. When you think you understand clearly, summarize that person's point of view as you see it. Work together until you both agree that the position is genuinely understood. Then switch places and go on to the next question.

FOR GIRLS: *What are the subtle and spoken messages you have gotten about rape as you grew up?*

FOR BOYS: *What are the subtle and spoken messages you have gotten about rape as you grew up?*

FOR GIRLS: *What scares or angers you most about rape?*

FOR BOYS: *What confuses or angers you most about rape?*

FOR GIRLS: *Tell your partner about one time or situation when you have felt frightened, harassed, or victimized because you are female.*

FOR BOYS: *Tell your partner how you felt and reacted as you listened to her experience.*

FOR BOYS: *Tell your partner about one time or situation when you have felt frightened, harassed, or victimized because you are male.*

FOR GIRLS: *Tell your partner how you felt and reacted as you listened to his experience.*

FOR GIRLS: *What do you think boys can do to prevent date rape?*

FOR BOYS: *What do you think girls can do to prevent date rape?*

How to Protect Yourself from Stranger Rape[15]

(This is written for girls, but the general ideas should be helpful for boys protecting themselves against any assault.)

Most rapists or assailants are looking for an easy victim—someone who appears helpless and submissive. You are less likely to be bothered if you walk confidently, aware of your surroundings. Research has shown that a rapist is more likely to pick out someone who is walking slowly, head down, hands in pockets, who looks like she will not put up a fight. Remember, rape is about power, not sex.

The most important thing you can do is to try to keep your mind clear and quickly evaluate your options. This is not easy. Fear can be immobilizing. TAKE A DEEP BREATH AND FOCUS ON WHAT YOU CAN DO TO PROTECT YOURSELF. *Is there help or escape available? What are your strengths or resources? How immediate is the danger? Can you stall until there is an opportunity to get away? Is the assailant coherent or drugged or agitated? Is there a weapon?*

Assess your assailant, environment, and options carefully. Every situation is different, so be flexible and look for a strategy that might work

- **Sexual Assault:** *Any unwanted sexual activity that has been forced or pressured without consent. This includes all of the areas listed below.*

- **Sexual Harassment:** *Verbal or physical harassment short of intercourse including unsolicited sexual threats or allusions to degrade, coerce, or threaten an individual. This includes obscene phone calls, unwanted sexual advances, graphic language, or unwanted physical contact.*

- **Rape:** *Unwanted sexual intercourse. This may or may not include excessive physical force. Legally, this requires penetration with the penis or other object.*

- **Date or Acquaintance Rape:** *Rape by someone that you know, i.e., boyfriend, date, co-worker, service person, doctor, etc.*

- **Drunk Rape:** *Sexual intercourse that takes place when the female is too inebriated to give consent or to resist.*

- **Statutory Rape:** *Sexual intercourse by a male over eighteen years of age with a female under the legal age of consent. This age varies from state to state, but is usually around sixteen to eighteen.*

for you in this situation. Physical confrontation may escalate the violent energy in a situation and should be used as a last resort. Keep your eyes open, your hands free, and your mind clear. You have many options to consider and use. You **can** protect yourself.

- **TRUST YOUR INTUITION.** If a person or situation makes you uncomfortable, get away. Don't dismiss your feelings or worry about looking silly. It is better to err on the side of caution.

- **GET HELP OR ESCAPE.** If you feel threatened, go somewhere where there is light and other people. If you are followed, give clear firm directions to someone who may help you—"You, call the police, I'm in danger." *If you have been stopped by the attacker, do not run* unless you are sure you can reach safety. If he can overtake you, it may escalate the situation.

- **BECOME A PERSON TO THE ATTACKER.** Humanize yourself. Don't antagonize him by being overly aggressive or passive. Get him to talk to you. Try different approaches—anything that keeps him talking and calm.

- **GAIN HIS CONFIDENCE.** Communicate with your words, eyes, or gestures that you are not a threat to him. You want him to lower his guard so that you can de-escalate the situation, escape, or fight. Build up his ego and try to set up a situation where you can get away. Con him, pretend to go along with him, lie—anything you can do to control the situation.

- **NEGOTIATE UNTIL SAFE.** Keep talking and maneuvering things until you can get away. If there are two or more assailants, identify the leader and negotiate with him. When you get to safety, call 911.

- **ACT UNDESIRABLE.** Some girls have avoided an assault by acting strange or undesirable. Feign deafness, epileptic fits, heart attack, or insanity. Claim to have VD or AIDS, that you are pregnant or have your period. Strange, unexpected behavior may scare the attacker off.

- **ACT ANGRY AND DETERMINED, NOT AGGRESSIVE.** Aggression or resistance may make your attacker more forceful or violent, but a firm show of confidence and assertiveness may take him by surprise, especially in the early stages. He expects weakness, fear, and submissiveness. If you can firmly tell him to leave you alone, he may back off.

- **FIGHTING BACK.** If you must fight, fight 100 percent—don't hesitate, flail randomly, or back down. Your resistance will both surprise and anger your assailant, so you must fight quickly and wisely.

If you are about to be tied up or your life is being threatened, fight, run, scream, bite, kick, scratch. Talking is no longer appropriate and statistics show that any kind of resistance will deter 60 percent of attackers.

A study of college campuses in 1985 found these statistics.[16]

- *52 percent of the women surveyed have felt some form of sexual victimization.*
- *One in eight women have been the victims of rape or attempted rape.*
- *47 percent of the rapes were by first or casual dates.*
- *Three-quarters of the women raped were between fifteen and twenty-one; the average age was eighteen.*
- *One in twelve men admitted to having fulfilled the prevailing definition of rape, yet none identified themselves as rapists.*
- *About a third of the women raped did not tell anyone; 90 percent did not tell the police.*

Do not resist if a gun or knife is being used—do as the assailant asks. He may put the weapon down at some point, giving you an opening to resist. If you are sure he is going to use the weapon anyway, wait for an opportunity to resist and go for it.

A woman can effectively fight a man, even if he is much bigger and stronger. She must use not only her strength, but her wits and the element of surprise. Strike vulnerable areas—the eyes, throat, nose, groin, knees, and head. Fight from the ground using your strong leg and hip muscles. Do not get into an upper-body fight—men's arms are much stronger. A strong, well-placed kick can incapacitate or knock out your assailant.

Don't lose heart. Keep your body fit and become familiar with its strengths. Don't hold your breath—yelling will keep you breathing and may intimidate your assailant. Focus your energy and fear into power, like a mother bear protecting her cubs. (Don't get in *her* way!) **Believe in your right and power to protect yourself. It is best to train your skills and awareness by taking a self-defense course designed especially for women.**

If You Are Assaulted:

1. Get to a safe place. Call 911 if there is any risk of your attacker finding you.

2. Call a friend or family member for assistance and support.

3. Try not to bathe, shower, douche, brush your teeth, use the toilet, or change your clothes. If you do, you will destroy evidence that could be used to help identify your assailant.

4. Get medical attention as soon as possible. In the emotional shock following an attack, you may not be aware of some physical injuries. You may want to be treated for possible VD or pregnancy. Physical evidence of your assailant (sperm, hair, skin traces) may be collected at this time.

5. You can call a rape crisis hotline to speak with someone who will be supportive and help you explore the options and decisions facing you. You will need to decide how and if you will report the crime and what sort of emotional and physical support you need.

6. If you are under eighteen, you should know that any doctor, professional, or rape crisis counselor is required by law to report your assault to a division of child protective services.

7. After a rape, most women go into a state of emotional shock. They often feel frightened, vulnerable, angry, ashamed, anxious, and confused. Eating problems, nightmares, and sleep disturbances are common. It may seem difficult to trust anyone—particularly if you have been raped by an acquaintance. Most women go through a period of feeling disempowered and vulnerable. Counseling and enrollment in a self-defense course may help you regain your sense of power and dignity.

Date or Acquaintance Rape

While stranger rape may be more violent, acquaintance rape can be equally devastating because it violates the safety with someone you have known or trusted. It is also probably the most common, and least reported, form of rape, particularly for girls ages fifteen to twenty-five. Date or acquaintance rape is forced sexual contact with someone that you know and may even be involved with on a social or romantic basis. Most often it involves a first date or someone you have just met at a party or bar, but acquaintance rape could also be initiated by a neighbor, repairman, doctor, teacher, relative, or close friend. It could even be with your steady boyfriend or husband if he forces you to have sex against your will.

The statistics of date rape on college campuses are pretty alarming. Estimates vary from one in nine to one in five females are raped during their college years. Ninety-six percent do not report the assault either because they do not want to prolong or publicize their trauma or because they feel ashamed and stupid—many feel that they should have been able to prevent the assault.

At the time of the rape, most girls can't believe what is happening, especially if it is with someone that they trust and care about. It is hard to imagine that a friend would take advantage of them in this way. Many girls are taught not to make a scene and may fear the physical strength of their partner. Some girls are actually taught not to resist or make him angry or they will really get hurt. Many girls lack confidence in their own boundaries and don't really believe they have the right and power to say no. In the Campus Project on Sexual Assault completed in 1985, almost three-quarters of the women who had been forced to have sex against their will did not identify their experience as rape. They blamed themselves for not being stronger or avoiding the situation or somehow provoking the attack. While it is important to think ahead and protect yourself, *no one has the right to force you to have sex.*

On the other hand, males are often confused about their role in date rape. In the study cited above, one in every twelve males admitted to forcing a girl to have sex without her consent, yet virtually none of them saw this as rape. Raised with the macho stereotypes of male as the aggressor, many of these men believed that women don't really mean it when they say no to sexual advances—that is just all part of the game. They often believed that a woman likes a man who will show her who is boss and that women actually enjoy forced sexual contact.

In many cases, poor communication may lead to mistaken assumptions:

- *She agreed to go back to his room to listen to his new music disc.*

- *He thought that meant she was agreeing to have sex—why else would she agree to go back to his room at 11:00 at night?*

- *He brings flowers and takes her out to a lavish night on the town.*

- *She thinks he is just trying to bribe her into sleeping with him.*

FOR GIRLS:

Learn how to be direct and clear about what you do and do not want. Don't just push away gently and sweetly say "Please don't . . ." Speak up! Firmly say "NO. I do not want to have intercourse/ you to touch me there/to go to your room."

*You have the right to set your own limits and insist that they be respected. When you say no, **mean** no, not maybe. Try not to give mixed messages.*

Boys sometimes may not understand how you can mean no to sexual intercourse and still want to kiss and snuggle. Let him know explicitly what you are and are not comfortable with.

If you DO want to have intercourse, take responsibility for that decision and communicate openly with your partner.

*AND REMEMBER to always respect **his** right to say no. Guys get a lot of pressure to be sexually active, but they have feelings and reservations just like you do.*

- *She loves to dance and flirt seductively.*

- *He thinks that she wants to have sex or that at least he should respond to her flirtation.*

- *He would like to express his love and commitment to her physically.*

- *She thinks that all he wants her for is sex.*

Any or all of these assumptions may be true. Or they may all be false. Mind reading is not a good basis for a relationship and is definitely not sufficient evidence of sexual consent or intent.

> *If you are thinking about having sex, **TALK TO EACH OTHER.***
> *If you are not sure what the other person wants or feels, **ASK HIM.***
> *If you are uncomfortable with what is happening, **SPEAK UP.***
> *If he or she doesn't seem to be listening, **YELL OR PHYSICALLY RESIST THE SITUATION.***

This is difficult to do with someone you know or care about, but you have the right and responsibility to protect yourself.

Alcohol or drug use is a quick way to reduce your power and ability to think clearly in a sexual situation. The vast majority of date rapes occur when one or both partners are high or inebriated. A girl may not make a sober decision or be able to physically resist unwanted sexual advances when she has had too much to drink. A boy may feel less interested in controlling his sexual urges or listening to a girl's resistance. And neither of them is probably thinking much about birth control or STDs or AIDS. Alcohol may help you relax and feel more sociable, but it doesn't do much for your judgment, safety, or personal power.

Male Awareness and Responsibility for Rape[17]

When faced with the violent and frightening realities of sexual assault, most men feel ashamed and angry. This may happen when you listen carefully to the fears and anger of your female friends. It may happen when a girlfriend, sister, or mother has been raped. It may happen because you have been a male victim of sexual assault.

Sexual assault and harassment have become headline news, but our legal and personal discussions are often clouded with defensiveness and misunderstanding. Men in our culture are taught to be sexually aggressive. You may have been taught that girls just say "no" to play hard to get. The media, jokes, and locker-room bravado suggest that it is your job to "score" and a girl's job to try to stop you. Fraternities sometimes use "scoring" as part of their initiation rights.

Men can help stop sexual violence against women. Most men do care and respect women in their personal lives. "This is good, but it is not enough. Men who resent having to bear any of the burden of what other men do should keep in mind that every woman would also like to be accepted as an individual human being," says Charlie Jones, a male rape crisis advocate. He suggests the following things that concerned men can do:

- *Speak out against sexual assault.* Rapists speak in a male voice and act in our name. If it's not OK, say so in your voice.

- *Examine your own attitudes.* Many men say they are against rape, but still believe it is OK to force sex under certain circumstances.

- *Report abuse, interrupt harassment.* Rape jokes are not funny.

- *Educate yourself about what sexual assault really means.* Read, talk, listen. Rape crisis centers often have male advocates that will be glad to talk with you.

- *Listen to women.* Respect their feelings and ideas about sexual assault. Let them know that there are men who will support and stand with them against sexual assault.

- *Talk with other men about sexual assault.* We have all been raised with myths and masculine stereotypes. Talking honestly together, we can reclaim our real masculinity that is not threatening to the women we know and care about.

WHAT CAN I SAY?

Have you ever thought of a perfect comeback or response to a sticky situation—only it is twelve hours later and no one is there to appreciate your self-composure and wit?

Either on your own or in small class groups, come up with some short, assertive responses to these typical sex lines. They may come in handy when you're too confused or pressured to come up with one on the spot.

BUT REMEMBER, YOU DON'T HAVE TO BE WITTY OR COMPOSED OR APOLOGETIC OR RATIONAL TO MAKE YOUR WISHES KNOWN. If you are uncomfortable or don't want something to happen, *just say no.* It helps to muster up as much firmness and determination as possible, but you *do not have to explain, justify, apologize, argue, or appease anyone.* You have the right to set your own boundaries and decide how you will use and share your body. No questions asked.

"If you really loved me, you would . . ." _____

_____

"I just want to show you how much I love you." _____

_____

"What do you mean 'no,' after all the money I spent on your tonight?" _____

_____

"You really want it, you're just playing hard to get." _____

_____

"We're the only couple who isn't doing it." _____

_____

"Have another beer, then maybe you won't be so uptight." _____

_____

"Why were you dancing so sexily (wearing a short skirt, flirting with me) if you didn't want to go all the way?" _____

_____

"You turned me on, you can't say no now." _____

_____

"You are so gorgeous, sexy, desirable, etc., etc., I just can't stop myself." _____

_____

"You knew when I asked you up to my room that this is what would happen." _____

_____

"We've done it before, you can't say no now." _____

_____

"You don't understand. I have these sexual needs. It's not fair to keep frustrating me." _____

_____

"I can't see much future for our relationship if it doesn't include sex." _____

_____

Sexual Abuse and Incest

A disturbing number of boys and girls have been sexually molested as children—by strangers, family acquaintances, or relatives. If this has happened with a parent, grandparent, or sibling, it is called incest. Both incest and sexual abuse are against the law and all doctors, teachers, or counselors are required to report any suspected cases to child protective services.

Inappropriate touching, sexual activity, or penetration are usually very frightening and confusing to a child. He or she does not have a sophisticated understanding of sex or appropriate behavior, but usually feels frightened and helpless. This may be further complicated by the negative and positive feelings provoked by the hushed secrecy and threats used by the adult. Many children block out any memory of what has happened.

These repressed memories frequently come back during adolescence and adulthood when the individual begins to experience adult sexual feelings and relationships. The teenager may not remember what has happened, but may feel unexplained emotions of fear, shame, or anger in sexual situations. She may completely avoid normal relations with the opposite sex and cling to more childish relationships. There appears to be a high incidence of sexual child abuse among teenage anorexics and bulimics. Some previously abused teenagers begin to have disturbing dreams or flashbacks of their molestation.

If you have any of these problems or know you are a survivor of child sexual abuse, it is important that you tell someone and try to get professional help. The fears and loss of power usually associated with child molestation can have long-term negative effects on your sense of yourself and your experience of relationships and sexuality. The worst is over, but most people need to heal and understand, on an adult level, what has happened. Counselors and therapists are trained to help you work through these issues.

Dear Quandary Master . . .

Here are some letters asking for advice and information about some sexual situations. Make your answers as realistic and helpful as possible. Be sure to include any relevant information or resources that might be helpful.

#1.

Dear Quandary Master,

I must be the most unlucky teenager alive. After five months of going with my boyfriend, we never had sex. I mean, we messed around a lot, but we always stopped before things went too far. Well, last month, we got a little carried away and before I really knew what was happening, we had intercourse. Of course, neither of us was using birth control because we never planned to go all the way. It just sort of happened. I was kind of worried, but my boyfriend assured me that he had pulled out in time and just one time wasn't a big deal.

Well, you guessed it. My period was two weeks late and I got one of those pregnancy tests from the drugstore. The results were positive. I can't believe it. Do these tests really work? Can you really get pregnant the first time—even if he pulls out before he ejaculated? It doesn't seem possible. I'm scared to tell my boyfriend—he is really going to be upset. Should I tell my mom? She will be furious and Dad will be so disappointed in me. I don't know what to do and I can't even believe that this is happening to me. What should I do?

Signed, Unlucky Ursula

#2.

Dear Quandary Master,

Boys can really be exasperating. I have been dating this perfectly nice guy. He's good-looking and always seems to go out of his way to do nice little things for me. We have a lot in common and we always have a lot of fun together. All my friends think we are the perfect couple. We talk about sex from time to time, but I don't want to rush things and that seemed to be OK with him. But lately that seems to be all that he thinks about. It seems so important to him that I finally agreed. Now that's all he wants to do. I don't even know if he likes me anymore. We hardly talk or go places with our friends. He just wants to be alone and have sex.

Do guys have a hormone problem or something? Is he just using me for sex? How do I know if he really cares about me? How can I say "no" when I've already said "yes"? He doesn't seem to notice or care how I'm feeling anymore. What should I do?

Signed, Feeling-Used Frieda

#3.

Dear Quandary Master,

I give up. The female half of the human race is totally bewildering to me. I have this girlfriend who is pretty nice most of the time, but when it comes to sex, she is absolutely mind-boggling. We have been dating a couple of months and she acts like she really likes me. We mess around a little bit and she seems to like that too. But whenever I try to make any moves, she says not to rush things. So I've been patient and we talk about it a while. Finally she says "OK, maybe, but we have to use birth control." Fine. So I go out and buy some rubbers and she gets that little spongy thing, and we plan this nice picnic on the beach. Well, I think we are having a good time, but as soon as we start to get down to business, she starts crying and says she's not sure.

I mean, really, what does the lady want? Is she a tease? We do everything her way and she still gets cold feet. What should I do? I really like her, but I can't figure her out. All of my other friends don't seem to be having this problem. Should I move on to greener pastures?

Signed, No-Action Nevil

#4.

Dear Quandary Master,

I am ashamed to be writing this letter, but I can't talk to anyone about this and it is driving me crazy. For the last couple of years, I have had this feeling that something is wrong with me. I have plenty of friends who are girls and I'm a good athlete and love to surf and I play in a band, but I'm just not interested in dating or being with girls sexually. I've never done anything or told anyone this, but I am much more attracted to boys. God, that sounds so awful. We had this gay panel at my school and I could really identify with what they were saying.

What should I do? Am I a homosexual? If anyone at school found out that I feel this way, they would hate me. I don't know what to think. Is this just a phase? Is there something I can do to change the way I feel? Am I making something out of nothing? I've tried not to think about it, but sometimes I feel so depressed I actually think about killing myself. What should I do?

Signed, Confused Caleb

#5.

Dear Quandary Master,

I may be the last living virgin over the age of fourteen in the United States. I've thought a lot about it and I've decided that I'm not ready to have sex. I know that I don't want to get pregnant and I don't feel comfortable with any of the birth control around. There are too many side effects and not enough reliability. And AIDS really scares me. I want my first time to be special with someone I really love and who cares about me. I want it to be someone I can trust and want to be with for a long time—maybe to marry, but definitely serious.

Well, in case you didn't know, this is not the most popular position these days. There have been several guys who have wanted to take me out, but I usually avoid them because I don't want to get in the position where they are expecting me to have sex with them. I am getting a reputation of being "stuck up" and it doesn't do wonders for my social life. I would like to date and even have a boyfriend—I just don't want to have sex yet. And I don't want to start caring about a guy if he's just gong to drop me when he finds out I won't go to bed with him. Is there something wrong with me? Am I being too "old-fashioned"? Am I gay? Should I just check into a convent until I'm ready?

Signed, Veronica Virgin

#6.

Dear Quandary Master,

I have known about AIDS since I was a kid—who hasn't? At first, everyone seemed pretty scared and when I was younger, we all swore we would never have unprotected sex or screw around. Then it was like everybody got bored with thinking about it or something. It was no longer new and scary, so most of the kids in my school acted like it didn't exist any more. Even when we heard all the reports about young people being the largest group newly infected with HIV, people just shrugged it off. There is so much sensationalism on TV and in the news, I guess it takes a lot to get our attention.

But I know better. Last year my uncle died of AIDS—actually, it was a pneumonia that his body couldn't fight off. He was twenty-eight and had HIV for over eight years—I didn't even know about it until about three years ago. You never would have guessed—Uncle Bob was in great shape, had a great job, and was always doing something cool, like mountain climbing or surfing. He wasn't gay and he didn't do IV drugs. He got HIV from a very nice girl that he had dated for a while back when he was in college. She didn't know she was infected and who knows where she got it. She died a couple years ago too.

I miss him a lot and my mom still can't talk about it—he was her youngest brother. I don't have intercourse, unprotected or protected. It is too risky. I see some of my friends sleeping around and acting like it was just a joke. They use protection if they have it and if they think about it, but they have no idea what could really happen. I want to do something that will get through to them.

Signed, Sadder-but-Wiser Sam

Do-It-Yourself Quandary

Identify an important dilemma related to sexuality in our culture today that was not discussed in this chapter.

- *What factors make this issue particularly complicated or difficult to resolve?*

- *What values or ethical considerations are involved?*

- *What solutions or choices are available?*

WEB SITES

Abortion
www.gynpages.com/nwho/index/html
www.rcrc.org
www.agi-usa.org

Adoption
www.calib.com/naic/index.htm
www.almanet.com
www.adoptioncrossroads.org

Birth Control
www.columbia.edu/cu/healthwise/about.html
www.igc.apc.org/ppfa/contraception/choices main.html
www.reproline.jhu.edu
www.birthcontrol.com
www.rubbertree.org
www.depo-provera.com
www.plannedparenthood.org
www.chebucto.ns.ca/health/TeenHealth/index.html

Menstruation
http://onewoman.com/redspot
www.mum.org/index.html

Pregnancy and Childbirth
www.teenpregnancy.org
www.childbirth.org.
www.mayo.ivi.com/common/html/pregpg.htm

Sexual Assault
www.worldchat.com/public/asarc
www.cs.utk.edu
http://incestabuse.about.com/health/incestabuse/blincest.htm
www.angelfire.com/wa2/silentnomore
www.cs.utk.edu/~bartley/other/RAINN.html
www.hdtl.org/index3.shtml
www.cs.utk.edu/~bartley/saInfoPage.html

Sexual Orientation
www.youth.org
www.hsl.mcmaster.ca/tomflem/gay.html
www.glsen.org/templates/index.html

www.chebucto.ns.ca/Health/TeenHealth/SexOrien/gay.html

www.apa.org/pubinfo/orient.html

www.cyberspaces.com/outproud

www.pflag.org/marriage/marriage rights.htm

Sexual Questions

www.teenwire.com/index.asp

www.sxetc.org

www.pathfinder.com/drruth

www.siecus.org

www.itsyoursexlife.org

www.notmenotnow.org

www.gyn101.com

www.columbia.edu/cu/healthwise/about.html

www.iwannaknow.org

www.advocatesforyouth.org

STDs/HIV/AIDS

www.columbia.edu.cu.healthwise/about.html

www.igc.apc.org.ppfa/stis/sti facts main.html

www.youthHIV.org

www.safersex.org

www.aegis.com

www.aidsnews.org

www.ama-assn.org/special/hiv/hivhome.htm

www.msnbc.com/news/AIDS

www.cdc.gov/hiv/stats

---

[1]*Teaching Materials and Strategies of Family Life Education Curriculum.* Adapted from the Sex Education Coalition of Metropolitan Washington.

[2]Adapted from the Human Relations and Sexuality program at Milton Academy. Developed by Ellie Griffin and Jack Starmer.

[3]Travis, Carol. The sexual lives of women over sixty. *MS* magazine, July, 1977.

[4]*Webster's College Dictionary.* New York: Random House, 1991.

[5]Schachter, Stanley. Deviations, rejection and communication. *Journal of Abnormal and Social Psychology,* 46 (1951): 190–207.

[6]Asch, Solomon. Effects of group pressure upon modification and distortion of judgment. In *Groups, Leadership and Men,* ed. M. H. Guetzkow (Pittsburgh: Carnegie, 1951), pp. 117–190.

[7]Milgram, Stanley. Behavioral studies of obedience and disobedience to authority. *Human Relations,* 18 (1965): 57–76.

[8]Written and choreographed by my teaching partner, David Mochel.

[9]UNAIDS Joint United Nations Programme on HIV/AIDS, "Report on the global HIV/AIDS epidemic June 2000."

[10]Henry J. Kaiser Family Foundation. National Survey of Teens on HIV/AIDS, 2000.

[11]Ibid., pp. 5, 6.

[12]Power, Carla, Tom Masland, Ester Pan, Iara Santoro, Ron Moreau, and Mac Margolis. Paying for AIDS (cost of AIDS drugs). *Newsweek International,* March 19, 2001, p. 16.

[13]Mukherjee, Siddhartha. Take your medicine—Why cheap AIDS drugs for Africa might be dangerous. *The New Republic,* July 24, 2000, p. 16.

[14]Ervin "Magic" Johnson at press conference on November 8, 1991, announcing that he had tested HIV-positive.

[15]Adapted from program materials prepared by Rita Ornelas, *Model Mugging of Santa Barbara,* 1991.

[16]MS magazine *Campus Project on Sexual Assault.* Funded by the National Center for the Prevention and Control of Rape, 1985.

[17]Adapted from *Male Responsibility for Rape and Rape Awareness* by Charlie Jones, 1987.

Index

Notes

Notes

Notes